AN ECONOMIC HISTORY OF TROPICAL AFRICA

Volume One

The Pre-Colonial Period

Z. A. Konczacki and J. M. Konczacki

AN ECONOMIC HISTORY
OF TROPICAL AFRICA

VOLUME ONE   : THE PRE-COLONIAL PERIOD
VOLUME TWO   : THE COLONIAL PERIOD

VOLUME THREE : AN ECONOMIC AND SOCIAL
                      HISTORY OF SOUTHERN
                      AFRICA

AN
ECONOMIC HISTORY
OF TROPICAL AFRICA

VOLUME ONE

THE PRE-COLONIAL PERIOD

Selected and Edited by
Z. A. KONCZACKI
Professor of Economics, Dalhousie University
and
J. M. KONCZACKI
Associate Professor, Mount St Vincent University

FRANK CASS

First published in 1977 in Great Britain by
FRANK CASS AND COMPANY LIMITED
Gainsborough House, Gainsborough Road,
London E11 1RS, England

and in the United States of America by
FRANK CASS AND COMPANY LIMITED
c/o Biblio Distribution Center
81 Adams Drive, Totowa, New Jersey 07512

ISBN O 7146 2919 7

Library of Congress Catalog No. 72 – 92967

Printed in Great Britain by offset lithography by
Billing & Sons Ltd, Guildford, London and Worcester

Contents

Introduction   vii

Part I   **AGRICULTURAL DEVELOPMENT**
   1   The Spread of Food Production in Sub-Saharan
      Africa   *J. Desmond Clark*   3
   2   Speculations on the Coming of the Banana to Uganda
             D. N. McMaster   14
   3   The Cultivation and Use of Yams in West Africa
             D. G. Coursey   31
   4   The Introduction and Spread of Maize in Africa
             Marvin P. Miracle   41

Part II   **LAND USE AND TENURE**
   5   Land Tenure: Group and Individual Rights
             M. Gluckman   55
   6   Land Tenure and Feudalism in Africa   *Jack Goody*   62
   7   Land Tenure Rights in Ancient Ruanda
      Jacques Maquet and Saverio Naigiziki   70

Part III   **INTRODUCTION AND USE OF METALS**
   8   The Iron Age in the Sudan   *A. J. Arkell*   79
   9   Early Records of Iron in Abyssinia   *G. A. Wainwright*   83
  10   An Essay on the History of Metals in West Africa
             Raymond Mauny   89

Part IV   **SOME ECONOMIC AND TECHNOLOGICAL
          ASPECTS OF THE IRON AGE**
  11   The Iron Age of Zambia   *Brian Fagan*   103
  12   Aspects of the Ushi Iron Industry
        G. Kay and D. M. Wright   115

Part V   **PATTERNS OF TRADE**
  13   Trans-Saharan Trade in the Middle Ages
          S. Daniel Neumark   127
  14   Trade Patterns in Ghana at the Beginning of the
      Eighteenth Century   *K. B. Dickson*   132
  15   Nineteenth-Century Trade in the Bamenda Grass-
      fields, Southern Cameroons   *E. M. Chilver*   147
  16   Slavery and the Slave Trade in the Context of West
      African History   *J. D. Fage*   166

17 Early Trade and Raw Materials in South Central
   Africa   *Brian M. Fagan* 179
18 The East African Coast. An Historical and
   Archaeological Review   *J. E. G. Sutton* 193
19 The East African Slave Trade   *Edward A. Alpers* 206
20 The East African Ivory Trade in the Nineteenth
   Century   *R. W. Beachey* 216

Part VI   TRADE ROUTES AND TRADE CENTRES
21 Some Reflections on African Trade Routes
                                          Gervase Mathew 231
22 Long-Distance Trade-Routes in Central Africa
                                          J. Vansina 237
23 Some Comments on the Origins of Traditional
   Markets in Africa South of the Sahara *B. W. Hodder* 253
24 Trade Centres in the Northern Interlacustrine Region
                                          John Tosh 269

**Part VII   MEDIA OF EXCHANGE AND STANDARDS
              OF VALUE**
25 Native and Trade Currencies in Southern Nigeria
   during the Eighteenth and Nineteenth Centuries
                                          G. I. Jones 274
26 Cowrie from North and South: an Episode in the
   History of the Dahomean Currency System
                                          Karl Polanyi 284
27 The Ounce in Eighteenth-Century West African
   Trade   *Marion Johnson* 289
28 Salt Currency in Ethiopia in the Zämänä Mäsafent
                                          M. Abir 299

Index   305

Introduction

The economic history of Tropical Africa has only recently begun to emerge as a distinctly specialised field of study. In the past, its problems have been occasionally dealt with by anthropologists, archaeologists, economists, ethnographers, geographers, and historians. With only a few exceptions, a more systematic work by economic historians is still lacking.

In order to narrow down the existing gap, the preparation of the present book was undertaken. It is only the first part of a larger study which will include the economic history of the colonial period.

The editors, having a large selection of articles at their disposal, preferred to limit the number of excerpts from books to a minimum. This decision was made on purely practical grounds. The bibliographical information on the latter kind of literature is far more satisfactory. Also, its availability presents no serious problems in a reasonably well equipped library. The position with regard to articles published in learned journals is quite different, especially when published in foreign languages and when such journals are not readily available. In undertaking this task, the editors desired to assist the student by providing guidance in an area which is new to him. The choice of the reading matter was not an easy one, as some very worthwhile articles could not be included owing to lack of space.

A few comments on the approach used while compiling this book of readings may be useful.

In order to obtain a comprehensive view of the material progress of man in Africa, one cannot neglect to study some aspects of the distant past. Bearing in mind that, according to the orthodox opinion, prehistory ends with the appearance of adequate written records, much of sub-Saharan Africa's past would not be considered history. Moreover, if one accepts the approach to periodisation which the Western historians adopted with regard to their own part of the world, much of the African past would have to be described as proto- or parahistory, since the information about the non-literate African societies was recorded in the literature of other cultures.

An economic historian can solve this difficulty by following in the footsteps of some modern historians of sub-Saharan Africa who eschew orthodoxy. Otherwise history would become mainly a study of European activity in Africa. The introduction of modern scientific methods of historical research revolutionised the old concepts of the nineteenth century, which neatly drew a line of demarcation between history and prehistory.

The standard methods of research in the field of African history make use of written documents, archaeological findings, linguistic analysis and oral tradition.* An economic historian of Africa, more than any other historian, must avail himself of botanical and zoological evidence and must take into account the influence exerted by the physical geography.

The investigation of the genetic relationships between domesticated plants and animals and their wild ancestors may provide answers to their geographical origin, and consequently produce evidence of contacts between different regions or continents.

The study of the physical geography of Africa, starting with a paleo-ecological approach, may provide at least a partial explanation in terms of environmental changes of the economic and social structures viewed in an historical perspective.

An economic historian of sub-Saharan Africa may also have good reasons for adopting a largely pragmatic approach to periodisation. Pure subsistence economies which existed in the distant past, certainly deserve a study. If, however, they represented a stationary system, they must of necessity be of limited analytical interest. Nevertheless such cases were an exception rather than a rule. It is the process of change that asks for analysis and explanation. Change occurs as a result of the appearance of an ecological imbalance generated endogenously, or it may come from outside, for example by way of a climatic change or as a result of contact with the external world. It is the appearance of a marketable surplus and the development of exchange which eventually leads to trade relations with other, often distant, regions. This in turn is accompanied by occupational stratification and specialisation which attracts the attention of an economic historian. It is, therefore, not surprising that he should not be opposed to the opinions of those historians who link the beginning

*Mistakenly, archaeology is often taken as a synonym for prehistory. In Africa, to a large extent archaeological findings refer to periods later than those with which prehistoric archaeology is concerned.

of the history of sub-Saharan Africa with the dawn of the African Iron Age and who consider that the world of the neolithic agriculturalist belongs to prehistory. But, at the same time, he should be capable of understanding those historians who were never anxious to draw a clear-cut dividing line between history and prehistory in Black Africa. This happened as a consequence of the close cooperation between the human and natural sciences. An economic historian is primarily interested in the general phenomena rather than in the specific facts. Because of the nature of his approach he may be permitted not to pay too much attention to the fine distinction between prehistory and history.

As we deal with sub-Saharan Africa a few words should be said about the meaning of this term.

To single out the sub-Saharan area from the rest of the continent, in a purely geographical sense, may lead to some ambiguities. Economic and cultural contacts with other areas of the continent, and North Africa in particular, explain a certain amount of regional overlapping which was unavoidable in the selection of material for this book.

The historical division into the pre-colonial and colonial periods rests on the assumption that the latter period began towards the end of the nineteenth century. The intention of the editors is to preserve this distinction even if, again, some measure of overlapping cannot be avoided. Notable exceptions are, of course, a large part of Southern Africa and the territorially insignificant coastal areas in different parts of Tropical Africa.

A few comments should be made concerning the subject matter of this book, which is arranged in seven parts.

The first part entitled, 'Agricultural Development', combines historical facts together with some speculations on the economic prehistory. The theme of J. Desmond Clark's article on the spread of food production is taken up in the remaining papers which concentrate on such aspects of agricultural development as the origin of some selected crops, their antiquity, cultivation and use. Some new facts were discovered since Professor Clark's article was written and also since this book of readings was put together. The date at which the knowledge of iron-working reached sub-Saharan Africa has recently been moved down to the middle of the first millennium B.C. Iron was then being smelted by the Negro peoples at Nok, in West Africa. Moreover, the typology of pottery of the Central African Iron Age has changed considerably. The importance previously attached to the Channel-decorated ware is not borne out by the recent discoveries (the reader is advised to consult D.W. Phillipson's 'Iron Age History and Archeology in Zambia', *Journal of African History*, vol.XV, No.1,

1974). But this new evidence does not alter the main conclusions arrived at by Professor Clark concerning African economic pre-history.

The second part considers the problem of the patterns of land use and tenure. With a few exceptions, the institution of land tenure was characterised by a high degree of permanence and in spite of its complexity there are many similarities among the various agricultural communities. Max Gluckman's study deals with the institutional side of land tenure. The question of the appropriateness of comparing the tribal and the feudal land tenure systems, which is hinted at there, is taken up by Jack Goody in his paper containing some seminal ideas.

This part is concluded with a case study of ancient Ruanda by Jacques Maquet and Saverio Naigiziki. The authors describe and analyse the land use and tenure arrangements in a society comprising two distinct groups: the pastoralists and the farmers. The former as conquerors dominated the latter. As there were parallel situations in other parts of Africa, this case study merits attention.

An attempt is made in parts three and four to throw some light on the question of the introduction of metals in general and of iron in particular. Mining and metal-working activities are discussed together with other important aspects of economic life during the different phases of the African Iron Age. Professors Raymond Mauny and Brian M. Fagan have brought up to date their papers especially for this reader. G. Kay and D. M. Wright strive to discover the nature of the primitive iron technology as it was practised in pre-colonial times. Their work represents one of the very few attempts to record the old methodology of iron smelting.

Work based on archaeological evidence is particularly exposed to the risk of rapid obsolescence as new findings are taking place at an increasing rate. This is especially well exemplified by the number of new radio-carbon dates published every year. Consequently the readers of this book are urged to consult reports which are published regularly, in order to up-date their information.

Parts five to six aim at providing a glimpse into some aspects of African trade. Many questions can be raised under these headings but only a few can be dealt with. What goods were produced for exchange? What were the patterns of trade? Who were the producers and the traders? What were the origins, the nature and the size of the markets? What were the trade relations with other continents? What were the effects of trade?

It is in the sphere of trade that various hypotheses have been put forward in recent years and discussions were carried on.

Let us take the Atlantic slave trade as an example. Professor Fage's paper on 'Slavery and the slave trade in the context of West African History' refers to Philip D. Curtin's revision of the views on the quantitative aspects of slave exports (see also P. D. Curtin, *The Atlantic Slave Trade: a Census*). An element of controversy is introduced by Fage, who questions some former statements concerning the local African attitudes to slavery. Fage's views in turn provoked comments from C. C. Wrigley (C. C. Wrigley, 'Historicism in Africa – Slavery and State Formation', *African Affairs*, Vol. 70, No. 279, 1971). Needless to say, limitations of space did not permit the editors to enter into details of such interesting discussions.

Professor E. A. Alpers's paper fills in the gap in the much neglected study of the East African slave trade by providing some new facts and insights.

The evolution of thought on the development of trade takes a prominent place in recent discussions. Jan Vansina's interest in and emphasis on the role played by the long-distance trade (see 'Long-distance trade-routes in Central Africa') has been recently questioned by Richard Gray and David Birmingham (editors of *Pre-colonial African Trade*), who maintain that in explaining the development of trade, instead of a geographical criterion one must employ an economic analysis. Thus, they emphasise instead 'the vital distinction resting not on spatial categories but on the contrast between the economic activities directly related to trade'. The difficulty is, that economic analysis cannot be divorced from economic theory on which it rests, and economic theory applies just as well to local trade as it does to long-distance trade relations. The principles of comparative or absolute advantage are the core of that part of economic theory which concerns itself with international or inter-regional trade relations. The answers depend on how various terms are defined. For example to equate long-distance trade with the trade in overseas commodities only, would not be a true reflection of pre-colonial African reality.

Another fruitful and largely untouched area of research is concerned with the origin of African markets. In a paper by Professor Hodder two theories concerning market origins are discussed. The author stresses the fact that there is not only the need to collect more data but also that there is a greater need to construct some general conceptual framework for analysing such little-understood phenomena as market institutions.

The last part of this volume concentrates on the various forms of 'money' in pre-colonial Africa, from the primitive to the more sophisticated media used in the trade with Europeans. The little-explored question of the standards, which was studied some years ago by the late Karl Polanyi, here receives attention by the inclusion of Marion Johnson's study of the role of the ounce in West African trade.

The problem of currencies is a challenging one and should be paid more attention by the economic historians of Africa, who may be able in the future to say more about the relationship between the emergence of new currencies and the growth of trade.

To conclude, the stage of development in which the economic history of pre-colonial Africa south of the Sahara finds itself, is still largely one of collecting basic data. As information accumulates, the formulation of new hypotheses and their testing will become possible. Nevertheless, it is safe to say that knowledge about the facts gathered so far and the partial conclusions that can be drawn from them, invalidate the opinion that the African economies of the past do not lend themselves to an analysis based on economic theory.

One cannot disregard the fact that the modern science of economics takes into account problems reaching far beyond Western industrial society and finds it fruitful to apply its theory to such areas. It goes without saying that this recent development strengthens the position of an economic historian. A limited number of institutions with a strictly economic aim within a given society provide no reason for neglecting their study.

Furthermore, the supporters of the extreme view that an economic history of pre-colonial Africa is not possible seem to lean heavily on a simplistic distinction between pre-industrial and industrial economies, thus leaving out of the picture a whole array of significant nuances. Between the extremes of non-literate, non-machine and non-pecuniary communities on the one hand, and the Western industrial society of our time on the other, there existed many societies endowed with varying degrees of economic complexity. And from this point of view, sub-Saharan Africa was no exception.

Z. A. KONCZACKI
J. M. KONCZACKI

PART I

Agricultural Development

1

THE SPREAD OF FOOD PRODUCTION
IN SUB-SAHARAN AFRICA*

J. Desmond Clark

After the end of the Pleistocene, sub-Saharan Africa seems to have been more receptive of than contributory to cultural progress in the Old World as a whole. By that time favourable localities in the sub-continent – the margins of lakes and watercourses, the sea coasts, the peripheral regions of the equatorial forest – were sometimes supporting nearly, or entirely, sedentary communities of hunting-collecting peoples who were enabled to live in this way due to the permanent presence of one or more staple sources of food: freshwater fish, water animals and plants, and sea foods; and forest foods (the *Dioscoreas, Elaeis guineensis,* and other oil-bearing plants), either perennial or capable of being stored. Evidence of such occupation is seen in the midden accumulations in both cave and open sites at this time (1). Populations could thus become more concentrated and an increase in density may be inferred, the limiting factor being the maximum that any one environment could support by intensified collecting methods (Fig. 1).

The two ecosystems in sub-Saharan Africa most significant in determining subsequent economic developments were the plateau grasslands and lakes of East and East Central Africa and the peripheral parts of the lowlands and montane evergreen forest zones of West and West Equatorial Africa. In the one, dependence would seem to have been predominantly on a protein diet based on game and fish, with vegetable foods of subsidiary importance, and, in the other, probably on a starch diet based on vegetable foods, supplemented to some extent by protein from fish and, to a lesser degree, from game. The introduction of cereal crops was, therefore, of the

*Reprinted by permission of Cambridge University Press from *Journal of African History*, Vol. III, No. 2, 1962. The original version of this paper was submitted to the Conference under the title, 'Reflections on the introduction of domestication and the change from stone- to metal-using economy in sub-Saharan Africa'.

greatest importance since it permitted the sedentary, Mesolithic population to occupy, widely and permanently, territory previously capable of supporting only temporary settlement. While the introduction of agriculture would have supplemented the perennial wild plants and encouraged plant cultivation, its chief importance in the plant-tending, 'vegecultural' communities would have been to encourage *permanent* occupation of areas previously uninviting to sedentary gatherers – dry savannah and continuous canopy forest. The chief development in food production in the higher rainfall, thicker vegetation region of the west and centre probably only took place, however, after the introduction of American and Asian food plants of the humid tropics and after metal-working had provided efficient tools with which to make effective inroads upon the forests.

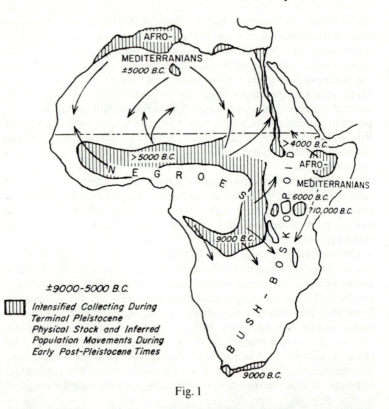

Fig. 1

Domestication of stock – cattle, sheep and goats – may be expected to have been equally as revolutionary an innovation for human economy in both types of country. It would, however, have particular significance in providing a permanent source of protein for those occupying the forest periphery, though here its distribution must originally have been controlled by the tsetse fly.

It is well to remember with regard to agriculture that there are two factors requiring recognition: the one the cultivation of cereal crops, wheat, barley, millets, sorghum, etc.; and the other the cultivation of plant crops, *ensete*, bananas, yams, oil plants and trees, fluted pumpkins, pulses, etc. The initial 'vegecultural' stages in domesticating the latter group were almost certainly local developments south of the Sahara, (1) while, on the archaeological evidence, there can be little doubt that cereal cultivation spread to Africa from South-West Asia sometime during the fifth millennium B.C., perhaps somewhat earlier. What is believed to be the earliest Neolithic in North-East Africa is represented by the Fayum A culture dated to ±4300 B.C. by radiocarbon. By the first half of the fourth millennium Neolithic culture had spread to the upper Nile at Khartoum, where the Khartoum Neolithic at Es Shaheinab dates to ±3200 B.C. Arkell, however, considers that these dates are unreliable and would make the initial introduction into Lower Egypt earlier and the spread to the Sudan more rapid (2). Some confirmation for Arkell's suggestion is found in the radiocarbon dating for three Saharan Neolithic industries with pottery occurring in rock shelters with paintings of cattle scenes in the Tassili. If the paintings can be associated with the industries, it would indicate that cattle were already domesticated in North Africa by the sixth millennium B.C. (3), (4).

The staple cereals cultivated in the lower Nile at this time were barley and emmer wheat, and the silos of the Fayum A peasants contained 80 per cent barley and 20 per cent wheat (5). The bifacially worked serrated sickle blade is an intimately related tool, and it seems probable, therefore, that the extent of the distribution of all forms of sickle blades in Africa may perhaps provide some indication of the extent of wheat and barley cultivation, and so of the use of these crops as staples in the continent in prehistoric times. In this distribution area can be included the Nile Valley, the Mediterranean coast west to Cyrenaica, the eastern oases of the Sahara, and perhaps the Western Sudan and the Tigré plateau of Ethiopia.

From the sixth to the third millennium B.C. the Makalian Wet phase in Saharan and sub-Saharan Africa, which would seem to be the equivalent of the Atlantic stage in Europe, permitted movement of human and animal populations from the Mediterranean littoral southwards, and from the savannah of West and Central Africa northwards. Such a favourable habitat enabled Later Stone Age Mesolithic hunters and fishers, with their improved methods of food getting, to populate the Sahara to an extent never before possible, and must have rendered these communities particularly receptive of and quick to adopt the new practices of cereal and crop cultivation and domestication of animals (especially the latter) when these were diffused (Fig. 2).

The material culture of the Mesolithic/Neolithic populations of the Southern Sahara, from Mauritania in the west to the Nile at Khartoum in the east, indicates a way of life based on hunting and fishing. This is shown especially in the bone harpoons, fish-hooks, and bifacially worked stone projectile points, and implies a reasonably well-watered and bush covered terrain that was very different from the desert conditions that exist there today (6). It would seem not improbable that the inhabitants of the settlements grouped round the pans and river courses of such sites as Asselar, Taferjit, Tamaya Mellet and In Guezzam were Negroids whose spread had been made possible by the northward displacement of the Sudan and Sahel belts. Skeletal remains of Negro-type have been found at Asselar, Tamaya Mellet, Early Khartoum, and several other sites in the central Sahara.

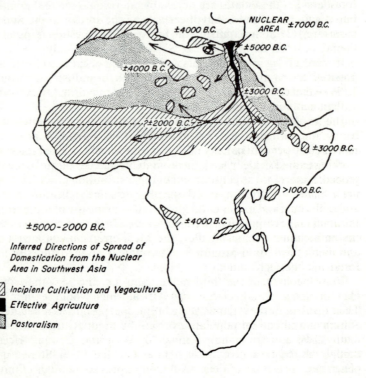

Fig. 2

Contact with populations living to the south of the desert during these millennia, and the later movement out of the desert that must have been forced on some of the inhabitants by the post-Makalian dry phase after the middle of the third millennium B.C., are likely to have been the causes whereby knowledge of and experiment in cereal crop cultivation passed to the sub-Saharan populations.

Dambo and waterside sites and the fringes of forests must have seen the first attempts at tropical agriculture and plant cultivation. Much surface material and a very few stratified sites together with one or two radiocarbon dates tend to confirm this. In tropical West Africa (Guinea, Mali, Mauritania (7), the Ivory Coast, Dahomey, Ghana (8), (9), and Nigeria (Nok Culture)) (10), (11) two stages of Neolithic culture were present or can be inferred, the main distinguishing feature being the absence of pottery from the earlier stage. In the north-eastern and north-western parts of the Congo basin only one stage has so far been distinguished (12). Almost nothing is known about the settlement patterns of any of these West African and Congo forest and savannah cultures except where rock shelters were used, but it can be inferred that the usual form was an open village consisting of, for Neolithic groups in the forest, a fair-sized population.

If Vaufrey (7) is correct in supposing that a proportion of the polished celt-like artifacts from Aouker and Hodh (15 – 17°N: 5 – 10°W) were used as hoes, it will imply that some incipient cultivation at least was being practised in this now desert region at some time during the Sahara Wet Phase (i.e., before 2000 B.C.) when suitable terrain for cultivation may be expected to have existed there. Alternatively, these hoe-like celts may have been nothing more than the working ends of digging sticks for collecting wild vegetable foods. If, indeed, some of these celt-like tools are hoes and the absolute dates are in any way reliable, it would seem that experimentation with yam and millet cultivation, which had been under way from the fifth to the third millennium, had, by the time of the Nok Figurine culture in the first millennium B.C., resulted in the appearance, firstly of incipient, and then of full, food-producing communities on the fringes of the forest and in the savannah.

These Neolithic communities were all equipped with wood-working tools, the axe and the adze, and, it would seem, with the hoe also. Their distribution covered what is now the Sahel belt of the southern Sahara and spread into the forest proper. Without adequate carbon dating, however, the age of these cultures cannot be determined, though the few dates that do exist show that the Neolithic had not penetrated to the Ghana coast before the beginning of the fourth millennium, while the Nok Culture seems to have lasted from ±918

B.C. to about A.D. 200 (13). It may be suggested that the soft stone hoe was the implement used for yam (*Dioscorea cayenensis* or other indigenous *Dioscoreas*) and sorghum cultivation in higher rainfall zones where a more broad-bladed tool than the pointed digging stick would be required for mound cultivation or for breaking up new ground under a thick vegetation cover.

In Ethiopia and the lake region of the East African Rift very different cultural assemblages are found. The most significant are those at Agordat near Axum in Eritrea (14), Quiha and Tuli Kapi on the northern and western parts of the Ethiopian high plateau, (15) and the settlements and burial mounds in the Nakuru-Naivasha basin in Kenya, and in Ngorongoro in Northern Tanganyika (16), (17), (18). The cultural associations of the hoe cultivators of central Abyssinia reported by Père Azais (19) in Woolega and Kaffa lie, presumably, more closely with the Southern Sudan and West Africa than with those of the Agordat and Gregory Rift Cultures, among which pastoralism seems to have assumed greater importance. It would seem also probable that there is an association between the stone hoe cultures of Western Ethiopia and *ensete* cultivation, since there is a measure of agreement in the distribution of both.

Most of the other East African Neolithic cultures made much use of obsidian for their smaller percussion flaked tools, knives, scrapers, burins, and projectile barbs. This suggests a somewhat more mobile hunting and pastoral form of livelihood. Some writers have suggested that the whole cattle complex of the Sahara Neolithic peoples was derived from Arabia via the Horn. The archaeological evidence, however, lends no support to this hypothesis, and the rock art in particular indicates that the pastoral groups depicted therein came *from* the Sahara or Nubia to the Horn, and not the other way round (20). Other than the pecked and ground stone axes, of which several distinctive types are found, these assemblages lack the heavy wood-working equipment of the forest and savannah cultures. The most characteristic domestic equipment consisted of stone bowls and palettes of various kinds, usually made from lava, together with flat grindstones and deep, bag-shaped pottery, sometimes with handles and spouts. In some instances, evidence of permanent dwellings (Hyrax Hill) and settlements (Lanet) suggests a different cultural tradition with a fairly long history and probably some form of incipient agriculture. Cattle were present in the northern part of the Horn by the second millennium B.C., if we can accept the evidence of the Deir-el-Bahari bas reliefs, and some of the later Kenya Neolithic peoples are known to have owned cattle (Hyrax Hill). Among this last, the zebu strain has been identified, so that it is likely to have been acquired sometime after the first half of the first millennium B.C.

when, it is believed, this stock began to be diffused across the straits from Southern Arabia.

The grindstones and bowls strongly suggest some form of crop cultivation. In Eastern Ethiopia these crops may have been wheat, barley and *teff* (21), while in the Gregory Rift area the plants are more likely to have been primarily finger millet (*Eleusine* sp.), with the addition of various sorghums and *Pennisetum*. The length of time during which these Neolithic communities occupied East Africa and Ethiopia is not known, but a carbon date of 1063 ± 80 B.C. (22) for a late phase of the Stone Bowl Culture suggests that they were already established there in the second millennium B.C., while another date of A.D. 1584 ± 100 for the late settlement site at Lanet probably represents the upper limit (23).

The earliest food producing population of Southern Africa (as distinct from East and West Africa) of which we have knowledge were the authors of a very characteristic pottery tradition. This comprised decoration involving channelling, grooving, incised hatching, and sometimes stamping on globular pots and deep and shallow bowls. It is referred to in East Africa (24) and also in Ruanda Urundi (25) and the Kasai (26) as Dimple-based pottery. In Rhodesia it is known as Channelled ware north of the Zambezi (27) and Bambata ware (28) south of the river. The uniformity of this pottery in Uganda, Ruanda, Kavirondo.and the Katanga indicates that its initial dispersal may have been quite rapid. A Dimple-based pot from Nsongezi rock shelter in Uganda has been dated to A.D. 825 ± 150 (29). Channelled ware has been dated to *c*. A.D. 100 ± 212 in Eastern Barotseland where it occurs on a buried land surface (30). A late and variant form, known as Gokomere ware, was present in A.D. 330 ± 150 on the Zimbabwe acropolis, and the typical Channelled ware occurs again at the Kalambo Falls where a late phase dates to A.D. 1080 ± 180. This last date probably marks the end of this culture as such, since by A.D. 1085 ± 150 it had been replaced at the Zimbabwe acropolis by pottery of a quite different tradition. In modified form it seems to have lingered in the Rhodesias and southern Tanganyika until fairly recent times.

Little is known of the settlement patterns or dwellings of these Dimple-based/Channelled ware peoples, but in Uganda, as also at Bambata and perhaps at Gokomere, rock shelters were sometimes occupied (31), (32). The usual type of settlement must, however, have consisted of free standing dwellings in the open. Of considerable importance, therefore, are Robinson's Mabveni excavations which show that the settlement there consisted of a small open village comprising several huts made of pole and daga with similarly constructed grain bins.

Nothing is known either about the physical characteristics of the Dimple-based/Channelled ware population, though the Stamped ware tradition south of the Zambezi is associated with a Bush-Bos-kopoid stock. North of the river no skeletal remains have been found with Channelled ware but later Iron Age remains show both Bush-Boskopoid and negroid features together with hybrids (33), (34). Afro-Mediterranean characteristics are apparent also in some of the Later Stone Age populations in Rhodesia and South Africa (35). Their presence in the south in association with certain cultural traits strongly suggests a movement of East African long-heads into the sub-continent in late prehistoric times. Such a movement would seem most likely to have taken place about the beginning of the present era, and to have been responsible for transmitting to the historic Hotten-tots their stock and characteristic pottery. Whether or not such a movement was connected with, or quite separate from, the Chan-nelled ware population is unknown, though it is thought most likely to have been separate. Channelling is a characteristic motif for decora-tion of some Hottentot pottery, but, apart from that, the two traditions have little in common. The general shape, and the pointed base form of the Hottentot pots, the lugs and spouts, are much more closely linked with the Neolithic Stone Bowl cultures of the Gregory Rift.

Such population movements, bringing with them fundamental improvements in food getting, must have profoundly affected the Later Stone Age inhabitants of Southern Africa, and, in fact, all hunter-gatherers with whom the Neolithic and Iron Age farmers came into contact. It has generally been assumed that there was a sharp cultural break between the Stone and Iron Ages in sub-Saharan Africa, with the proviso that some peoples at the Stone Age level persisted in their way of life living in symbiosis with Iron Age food producers until quite late times – where some Bushman, Pygmy, and other groups are concerned, for example, until the present day. Ample evidence exists, as has for long been appreciated, for this overlap and contemporaneity of stone- and metal-using peoples, but what has not been appreciated is the potential and degree to which cultural adaptation must sometimes have taken place, thus enabling some of the Later Stone Age food-gathering populations to change their economy and so to compete favourably with the metal-using immigrants. Such a change would generally mean the abandonment of sites favourable for hunter-collectors and the settlement of others more suitable for stock raising and cultivation. That such changes did not, however, come about all at once is evident both from the archaeological record and from oral tradition (36), which indicate that processes of acculturation leading to economic revolution had been under way from the beginning of this era up to the present day. It might, therefore, be expected that some of these successful communities may have evolved into Bantu tribal groups we know today, and that these would show to a varying degree evidence in their physical composition of their Bush-Boskopoid ancestry. Indeed, this is precisely what we do find in those parts of South Central Africa where skeletal remains of proto-historic times have been studied (37), (38), (39).

In summary, knowledge of cultivation of cereal crops was, on the existing available archaeological evidence, transmitted across the Sahara from South-West Asia via the Nile and perhaps the Maghrib, and with this agricultural knowledge must have come domestic stock – long- and short-horned cattle, sheep, and goats. The sedentary hunters and fishers, as also the 'vege-culturalists' of the savannah dambos and forest fringes, were not slow to develop by experiment and adaptation their own domesticates, and to occupy territory which formerly had permitted only temporary settlement. This change in the economy and accompanying movement of populations seems to have begun during the second millennium at the latest. The continued dessication of the Sahara, the transmission of the knowledge of metallurgy to West and South Central Africa, and also, no doubt, the conquests of the Axumite empire in Ethiopia, caused a further movement of stock owners and cultivators from the Sudanic belt and the Horn southwards into the Congo Basin, South Central and Southern Africa. Here symbiotic existence of hunters and cultivators resulted, it is suggested, in many of the former forsaking their nomadic life and becoming semi- or fully-sedentary cultivators and pastoralists. Most of them must have conducted their lives on a simple pattern of transhumance, as did the Bantu and Hottentot communities of the south-east coastal regions in the sixteenth and seventeenth centuries (40).

The introduction of metallurgy helped considerably to speed up and intensify this process of transformation from a collecting to a food-producing economy, which in most areas must have been completed by the end of the sixteenth century.

REFERENCES

(1)   Clark, J. D., 'From Food Collecting to Incipient Urbanisation in Africa South of the Sahara'. In Braidwood, R. J., *Courses Towards Urban Life* (1962), Viking Fund Publications in Anthropology, No. 32.

(2)   Arkell, A. J., 'Khartoum's Part in the Development of the Neolithic', *Kush* (1957), v, 8-12.

(3)   Lhote, H. Personal communication.

(4)   Mori, F., *Arte preistorica del Sahara Libico* (De Lucca, Rome, 1960).

(5)   Cole, S., 'The Neolithic Revolution', British Museum (Natural History) (London, 1959), II.

(6)   Monod, T., and Mauny, R., 'Découverte de nouveaux instruments en os dans l'Ouest Africain'. In Clark, J. D., and Sole, S., *Proceedings of the 3rd Pan-African Congress on Prehistory, Livingstone, 1955* (Chatto and Windus, London 1957), 242-7.

(7)   Vaufrey, R., 'Le Néolithique paratumbien: une civilisation agricole primitive du Soudan', *La Revue Scientifique* (1947), No. 3, 267, 205-32:

(8)   Davies, O., 'Neolithic cultures from Ghana', C.R. *4th Pan-African Congress, Leopoldville, 1959* (1962). In press.

(9)   Shaw, C. T., 'Report on excavations carried out in the cave known as "Bosumpra" at Abetifi, Gold Coast Colony', *Proc. Prehist. Soc.* (1944), X, 1-67.

(10)   Fagg, B. E. B., 'An outline of the Stone Age of the Plateau Minesfield', *Proc. Int. West African Conference* (1949).

(11)   Willett, F., 'Investigations at Old Oyo, 1956-7: An Interim Report', *J. Hist. Soc. Nigeria* (1960), II (1), 59-77.

(12)   Mortelmans, G., 'La préhistoire du Congo Belge', *Revue de l'Université de Bruxelles* (1957), 2-3.

(13)   Deevey, S. E., *et al.*, 'Yale natural radiocarbon measurements III', *Science* (1957), CXXVI, 908-19.

(14)   Arkell, A. J., 'Four occupation sites at Agordat', *Kush* (1954), II, 33-62.

(15)   Clark, J. D., *The prehistoric cultures of the Horn of Africa* (Cambridge University Press, London, 1954).

(16)   Leakey, L. S. B., *The Stone Age Cultures of Kenya Colony* (Cambridge University Press, London, 1931; reprinted with a new introductory note by the author, Frank Cass, London 1971).

(17)   Leakey, M. D., 'Report on the excavations at Hyrax Hill, Nakuru, Kenya Colony', *Trans. Roy. Soc. South Africa* (1945), XXX, iv, 271-409.

(18)   Leakey, M. D., and Leakey, L. S. B., *Excavations at the Njoro river cave* (Oxford University Press, London, 1950).

(19)   Bailloud, G., 'La Préhistoire de l'Ethiopie'. In *Mer rouge – Afrique orientale. Cahiers de l'Afrique et de l'Asie* (Paris, 1959), 15-43.

(20)   See (15) above, 295-315.

(21)   Simoons, F., 'Some questions on the economic prehistory of Ethiopia'. Paper read at the Third Conference on African History and Archaeology, School of Oriental and African Studies, July 1961, University of London (1961).

(22)   Leakey, L. S. B., *Annual Report of the Coryndon Museum* (Nairobi, 1956).

(23)   Deevey, E. S., 'Yale natural radiocarbon measurements, V', *Amer. Journ. of Science* (1960), Radiocarbon Supplement II, 58.

(24)   Leakey, M. D., Owen, W. E., and Leakey, L. S. B., 'Dimple-based pottery from Central Kavirondo', *Coryndon Museum Occasional Paper*, No. 2 (Nairobi, 1948).

(25)   Hiernaux, J., and Maquet, E., 'Cultures préhistoriques de l'âge des métaux au Ruanda Urundi et au Kivu, Congo Belge', *Acad. roy. des sciences d'Outre mer; Classe des sciences nat. et méd.*, New Series (1960), LX, No. 2, 1-102.

(26)   Nenquin, J., 'Dimple-based pots from Kasai, Belgian Congo', *Man* (1959), 242.

(27)   Clark, J. D., *The Prehistory of Southern Africa* (Penguin Books, Harmondsworth, 1959), pp. 287-9.

(28)   Summers, R. F. H., 'The Southern Rhodesian Iron Age', *Journ. Afr. Hist.* (1961), II (1), 1-13.

(29)   Posnansky, M., 'Pottery types from archaeological sites in East Africa', *Journ. Afr. Hist.* , (1961), II (2), 177-98.

(30)   Fagan B. M., 'Radio-carbon dates for sub-Saharan Africa I', *Journ. Afr. Hist.* (1961), II (1), 137.

(31)   Lowe, C. van Riet, 'The Pleistocene Geology and Archaeology of Uganda, Part

II, Prehistory', *Geol. Survey of Uganda Mem.* (1952), VI.

(32) Gardner, T., Wells, L. H., and Schofield, J. F., 'The recent archaeology of Gokomere, Southern Rhodesia', *Trans. Roy. Soc. S. Africa* (1940), XXVIII, 219-53.

(33) Tobias, P. V., 'Skeletal remains from Inyanga'. In Summers, R. F. H., *Inyanga* (Cambridge University Press, London, 1958), 159-72.

(34) Tobias, P. V. Unpublished report on skeletal remains from Northern Rhodesian sites.

(35) Wells, L. H., 'Late Stone Age human types in central Africa', *Proc. 3rd Pan-African Congress on Prehistory* (1957), Clark, J. D., and Cole, S., 183-5.

(36) Clark, J. D., 'A note on the pre-Bantu inhabitants of Northern Rhodesia and Nyasaland', *S. Afr. Journ. Sci.* (1950), XLVII, No. 3, 42-52.

(37) Wells, L. H., 'Fossil man in Northern Rhodesia'. In Clark, J. D., *The Stone Age Cultures of Northern Rhodesia* (South African Archaeological Society, Cape Town, 1950).

(38) See n. (33) above.

(39) Galloway, A. (ed.), 'Symposium on human skeletal remains from the northern and eastern Transvaal', *S. Afr. Journ. Sci.* (1935), XXXII, 616-41.

(40) Boxer, C. R., *The tragic history of the sea, 1589-1622*, Hakluyt Society (1957), Second Series, CXII.

2

SPECULATIONS ON THE COMING OF THE BANANA TO UGANDA*

D. N. McMaster

Bananas (*Musa* spp.) are the great staple food crop of southern Uganda (Fig. 1). In 1958 they occupied a total area of over 1,200,000 acres and supplied the main subsistence of roughly 2,500,000 people, or 35 per cent of the total population of Uganda. Banana cultivation also supports densities of population well above the average for the country. In many areas, where the crop is paramount, densities of over 200 persons per square mile are frequent, rising in central Buganda to over 500 per square mile, and among the Gisu of the western slopes of Mount Elgon it reaches 1,000 per square mile. The close association between banana cultivation and the Bantu-speaking tribes is demonstrated by Figs. 1 and 2. The nature of the association varies. The dominant importance of bananas is most clearly marked among the largest single tribe, the Ganda. This is true both of the past (1) and the present. A similar relationship continues into Tanganyika among the Haya of Bukoba District. The traditional dominance of bananas in the agriculture of the Soga and the Amba is also attested by Fallers (2) and Winter (3) respectively. Today, bananas are also the staple crop of the Gisu, although the extent of their former reliance upon them is uncertain (4). Among many of the remaining Bantu-speaking tribes of southern Uganda, notably the Nyoro, Toro, Ankole, Hororo and Gwere, the status of bananas is somewhat different. Formerly they appear to have been of subsidiary importance to finger millet (*Eleusine coracana*), but in the present century banana cultivation has expanded steadily in both acreage and popularity.

Baker and Simmonds believe there are about fifty varieties of banana in the inland areas of East Africa, and they consider this to be a probable 'secondary centre of diversity of the crop' (5). Buganda

*Reprinted with permission of the editor from the *Journal of Tropical Geography*, Vol. 16, 1962, pp.57-69.

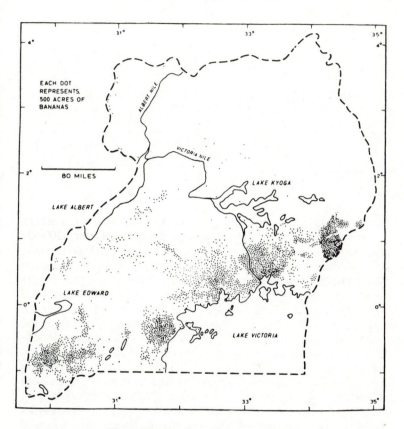

Fig. 1 Distribution of bananas, 1958.

again predominates. As early as 1902 Sir Harry Johnston recorded thirty-one local varieties. This wide range, much exceeded in later counts, is a reminder of the importance of bananas to the Ganda. They are focal in the life and economy of the people. All other foodstuffs are considered secondary and second-best. Legend associates the banana with Kintu, the mythical father of the tribe. The techniques of banana cultivation are elaborate and give every indication of being long established. Four main groups of bananas are recognised: cooking bananas (or *matoke*), beer bananas (*mbide*), roasting bananas (*gonja*) and dessert, yellow bananas (*menvu*). Within these broad groups there are great refinements in variety, nomenclature, management and usage. Besides the fruit, almost every portion of the plant has traditional usages for fibres, wrapping, fuel and so on.

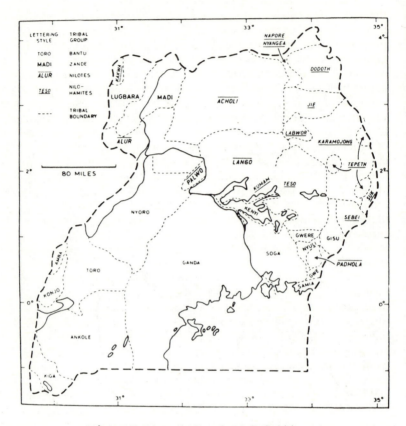

Fig. 2   Tribal boundaries (after J. E. Goldthorpe).

The broad outlines of the banana problem in relation to Uganda may now be stated. Here is a crop which, on botanical, anthropological and agricultural evidence, shows every sign of being anciently entrenched in local cultivation. Simmonds, who has made a particular study of the crop, writes, 'I find it difficult to believe that a banana civilisation such as that of the Baganda has developed in a mere 1,000 years or so' (6). Yet the cultivated bananas are not, in their origins, indigenous to Africa, being quite distinct from the native genus *Ensete*, none of which bear edible fruits (5). The great majority of edible bananas had their origin in only two wild species, *Musa acuminata* and *M. balbisiana*, or in crosses between them (7).[1] The apparent homes of these ancestors lie in the monsoon coastlands of eastern Asia in the area bounded by the Bay of Bengal, the Malay Peninsula and the southern ranges of the new fold mountains. Today, the banana is a true cultigen: a plant made over by man for his own uses, no longer bearing viable seeds, and dependent upon man for its propagation by means of corms or suckers taken from existing plants. Under such conditions the sole method of genetic variation is by somatic mutation (or 'sporting'), and mutation rates are practically constant (6). It may be deduced from these facts and from the great variety of cultivated bananas existing today that the domestication is very ancient. This may indeed be among the oldest of domesticated food plants. If so the origins of the banana are tied up with the origins of agriculture itself. The broader aspects of the problem may, however, be approached from a consideration of the local situation.

It is unprofitable to give much consideration to the possibility of an autochthonous East African agriculture to which, later, attractive food plants might have been added as they became available by introduction. The attempt is soon checked by the apparent poverty of choice of important food plants that may be assumed to have been locally available. Greenway has summarised the evidence on the origins of cultivated food plants in their application to East Africa (8). Sorghum (*S. vulgare*), finger millet and simsim (*Sesamum indicum*) may have originated in eastern Africa, the Ethiopian Highlands being the most likely centre. The Bambara groundnut (*Voandzeia subterranea*) is more likely to have been locally developed. It may be noted that these are seed crops which might be expected to yield some archaeological evidence of early cultivation in East Africa. Virtually all the important planted crops have been introduced. A more fundamental objection to the localised invention of agriculture is found in the consideration of the time scale of man's technological progress. In perhaps one million years of experience, man has been an agriculturalist for a few millenia. In relation to Africa the time span is certainly reduced. The first attested evidence from radio-carbon dating of agriculture in lower Egypt – admittedly in a fairly advanced form – is about 4500 B.C. However obvious the ideas of cultivation may appear in retrospect, they did not come quickly or easily to man. It is probable that diffusion of the basic techniques considerably outstripped and outweighed independent invention.

The nature of the African continent in relation to crop transmission is therefore important. Fig. 3 attempts an evaluation in such terms. It relates particularly to planted crops for two reasons: firstly, because the banana is such a crop; secondly, because the thesis of Hahn and others that planted agriculture evolved before seed agriculture seems to be a valid premise. Technique is at least as basic to agriculture as crop choice. Vegetative propagation and selection on the one hand, and sowing and cross-breeding on the other are very different modes of cultivation, which must have taken the early cultivators long ages to

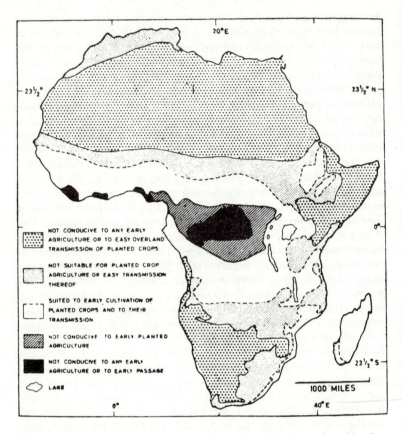

Fig. 3. An ecological evaluation of Africa in relation to the early cultivation and transmission of planted crops. Ecology after Phillips (10). Madagascar after Maurette (20).

master and to combine. Sauer also makes the significant observation that for the earlier cultivators, working with the digging stick and similar primitive tools, the moulds and moist soils of forest margins must have offered easier opportunities than the knotty tussocks and matted roots of the savannas. River terraces and alluvial fans would also present advantages. Agriculture in the savanna may well be derivative (9).[2] In Fig. 3, therefore, the zones designated as best suited to the early transmission and cultivation of planted crops constitute the margins of the humid tropical forest, the humid sub-tropical and montane forests, and the sub-humid wooded savanna. The designations are those of Phillips (10). Without starting the hare of possible climatic change, it is reasonable to conceive of the sub-humid wooded savannas having become progressively more open during centuries of human activity, with consequent effects upon their water resources and soils. On the flanks of the favoured zones, heavy forest, particularly where it is marshy, drier savanna, semi-deserts and deserts progressively limited the opportunities.

The ecology of East Africa is peculiar. A favoured region – the plateau of the great lakes – is surrounded by barriers of varying degrees of difficulty. To the north, the *sudd* and the *toich* are formidable zones. To the north-east, below the tabular edge of the Ethiopian Highlands, lies a belt of semi-desert, intensifying into true desert around the southern end of Lake Rudolf. To the east, backing the Indian coast, lies the Nyika, a tract of inhospitable, sub-arid thorn bush. To the west, the highlands and troughs of the western rift valley system and the extensive forests of the Congo Basin pose difficulties. The history of the nineteenth century European exploration of East Africa provides ample testimony to the reality of these barriers. Only to the north-west, via the Congo-Nile divide, and to the south, via the rift valley lakes, are there attractive approaches to the East African plateau. The Congo-Nile divide is the easier route. Physically, this major watershed between two great African rivers is surprisingly unimpressive. Often, its contemporary treelessness, consequent upon generations of human activity, underlines this effect.

Divergent views on the introduction of the banana to Uganda may be set against this ecological background (Fig. 4). Firstly, the ideas of the Ganda themselves deserve consideration. These ideas are fairly specific and circumstantial: the banana was brought by Kintu from the north or the north-east (1a). Opinions vary widely on the value of tribal myth in historical interpretation. Unaided, it scarcely supports the superstructure of a thesis. The story of Kintu prevails in some detail, not only among the Ganda but also among the Nyoro and the Toro (11). In Buganda there are perhaps two strata in this myth; the first embedding cryptic elements concerning a long-distance folk migration, the second partially derived from the first and relating to the incoming of Hamitic overlords from the north-east. In the orthodox view the latter elements founded a dynasty in Buganda, probably between 1,000 and 500 years ago. They may well have taken over existing tribal legends to underwrite and confirm their own power. However this may be, certain points of the legend of Kintu as given by Roscoe deserve note. When he first came to Uganda, Kintu found no food. He brought with him one cow but no crops or domestic stock until Nambi, his wife, accompanied him, when a goat, a sheep, a fowl and a banana plant were also brought. The banana was established in a named locality. Kintu's wife is thus depicted as the first Buganda agriculturalist. The immigration of an agricultural people into a

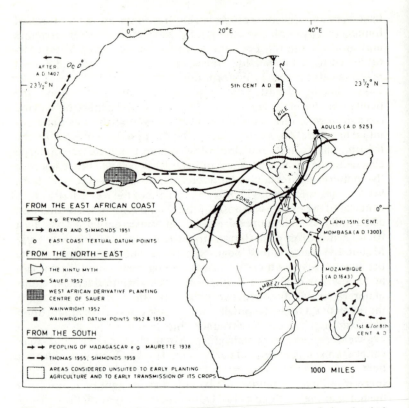

Fig. 4. Some suggested routes of possible banana transmission in their relation to Uganda.

thinly populated territory of hunter-gatherer and fishing groups is consonant with modern views on Uganda's pre-history. There is also some indication that this incursion and overlapping progressed southwards through the continent (12). As a record of folk migration the approach of Kintu from the north would also agree with the postulates of Greenberg (13), who, upon linguistic evidence, assigns to the Bantu-speaking peoples an origin in the area of the Cameroons, the expansion therefrom having occurred within the last 3,000 to 2,000 years. Kintu, then, hints at a possible southward entry of the banana into Uganda, but the more distant routes remain obscure.

Wainwright (14) has directed attention to the possibility of the banana having entered Uganda from the north-east by way of the Ethiopian Highlands. He presents probable documentary evidence for its presence on the Red Sea coast at about A.D. 525. It could thus have been brought to Uganda by Kintu, conceived as the Hamitic founder of a dynasty. Neither the final stages of the route through the north-eastern approaches, nor the carriage by a predominantly cattle-centred group are fully satisfying.

It is sometimes maintained that a direct entry of the banana into the Lakes Plateau from the East African coast poses no particular difficulty. This is not so. The Nyika forms a forbidding hinterland to the coastal fringe of such significance that it is probably a valid generalisation to say that before the nineteenth century it was the East African interior that 'discovered' the coast rather than the reverse. Archaeology offers no evidence for penetration inland from the coast. 'No pottery or porcelain or other objects imported to the coast have yet been traced inland' (15). Nor is there yet any documentation of contacts between Uganda and the coast earlier than the eighteenth century. Baker and Simmonds suggest, as an alternative to a southern route, that the line from the coast via the Usambara Mountains and Mount Kilimanjaro is a feasible one for the introduction of the banana, but their own work on varieties goes some way to rule it out, and Simmonds confirms the difficulty (5, 6). The varietal populations of the inland and the coastal areas are markedly different, and most of the overlap can readily be explained as a modern development. There may, further, be a chronological problem. The archaeological evidence for coastal settlement by sea-going peoples does not go back earlier than the late thirteenth century (16). The banana seems to have been present on the East African coast by A.D. 1300 (8). Unless, however, it was already of some antiquity, these datings allow quite inadequate time for diffusion inland and the subsequent development of new varieties. A much longer time interval would be needed. There is reason to infer Arab, and perhaps Indonesian, contacts considerably earlier, although Kirkman is sceptical regarding the latter. According to documentary evidence, the earliest contacts were made about the first century A.D. *The periplus of the Erythraean Sea* contains references to the maritime trade of the East African coast, but no points have been confidently identified (17).

Thomas (18) and Simmonds (6) urge the claims of the southern route of entry for the banana, via the Zambezi valley and the great lakes. It has, indeed, strong claims to consideration and its geographical suitability has already been noted. Indonesian settlers, arriving almost certainly along the monsoon routes, are known to have reached Madagascar in the eighth century, and earlier migrants may have arrived as early as the first century A.D. (19). Various workers, including Hornell (20) and Culwick and Culwick (21), have indicated positive and possible Indian echoes within mainland Africa. These are summarised by Posnansky (22). The form and decoration of sewn

boats in East Africa are the most material traits, musical influences
the most wide-spread. The banana is an important food crop in
Madagascar. It, and other Asiatic crops including taro, or the coco-
yam (*Colocasia antiquorum*), could also have been among the introductions that diffused gradually northwards and westwards
through tropical Africa.

A number of reservations concerning this route should be set out.
Firstly, the problem of bulk carriage of a considerable variety of
planting stock over extended ocean routes should not be minimised.
Secondly, it may be noted that the route when applied to East Africa,
though certainly feasible, runs counter in direction to general views
on the diffusion and migration of a number of other elements in
Africa, including cattle (23), the movements of Bantu-speaking peoples (13), with the consequent recessions of the Bushman-Hottentot
groups (12), and the spread of iron working (24). The human implications seem especially significant. The carriage of a staple crop of
such importance and variety, as the banana assumes in Uganda, must
surely be associated with folk migrations. The time range of up to
2,000 years, which is available if a spread from Madagascar is pos-
tulated, may be sufficient, but it is difficult within the existing
framework of the Bantu expansion to envisage the main human
groups moving south-eastwards and southwards from West Africa,
whilst crops of basic importance to them today were transmitted

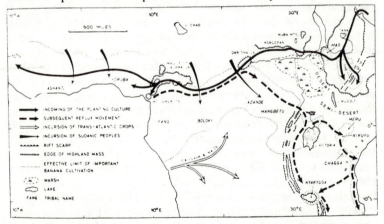

Fig. 5. Some features and relationships along a suggested northern route.
The northern limits of banana cultivation shown here are determined mainly
on climatic grounds, and draw on plates 18 and 23 of the 'Atlas des Colonies
Françaises' (Paris, 1934), and on Tothill (36). The southern limits accord
mainly with the importance of contemporary cultivation; for West and
Central Africa they draw on the maps of Johnston (42).

northwards by other agents. Thirdly, the present areas of important banana cultivation are best developed in a broad wedge of country situated chiefly north of the Equator and extending from West Africa to the East African plateau. Southwards the distribution of African banana-cultivating groups becomes more fragmentary (Fig. 5). Although there are climatic patterns supporting this distribution, it does not accord too well with an entry from the south. Fourthly, if the banana did enter the continent via the mouth of the Zambezi, some early diffusion might well have been expected southwards along the trade-wind coastlands of Mozambique and Natal, where bananas are appreciable commercial crops today. The writer knows of no suggestion that this occurred. It is felt that the general mode of entry of the banana into the continent still remains an open question.

Brief note should next be taken of the broad synoptic picture given by Murdock (25) of the sequential development of African agriculture. Murdock does not himself express this in a map. Fig. 6 is an attempt at such an interpretation in general terms. Any errors or mis-readings that it contains are due, therefore, to the present writer. An entry of the banana from Indonesian settlements on the east coast is proposed. This possibility has been discussed above. A central point in Murdock's thesis is the independent invention of agriculture in a Sudanic area of West Africa which he terms Nuclear Mande. Origins between 5000 and 4000 B.C. are suggested. The range of staples proposed includes both planted and sown crops. Some implications of these views have also been discussed above. Murdock does a service in drawing attention to the probability that agriculture existed in West Africa in much earlier times than has often been assumed. However, the suggestion of independent invention scarcely has sufficient warrant, particularly in view of the broadly contemporaneous evidence of agriculture in lower Egypt, and the demonstration, by the British Ennedi expedition (26), of regular contacts by about 4000 B.C. between the middle Nile and the Lake Chad area. Posnansky (22) concludes that the archaeological evidence is overwhelmingly against the independent invention of agriculture anywhere in northern or central Africa. This, again, prompts the consideration of Sauer's work (27). Although a brief synopsis must do scant justice to the cogency of his arguments, the main relevant points in his thesis should be noted.

Sauer argues that the origins of agriculture should be sought among settled communities, and suggests that fishing societies in tropical areas of diversified topography agree best with this tenet. Whilst men engaged in fishing, women may have developed the earliest agriculture, based upon the vegetative reproduction of planted crops. Geographical and botanical pointers lead Sauer to propose south-eastern Asia as the hearth of this original agriculture.

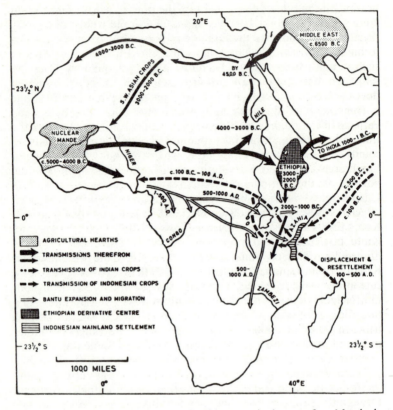

Fig. 6. Sequential development of African agriculture (after Murdock, 1959).

In this setting the achievements may have included the domestication of a range of important crops including bananas, taro, certain of the yams (*Dioscorea alata* and *D. esculenta*), and a number of plants used for the preparation of fibres, dyes and spices. The domestication also of the dog, the pig and the chicken as household animals, and the development of such techniques as the preparation of bark-cloth and the use of certain stupefying vegetable juices in fishing are also credited to this hearth. Agriculture was women's work. It did not yield a balanced diet, since fish was also produced by the men.

This ancient planting culture is seen as diffusing in slow folk migrations north-eastwards into China, south-eastwards into the Asian and Pacific archipelagoes, and westwards into India, the Middle East and tropical Africa (Fig. 4). The Guinea Coast of West Africa is accorded importance as a subordinate centre of vegetative domestication, the two yams *Dioscorea rotundata* and *D. Cayenensis* being among its contributions. In favoured areas along the migration routes there evolved, under the earlier planting stimulus, new crops and new techniques of seed agriculture. Following Vavilov, Sauer attributes such derivative importance to the Ethiopian Highlands, where a range of crops including sorghum, finger millet and simsim may have developed.

There is great attraction in the bold synoptic view just outlined. Patterns of life in the more humid parts of western Africa often agree well with features attributed to the planting culture. Summary accounts of the Fang (28), the Boloki (9), and the coastal Bantu of the Cameroons (29) may be cited as examples. Furthermore, numerous possible parallels may be traced among the Bantu-speaking tribes of Uganda, particularly among those which appear to have been least affected by later Hamitic influence, as for example, the Kenyi, Gisu, Konjo and Ganda. Some of these parallels have been set out in the Kintu myth.[4] The Kenyi are predominantly a fisher folk, whose limited agriculture is almost wholly by planting techniques. The Konjo of the Ruwenzori slopes were found sixty years ago to be subsisting on a diet 'mainly of bananas, sweet potatoes and colocasia' (30). Indeed, even allowing for the modern spread of cassava cultivation, the correspondence between the distribution of Bantu-speaking tribes in Uganda and the general dominance of planting techniques in agriculture are close (31). Use is made of vegetable fish poisons by a number of tribes, including the Gisu.

There are, however, appreciable problems in applying Sauer's thesis as it stands. The feasibility of a major migration of the banana through the Arabian realm has been questioned by Thomas (18) and Simmonds (6). Sauer discusses the point. He envisages a route through the coastal fringes of Southern Arabia, where there are a number of oases sited below mountain ranges which rise to 3,000 feet and more. The importance of this coast-wise route in general agricultural migrations was subsequently stressed by Burkill (32), who terms it the Sabaean Lane. Dale (33) hints at possibilities of climatic deterioration in this zone, but, even setting this aside, something can be allowed for man's progressive impoverishment of the natural vegetation of the highlands. The banana will grow in oasis conditions, provided it has shelter and sufficient non-saline water at its roots. It is cultivated under such conditions in the modern Sudan Republic and in Egypt (34). Sauer notes that, for carriage, the root stocks can be thoroughly dried out and left exposed for months before replanting. The pseudostem may also be used for a starchy foodstuff in times of famine. Even so, the route raises doubts, and, since these are most strongly expressed by botanists, the difficulty cannot be considered as fully resolved.

The Ethiopian Highlands provide a suitable line of entry into Africa for a planting culture, including the banana. Traces of old racial and cultural influences are indicated among the Mao and the Ometo group of Sidamo (35). But, concerning the banana, it is in these areas of Africa alone that there exists today a strongly developed cultivation, not of the *Musa* species but of the indigenous African genus *Ensete* (36, 37). This plant forms a staple food, cultivated at altitudes between 5,000 and 9,000 feet for its pseudostem, from which an edible starch or bread is prepared. This evidence is distinctly equivocal: the techniques of agriculture are in accord with planting ways. But, if the edible banana became available early, why did it not supplant *Ensete*? The question cannot at present be answered. Simmonds may, however, provide a pointer when he notes that 'it is hard to conceive of *Ensete* agriculture existing (at least in its intensive form) without the stock upon which it depends for manure.'

There remains a material chronological problem regarding Ethiopia. The postulate of a derived Ethiopian seed centre requires the passage of the planting culture through this realm long before there is any warrant for assuming its diffusion southwards into East Africa. This objection does not, however, apply to West Africa. Sauer's own diagrammatic lines of diffusion into Africa do not meet this objection, nor do they fit in well with the natural barriers to the north and north-east of the East African plateau.

Objections to Sauer's scheme have been set out fairly fully because, despite them, this is felt to be the most satisfying approach to the banana problem. The case for the planting culture is better than the specific case for the carriage of the banana, but it seems likely that if Africa did get agriculture by this route one of the oldest cultivated plants was introduced as part of the endowment.

A modification of Sauer's thesis is now proposed which meets some of the difficulties within Africa. The planting culture, including the banana, is seen as entering Africa through the Ethiopian Highlands during folk migrations at a very early date. Barriers of swamp and desert prevented a direct transmission towards East Africa. Instead, the main diffusion was towards West Africa. The route suggested is from Ethiopia towards the present site of Malakal, and thence along the southern edge of the plateau of Kordofan to the Dar Shalla. This tract admittedly raises difficulties, but water and alluvial soils would enable settlement to take place in favoured sites along the scarp foot. The Dar Shalla lies on the northern edge of the general zone suited to banana cultivation. Thence, transmission westwards, skirting the margin of the high forest and taking advantage of the natural 'stepping stones' of the Massif de L'Adamaoua and Mount Cameroon, could readily occur. Thereafter, the more humid regions of West Africa and the Cameroons are seen as the main setting for the evolution and the expansion of agriculture in tropical Africa for many centuries. Additional domestications were made, variation among bananas may have proceeded, and agriculture in the West African savannas may have developed, with their further stimulus of contacts along the east-west Sudan zone south of the Sahara. This has been a great route for migrations and trade throughout many generations.

Evolved societies based on planted crops are not highly or readily mobile. Their methods do not make undue demands upon the soil and may support considerable rural population densities. The stimulus to later folk movements is therefore an open question. Posnansky (22) links the Bantu expansion with the spread of iron. This connection may be valid but it may have operated indirectly. Ganda tradition is that iron-working was acquired from Bunyoro, to the north-west: there is no mention of Kintu having brought it (24). This suggests that the Ganda were already established in their present area when iron arrived. However, the suggestions of stability and population balance in western Africa emphatically do not apply to the savanna or to the Sudanese zones. Therein generations of seed agriculture, with the accompanying tree destruction, operating on soils of moderate potential, will have impoverished certain areas and opened the ways to movement southwards. Cattle-ownership would accentuate this mobility, and iron-technology, moving easily along the Sudan belt, would furnish new and potent weapons for conquest. The migrations of the Bantu may have been a response to such invading pressures from the north. Forde's analysis of the Yoruba would accord with this general pattern of development (9).

Under pressure, an eastward reflux movement of planting peoples, carrying the banana, taro and yams among their. crops[5] is likely, moving along the forest-savanna corridor, now somewhat more open and extended further southwards. The entry to East Africa would be by way of the easy Congo-Nile divide, with an ultimate arrival in Buganda from the north. Such a movement could have brought the Bantu-speaking agriculturalists to Uganda within the last 1,500 years and with them the main planted crops. If the banana was among them, considerable variation would already have been present upon which later selection has drawn. No accuracy is claimed for the further movements within East Africa shown on Fig. 5. Bantu-speaking groups undoubtedly moved coastwards as well as southwards, but it is certain that new banana varieties must subsequently have been brought to the East African coast and spread inland from there. Once Bantu agriculturalists reached the coast new crops can easily have been added to their range.

In later ages, southward drives of invaders from the Sudan zone certainly occurred. Earlier societies have often been part overridden, part absorbed and in other instances driven deeper into the Congo forests. The descriptions of the Mangbetu and the Azande, as summarised by Baxter and Butt (38), may exemplify successive stages in the absorption of earlier planting societies. Banana cultivation flourishes in stable or sheltered societies. In times of pillage and invasion the crop itself is vulnerable to theft and destruction. Invading peoples may also have brought with them new grain crops. The adoption of finger millet as a staple by the Nyoro and Toro could reflect such influences. Furthermore, agricultural economies have been greatly modified in recent centuries by New World crops, particularly cassava, sweet potatoes and maize, driving into the continent from the Congo and the Guinea Coast. The adoption of these crops may have helped to check the southward extension through the Congo Basin of the banana as a major food crop (Fig. 5).

Within Uganda, the modern extensions of the banana in Bunyoro, Toro, Ankole, Kigezi and Bukedi are more readily explicable. The last sixty years have witnessed a new regime of stability and order. Even more significantly, in the early decades of the present century this was carried over most of southern Uganda, and as far north as Lango, by subordinate Ganda administrators. They bore with them their favourite food crop, the banana. To local Bantu eyes, it also seems to have become endowed with some of the prestige of the Ganda. The modern expansion of the crop seems to spring mainly from these causes, the desire to copy Ganda ways perhaps becoming at the same time stronger and less explicit as development proceeded.

No finality is claimed for the suggestions put forward in this paper. They will serve their purpose if they draw attention to certain key areas and fields of study, from which the different arguments may be strengthened or undermined. The writer considers that a northern sequence solves more problems than it raises, but it certainly lacks proof. The northern forest fringes, the Zambezi-great lakes route, and the Angolan Plateau are key areas, but the extent to which later tribal movements and modern sophistication complicate the reconstruction of earlier patterns of agriculture must be recognised. Archaeology and botany are key fields of study. The evidence from archaeology is likely to be indirect, since bananas and other planted crops yield little lasting material imprint. Simmonds (6) points out, also, that bananas are inherently unpromising material for the recognition of subtle mutations, but he also notes that little is yet known of the relationships of the varieties grown in West Africa. Botanical research on these types and on those of Madagascar may in time yield more positive pointers than those now available.

NOTES

1. Following the work of Cheesman, the former distinction between 'bananas' and 'plantain', for long blurred, has become invalid for general purposes.
2. There appear to be two phases of hoe cultivation in Africa: an earlier, associated with root crops and dominantly female; and a later, probably developed primarily in the savanna lands in connection with millet growing, in which men share in or take over nearly all agricultural pursuits.
3. Allen has presented a case for identifying Rhapta, the southern-most port mentioned, with the Pangani estuary.
4. It is notable that the association between Kintu and the coming of the banana is particularly strong among the Mushroom Clan, traditional makers of bark-cloth (1b).
5. It is probable that other crops will have been acquired, for example, simsim.

REFERENCES

(1) Roscoe, J., *The Buganda* (1911; reprinted with a new bibliographic note, Frank Cass, London, 1965); (a) pp.460-4, 151 and 186; (b) p.151.
(2) Fallers, L. A., *Bantu bureaucracy; a study of integration and conflict in the political institutions of an East African people* (Cambridge, 1956).
(3) Winter, E. H., *Bwamba economy* (Kampala, 1955).
(4) La Fontaine, J. S., *The Gisu of Uganda* (London, 1959).
(5) Baker, R. E. D. and Simonds, N. W., 'Bananas in East Africa, Part 1: The botanical and agricultural status of the crop', *Empire Journal of Experimental Agriculture,* Vol. 19, 1951, pp.283-90.
(6) Simmonds, N. W., *Bananas* (London, 1959).
(7) Cheesman, E. E., 'On the nomenclature of edible bananas', *Journal of Genetics,* Vol. 41, 1948, pp.293-6.
(8) Greenway, P. J., 'Origins of some East African food plants', *East African Agricultural Journal,* Vol. 10, 1944, pp.34-9, 115-9, 177-80, 251-6, and Vol. 11, 1945, pp.56-63.
(9) Forde, C. Daryll, *Habitat, economy and society* (London, 1934), p.172.
(10) Phillips, J., *Agriculture and ecology in Africa* (London, 1959).
(11) Richards, A. I. (ed.), *East African Chiefs: a study of political development in some Uganda and Tanganyika tribes* (London, 1960).
(12) Heinzelin de Braucourt, J. de., *Exploration du Parc National Albert Pt. 2, Les fouilles d'Ishango* (Brussels, 1957).
(13) Greenberg, J. H., *Studies in African linguistic classification* (New Haven, 1955).
(14) Wainwright, G. A., 'The coming of the banana to Uganda', *Uganda Journal,* Vol. 16, 1952, pp.145-7.
(15) Freeman-Grenville, G. S. P., 'The times of ignorance: a review of pre-Islamic and early Islamic settlement on the East African Coast', in *Discovering Africa's past* (Kampala, Uganda Museum, 1959, Occasional paper, No. 4).
(16) Kirkman, J. S., 'Archaeological research on the coast of Kenya', in *Discovering Africa's past* (Kampala, Uganda Museum, 1959, Occasional paper, No. 4).
(17) Allen, J. W. T., 'Rhapta', *Tanganyika Notes and Records,* No. 27, 1949, pp.52-9.
(18) Thomas, A. S., 'The coming of the banana to Uganda', *Uganda Journal,* Vol.19, 1955, p.211.
(19) Maurette, F., 'Afrique équatoriale, orientale et australe', *Géographie Universelle* (Paris, 1938), Tome XII, ch. 23.
(20) Hornell, J., 'Indonesian influence on East African culture', *Journal of the Royal Anthropological Institute,* Vol. 64, 1934, pp.305-32.
(21) Culwick, A. T. and Culwick, G. M., 'Indonesian echoes in Central Tanganyika',

      Tanganyika Notes and Records, No. 2, 1936, pp.60-6.
(22) Posnansky, M., 'Bantu genesis', *Uganda Journal,* Vol. 25, 1961, pp.86-93.
(23) Epstein, H., in *The indigenous Cattle of the British dependent territories in Africa* (London, 1957), Part IV, and Fig. 9 on p.141.
(24) Wainwright, G. A., 'The diffusion of *-uma* as a name for iron', *Uganda Journal,* Vol. 18, 1954, pp.113-36.
(25) Murdock, G. P., *Africa: its peoples and their culture history* (New York, 1959).
(26) Arkell, A. J., 'Preliminary report on the archaeological results of the British Ennedi Expedition, 1957', *Kush,* Vol. 7, 1959, pp.15-27.
(27) Sauer, C. O., *Agricultural origins and dispersals* (New York, 1952).
(28) Brunhes, J., *Human Geography* (London, 1952, translation by E. F. Row), pp.152-6.
(29) Ardener, E., 'Coastal Bantu of the Cameroons', *Ethnographic Survey of Africa* (London, 1956), Pt. XI.
(30) Johnston, Sir Harry, *The Uganda Protectorate* (London, 1902), Vol. 2, p.576.
(31) McMaster, D. N., *A subsistence crop geography of Uganda* (Ph.D. thesis of the University of London, published in 1962 by Geographical Publications Limited as World Land Use Survey, Occasional Paper No. 2), Fig. 12.
(32) Burkill, I. H., 'Habits of man and the cultivated plants of the Old World', *Proceedings of the Linnean Society, London,* Vol. 164, 1953, pp.12-42.
(33) Dale, I. R., 'The Indian origins of some African cultivated plants and African cattle', *Uganda Journal,* Vol. 19, 1955, pp.68-72.
(34) Tothill, J. D. (ed.), *Agriculture in the Sudan* (London, 1948).
(35) Cerulli, E., 'Peoples of South-west Ethiopia and its Borderlands', *Ethnographic Survey of Africa* (London, 1956), Pt. III.
(36) Smeds, H., 'The *Ensete* planting culture of eastern Sidamo, Ethiopia', *Acta Geographia,* Vol. 13, 1955, and 'Ensete-odlingen i Syd-Ethiopien', *Saertryk af Kulturgeografia* (Aarhus), No. 73, 1961, pp.49-59.
(37) Simmonds, N. W., '*Ensete* cultivation in the southern highlands of Ethiopia; a review', *Tropical Agriculture,* Vol. 35, 1958, pp.302-7.
(38) Baxter, P. T. W. and Butt, A., 'The Azande and related peoples', *Ethnographic Survey of Africa* (London, 1956), Pt. IX.

3

THE CULTIVATION AND USE OF YAMS IN WEST AFRICA*

D. G. Coursey

Introduction

A major part of modern West African dietary is furnished by crop plants which are not indigenous to the area, but which have been introduced to West Africa mostly in historic times. It is only necessary to consider the list of crop plants known to have been imported – bananas, citrus fruits, pineapples, maize, several varieties of rice, coconuts, groundnuts, several legumes, some of the cocoyams (taros) and, most important, the ubiquitous cassava (manioc) – to realise that African diets in the period before European contact must have been very different, and more restricted, than they are today. Most of the above-mentioned plants were introduced by European traders in the sixteenth and seventeenth centuries, although bananas and cocoyams, which are of Asiatic origin, probably entered the area with Arabic or Sudanese migrations, and there is evidence that maize (which is American in origin) entered West Africa not only directly, but also *via* the Mediterranean. In recent years, diets have been further diversified by the substantial and increasing imports of temperate zone foods as such – notably milk, wheaten flour, dried Atlantic cod and preserved meat and fish.

There is no doubt that many food crops were formerly utilised to a great extent, which are now neglected entirely – except, perhaps in the remotest areas – or are only used in time of famine (20), (28). These would have added some diversity to the diets of the pre-contact era. Two food plants which are still of the greatest importance are, however, indigenous to West Africa; these are the yams (*Dioscorea* spp.) and the oil palm (*Elaeis guineensis* Jacq.) It is with the former of these that the present paper is concerned.

---

*This article, abridged by the editors and revised by the author, is reprinted by permission from *Ghana Notes and Queries* (Kumasi), Vol. 9, 1966.

Botany and classification

Before proceeding, it may be useful to those not familiar with tropical agriculture, to clear up misconceptions that exist over the use of the word 'yam'. The word is strictly applied only to members of the genus *Dioscorea L.* and it is in that sense that it is used here. It is often misapplied, however, especially by American writers, to cover a surprising range of tropical and sub-tropical root and tuber crops, principally the sweet potato (*Ipomea batatas (L.)* Lam.) but also the cocoyams or taros (*Xanthosoma* and *Colocasia* spp.) and arrowroots (*Maranta* spp.) The so-called 'yam belt' of the southern U.S.A. is actually a region where sweet potatoes are extensively grown. In West Africa, a tuberous-rooted legume (*Sphenostylis stenocarpa* Harms.) is commonly referred to as the 'yam bean', on account of the form of its root: this term is also applied in Asia and America to *Pachyrhizus* spp.

Botanically, the genus *Dioscorea* is the type genus of the family Dioscoreaceae and the order Dioscoreales, a family of monocotyledons closely related to the Liliales. Over 600 species are known (22) which are widely distributed throughout the tropical regions of the Old and New Worlds. A few species (of no economic importance) penetrate as far into the temperate zone as Albania, the Pyrenees and New England (16), (2).

Most species, and all the edible ones, develop an underground tuber or group of tubers, from which an herbaceous 'vine' is produced annually, to die away at the end of the growing season. These tubers are natural storage organs, which enable the plant to survive during periods of inclement conditions – e.g. from one rainy season to the next. It is the tuber that forms the edible part of the plant. Available evidence suggests that, like the potato, the yam tuber is, organographically, derived from the stem rather than the root (10), (26), though recent investigations (23) indicate that it is derived from the hypocotyl.

Only a few of the species, however, are of any value as food plants. The majority form only small, hard and unpalatable tubers, while many are actually toxic. The most important as cultivated crops are the following (3), (13), (34), (21), (15), (16):

D. alata L. Water Yam, Winged Yam, Greater Yam.
D. rotundata Poir. White Yam, Guinea Yam.
D. cayenensis Lam. Yellow Yam, Yellow Guinea Yam.
D. esculenta (Lour.) Burkill. Chinese Yam, Lesser Yam.
D. bulbifera L. Potato Yam, Aerial Yam.
D. trifita L. Cush-cush, Yampi.

Other species may be of local importance. In West Africa, *D. dumetorum, D. macroura, D. praehensilis, D. smilacifolia, D. hirtiflora* and *D. preussii* are utilised to some extent: they are, however, of minor importance. It has been estimated by Torto (1956) that 80 per cent of the yams produced in Ghana are derived from two cultivars of *D. rotundata*, 'Puna' and 'Labeco': the writer's experience with the crop in Nigeria leads him to suppose that similar considerations apply in that country, and elsewhere in West Africa.

Etymology of the term "YAM"

The origins of the term 'yam' are obscure. It has already been noted that the word is sometimes used to cover a number of other root crops, but this use is largely confined to the North American continent, and is probably a recent development.

There is no reason to suppose that the word is original to any European language, as no edible yams occur in Europe. Furthermore, there is a great similarity in the words used in different European languages for this plant:

English–	Yam (Jugnamis, Yammes in early documents)
French–	Igname
Spanish–	Name
Portuguese–	Inhame (Ynhame, in early documents)
German–	Ignam (kolle)
Dutch–	Ignom (?), Iniamas

The Arabic 'Ighnām' is also noteworthy in this context.

It would appear that the word entered the European languages from a source in a yam-producing tropical country during the period of paleo-Colonial expansion in the fifteenth and sixteenth centuries.

According to Chevalier (1946) the word 'igname' was derived by the French from the Mande 'niam', and cites an unspecified French dictionary of 1575, in which it occurs. The derivation from the Mande appears plausible, but it should be noted that 'ynhame' is used in much earlier Portuguese (29), and 'niam' by Columbus in 1492 (14). The subject has been discussed in detail by Burkill (1938), who supports the theory that the word passed from the Mande, through Portuguese, into European languages.

Origins of the edible yams

As indicated above, the genus *Dioscorea* is widely distributed throughout the tropics. It would appear *a priori* likely, therefore, that cultivation and use as food should have arisen independently in different parts of the world, different species being used. This view is supported by Chevalier (1946) Burkill (1960) Coursey (1967) and by Alexander and Coursey (1969) but the opinion has been widely expressed that yam cultivation originated only in South-East Asia, and that West Africans were 'shown how to grow yams'. There is no justification whatever for this view, which appears to be based on the remarkable pseudosyllogism:

Many important West African food crops are exotic in origin.

Yams are important West African food crops.

Therefore yams are exotic in origin.

Little knowledge of logic is required to appreciate the faults of this argument. The psychological climate of much of the Colonial era in West Africa was however unfavourable to the idea that African races could possibly have developed any useful crop.

Rational appreciation of the problem is also complicated by the fact that some species of yam, which are currently cultivated in West Africa, are undeniably of Asiatic origin.

One of the economically important yams of the Enantiophyllum group *D. alata,* although unknown in the wild state, is generally accepted as having been cultivated originally somewhere in the region of Burma, Siam or Malaysia, and to have been derived from the wild *D. persimilis* (5), (6) and to have spread through most of South-East Asia at an early date. It probably reached Madagascar in the eleventh century (30) and Zanzibar and the East African coast not much later. It was doubtless introduced to West Africa by the Portuguese (9) and its cultivation here is now widespread, although it is much less favoured than the indigenous species. It is significant that it is commonly known in the West Indies as the Lisbon Yam: the term Water Yam used in West Africa may, perhaps, indicate its overseas origin.

The Lesser Yam, *D. esculenta,* is grown to a very limited extent in parts of West Africa. It is probably ultimately of southern Chinese origin (31) but was widely disseminated throughout South East Asia before European penetration of that area (4), (6). It was probably carried by the Portuguese both to West Africa and the West Indies, but its cultivation in the former area does not seem to have persisted. It was deliberately introduced into West Africa in recent years (25), because it is higher-yielding than the local species, and because it was felt that it would be adaptable to mechanical cultivation, but has not become popular, as it does not yield a satisfactory 'fufu'.

The Cush-cush, *D. trifida,* is of South American origin (Chevalier, 1946) and there, and in the Caribbean, is one of the most highly prized types of yam. It is little used in the Old World, however, except in Ceylon: its cultivation in West Africa is negligible (34).

The Aerial or Potato Yam, *D. bulbifera,* which is remarkable in that the aerial tubers formed in the axis are generally larger than the normal underground tuber, is distributed naturally throughout Asia and Africa. It is not popular in West Africa probably for the same reason as *D. esculenta*. Some African forms are toxic.

D. dumetorum, which occurs through most of the savanna of Africa, and the other minor species mentioned earlier, are generally accepted as being indigenous to the continent.

The main controversy arises in connection with *D. rotundata* and *D. cayenensis*, which, as already indicated are by far the most important edible species in West Africa. Nearly all botanists and agriculturalists – including such eminent authorities as Chevalier and Burkill – agree that they are indigenous to the area. Brown (1931) is a notable exception: he regards the species as forms of *D. alata*, and therefore presumably Asiatic; this view is, botanically, quite indefensible. Some historio-geographers, however, find this view difficult to accept, and prefer an Asiatic origin. Goodwin (1939) has even suggested that yams were brought from Asia to Africa by the migrations of the 'proto-Negro'.

The only reasonable supposition is that these species are indigenous. They are far more extensively grown than other, exotic species, and are generally much preferred (e.g. the Ewe *te gba* = 'proper yam', for *D. rotundata*). In the West Indies, where these species are extensively grown – having largely displaced the local varieties – they are known as 'Guinea Yams'. Wild forms of *D. cayenensis* have been reported by Chevalier (1936, 1946) as being widespread in various parts of West Africa.

Origins of yam cultivation

The cultivation of yams in West Africa certainly antedates European contact. They are mentioned as important food crops in what are now Portuguese Guinea, the Nzima area of Ghana, and Eastern Nigeria, by Pacheco Pereira (1505-8), whose knowledge of the Coast is at least fifteen years earlier than the date of his writing.

In all probability, their cultivation is extremely ancient and played a most important part in the development of agriculture in sub-Saharan Africa.

The following pattern of development is suggested as likely. Palaeolithic man in West Africa, while still in the hunting and food-gathering stage, would doubtless have encountered, with other edible roots, several varieties of yam, and found some of them to be acceptable as food. The nature of the yam is such that, if the tuber is removed without excessive damage being done to the roots and vine, the plant will, at certain times of the year, recover, and produce another tuber in the place of the one removed. At the period of most rapid growth, this process could take only a few weeks. This would readily be noticed by the collectors, who would thus become habi-tuated to returning periodically to the same wild yam plants. From this practice, the transition to a proto-agricultural phase, when deliberate care is taken to minimise damage to the plants when removing the tubers, in anticipation of a future supply, is a compara-tively simple step. This, in turn, would lead to the transfer of wild plants to more convenient sites, hence to selection of the most pala-table forms leading gradually to ennoblement and the formation of different local cultivars, and thus to a true agriculture. It is considered that the New Yam Festival, which is of great cultural importance throughout the yam-growing parts of West Africa, and which ritually prohibits the consumption of yams at certain times of year, is a socio-cultural survival from this period (Coursey and Coursey, 1971). Even today, though, yam cultivation retains some proto-agricultural characteristics (11), (8). The origins of African yam-based agriculture are discussed in detail elsewhere (Coursey 1972).

The exact area where this type of yam cultivation originated will probably never accurately be determined, but the writer is inclined to favour a location on the borders of the Dahomey Gap, which lies approximately centrally within the main yam zone of West Africa: in any case, it would have been at or near the forest/savanna ecotone. It is not unreasonable to assume that the development of this form of agriculture triggered off a population explosion, which led to the penetration of the forest zone by people, and a crop, which had originated in savanna conditions. In this connection, it is interesting to note that the area of West Africa in which yams are the major food crop (or were, prior to the introduction of exotic food crops in recent times) coincides closely with the area occupied by people speaking languages of the Kwa group. This penetration would have been greatly accelerated by the development of iron tools, but would have been possible, to a more limited extent, even in Neolithic times, using fire as the principal method of forest clearance. It must be borne in mind, too, that yam cultivation can be carried out in the forest with only a minimum of clearance, far less than is required for grain, or most other types of crops. In many parts of West Africa, even today, land to be used for yam growing is often only partly cleared, trees of any economic value being left standing, and used as supports for the yam vines.

In referring to the yams as savanna crops, it is, however, necessary to realise that the major yam-producing areas of modern West Africa lie not within the true savanna zone, but within the Derived Guinea Savanna, which has only recently – in some areas only within living memory – been degraded from High Forest as a result of human activity. It is not impossible that the ennoblement of the yams originally took place in these very areas, but under High Forest conditions. The increased populations that developed as a result of the increased availability and reliability of food supply were ultimately responsible for the destruction of the forest environment: a process that has been accelerated by the more recent introduction of exotic crops which require more thorough forest clearing for their cultivation. Origin of yam cultivation in the area that is now the Congo has been suggested by Burkill (1939) and supported by Waitt (1961).

Unlike many other possible early food crops, the yams would have been comparatively little affected by the change in environment from forest to savanna, as they are well adapted to survive a prolonged dry season. This may well have been a major factor in bringing them to a dominant position in West Africa food economies.

Yam cultivation doubtless evolved independently, probably on essentially similar lines in the other main areas of origin, South-East Asia and Central and South America (in the West Indies, yam cultivation was probably introduced, and certainly greatly expanded, by early West African immigrants), different species being concerned in each instance (18).

As international maritime traffic developed in the fifteenth and sixteenth centuries, the main edible species of yam were rapidly disseminated throughout the tropics; a rough indication of the process is given in the map on p.40. This dispersion arose, probably, not so much from a deliberate policy of plant introduction (except, perhaps, in the case of the West Indies), but from the use of yams for the victualling of ships, especially slavers. Where available, yams were well adapted for this purpose, as they store well (though with some loss in weight) and are not liable to attack by the insects that so readily infest grain and similar products. Their antiscorbutic properties may also have been noted, and appreciated, by these early mariners. Yam tubers do however sprout spontaneously after protracted storage, and would then become less attractive as food. After a prolonged voyage, any uneaten stocks of yams would certainly have sprouted, and could well have been dumped ashore at some port-of-call, or bartered at cut prices for new stock.

The dissemination of *D. alata* in the Indian and Pacific Oceans certainly antedates European contact with this area, and was presumably effected by Indo-Malayan and Polynesian peoples (30), (9).

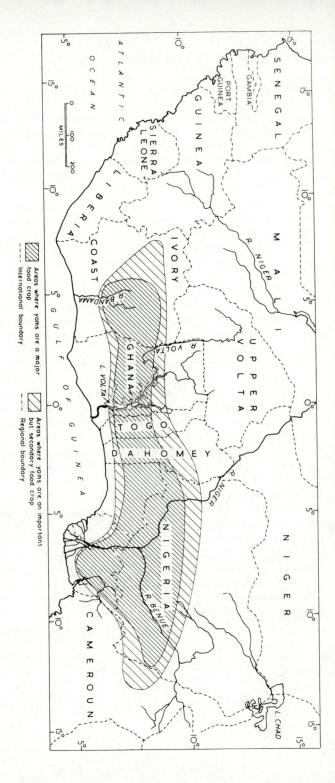

38

The Yam Zone of West Africa

From D. G. Coursey, *Yams* (Longman, 1967)

Areas where yams are a major food crop

Areas where yams are an important but secondary food crop

International boundary

Regional boundary

MILES
0   100   200

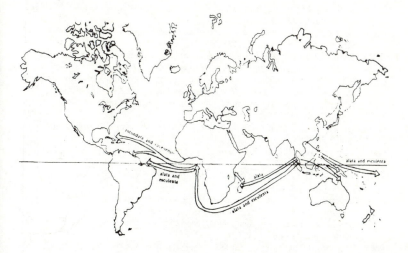

Routes of diffusion of yam cultivation

REFERENCES

(1) Alexander, J. and Coursey, D. G. 'The origins of yam cultivation' in Ucko, P. J. and Dimbleby, G. W., *The domestication and exploitation of plants and animals*, G. Duckworth, (London, 1969).

(2) Ayensu, E. S. 'Dioscoreales', Vol. VI of *The anatomy of the monocotyledons*, C. R. Matcalfe, edit., Clarendon Press, (Oxford, 1972).

(3) Brown, D. H. 'The Cultivation of Yams', (Trop.) *Agric. Trin.* 8, 8, (1931) pp. 201-6; 8, 9, pp. 231-6.

(4) Burkill, I. H. 'The Lesser yam – Dioscorea esculenta', *Gdnr's Bull.* (1917), 1, 11-12, p. 396.

(5) Burkill, I. H. 'Dioscorea alata', the greater yam', *Gdnr's, Bull.* (1919), 2, 5, p. 158.

(6) Burkill, I. H. *A Dictionary of the Economic Products of the Malay Peninsula.* Crown Agents, London, (1935).

(7) Burkill, I. H. 'The contact of the Portuguese with African food plants which gave words such as "Yam" to European languages.' *Proc. Linn. Soc.* (1938), 150, 2, pp. 84-95.

(8)   Burkill, I. H. 'Notes on the genus Dioscorea in the Belgian Congo', *Bull jard. bot. Bruxelles*, (1939), 15, 4, pp. 345-92.

(9)   Burkill, I. H. 'The rise and decline of the Greater Yam in the service of man', *Advance-Science*, London, (1951), 7, 28, pp. 443-8.

(10)   Burkill, I. H. 'Organography and evolution of Dioscoreaceae, the family of yams', *J. Linn.*, Soc., (1960), 56, pp. 319-408.

(11)   Chevalier, A. 'Contribution à l'Etude de quelques espèces Africaines du genre Dioscorea', *Bull. Mus. Nat. Hist. Naturelle*, Paris (1936), 8, 6, pp. 520-55.

(12)   Chevalier, A. 'Nouvelles recherches sur les ignames cultivées', *Rev. int. bot. appl.*, (1946), 26, 279-80, pp. 26-31.

(13)   Cobley, L. S. *An Introduction to the Botany of Tropical Crops.* Longmans, London, (1957).

(14)   Corominas, J. *Diccionario Critic Etimologico de la Lingua Castellana.* Editorial Franke, Beru, (1954).

(15)   Coursey, D. G. 'The role of the yams in West African food economics', *World Crops*, (1965), 17, 2, pp. 74-82.

(16)   Coursey, D. G. *Yams.* Longmans Green, London, (1967).

(17)   Coursey, D. G. 'The origins and domestication of yams in Africa', paper prepared for the Wenner-Gren Symposium on The origin of African plant domesticates, London, (1972).

(18)   Coursey, D. G. and Alexander, J. 'Agricultural patterns and the sickle cell', *Science*, London, (1968), 160 (3835), pp. 1474-5.

(19)   Coursey, D. G. and Coursey, Cecilia K. 'The New Yam Festivals of West Africa', *Anthropos*, (1971), 66, pp. 444-84.

(20)   Irvine, F. R. 'Supplementary and Emergency Food Plants of West Africa', *Econ. Bot.*, (1952), 6, 1, pp. 23-40.

(21)   Irvine, F. R. *A Textbook of West African Agriculture.* O.U.P., (1963).

(22)   Knuth, R. 'Dioscoreaceae', *Pflanzenreich*, 87, (1924), (iv, 43) pp. 1-278.

(23)   Lawton, June R. and Lawton, J. R. S. 'The development of the tuber in seedlings of five species of *Dioscorea* from Nigeria', *Bot. J. Linn. Soc.*, (1969), 62 (2), 223-32.

(24)   Murdock, G. P. *Africa – its peoples and their culture history.* McGraw-Hill, New York, (1959).

(25)   Miege, J. 'Le Dioscorea esculenta Burkill en Côte d'Ivoire', *Rev. int. bot. appl.* (1948), 28, 313-14-, pp. 500-14.

(26)   Nioku, E. 'The propagation of Yams by vine cuttings', *J. West Afri. Sci. Assoc.*, (1961), 8, 1, pp. 29-32.

(27)   Goodwin, A. J. H. 'The origins of certain African food plants', *S. Afr. J. Science*, (1939), 36, pp. 445-63.

(28)   Okiy, G. E. O. 'Indigenous Nigerian food plants', *J. West Afr. Sci. Assoc.*, (1960), 6, 2, pp. 117-21.

(29)   Pacheco Pereira, D. *Esmeraldo de Situ Orbis.* (1505-8) Reprinted in English by the Hakluyt Society. 1937.

(30)   Sampson, H. C. Additional Series No. 12. *Kew Bull.* (1936).

(31)   Ting, Y and Chi, C. W. 'The Chinese sweet potato', *J. Agric. Assoc. China*, (1948), 186, 1, pp. 23-33.

(32)   Torto, J. O. 'The Cultivation of Yams in the Gold Coast', *New Gold Coast Farmer*, (1956), 1, 1, pp. 6-8.

(33)   Waitt, A. W. 'Yams – Dioscorea species', paper presented to the Conference on History and Archaeology in Africa, S.O.A.S. London, (1961).

(34)   Waitt, A. W. 'Yams – Dioscorea species', *Field Crop Abstracts*, (1963), 16, 3, pp. 143-57.

4

THE INTRODUCTION AND SPREAD OF MAIZE IN AFRICA*

Marvin P. Miracle

Although maize is often listed as one of many food crops introduced in Africa by the Portuguese, how and when maize was brought to the continent cannot yet be established with certainty. This paper examines, with respect to African territory south of the Sahara, such evidence as may be found, chiefly in early travel accounts, of the introduction and spread of maize.

Two important aspects of the problem, however, are not scrutinised here. One is the view that maize is a plant of New World origin; the other is the view that, whether or not there was pre-Columbian contact between Africa and the Americas, maize was unknown outside the New World prior to Columbus's voyages. Although both views have been challenged, they have been widely accepted by competent scholars and are accepted here pending the appearance of additional convincing evidence to the contrary.

Perhaps more is known about the time when maize began to be important in parts of Africa than about the precise points of introduction or the responsible agents. At best only a rough history can be sketched at present, and, considering the size of Africa, that history would presumably vary from region to region. Here we look first at western tropical Africa, next at areas farther inland and southward, and last at the eastern tropical coast.

The earliest reference to what may have been maize applies to western Africa. There is mention of *milho zaburro* in a description of the West African Coast by the Portuguese writer, Valentim Fernandes, made in 1502 (24b).[1] But it is not certain whether his reference is to maize or a millet or sorghum. There is fairly good evidence that the term meant maize in 1550. M. D. W. Jeffreys (16) shows that in 1554 the Italian historian Gian Battista Ramusio refers to maize as

*Reprinted by permission of Cambridge University Press from *Journal of African History,* Vol. VI, No. 1, 1965.

miglio zaburro in his *Del Navigatione e Viaggi* and illustrates his discourse with a drawing of an ear of maize, unmistakably indicating the plant to which he was referring.[2]

R. Portères argues that maize was introduced from the north, across the Sahara, by Arab traders, as well as along the coasts by the Portuguese (28). Much of Portères's reasoning about the Portuguese introduction into western tropical Africa is based on the belief that maize with soft starch, the 'flour types', which are found more along the coast, came from Brazil, whereas the types with harder starch, the 'flint types', came from the Caribbean. Portères suggests that these 'flint types' came by way of Spain, through the Mediterranean to Egypt, and thence to inland areas of western Africa. It is possible, of course, that the distribution of maize types has changed considerably during the intervening centuries.

W. R. Stanton cites the diversity of maize types along the north-south trade routes of the interior of western Africa as evidence of the trans-Saharan route of introduction (31, p.4). But this also does not necessarily tell us anything about when or how maize was introduced; it may have no more value than to suggest the direction from which varieties now found in West Africa came. The types of maize in Africa may have been changed several times by introduction of new varieties since maize first made its appearance.

Teixeira da Mota reports that *milho basil*, the name by which maize is known in Portuguese Guinea, may be a corruption of *milho brasil*, i.e. Brazilian grain (25). On the whole, however, linguistic evidence supporting the introduction of maize by the Portuguese is meagre compared with that suggesting entrance from the Mediterranean (28; 23, p.106 & 15).

The first documented report of maize deep in the interior of western Africa dates from the second half of the eighteenth century. In 1788 the Association for Promoting the Discovery of the Interior Parts of Africa obtained from a man of Tripoli, referred to simply as Imhammed, a description of the Bornu Empire (located near Lake Chad) and Cashna, south-west of it (presumably Katsina in Northern Nigeria), which he had visited some years earlier. He listed maize as the principal grain cultivated in the first of these kingdoms and as an important crop in the second (1, p.202). Imhammed's report was verified by Ben Alli who independently gave the Association an account of the same countries.

Mungo Park noted maize along much of the route of his journey up the River Gambia to the Niger and thence back to the mouth of the Gambia in 1795-7, but gave no indication that it was a staple food. A similar report was made in 1818 for the same area and for the Futa Jallon by G. Mollien (22).

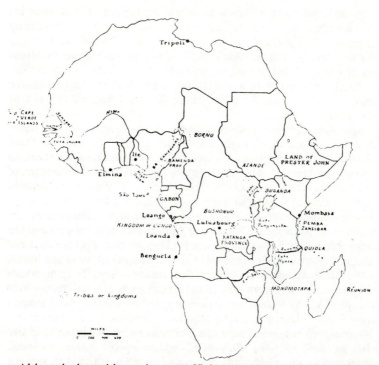

Although the evidence is not sufficient to support the hypothesis that the Portuguese were the first or sole agents to introduce maize to western Africa, there is good reason to think they would have tried to introduce maize to at least some areas. Aside from curiosity about whether maize would grow in this new land they had discovered, there was at least one economic motive for trying it.[3] the need for a cheap staple food for slaves, which became particularly pressing after 1517 when the development of the New World market greatly swelled the volume of slaves sold and increased considerably the average distance they were transported.

Barbot emphasises the importance of maize in the slave trade (4, p.197):

Tis generally observ'd, that *Indian* corn rises from a crown to twenty shillings betwixt *February* and harvest [August according to Bosman], which I suppose is chiefly occasion'd by the great number of *European* slave ships yearly resorting to the coast . . .

He also refers to the vast profits maize farmers made 'by selling it [maize] to the *European* forts, and slave ships; as also to all the other nations about them' (4, p.197).

A little later, in 1721, John Atkins observed that vegetables, horse-beans, rice, maize, and manioc meal were the 'common, cheapest, and most commodious Diet . . .' (2, p.171) for slave ships, but he does not indicate which commodities the slaves received, or the relative importance of each in slave rations.

Jean-Baptiste Labat, in a narrative published in 1728, states that maize was the staple for slaves along the River Senegal (18, pp.166 and 167).

Only linguistic evidence is available on the introduction of maize into the Sudan, the Congo Basin, and Angola. Two routes of introduction are suggested: one across the Sahara to the western and Central Sudan, and the other from the Atlantic coast. Reference has been made previously to the route across the Sahara to tropical Africa; introduction from the coast is suggested by Duarte Lopez's note in 1591 that maize was known in the kingdom of Congo as *Mazza Manputo,* which Filipo Pigafetta explains means grain of Portugal, Manputo being the local adjective for Portuguese.[4] This account also alleges that maize was the vilest of grain and only fit for swine.

Additional evidence of a similar nature comes from northern Angola, where it is reported that in 1600 maize was called *Masimporto* (13, p.312), which could be an indication of the Portuguese introduction. There is also early evidence of maize in these four centuries in a fragment of Bushongo oral tradition that can be dated by an eclipse of the sun on 30 March 1680, the only eclipse visible in the area in the seventeenth and eighteenth centuries (33, p.142). Using this as the base for calculations, E. Torday estimated that the Bushongo, who are found in the South-Central Congo Basin, were not acquainted with cassava (manioc) until about 1600; and, according to their tradition, maize and millets had been their staples until that time (33, p.143). However, Jan Vansina's analysis of Bakuba oral tradition suggests that maize was not introduced to the Bushong before the reign of Shyaam a Mbul a Ngoong, which began about 1630 (33a, p.261).

In any event, Bushong tradition seems to suggest that maize had not only made its way into the heart of Africa fairly rapidly, if introduced by the Portuguese, but was also recognised as a valuable food. This is not unlikely: it is easily transported, and would have been a convenient object of trade or means of provision for travellers, warring parties, and the like; and there is little technique to be learned in order to grow it or to convert the harvest into an edible form, crushing and boiling the grain being enough.

There is an additional reason to think that maize may have spread quickly through the Congo Basin: if these people had a narrow range of staple foodstuffs prior to maize, say mostly millets and sorghums, as seems likely, they may have welcomed variety and therefore readily adopted maize. Moreover, the similarity between these crops could have hastened the adoption because not only are they alike in appearance, but they require similar care and processing. Addition of maize to the diet would have necessitated little or no learning of new techniques. And it is quite possible that maize gave a higher yield than millets or sorghums, then as it does now, under the rainfall conditions of most of the Congo Basin. Thus, it may well be that maize was brought by the Portuguese to the Congo some time after 1493, and spread so rapidly that by 1600 it had become established as a staple 600 miles or so inland.

In northern Gabon, the Bulu maintain they had no maize until the latter part of the nineteenth century, when they obtained it from Hausa traders who came from the north-west (14).

Livingstone was much impressed with the extent to which maize was grown on the eastern edge of the Congo Basin, in the country bordering Lake Tanganyika on the east, which he visited in 1871. He leaves little doubt that it was a staple in some areas of that region (20, p.42). By 1885 it is reported to have been replaced by cassava among at least one tribe of the southern Congo Basin (34, pp.232 and 307).

Two fragments of evidence suggest that maize reached parts of the northern Congo Basin some time after 1830. Belgian agricultural officers in the early part of the present century say that, according to oral tradition, the Azande introduced maize to tribes now adjacent to them to the south (19, p.105), and the Azande are said to have invaded northern Congo about 1830 (24a, p.379). George Schweinfurth found maize grown only as a garden crop in northern Congo in 1870; but in the extreme north and extending into southern Sudan, in Azande country, it was depicted as the most important crop thirty-five years later by A. de Calonne-Beaufaict (30, p.87 and 10, p.210). Today, however, it is said to be only a secondary crop in Azande agriculture (29, p.228).

Among the Logo, a tribe adjacent to the Azande to the south-east, maize is said to have replaced millets and sorghums some time prior to the present century, but to have lost its place as the primary staple to cassava and sweet potatoes after the advent of European rule (19a, p.300). M. H. Lelong reports that cassava was unknown in pre-colonial times and that sweet potatoes, although known, were little cultivated. How and when these crops assumed importance is not clear, but a severe invasion of locusts in 1930 probably accelerated the shift away from maize. Because neither sweet potatoes nor cassava are nearly so vulnerable to locust attack, for a number of years following 1930, the Belgian administration forced the Logo to grow relatively large acreages of these crops to ensure that there would be a reserve in case of famine (19a, p.300).

Frans Pauwels notes that among the Congo Alur, a tribe inhabiting an area adjacent to the north-western corner of Lake Albert, maize is today the second most important food in the diet, and that it and cassava, the major starchy staple of the area, have almost completely replaced sorghum, which was originally the most important cereal (26, p.236). Unfortunately, information is not given on the timing of the shift to maize, but one comment suggests that expansion of maize has been limited by the recent introduction of cassava. Pauwels states that cassava was introduced only in 1948, and that by 1960 it had become the principal starchy staple in the diet (26, p.236).

Documentation of a Portuguese introduction of maize to the coast of eastern Africa is no better than for other regions. Linguistic evidence is perhaps better than for western Africa, but is not as persuasive as that for Angola and the Congo Basin. A. C. A. Wright argues (1) that tribes of the Nyika group have the root name *pemba* for maize, hence they probably got it from the island of that name; and (2) that the Sena of Nyasaland call maize 'sorghum of the sea coast' (37, pp.66 and 67).

The earliest reference to maize in eastern Africa is possibly one made by João de Barros. If M. D. W. Jeffreys, who attempts to prove that maize had a pre-Columbian introduction to Africa, is correct, Barros mentions maize in the Land of Prester John (Ethiopia) for a date that can be established as 1516 (16, p.116).

There is no record of maize in south-eastern Africa in the first part of the sixteenth century. The chronicles of Cabral's voyage in 1501 contain no mention of it. Duarte Barbosa's description of the towns he visited in 1501-16 mentions *milho* several times along the coast and in Madagascar, but he does not specify *milho zaburro,* and so seems to have been referring to the millets and sorghums (21). Perhaps the first clear reference to maize in this region is found in an early Portuguese account of Monomotapa. This notes that in 1561 a priest there lived mainly on *milho zaburro* (32, p.127). Sir Harry Johnston categorically states that it was introduced into Mozambique in about 1570 (17, p.426), but provides no documentation.

Regardless of how long maize may have been established in eastern Africa, it was little observed before the end of the sixteenth century. At least it did not attract the attention of travellers, and they rather consistently discussed the foods of the strange lands they had visited. Therefore maize seems unlikely to have been a common staple. I have found two references to it in eastern Africa during the next century, but neither suggests that it was important. For 1643 there is an account of Portuguese settlers on Zanzibar and Pemba growing maize, among other crops, to supply the Portuguese garrison at Mombasa, which at that time had difficulty in obtaining provisions from the tribes of the mainland.[5] The second reference is contained in Dapper's description of Africa, published in 1668, which mentions maize at Quoila (11, p.675).

The record during the next century is a little more substantial, but not notably so until the last few years. According to one account, maize seems to have been found in Madagascar in 1717 (12, p.25). However, Perrier de la Bathie claims that maize was introduced to Réunion in 1735 by the French, and speculates that it spread from there to Madagascar (5, p.836). However, this is almost certainly speculation based on the fact that de la Bourdonnais, who was first governor of the island, and began his administration in 1735, seems certainly to have introduced cassava to feed slaves working on the island's sugar plantations. According to the memoirs of Baron Grant, who lived on Mauritius as early as 1740 and spent twenty years there, Governor de la Bourdonnais (12a, pp.199-200):

> ... introduced, though not without considerable difficulty, the cultivation of *manioc*, which he at length obtained from the island of St Jago [Santiago, Cape Verde Islands] and Brazils.[6] He was, indeed, obliged to employ his authority to compel the people to cultivate this plant ... He published an ordinance, by which every inhabitant was obliged to plant five hundred feet of manioc for every slave he possessed ...

Gilbert Cours adds that cassava was brought to Réunion in a ship named *Le Griffon*, that it arrived in 1738, and that the first Africans to eat it were fatally poisoned because they did not know correct processing methods (10a, p.1).

An extract from a 1690 narrative by M. du Quesne published by Charles Grant, Viscount de Vaux, along with his father's memoirs, clearly indicates that maize was known in Réunion in 1690, almost half a century before 1735, but the statement suggests that maize may have been recently introduced there, for it is listed with crops that were 'experimentally known to flourish'[7] (12a, p.154). Moreover, whatever the date when maize was introduced to Réunion, there seems to be no clear evidence that it spread thence to Madagascar.

Francisco de Melo de Castro, Governor of Mozambique in 1750, in a report on that colony gave *milho grosso* as one of the crops grown there (8, pp.178 and 179). He probably meant maize, since during the eighteenth century, and even until recently, *milho grosso* was one of the Portuguese designations for maize (8, pp.178 and 179; 7, p.196 and 24, p.12). In 1798, maize was described as the staple of Mozambique (36, p.35), and in the same year, Lacerda is recorded as having encountered it deep in the interior, in what is now eastern Zambia. According to R. F. Burton, the translator of Lacerda's account, he purchased a small basket of millet heads, but in parenthesis Burton notes they were *corn-cobs*, a term now commonly used in the area for ears of maize; moreover, in an earlier note Burton comments that (9, p.17):

> The greater Millet (milho grosso) is the Jowarri, Durrah, Ta'am, Mtam, or *Holcus Sorghum*. Monteiro and Gamitto, however, translate Milho Grosso by 'Zea Maiz'.

Thus there is a good chance that it was *milho grosso* (maize) that Lacerda purchased. In any event, there is verifiable mention of maize, in the same area thirteen years later (6, p.223).

In summary, linguistic evidence strongly suggests that maize penetrated the interior of tropical Africa from the coastal regions, but the timing and mode of its introduction cannot be established. The commonly repeated assertion that the Portuguese brought maize to tropical Africa from the New World cannot be documented at this juncture, although they seem certainly to have had economic motives for doing so.

Maize was probably introduced to tropical Africa at more than one point and at different times. Even though the Portuguese may have been the first to introduce maize to the African continent, it is unlikely that they were the responsible agents at all points of its introduction. Linguistic evidence suggests that many areas of northern tropical Africa received maize across the Sahara, and Arab traders may also have introduced it to other areas.

Very little can be established about how maize spread from tribe to tribe in the interior, although a little more can be learned about when maize became an important crop.

The first mention of maize in tropical Africa is probably by Valentim Fernandes in his description of the western African coast he explored in 1502, but he may have been referring to some other grain. Other data suggest that maize was widely grown along the coast from the River Gambia to São Tomé, around the mouth of the River Congo, and possibly in Ethiopia, in the sixteenth century. There is reference to it in all these places, in Zanzibar, and around the mouth of the River Ruvuma in the seventeenth century; and it was not only mentioned but described as an important foodstuff and a major provision for slave ships between Liberia and the Niger Delta during the same century.

Much less information is available for the interior, but some evidence indicates that maize reached the northern Congo Basin after 1830; it clearly seems to have been unknown in Uganda as late as 1861. Until well within the present century, it was neither a major export nor a mainstay of the diet in most of eastern and central tropical Africa, the bulk of the areas where it is now of major importance.

NOTES

1. The numbers in brackets refer to the works listed at the end of the article.
2. That is, assuming that Ramusio was responsible for the illustration. Mr Frank Willett speculates that it may have been added by an editor (36a, p.3).
3. Another economic motive, introduction of maize to supply Portuguese sailors on ships engaged in the spice trade by the newly discovered route to the Orient, seems unlikely. It is probable that the Portuguese did not readily accept maize as a staple. Gerarde summarises what was probably the consensus of European attitudes in 1597 with these words (quoted in 35, p.45): '. . . We may easily iude [sic] that it nourisheth but little, and is of hard and evil digestion, and a more convenient food for swine than men.' One of the Portuguese writers of the same period, Duarte Lopez, noted in 1591 that maize was the vilest of grain and only fit for swine (27, p.40). Moreover, descriptions of the diet of ships' crews and of garrison provisions of Mozambique for 1505-7 make no mention of maize (3, p.132); and, as late as 1721, maize is described as a provision crews would use only in emergencies (18, p.167). However, this concerns the use of maize flour or maize meal; we do not have evidence on when roasting ears, a popular but not staple use of maize, gained acceptance by Europeans. It could well be that maize was grown around provisioning stations at an early date as a vegetable to be used by shore personnel and by ships while they were in port.
4. 'Vi è il miglio bianco nominato Mazza di Congo, cioè grano di Congo & il Maiz che e il più vile de tutti che dassi a porci, & cosi anco il riso è in porco prezzo, & al Maiz diccono Mazza Manputo cioè grano di Portugallo, apollando essi Manputo Portugallo' (27, p.40).
5. Correspondence between Sir John Gray and A. C. A. Wright cited in 37, p.64.
6. At another point (12a, p.49), Viscount Grant states that Governor de la Bourdonnais had cassava brought from the island of Madeira.
7. 'There are also the aloes, indigo, sugar canes, cotton, the anana, the banana, tobacco, the potato, the pumpkin, land and water melons, cucumbers, and a hundred and other plants, fruits, and roots, which grow everywhere, and without cultivation, even on the mountains. Turkey corn, or maize, millet, rice, wheat barley, and oats, are also experimentally known to flourish there; and a twofold harvest of these grains may be annually gathered. All the plants and herbs of our European gardens have been cultivated there with great success' (12a, p.134).

REFERENCES

(1)   Association for Promoting the Discovery of the Interior Parts of Africa, *Proceedings* (London, 1791).
(2)   Atkins, John, *A Voyage to Guinea, Brasil and the West Indies* (London, 1737; reprinted Frank Cass, London, 1970).
(3)   Axelson, Eric, *South-East Africa 1488-1530* (London, 1940).
(4)   Barbot, John, 'A Description of the Coasts of North and South Guinea: and of Ethiopia Inferior, vulgarly Angola: . . .', in A. Churchill (comp.), *A Collection of Voyages and Travels*, Vol. V (London, 1732).
(5)   Bathie, Perrier de la, 'Les plantes introduits à Madagascar', *Rev. de Bot. Appliquée et d'Agric. Trop.*, September-October 1931.
(5a) 'The strange adventures of Andrew Battel', in John D. Pinkerton (comp.), *A General Collection of the Best and Most Interesting Voyages . . .*, Vol. XVI (London, 1814).
(6)   Beadle, B. A. (trans.), 'Journey of the Pombeiros, from Angola to the Rios de Senna . . .', in R. F. Burton, *Lacerda's Journey to Cazembe in 1798* (London, 1873).

(7)   Botelho, Sebastião Xavier, *Memória Estatistica Sôbre os Dominios Portuguezes no Africa Oriental* (Lisbon, 1835).
(8)   Boxer, C. R., 'Maize Names', *Uganda Journal*, September 1952.
(9)   Burton, Richard F. (trans.), *Lacerda's Journey to Cazembe in 1798* (London, 1873).
(10)   Calonne-Beaufaict, A. de, *Azande* (Brussels, 1921):
(10a)   Cours, G., 'La Revue du Madagascar', *Le Courrier Agricole de l'Afrique*, 14 February 1946.
(11)   Dapper, Olfert, *Naukeurige Beschrijvinge der Afrikaensche Gewesten* . . . (Amsterdam, 1668).
(12)   Grandidier, A. (ed.), *Collection des ouvrages anciens concernant Madagascar*, Vol. V (Paris, 1903).
(12a)   Grant, C., *The History of Mauritius* . . . (London, 1801).
(13)   Hambly, Wilfrid D., *The Ovimbundu of Angola*, Anthropological Series of the Field Museum of Natural History, Vol. XXI, No. 2 (Chicago, 1934).
(14)   Communication from George R. Horner, 1958.
(15)   Jeffreys, M. D. W., 'The History of Maize in Africa', *South African Journal of Science*, March 1954.
(16)   ―― 'The Origin of the Portuguese Word Zaburro as their Name for Maize', *Bulletin de l'I.F.A.N.*, Series B, Vol. XIX, 1957.
(17)   Johnston, Sir Harry, *British Central Africa* (New York, 1897).
(18)   Labat, Jean-Baptiste, *Nouvelle Relation de l'Afrique Occidentale* (Paris, 1728).
(19)   Lacombez, M., 'L'Agriculture chez les Mangbetu de l'Ituri', *Bull. Agri. Congo Belg.*, March-December 1918.
(19a)   Lelong, M. H., *Mes Frères du Congo*, Vol. II (Brussels, 1946).
(20)   Livingstone, David and Charles, *Narrative of an Expedition to the Zambesi and its Tributaries;* . . . (London, 1865).
(21)   Machado, Augusto Reis (ed.), *Livro em que da relação do que viu e ouviu no Oriente Duarte Barbosa* (Lisbon, 1946).
(22)   Mollien, G., *Travels in the Interior of Africa to the Sources of the Senegal and Gambia* . . . (London, 1820).
(23)   Masefield, G. B., 'Maize Names', *Uganda Journal*, March, 1950.
(24)   Melo, C. Vieria de, *L'Agriculture* [Mozambique]. Published for the Exposition Colonial International (Paris, 1931).
(24a)   Merriam, Alan P. *et al.*, 'The Concept of Cultural Clusters Applied to the Belgian Congo', *Southwestern Journal of Anthropology*, Winter 1959.
(24b)   Monod, T., A., Teixeira da Mota, and R. Mauny, *Description de la Côte Occidentale de l'Afrique par Valentim Fernandes* (1506-1510) (Bissau, 1951).
(25)   Communication from A. Teixeira da Mota, 1958.
(26)   Pauwels, Frans M., *Landuishoudkundig Onderzoek Bij de Japaliri* (Gent, 1960).
(27)   Pigafetta, Filipo, 'Relatione del Reame di Congo . . .' (Rome) quoted in Conde de Ficalho, *Plantas úteis da Africa Portugueza* (Lisbon, 1884).
(28)   Portères, 'L'introduction du mais en Afrique', *J. Agric. Trop. et Bot. Appliquée*, Nos. 5-6, 1955.
(29)   Schlippe, Pierre de, *Shifting Cultivation in Africa* (London, 1956).
(30)   Schweinfurth, George, *The Heart of Africa*, Vol. II (London, 1874).
(31)   Stanton, W. R., 'Progress Report on a Maize Survey of West Africa, II' (unpublished manuscript, Moor Plantation, Nigeria, 1958).
(32)   McCall, George, *Records of South-Eastern Africa*, Vol. II (Capetown, 1898).
(33)   Torday, E., *On the Trail of the Bushongo* (London, 1925).
(33a)   Vansina, J., 'Recording the Oral History of the Bakuba: II – Results', *J. African Hist.*, 1, 2, 1960.
(34)   Verhulpen, Edmond, *Baluba et Balubaisés du Katanga* (Antwerp, 1938).

(35)   Weatherwax, Paul, *Indian Corn in Old America* (New York, 1954).
(36)   White, William, *Journal of a Voyage Performed in the Lion Extra Indiaman* . . .
       (London, 1800).
(36a) Willett, Frank, 'The Introduction of Maize into West Africa: An Assessment of
       Recent Evidence', *Africa*, January 1962.
(37)   Wright, A. C. A., 'Maize Names as Indicators of Economic Contacts', *Uganda
       Journal*, March 1949.

PART II

Land Use and Tenure

5

LAND TENURE: GROUP AND INDIVIDUAL RIGHTS*[1]

M. Gluckman

Widespread sharing of produce is the rule in tribal societies. Some early Western observers therefore concluded that they were 'communistic', and that individual rights in land and other goods did not exist. There is implicit in this judgment a false antithesis between 'communistic' and 'individualistic', arising from the way in which we say that a person or a group 'owns' a piece of land or some item of property. We are speaking loosely when we use this sort of phrasing: what is owned in fact is a claim to have power to do certain things with the land or property, to possess immunities against the encroachment of others on one's rights in them, and to exercise certain privileges in respect of them. But in addition other persons may have certain rights, claims, powers, privileges, and immunities in respect of the same land or property. Hence, when we say that a particular group of kinsmen owns land, we are also saying that all the members of that group have claims to exercise certain rights over that land – maybe equally with one another, maybe varying with their status. The incidence of rights over land varies with the technology of the tribe concerned, from those who live by hunting and collecting wild products to those who have elaborate systems of agriculture. Even when, as in hunting tribes, each member of the tribe has the right to hunt freely over the extent of the tribe's territory, this reduces to a right of every individual to hunt without let and hindrance from others; and this particular right to hunt freely may exist among agriculturists whose arable land is allocated specifically to smaller groups and to individuals within the tribe. Rights of this kind can vary with the methods of exploiting the land: thus hunting with bow and spear may be free, while

*Reprinted by permission of the International African Institute from Chapter XII: 'Property Rights and Status in African Traditional Law', in *Ideas and Procedures in African Customary Law,* 1969, edited by Max Gluckman, published by the Oxford University Press for the International African Institute.

particular groups may own rights to hold game drives or to set game-nets in particular areas.

Similar variations occur in the use of pasturage among herders. There may be areas where rights to graze stock are free, in the sense that any member of the tribe may exercise such rights, while rights to use particular areas around water-holes are restricted. In Bechuanaland no man may own grazing land, which is open to all members of the tribe, but the chief in practice gives rights to men to graze their cattle in particular places and will protect them against trespassers. In that arid land the main problem is shortage of water: and rights to water are granted by the chief especially when a man has sunk a water-hole (Schapera). In most tribes with a mixed husbandry, cattle graze freely on the crop stalks in anyone's fields, though if cattle stray into the fields before harvesting, suit for damages lies.

The position among agriculturalists is more complicated; but in Africa land-tenure laws seem to fall into a general pattern, of which the Lozi (Barotse) tribe who dwell in the great flood-plain of the Upper Zambezi River are strikingly representative.[2] Because the river floods every year during the summer rains the people have to build their small villages on mounds in the plain which will stand above the waters. Even from these they move at the height of the flood to temporary villages on the margins of the plain. Each village on its mound is the centre of a number of pockets of arable land, scattered over the main expanse of uncultivable land in the plain and variously affected by flood-waters or by rainfall. The village is also the centre of sites suitable for fishing.

Ultimately the Lozi consider that all the land, and its products, belong to the nation through the king. Though one right of Lozi citizenship, to which all men who are accepted as subjects are entitled, is a right to building and to arable land and a right to use public lands for grazing and fishing, it is by the king's bounty that his subjects live on and by the land. Commoners think of themselves as permanently indebted to the king for the land on which they live and its wild and domesticated products which sustain them. The Lozi say this is why they gave tribute and service to the king and still give gifts. Since tribute was abolished by agreement with the British Government the king has had to purchase many of his necessities from his people, and this is the standard by which the Lozi assess their present poverty.

The king is thus the 'owner' of Loziland and its cattle and wild products, in the sense that he ultimately claims rights over all land. These rights entitle him to demand allegiance from anyone who wants to settle on the land; he has the power to distribute to people any land which has not been allocated by him or any of his predecessors; he has a right to ask subjects to give him land which they are using, but he cannot dispossess them; he has the right to claim any land (or other goods) which has been abandoned or for which family heirs cannot be traced; he has the power to control where men are allowed to build their homes; he has the right through his appropriate councils to pass laws about the holding and use of land; and he can expropriate land for public services, subject to giving the holders other land.

To balance his rights and powers, the king is under duty to do certain things with the land. He is obliged to give every subject land to live on and land to cultivate, and he must allow every subject to fish in public waters, to hunt game and birds, to gather wild fruits, and to use the clay, iron ore, grasses, reeds, and trees with which the Lozi make their pots, utensils, mats, baskets, weapons, implements, nets and traps, furniture, huts, medicines. The king must protect all subjects against trespassers or anyone attempting to prevent them from exercising their rights. Once the king has given land for cultivation, or a fishing site, the subject has in it rights which are protected against all comers including the king himself. Should he desire the land, either for his own use or to give to another, he must ask for it: 'The king is also a beggar'.

In practice, the ruling king has not granted most of the land to its present holders: they were given their rights by his predecessors, in some cases under a tradition reaching back to legendary times. The king should not interfere with these past dispositions of land, and his own courts protect his subjects against any attempt he may make to do so. The major distribution of land is to the villages on the mounds, and it is vested in the title of each village's headman. Whenever land is given to a man he acknowledges the gift by giving the royal salute to the palace of the king, or to the king sitting in council. When a headman of a village dies and his heir is installed, the latter gives the same royal salute and to this are referred the continuing rights of his title to control the land allocated to it.

A headman thus gets from the king rights to administer this land, not to work all of it. The headman in his turn is obliged to give sufficient land, if it is available, to all heads of households in the village, including himself; and each head of a household can take his own share to cultivate but must distribute lots among all his dependants. These rights to claim some of the land attached to a village inhere in membership of the village, and Lozi insist that, by their law, if a man (or woman) leaves the village he loses his rights in the land. Nevertheless, one frequently finds people who are not resident in the village but are working its land. This they do under another law: all kinsmen, in all lines, of the main family group of a village are entitled to make use of its wealth, provided that there is more than sufficient land for the members resident in the village. This was made clear in a case where a bad-tempered headman drove his villagers away. When his son succeeded to the headmanship he found himself head of a relatively empty village. Sons of two of his sisters who resided in other villages were working fish dams which had been allotted to their mothers by the dead headman. The new headman sued to have them ordered either to move to reside with him or to return these dams to him. This case put the judges in a moral dilemma: for while they were reluctant to find for the headman because he was behaving ungenerously by wishing to expropriate from the family property kinsmen who had done no wrong to him, they appreciated that were they to find against him they would be upsetting a basic rule of land-holding – that land is vested in the headman's control as representative of the resident villagers. In a Lozi court, judgment proceeds from the most junior of the many judges to the most senior. The judges wavered in their decision: some ruled the headman was entitled to expel his kinsmen but urged him not to, while others ruled that he could not expel them. Eventually the head of the court found a brilliant solution to the dilemma; clearly the dams belonged to (expressed in Lozi by a possessive prefix to the headman's name) the headman and this law could not be varied against him because he was ungenerous; but the court could invoke its powers to discharge an unsatisfactory headman. He threatened that unless the headman were generous and allowed his nephews to use the fish dams, the court would discharge him and find a more generous man to be headman. This case brings out clearly that rights to control the land vest not in an individual but in the title of headmanship. It emphasises a point of great importance: we must continually differentiate between a society as a structure of social positions (titles) and as a structure of relationships between incumbents of these positions.

This example of land-holding in a large African kingdom emphasises firstly that in kingdoms of this kind we are not dealing with 'feudal-type' states, as is often loosely alleged. Despite their common insistence on personal allegiances between lords and underlings, which is one of the main characteristics of both a tribal and a feudal system, rights to land are quite different in the two types of state. The right of all subjects to claim sufficient land, as an inherent attribute of citizenship, marked the political systems of the Ancient Germans and Celts, and not the land-tenure system of feudalism. Under feudalism a vassal entered into a special contract with his immediate lord in which he gave service of a demarcated kind in return for control over land and those attached to it. No one in those times could go to the king and demand land as of right, as men could do in Africa. Nor in African systems were there the means to build castles in which lords could live a different style of life from that of their underlings. All men also carried the same simple weapons, from king to meanest soldier (spear, club, bow-and-arrow, and hide-shield). No knights superior in armour on horseback formed a class of chivalry.

Secondly, this system of land-holding was an essential part of the organisation of social relations from the king downwards through the political units of villages, into the hierarchy of kinship relationships. The king may be called 'owner of the land' only as trustee or steward for the nation. He granted what I call a primary estate of rights of administration to all titles of heads of villages, including himself in his capacity as head of many villages. Each head of a village then broke his estate into secondary estates with rights of administration which he allotted to the heads of households in the village, including himself. These holders of secondary estates might allocate tertiary estates of this kind to dependent heads of household, but usually secondary estates were broken up and allocated in parcels of land to be worked as arable or as fishing sites by the holders, including the administrator of the secondary estate of administration. Thus at the bottom of the series there is an 'estate of production'. Land-holding in these tribes is thus an inherent attribute not only of citizenship but also of each social position in the total political and kinship hierarchy.

Each parcel of land was therefore not communally owned but was subject to a series of retreating or reversionary[3] rights from the final user up to the king. And every one of these rights was effective. If a user of land – a holder of an estate of production – left the village, the land reverted to the holder of the secondary estate of administration of which he was a member; and if the secondary holder in turn left, his estate reverted to the primary holder of the estate of administration; and only if he, and all who might replace him, departed from the area, was the king as ultimate owner of all land entitled to claim the whole estate. All these rights are not only valid in African law but they have also been recognised by British courts. In a Nigerian case in 1930 where land was required for public purposes, the British Privy Council held that the individual African holders were entitled to compensation, and the chiefs only to compensation for their reversionary[4] rights. This was a major recognition of African law and showed a change of outlook from the time when the same Council held that only the Ndebele king and not individual subjects had rights in land, which hence could all accrue to the conquering British South Africa Company.

In short, if we are to understand the use of land as a unit of production in these tribal societies we have to appreciate that it is too simple to talk of them as marked by either communism or individualism. Clearly land, as it is ultimately cultivated, is worked by individuals with secure and protected rights, but representatives of their family, of their village, and of the nation have claims on the land. No superior can arbitrarily oust a junior from his holding, and the heir of each junior enters on succession into this holding. What the junior cannot do is dispose of the land to any outsider or invite an outsider to come and use the land without consulting his superiors, up to that point in the social structure where the invitee ceases to be an outsider. That is, a junior inside a secondary estate cannot give land to a villager from outside the group which has rights in that particular estate unless he secures the approval of the secondary estate-holder; that secondary holder must consult the primary holder, the village headman, before he thus invites on to his land someone from outside the village; and a village headman must consult the king before he accepts into his village someone who is not a subject of the king. Correspondingly, a superior holder cannot force an outsider on the holder of a junior estate, without the latter agreeing.

The terminology I am using here may sound complicated, but I have adopted it for comparative analysis for two reasons. First, there is no suitable terminology extant in European languages or in African languages in general. Many writers use various terms from European languages, but all have connotations quite different from those involved in tribal tenure. 'Possession' is too weak a term, since it does not emphasise the strength of the rights owned by the holders of the land. 'Usufruct', defined by the *Oxford English Dictionary* as a 'right of enjoying the use and advantages of another's property short of destruction or waste of the substance', is often used. The dictionary definition also does not cover the strength of rights of African holders; and those who use the word, with the meaning to enjoy the fruits, similarly fail to recognise this strength. The land is not 'another's property'. Moreover, in Roman law a grant of 'usufruct' was for use of fruits during the holder's lifetime, not transmissible to heirs, as African land-holding is. Second, since there was no suitable term available it seemed sensible to find a terminology which described the rights and duties involved and the manner in which they inhere in status itself: status as a citizen, status as a villager, and status as a dependant in a family. Each status gives rights to claim land in the appropriate estate. 'Estate' is a term deriving from status. 'Administration' and 'production' describe the rights involved at different levels of 'status'.

One term can be used for all levels of the hierarchy, since the rights and duties obtaining between adjacent holders in the series are identical: the junior must give support and respectful allegiance to the senior, who must give support and land to the junior. In addition, however, each junior holder in the series owes his duties to all seniors, and he can be expelled from all his estates up to that held by the senior whom he offends. A young man working land can be expelled from the village if he offends the headman, and from the kingdom if he offends the king sufficiently.

This system of land-holding can be worked out among almost all the tribal peoples of whom I know, though some of them, in West Africa and South-East Asia, in more recent times began to allow pledging and sale of land, rights which are excluded in most of Negro Africa because of the ultimate reversionary[1] rights of the chief, or the reversionary[1] rights of the tribal community as a whole in those tribes which do not have chiefs. The hierarchy of estates may appear as a delegation of the primary estate of administration from king or paramount chief to district chiefs, then from them to sub-district chiefs, then to ward-heads, then to village headmen, as among Basuto and Zulu. It is least clearly marked where land is plentiful, as among the Bemba of Northern Rhodesia. Its main effect, seen even there, is that as citizenship gives a right to claim land, so if one enters on the use of land, this founds a claim by holders of superior estates to demand one's allegiance.

NOTES

1   A fuller justification of the argument of this essay exists in Chapters III-IV of my *The Ideas in Barotse Jurisprudence* (1965), with many bibliographical references.

2.   I write of the situation as I observed it in the 1940s.

3.   The discussions brought out that the rights were not 'reversionary' only, since they subsist all the time.

4.   See preceding footnote.

6

LAND TENURE AND FEUDALISM IN AFRICA*

Jack Goody

It has been claimed by some writers that African land tenure was feudal in kind; others have disputed this contention, denying the utility of the concept of a landed fief in Africa. Most of this discussion has taken place on a politico-legal level, but there is one crucial and obvious difference which has been largely overlooked. It is a difference which means that land tenure (and hence vassalage and landed fiefs) in Africa were basically different from Europe and indeed from the Eurasian continent generally; and it has to do with the means of production rather than with productive relations, though its influence upon these relations is of some importance. Basically Africa is a land of extensive agriculture.[1] The population is small, the land is plentiful, and the soils are relatively poor. Moreover, one fundamental invention that spread throughout the Eurasian continent never reached Africa south of the Sahara, with the exception of Ethiopia. I am referring to that Bronze Age invention, the plough.

What effect does the plough have? In the first place it increases the area of land a man can cultivate and hence makes possible a substantial rise in productivity, at least in open country.[2] This in turn means a greater surplus for the maintenance of specialist crafts, for the growth of differences in wealth and in styles of life, for developments in urban, that is, non-agricultural, life.[3] In the second place, it stimulates the move to fixed holdings and away from shifting agriculture. Thirdly (and not independently), it increases the value (and decreases the availability) of arable land.

In Africa, then, there was little use of machines, even elementary ones; agriculture meant hoe farming, which was carried out by men and women or both, depending upon the particular society. Indeed animal power, that drew the Eurasian plough, was not used for any

*Reprinted by permission from 'Economy and Feudalism in Africa' in *The Economic History Review*, Second Series, Vol. XXII, No. 3, December 1969.

form of traction. One immediate reason was that the wheel,[4] though it
crossed the Sahara, both in the West (as evidenced in the two-wheeled
chariots liberally engraved upon Saharan boulders) and in the East
(in Ethiopia and in the early Sudan), never penetrated pre-colonial
Africa (or rather was never adopted there). Nor was this because of
the lack of a metal technology. While Black Africa escaped the
civilising influence of the Bronze and Copper ages, the smelting of
iron diffused from the Mediterranean down both sides of the continent.

In the East the technique of iron-smelting travelled to the Sudan,
where Meroë has been described, with some exaggeration, as the
'Birmingham of Africa'; this movement occurred in the sixth century
B.C., roughly the same time as iron was found in Ethiopia. From there
it spread to Chad in the first century A.D., together with horsemen
using a long lance. In the West, iron-working was transmitted from
Carthage and the Barbary Coast to the Niger towns in the third
century B.C. The technique spread down eastern Africa, being introduced to Zambia in 'the first few centuries A.D.' by a number of
small related groups of immigrants who brought not only metallurgy
but also food production and pot-making from the area west of Lake
Tanganyika. Copper and bronze were employed in many parts of
pre-colonial Africa, but before the coming of iron the extent of this
use was negligible.

The absence of the wheel meant that man was unable to use not
only animal power but hydraulic power and wind power as well. This
is why the recent introduction of the lorry, the bicycle, and the
engine-driven mill has been so important for the rural economy of
Africa. But the lack of the wheel had another consequence for
agriculture, since it limited the possibilities of water control. In the
drier regions of the Eurasian continent the wheel has played a
dominant part in raising water from wells to irrigate the land. Simple
irrigation there is in Africa, as in almost every agricultural area. Some
of the inhabitants of Birifu (Lo Wiili) in northern Ghana channel a
permanent water supply to run among their fields, and thus get two
crops a year in place of one. The Sonjo of Tanzania practise more
developed water control. Rice-growing in the Western Sudan (and it
should be remembered that *Oryza glaberima* was domesticated independently of Asian rice in the Senegal – Mali region) demands yet
more positive measures.

There are other means of water control that do not involve the
wheel, using various techniques of temporary storage. Methods of
this kind did of course exist. Everywhere there was some im-
provement of natural pools. In Gonja and in neighbouring areas of
northern Ghana there are many ancient cisterns hollowed out of the

laterite; in the famous market town of Salaga, the city of 1,000 wells, these are cylindrical in form and do not seem wholly dependent upon surface water. But these storage systems are very different from the village tank of South-east Asia; while there is no lack of water in Africa, the problem of its distribution is enormous. And in terms of agriculture what is lacking is any mechanical device for drawing water, such as is used in the Middle East and even in the Saharan oases.

One example of the pragmatic effects of the technological gap between Africa and Eurasia lies in the military field. When the Portuguese spearheaded European expansion into other continents, they succeeded largely because of their use of gun-bearing sailing ships.[5] Through these they could dominate their African opponents who were armed only with sword, spear, bow and arrows. But, by the end of the fifteenth century, when the expansion of Europe began, their guns were also far in advance of Asia as well. These technological innovations soon spread from Europe, just as simpler forms of gunpowder and 'cannon' had earlier diffused there from China and the Middle East. But the way in which they did so is of interest. Beachy notes that 'the Africans never seem to have learnt to make fire-arms as good as those of the Europeans, unlike the sixteenth and seventeenth-century Japanese and Sinhalese, who soon achieved virtual parity with the Portuguese in this respect'.[6] Already in the mid-sixteenth century the Japanese were producing matchlocks and in the 1590s they were followed by the Koreans: Ceylon had become a centre of production by the end of the sixteenth century, when muskets and cannon were made at many different points in the Indian sub-continent. By the seventeenth century the inhabitants of the Malabar coast were exporting muskets to Arabia.[7] The reason for the failure of Africans successfully to take up the manufacture of this powerful new weapon is a simple one. They did not possess the requisite level of craft skill in iron-working. As a result, Africans were at an enormous disadvantage when the scramble for their continent began, since they had to fight against the very people who were supplying them with arms.[8]

What does all this add up to in socio-economic terms?

Firstly, rights in land were less highly individualised in most of Africa, partly because land was not a scarce commodity.[9] Among the Bemba of Zambia rights in the productive use of land, other than the small proportion under cultivation at any one time, hardly existed; the same is still true among the Gonja in northern Ghana. Under such conditions neither individuals nor kin groups bother to lay specific claims to large tracts of territory, since land is virtually a free good. Elsewhere, among the Lo Wiili or Tallensi of northern Ghana, the population densities are around 100-200 per square mile and rights in land more highly developed; productive resources tend to get tied down to small kin groups, minimal lineage segments, although residual rights are vested in larger descent groups which often see themselves as property-holding corporations. But in fact rights to the assets are divided up among the smaller units, which are themselves constantly splitting and reuniting, depending upon the distribution of the births of male children. But, overall, people were thin on the ground. Even today, the total figure for Black Africa is not much more than the population of the United States, although the surface area is four times as great.

Not only was land plentiful; it was also less productive than on the Eurasian continent, partly because of the technological limitations and partly because tropical soils are often of poor quality. Moreover, since processes of soil regeneration (either by manure or by special cropping) were limited in nature, the fertility of land soon fell off. Under these conditions, the answer usually lay in moving one's farm to a new site (though not necessarily one's residence), that is, in shifting cultivation.

The social consequences were twofold. Politically, chiefship tended to be over people rather than land, and these a leader tried to attract as well as restrain. The conditions for the forms of domination that obtained in the European Middle Ages hardly existed, with the exception of slavery.[10] It is highly significant that only in Ethiopia, which had the plough, was there any landlordism in Africa; here, in true medieval fashion, estates in land supported a nobility that filled the important offices of state in both the staff and line organisation, a nobility that was at the same time a leisure class in Veblen's sense. Besides the nobility one also found ecclesiastical landlordism – functionaries whose time was devoted to the glory of God (though individual commitment to the monastic life was often temporary rather than permanent in character) derived their 'living' from the church with which God had been endowed.[11]

If there are landlords, there can also be tenants and serfs; unfree tenancies mean little unless land is highly valued and the peasantry has nowhere else to go.[12] Under conditions of shifting cultivation, it means little. Slavery was important throughout most of Africa: war captives were given household or agricultural work to perform for their victors or their purchasers. But ties of subordination arose not out of shortage of land but as the result of purchase or conquest, giving rise to slavery rather than to serfdom.

Though there were no landlords, there were of course lords of the land – the local chiefs of centralised states who, from the standpoint of food production, were in a sense carried by the rest of the population;

we may look at this either as a return for services rendered or as the exploitation of the weak, for there is, I think, no real test. Chiefs could not be expected to hear complaints on an empty stomach. Their families did better than those of commoners; they rode where others walked. But in general, owing to the limited nature of the technology and to the relatively low differentiation in terms of levels of consumption, standards of living, as measured by the usual tallies, were not markedly different. As Gluckman has remarked of Zulu chiefship, one man can eat only a limited amount of porridge; the rest has to be distributed.[13] Probably the maximum differentiation in terms of what Weber called 'styles of life' was to be found in the trading states of the coast, in the empires of the Niger bend, and in the emirates of northern Nigeria, where there were certain modes of behaviour that distinguished the urbanites of the capital (the dynasty, the merchants, the learned men, the specialist workers and their hangers-on) from the rural population. But in most cases such differentiation was confined to chiefs themselves rather than to the dynasty as such, being a function of roles rather than social strata; and the most noticeable aspect of the difference lay in control over women and slaves (war booty), and guns and horses, rather than goods and land. The exceptions were to be found in the coastal strip, where ruling and merchant groups financed themselves out of the European and Asian trade: there are certainly some sumptuary distinctions reported by travellers from Dahomey and Ashanti. But these differences do not come near to those of medieval Europe, or even of Ethiopia, where a series of sumptuary rules confined to the nobility the playing of certain musical instruments, the brewing of honey wine, and similar forms of behaviour that were by definition of high prestige.[14]

I have been arguing that although there existed local chiefships (a line organisation) supported partly out of agriculture, partly from trade, there was nothing equivalent to estates in land of the European kind. This should perhaps be qualified by 'only in some places and under limited conditions'. For, turning from the line to the staff organisation, the suggestion is found that the large-scale development of central government, which as Weber had argued involves the creation of appointive (as distinct from hereditary) office, was possible in only a few African states because of the land situation that I have described.[15] The southern Bantu failed to develop in this way. But some states succeeded. Among those that did were the highly centralised kingdoms of Buganda,[16] of Barotseland (Zambia), and of Dahomey. In each of these special conditions existed. In Buganda, the banana provided the basis for continuous cultivation; in Barotseland, there were the fertile mounds of the Zambezi flood plain; in Dahomey there was the development of some plantation agriculture.[17] In all these states there was a system of 'office estates' (rather than fiefs proper), i.e. estates attached to the staff rather than the line organisation.

NOTES

1. The difference between extensive and intensive modes of agricultural production is clearly relative, and one which has to be related to the nature of the soils, the labour force, and the terrain; shifting cultivation continued in less fertile and accessible parts of medieval Europe long after the plough dominated the agricultural scene, and the same is of course true of Ethiopia today.

2. In forests it clearly has many limitations. Nor does the plough improve vegeculture to the same extent as it does the cultivation of cereals. The main point, however, was effectively made by V. G. Childe. See also W. M. McNeil, *The Rise of the West* (Chicago, 1963): 'The harnessing of animal power for the labor of tillage was a step of obvious significance. Human resources were substantially increased thereby, since for the first time men tapped a source of mechanical energy greater than that which their own muscles could supply. The use of animal power also established a much more integral relation between stock-breeding and agriculture. Mixed farming, uniting animal husbandry with crop cultivation, was to become the distinguishing characteristic of agriculture in western Eurasia. It made possible a higher standard of living or of leisure than was attainable by peoples relying mainly or entirely upon the strength of merely human muscles' (pp. 25-6).

3. Urban centres of course existed in pre-colonial Africa; they ranged from the agro-cities of the Yoruba to the trading and administrative towns of the Saharan fringes and the coastal regions.

4. Animal disease was another factor limiting the use of the plough. Of Ethiopia, which may have obtained the plough from South Arabia or Egypt even in pre-Semitic times (about 1000 B.C.), F. J. Simoons has written: 'Where there are animals suitable for ploughing, both Cushites and Semites use the plough; but where, as along the Sudan border, these animals are excluded by disease, even Semites turn to the hoe or digging stick for preparing their fields.' – 'Some Questions on the Economic Prehistory of Ethiopia', *Jnl. African Hist.*, VI (1965), 11. Iron-working, however, appears to have arrived from South Arabia at about the same time as writing, that is, in the fifth century B.C. – Anfray, 'Aspects de l'archéologie éthiopienne', *Jnl. African Hist.*, IX (1968), 352.

5. At first they depended upon the cannon on their floating castles, later upon hand-guns. See Cipolla's useful discussion where he quotes Pannikar as saying that by 1498 'the armament of the Portuguese ships was something totally unexpected and new in the Indian (and China) seas and gave an immediate advantage to the Portuguese'. C. M. Cipolla, *Guns and Sails in the Early Phase of European Expansion, 1400-1700*, p. 107.

6. Review of B. Davidson, *Jnl. African Hist.*, III (1962), 510.

7. See Cipolla, op. cit., pp. 127-8, and Al-Djamūzi's history in R. B. Serjeant, *The Portuguese off the South Arabian Coast* (Oxford, 1963), p. 117. 'These Malabaris are Muslims: the Munaibāri muskets are called after them.'

8. The position was not quite as desperate as it first appears, since one European power was quite willing to benefit at the expense of another; the sources never entirely dried up. And even within the same political unit (e.g. the British-administered Gold Coast), the interests of merchants and administrators were often at odds. It should be added that, though sulphur had to be imported, there

was certainly some manufacture of local gunpowder (e.g. in northern Ghana) but this was recognised to be of inferior quality (because it was not 'corned'). Equally guns could be repaired. But there is no evidence of any extensive manufacture of components. Even today it is imported bicycle tubes that are often used to replace barrels.

The one exception may have been the late nineteenth-century Mandingo warrior Samory. In 1898 Nebout was reported to have been shown a small-arms factory 'which was capable of turning out three repeaters a week'. The gun is described 'as a wonderfully close copy of the French article, but not bearing near inspection as to its details, more particularly in the matter of *rifling*'. – Dir. Mil. Intell. to C.O., 14 January 1898, C.O. Confid. Print, African (West), No. 549. Legasick quotes a similar report ('Firearms, Horses and Samorian Army Organisation, 1870-1898', *Jnl. African Hist.*, VII (1966), 104). Peroz and Binger, who separately visited Samory in 1897, make no mention of locally made guns; Henderson, who was captured in 1897, writes only of a cartridge factory. Local *numu* blacksmiths may have learnt new techniques from the invaders, but it is difficult to see how the low-temperature forge could be used for the manufacture of guns from scratch, as distinct from the kind of repair work that Binger describes (*Du Niger au Golfe de Guiné* (Paris, 1892), I, 191-2). In Europe the temperatures needed to emerge from the wrought-iron phase were first produced in the fourteenth century by using water-powered bellows for blast purposes, and this in turn depended upon rotary motion. But whether or not Samory succeeded in manufacturing firearms, his continued attempts to secure imported guns by exchanging captives or by more direct methods indicate that his efforts in this direction met with little success. Indeed right to the end the military economy of this empire-building was based upon the necessity of acquiring sufficient income from booty to import guns, powder, and percussion caps. – J. Goody, Introduction, *Ashanti and the North-west,* Institute of African Studies (Legon, 1965), pp. 75-8.

9. The tendency for rights in land to be more highly individualised the greater the population density has been noted by C. K. Meek, *Land Law and Custom in the Colonies* (1946, 1949; reprinted Frank Cass, London 1968), pp. 149-50. See also G. I. Jones, 'Ibo Land Tenure', *Africa,* XIX (1949), 313, and J. Goody, *The Social Organisation of the Lo Wiili* (1956), p. 37. Of course, land shortage is always relative to the available resources of labour, etc. But the tractor can create a shortage more easily than the plough, the plough more readily than the hoe. In my view there is no doubt that the 'communal' nature of African land tenure must break down rapidly with the introduction of plough or tractor, just as the economy of large households must tend to fragment when individual members acquire their own pay-packets, by selling their labour outside the domestic group.

10. Prof. Edward Miller has pointed out to me that there is another situation which leads either to serfdom or to plantation slavery. Both institutions can emerge under conditions where land is relatively plentiful and where it is necessary to prevent the escape of rent producers or labour producers which a chief or land requires. Perhaps an extreme form of this is the slavery found in pioneer settlements in certain parts of early medieval Europe. However, in Africa labour requirements led to slavery but not serfdom; trading towns like Kano and Bida in northern Nigeria, or Salaga and Bole in northern Ghana, were surrounded by villages of slaves which supplied the ruling and commercial groups. Domestic slaves, dependent kinsfolk, and clients filled other servile roles, but the supply of land and the degree of control made it difficult to exploit labour by anything other than slavery.

In Middle America, despite ample land, the Spanish conquerors imposed on the population a system of peonage, which was something less than slavery. But the conditions of productivity (the plough, soil, crops) and control (guns and horses) were very different.

11. In Ethiopia the church was the largest landowner after the Emperor. Some of these lands were worked by the monks; others were farmed by peasants. The landlord's rent, lay or ecclesiastical, could be enormous. At the end of the eighteenth century, Bruce stated that the tenants of Tigre usually surrendered at least half their crop, the landlord supplying the seed. But it was 'a very indulgent master that does not take another quarter for the risk he has run'. – See Richard Pankhurst, *An Introduction to the Economic History of Ethiopia* (1961), pp. 193-5. A similar situation existed in Egypt with regard to the *waqf* lands. See, for example, Ibn Khaldun's reference to chieftains who 'are wont to build Mosque schools, shrines and almshouses and to endow them with Waqf [Mortmain] lands...' – Charles Issawi, *An Arab Philosophy of History* (1950), p. 144.

Of course, monasticism could also be supported by means other than land – e.g. by 'taxes' on trade or by providing services for travellers. But this was not, I think, possible to any great extent under pre-colonial conditions in Africa.

12. The reduction of population in relation to resources can have the opposite effect on serfdom. When in the fourteenth century land in Europe became relatively plentiful (through either the Black Death or other causes) rents were halved in a decade, wages doubled, and the institution of serfdom was greatly weakened.

13. Gluckman suggests that the failure of the south-east Bantu to develop more extensive political units before the time of Dingiswayo at the beginning of the nineteenth century may have been due to the limited technology and the availability of land, so that there was possibly little point in building up power. 'The tribal economy was simple and undifferentiated; even in a good year the available technology did not allow a man to produce much beyond his own needs. There was little trade and luxury, so even a conqueror could not make himself more comfortable than he had been before. One cannot build a palace with grass and mud, and if the only foods are grains, milk and meat, one cannot live much above the standard of ordinary men.' – M. Gluckman, 'The Rise of a Zulu Empire', *Scientific American*, CCII (1960), 157-68. In West Africa the economy was more developed in these respects, particularly the military economy insofar as it depended upon cavalry and the importation of firearms and gunpowder. But the general point still holds.

14. Levine notes that the upper stratum of Abyssinian society 'created and shared what might be called a "gentry sub-culture", even though it was not so differentiated from the general culture as was the case in Europe and China'. – D. H. Levine, *Wax and Gold* (Chicago, 1965), p. 156. It should be added that sumptuary laws in the strict sense often arise when certain individuals or groups are challenging the prestige behaviour of old-established classes; they are a defensive mechanism to help maintain the existing social hierarchy. See, for example, Edward II's Ordinance against extravagant housekeeping, 6 August 1316. – W. Stubbs, *Chronicles of the Reigns of Edward I and Edward II*, I (1882), 238-9.

15. E. Colson speaks of the variable as the 'attitude to land', but the context of her remarks allows us to give this a more concrete reference. See 'The Role of Bureaucratic Norms in African Political Structure', in *Systems of Political Control and Bureaucracy in Human Societies,* ed. V. F. Ray, Proceedings of the American Ethnological Society (Seattle, 1958).

16. See. C. C. Wrigley, 'Buganda: an Outline Economic History', *Economic History Review*, 2nd ser., X (1957), 69-80.

17. And more importantly, perhaps, the European trade.

7

LAND TENURE RIGHTS IN ANCIENT RUANDA*

Jaques Maquet and Saverio Naigiziki

In Ruanda, as in most other regions of Black Africa, the concept of land ownership, which exists in the Western legal tradition and is based on the Roman Law, is not applicable. The rights resulting from manifold utilisation of land remain separated, whereas in the Western system these rights constitute a whole which is vested in the owner. It is an exclusive right to various uses to which a thing can be assigned. In Ruanda, the multiplicity of usage rights and the distinction between them are particularly marked, because the population of Ruanda consists of two groups: the pastoralists and the agriculturalists. As a result, the lands, at least the best part of them, being capable of a large number of pastoral and agricultural uses, give rise to a great diversity of rights.

Another reason which contributes to the complexity of the system of tenure in Ruanda is the fact that the group of agriculturalists is dominated by the pastoralists. The conquering pastoralists arrived in a country which was already settled. Thus, a system of pastoral customs utilising soil in a new manner was superimposed upon that of the existing agricultural rights. The former agricultural rights were not completely destroyed but the caste which seized political power controlled them.

Ancient Ruanda represents Ruanda prior to the changes which the local society underwent as a result of European influence. These changes did not take place simultaneously in all the areas of local culture.

The first Europeans settled in the kingdom about the year 1900. As far as tenure rights are concerned, it seems, that the ancient system had survived almost without change until about 1930. At that time the Belgian administration did away with numerous small administrative

*Translated and abridged by the editors. The original article, 'Les droits fonciers dans le Ruanda ancien', appeared in *Zaire: Revue Congolaise*, Vol. III, No. 4, 1957.

units, which had less than twenty-five taxpayers and re-grouped the chiefdoms. Owing to close relationship between the political organisation of the territory and the system of tenure, the re-grouping of the chiefdoms had important repercussions with regard to the rights of tenure.

Tenure rights of Mwami

One of the authors of this article has already pointed out (1) that the rights over all the lands of the country, as exercised by the king of Ruanda, combined two concepts – those of sovereignty and ownership, which are clearly distinct in the Western tradition. The Mwami was an absolute ruler, in the most complete sense of this term. Being a representative of Imana and identifying himself almost with the supreme God, he claimed to be a supernatural being responsible only to the deity itself. The latter, however, did not care much about human activities (2). Also, the Mwami was a supreme master and ultimate authority over his people, the lands, and cattle. Hence the saying that the Mwami is the owner of the soil. He is like a sovereign who possesses the 'dominium eminens' or 'imperium' over the land. This sovereignty was not only the notion of public ownership exercised by the state over its territory. It was a true ownership, in the sense that the king could enforce his rights over any piece of land against his subjects. But, as a matter of fact, he exercised these rights very seldom. He did so only to punish a disobedient subject. In principle, however, he was permitted to take possession of all property belonging to any of his subjects.

There is no confusion between the two distinct ideas, and this approach makes it possible to view legal realities in a different light. The king has an exclusive right to all land usage, which is a superior right to that exercised by any of his subjects. In fact, he does not take advantage of his position. His subjects can enjoy exclusive rights of tenure with regard to their lands but on a lower level: demands of a third party concerning these rights can be opposed.

The rural and forest regions

In order to describe different forms of tenure a fundamental distinction must be made between the rural and the forest regions. In each of these two regions of ancient Ruanda tenure rights were acquired and held differently. Rural regions consisted of dwellings, cultivated areas and pastures, whereas forest regions were covered with natural vegetation and had areas destined for clearance. The principle on which this distinction is based is not very clear as a greater part of the rural regions obviously consists of the forests that had been cleared in the past and it is difficult to say when exactly a clearing ceases to be recent and becomes old. Since the two spheres of rights differ, there is good reason for making this distinction, even if it is not always clear cut.

This distinction is based on time factor and it refers to the final stage of the old system. It is likely that tenure rights, as described here, existed long before reforms put an end to the old system. But it is not possible to assess the length of that period with any degree of precision.

The rural regions obviously lacked uniformity. Some were predominantly agricultural. They were situated on hill tops, on the plateaux and on the ridges. They were densely populated, and inhabited mostly by the Hutu. For this reason they were commonly described as ibu-hutu.[1] The Tutsi who lived there were either poor shepherds, or rulers, forming part of the administrative hierarchy and appointed by a higher authority. The latter, in order to provide pasture for milch cows (inya-rurembo) attached to their homes or enclosures, resorted to a pure and simple occupation (gu-koma) of fallow land (ibi-sambu), inhabited slopes (imi-evamu), lowlands (ibi-kuka), and swamps (imi-bande). Other parts of the rural regions, described as ibu-tutsi, were sparsely populated. These regions were inhabited by primitive pastoralists, who used large areas for pasture. They had gardens cultivated by the Hutu, who were, in one way or another, dependent on the livestock breeders.

Lastly, some parts of the rural regions which were either unsuitable for cultivation, or were never touched by the hoe, were predominantly pastoral. These parts were called imi-kenke and consisted of pastures, generally available to all livestock breeders. Some areas, however, were reserved by the Mwami (gu-koma) or by the chief supervisor of pastures (umu-tware w'umu-kenke). There the pastoralists permitted their cattle to graze temporarily (gu-ca ibi-raro) or they would take them there (ku-gishisha) if there was lack of fodder elsewhere.

Pastures in the rural regions

According to some old informants whom we have interrogated, the privative rights of pasture over certain lands did not always exist. They were introduced by Mwami Yuhi Gahindiro, the fourth predecessor of the present Mwami, Mutara Rudahigwa. Until his reign access to pastures was free for all livestock breeders. This would only continue for as long as the pasture land could adequately support the existing number of cattle. It is very likely that prior to the arrival of the Europeans the high density of both human and livestock population became obvious in Ruanda. At some stage, possibly during the reign of Gahindiro, lands suitable for grazing could no longer be considered as 'res nullius'. Exclusive rights to pasture came to be linked with certain lands which were given the name of ibi-kingi. The ibi-kingi were granted by a political authority, that is by Mwami, or his representatives. This grant required some payment which consisted of one or more heifers that had to be presented to the authority granting the rights of pasture. Furthermore, gift of cattle had to be made when a new representative of the authority was invested with his power. Hence, pasture lands provided an inexhaustible source of continuous profits to the governors. These officials had no salaries except for various payments which they collected on behalf of the Mwami and who authorised them to retain some part of them.

What were the rights of an igi-kingi tenant, who obtained such a concession from a political authority? He had the right to graze his herds. But as he was head of a primary patrilineal group (umu-tware w'in-zu) to whom the land concession was originally granted, the right to graze cattle on the igi-kingi was extended to his dependants. Furthermore, the tenant could let out the pasture land which he was granted. Jugs of beer constituted payment for one season, a young bull for a year, and one heifer for two years. Rent was payable in advance. The ibi-kingi were never divided up. Cows of the sub-tenants grazed together with the animals of the original tenant. When the cows of the sub-tenant had calves while they were kept in the tenant's enclosure, the latter could milk them for a period of two or three months. This was an additional form of payment made by the sub-tenant to the original tenant and was called kw-eza. To regain the right to milk his cows, after the period of kw-eza was over, the sub-tenant had to offer a jug of beer to the tenant; otherwise the right to milk belonged to the former.

One the death of the tenant his concession was inherited by his male descendants. Thus they became co-tenants, as igi-kingi could not be divided. In principle a concession was hereditary; women, however, never inherited pasture land, either from their fathers, or from their husbands.

Agricultural land in the rural regions

Agriculture necessitates a much more stable relationship between man and his land. Land deteriorates under the status of 'res nullius'. It seems that prior to the arrival of the Tutsi – the pastoralists – the tenure rights over cultivated lands in Ruanda were similar to those prevalent among the numerous groups of agriculturalists in Central

Africa (3) (4). Groups based on kinship exercised collective rights over a certain area which was cultivated by all their members.

In Northern Ruanda (Mulera, Rwankeri, Bushiru, Bigogwe) where Tutsi occupation was more superficial, patrilineal groups (in-zu) enjoyed collective rights till the old order of things (in-gobyi y'igi-sokuru) had come to an end.

When the Tutsi invaders established themselves as a dominant caste, agriculture was of interest to them only in so far as it supplied them with the necessary food without any effort on their part. They did not enter into competition with the Hutu for the farming lands. Nevertheless it appears that the Tutsi were responsible for a form of tenure called i-sambu. The i-sambu was created by dividing collective domaines which were up till then controlled by lineage groups. Should a dispute arise between the members of an in-zu concerning part of a collective domain, arbitration by a Tutsi was resorted to. The latter was either the holder of a political office or else a rich and respected man. To end the dispute the Tutsi assigned to each plaintiff a part of the collective domain. This course of action gave the Tutsi three advantages. Firstly, there was an increase in the number of contributors from whom payments in kind, or in the form of services were due.

The political authority demanded statute labour-and taxes not from individuals but from the heads of lineage groups who controlled the collective domain. Thus payment was made by the group as a whole. By granting to a head of a household tenure rights, over parts of the former collective domain, the Tutsi made him responsible for payments for his land, his i-sambu. This tended to augment the total amount of consumption goods which the Tutsi, both as individuals and as a caste were able to obtain from the farmers.

The second advantage of the arbitration by a political authority, or by a powerful lord was, that henceforth the holder of an i-sambu made payments to the arbitrator who settled the boundaries and granted tenure rights, for the protection of which he was responsible.

Finally, the third advantage was that when parts of the land held by the members of a lineage group were divided up by arbitration, instead of being returned to the collective holdings were acquired by escheat by the political authority.

In the regions where population was dense, all the fields were occupied. One could obtain land, if its owner died without heirs, or if it was abandoned by its rightful user, or if the latter was expelled. These lands which had no owner were called in-kungu and were returned to the representatives of political authority, who could redistribute them. Concessions were free, but gifts (ama-turo) were expected. These were repeated in a less regular manner than our taxes.

The lands called umu-kenke were free areas which were acquired also by way of a concession granted by the authorities and against the payment of ama-turo.

The areas designated as in-deka were also free areas, which due to the nature of the soil could not be cleared. These were located in sparsely inhabited zones. There was enough of this type of land to acquire it by simple occupation, without having first to apply to an administrative authority for permission. The latter was duty-bound to fix boundaries, should other persons intend to take possession of the adjacent land. But, in spite of the fact that in-deka was obtained by an act of simple occupation, customary payments had to be made to a local representative of the political authority.

Expulsion of a member of lineage group from a collective domain was based on custom established after the arrival of the Tutsi conquerors. The case was dealt with, and as far as possible decided upon by the lineage head. Reasons for expulsion were unsocial behaviour towards the group, paternal malediction, repeated breach of the law, and disinheriting before witnesses.

The excluded member of the group had to leave the collective domain. If he held a piece of land it passed into the hands of his paternal relatives. Should he reform himself and be reinstated as a member of the group, the tenure rights were restored to him. His children, even if born elsewhere, preserved their rights.

To sum up, tenure rights belonged to either of the two categories: domains of lineage groups held collectively (ama-zu), and fields granted to family heads (in-go). The former was the traditional system common among the peasants in Central Africa; the latter was the result of political pressure exercised by a centralised regime which pursued economic exploitation of a majority by a dominating minority. In both these cases, the group of Tutsi succeeded in controlling agricultural land usage, in a way which reduced the cultivators to the status of precarious tenancy. This enabled the Tutsi to prevent the growth of wealth and power outside their own sphere of activity.

At the same time, without working on land themselves, they could appropriate the whole agricultural surplus produced by the peasant class (5).

NOTES

1.   According to the practice which is being brought into general use, in Ruanda, the proper names were reduced to their root: Tutsi, Hutu, Twa. In the case of common nouns, the singular or plural prefix, as the case may be, has been preserved and it has been separated by a hyphen from the root. Hence: umu-garagu, aba-garagu, igi-kingi, ibi-kingi, etc.

REFERENCES

(1) Maquet, Jacques J., 'Le système des relations sociales dans le Ruanda ancien', (Tervuren, Musée royal du Congo belge, 1954), p. 109.

(2) Maquet, Jacques J., *The Kingdom of Ruanda in African Worlds*, edited by Daryll Forde, (London, International African Institute, 1954), p. 169.

(3) Bourgeois, R., *Banyarwanda et Barundi*, Vol. II, *La Coutume*, (Bruxelles, Institut Royal Colonial Belge, 1954), p. 187.

(4) Vanhove, J., *Essai de droit coutumier du Ruanda*, (Bruxelles, Institut Royal Colonial Belge, 1941), p. 41.

(5) Maquet, Jacques J., 'Le problème de la domination tutsi', (*Zaire*, 1952), Vol. VI, No. 10, pp. 1011-16.

PART III

Introduction and Use of Metals

8

THE IRON AGE IN THE SUDAN*

A. J. Arkell

It was in the seventh century B.C. that the Nile Valley felt the impact of the Iron Age. It was not a gentle impact, for the driving force was the army of Assyria, by then fully equipped with iron weapons. About the middle of the eighth century B.C., the King of Cush, fully Egyptianised if he was not of Egyptian stock, imposed his rule on Egypt, uniting it, and then set about to restore the ancient glory of Egypt by bringing back the old customs and beliefs that it had abandoned under the New Kingdom, *circa* 1500 B.C.

When the King of Cush, advancing from his capital at Napata near the Fourth Cataract, occupied Lower Egypt, he learned of the approach towards his north-eastern frontier of the expanding power of Assyria. First Syria and then Israel fell to the Assyrians, and Hezekiah, King of Judah, was vacillating between submission to Assyria and cooperation with the Cushite King of Egypt. When the Assyrians laid siege to Jerusalem in 721 B.C., the Cushites sent an army to relieve the siege; but before the armies met, an outbreak of plague caused the Assyrians to withdraw. After 50 years of cold war, the Assyrians advanced again and defeated the Cushite army on the frontier of Egypt; they then took Memphis, the capital of Lower Egypt, by assault. Two years later the Cushites took it back only to lose it again, and the Assyrians then advanced and occupied Thebes in Upper Egypt for a short time, one of their master carpenters leaving behind an Assyrian helmet and a set of iron tools found there long afterwards by Flinders Petrie (see Petrie 1917). About 661 B.C., the next King of Cush advanced again as far as Memphis; but he soon had to flee back

* This paper is part of a symposium, followed by comments (*Current Anthropology*, Vol. 7, No. 4, 1966 pp.469-478) from: J. H. Chaplin, Elizabeth Colson, Oliver Davies, Jean Hiermaux, Jacques Nenquin, Richard Pittioni, Merrick Posnansky, K. R. Robinson, J. Rudner, H. v. Sicard, and R. Raymond Wood. The comments are followed by replies from the authors (pp.478-481).

to Napata, pursued as far as Thebes by the Assyrians, who now sacked the city.

The Assyrians had demonstrated convincingly in Egypt the superiority of iron weapons over the copper, stone, wood, leather, and bone weapons of the Cushites and Egyptians. But Egypt is short of both fuel and iron ore, except in the neighbourhood of the First Cataract, and even there fuel is practically non-existent. The first iron-working in Egypt was by Greek and Carian mercenaries, who were employed by the Saite kings set up by the Assyrians as tributary rulers of Egypt after the expulsion of the Cushites. These mercenaries worked imported ore at Naukratis and Daphnae in the Delta. In 591 B.C. a number of them were the spearhead of an expedition sent by the Saites to forestall a threatened reinvasion of Egypt by Cush, while the Saites themselves were embroiled on their eastern frontier with Babylon (which had replaced Assyria as the great power on the Euphrates). Even in defence of their homeland, the Cushites once again failed to stand up against troops armed with iron weapons, and Napata was sacked. The capital of Cush was now moved to Meroe above the Fifth Cataract. At Meroe there were both ample supplies of iron ore from the Nubian Sandstone and of wood fuel, and it is probable that the King of Cush started working iron there as soon as he could obtain the services of skilled craftsmen. This may have taken some time, but when it occurred, it is probable that one or more renegade Greeks from Egypt supplied the necessary skill: the shape of the only iron ingots found in the Sudan is exactly the same as that of the ingots used by the Greeks at Naukratis (see Wainwright 1945).

By the time Meroe came to an end, perhaps not long after A.D. 300, there were 12 large mounds of iron slag that are still visible in the town (see Arkell 1961), and at least one of them had been in existence so long that in the first century B.C. it was chosen as the site of the Lion Temple. Cemeteries that have been excavated so far have not disclosed what happened to more than a tiny fraction of the iron manufactures of Meroe. The pyramids of Aspelta, the king who moved the capital to Meroe, and of his successors have only bronze model tools in their foundation deposits; Harsiyotef, who reigned about 404-369 B.C., is the first king who had model iron tools in the foundation deposits of his pyramid. So we can be sure only that iron-working was carried out on considerable scale at Meroe from the beginning of the fourth century B.C. It is not till very much later that iron objects appear in any quantity in tombs. Out of 1,550 graves at Napata that mostly precede Harsiyotef, only 18 contained iron objects, and all (except one spearhead) were small objects (arrowheads, bangles, razors, and tweezers). At Faras and in other Meroitic cemeteries which date between the second century B.C. and the third century A.D., the typical iron arrowhead with its single barb does not appear until the first century A.D. And it is about mid-second century A.D. that quivers, full of about 70 arrows each with iron heads, are common. Heavy iron objects have not been found in Meroitic graves. It is only in the post-Meroitic X-Group graves, dating between fourth and sixth centuries A.D., and then chiefly in the royal graves at Ballana and Qustul north of the 2nd Cataract, that spears, swords, hoes, saws, and axes are frequent. Even an iron cooking tripod occurred, and some 'camp-stools' made of iron. Horse bits and bells for horse trappings were also of iron; but strangely enough, although bows were used, iron arrowheads are rare. It is clear from other grave goods that the ramifications of trade with Byzantine Egypt were widespread at this time, and two unmistakable though crude copies of Byzantine bronze lamps from the Gold Coast show that Egyptian trade goods probably reached as far as West Africa (Arkell 1961 : 183, fig. 23).

How the knowledge of iron-working spread south and west from Meroe must await further archaeological excavation, but pottery from sites along the Blue Nile as far as Roseires and along the White Nile as far as the mouth of the Sobat suggests connections with Meroe. Spread of the knowledge of iron-working further up the White Nile may have been checked by the swamps of the Sudd, and an alternative route to Central Africa would have been due west to the Lake Chad area and thence southwest through the Azande and Bushongo country. Indeed, whether the knowledge of iron-working travelled along the foothills of Abyssinia to the east of the Sudd, or via Lake Chad and then south-eastwards, it seems that the early Iron Age Cultures of Central Africa that are probably associated with the Bantu movement must owe their origin indirectly to Meroe.

Stone walling and terrace cultivation (Summers) in Darfur west of the Nile (and on the way to Lake Chad) appear possibly to have been introduced by monks from Christian Nubia, a kingdom in Dongola between the 3rd and 4th Cataracts, which succeeded the X-Group people and flourished between the eighth and thirteenth centuries A.D. (Arkell 1961 : 194).

There is also a slight possibility that a knowledge of iron-working travelled to East Africa along the coast of the Red Sea. Mercenaries who hunted elephant for the Ptolemies in the third century B.C. along the coast of Abyssinia may have introduced the knowledge of iron weapons to those parts (see Wainwright 1945), but not necessarily of iron-working. In the first century A.D. 'Greeks' were bartering ready-made iron in the same area (see Schoff 1912 : 24-26).

REFERENCES
Arkell, A. J., 2nd edition revised, *A History of the Sudan to 1821*. (London: Athlone Press, 1961).

Petrie, W. M. Flinders, *Tools and weapons*. (London: British School of Archaeology in Egypt, Constable and Quaritch, 1917).

Schoff, Wilfred H., *The Periplus of the Erythraean Sea* (London, Bombay, and Calcutta: Longmans Green, 1912).

Wainwright, G. A., 'Iron in the Napatan and Meroitic Ages'. *Sudan Notes and Records*, 26:18 (1945).

9

EARLY RECORDS OF IRON IN ABYSSINIA*

G. A. Wainwright

The introduction of iron to these regions clearly originated with the Ptolemaic hunting expeditions, which were organised for the capture of elephants. Their influence would have begun under Ptolemy II, 283-245 B.C.., but he did not go farther south than Philotera-Qosseir which is still in Egyptian territory, and Ptolemais Epitheras which is probably near Suakin (1: §§ 5, 7). Ptolemy III, 245-222 B.C., is the first to interest us here, and the establishments were maintained until the time of Ptolemy V, 203-181 B.C. Thus, the influence of Ptolemaic Egypt was felt for a couple of generations, and was exercised from a series of establishments strung out along the coast nearly as far as Notu-ceras, the Horn of Africa (1: §§ 14, 15).[1] Even as far away as the Somali coast between Deire (the Straits of Bab el Mandeb) and Notu-ceras the coastlands were sufficiently well occupied for five of the chief huntsmen – Pytholaos, Lichas, Pythangelos, Leon, and Charimortos – to set up pillars and altars (1: § 15).

North of the Straits of Bab el Mandeb, near the modern Massawa, Addulis was an important centre of activity. Here Ptolemy III set up an inscription in Greek recording that he captured elephants (2). From here the huntsmen spread inland, and clearly had a centre at Aksum, a place which later was to become the capital of a kingdom and the sacred city of the Ethiopians. At Aksum a block of stone has been recorded which at the time of its discovery still preserved the name of Ptolemy III Euergetes in Greek. There was also found there one of those magical hieroglyphic tablets so well known in Egypt from the fourth century B.C. onwards, and called by archaeologists *cippi* of Horus (3: i, pp. 417, 418ff; iii, p. 132). They are charms against every sort of noxious beast: crocodiles, serpents, scorpions, lions, etc. The Aksumite specimen must have been brought from Egypt by one of the

---

*Reprinted by permission of the Royal Anthropological Institute of Great Britain and Ireland from *Man*, No. 43, July-August, 1942.

huntsmen, though it is of some size, in fact about as large as they are commonly made, being 17 in. by 6 in.

The activities of these huntsmen opened up Africa to trade. We have a papyrus which was written in the first half, or possibly the middle, of the second century B.C., that is to say, at the time that the hunting establishments were being closed down. It is the bond for a loan which five men were raising for a trading voyage to the Incense Country (4), and of this more in the next paragraph. In East Africa itself trade was already filtering down as far as Durban in Natal. At that place a coin of Simon Maccabaeus, 143-136 B.C., has been dug up at Marianhill just behind the harbour (5). At Msasani, a little north of Dar es-Salaam, a coin of Ptolemy X Soter, 115-80 B.C., has been found (6). Not very far from Msasani it has been shown that certain customs to be found on the mainland and on the island of Zanzibar clearly originate in Egypt and Greece(7).

The date of the above-mentioned papyrus combined with the status of the partners in the trading company suggests an interesting sidelight on the growth of this trade. Four of the company were officers of the mercenaries, and the fifth was a seafaring man in the merchant service. It looks as if the officers had been employed in the elephant hunts, and that the shutting down of these stations had deprived them of their living, and so they took to trade instead. Being no sailors they took a sea-captain into partnership; clearly to sail their ship for them. They had not much money as they had to raise a loan with which to get started. If they had already been hunting elephants on the coast of Somaliland, they would know the conditions and prospects down south, and it would be natural for them to turn to the south seas when thinking of making their fortunes. They must have known all about the frankincense trade, for the tree grows on the African coast of the Gulf of Aden (1: § 14; 8: pp. 25, 26, §§8-12; 2: p. 51; 9: i, p. 426)[2] just where the hunting-grounds had been established. Moreover, the incense trade must have offered splendid profits to those who were not afraid to adventure into foreign parts.

Although they came to East Africa from Egypt, the leaders of the hunting expeditions were largely adventurers from Greece and Asia Minor. Lichas was an Akarnanian, Charimortos was an Etolian, Alexander an Oroandian from Pisidia, and his second in command, Apoasis, was also a Pisidian coming from the not far distant city of Etenna (10).[3] The trading company was an even more cosmopolitan affair, the five partners being a Thessalonican, an Elean from southern Italy, a Massaliot, a Carthaginian, and a man who bore the same Celtic name, Cintus, as the Massaliot and so probably came from Marseilles also (4).

Probably all of them were disreputable characters. We actually know that Charimortos was a man 'of coarse manners and drunken habits' with whose help the avaricious General Scopas 'had absolutely pillaged the kingdom' (11). In fact conditions in East Africa must have been very like those at Khartum in the early and middle nineteenth century. Society there was composed of little else but every sort of scoundrel and ruffian from every country of the Near East mixed with similar characters from various European countries. In fact, it was said that anyone who had made his own country too hot to hold him migrated to Constantinople, when that place became uncomfortable he moved on to Cairo and if he were too bad even for that, he drifted up to Khartum. Thus, we find that the opening up of Africa in the last centuries B.C. was taking place under the auspices of Egypt, just as it did some two thousand years later, and on each occasion the majority of the agents were not Egyptians but were mostly from the north side of the Mediterranean.

The ancient opening up of Africa was carried out by people coming from countries where the Iron Age had long been established. One must, therefore, presume that these pioneers of progress were using tools and weapons of iron, and so would have introduced a knowledge of that metal to the countries they visited. Anyhow, it is the fact that some time after these activities the first written document we have concerning trade in these parts shows the desire for iron on the part of the natives. It is especially prominent round about the Ptolemaic centre of Adulis, and the iron was used there for the same purpose that the Ptolemaic expeditions had gone there, i.e. for elephant hunting.

This document is the Periplus of the Erythraean Sea, and it was written within a few years of A.D. 60, (8: p. 15) about two hundred and fifty years after the shutting down of the Ptolemaic hunting establishments. In it we are told that on the coast round about Adulis, near the modern Massawa, 'There are imported into these places ... iron, which is made into spears used against the elephants and other wild beasts, and in their wars. Besides these, small axes are imported, and adzes and swords; . . . . Likewise from the district of Ariaca (the north-west coast of India) across this sea, there are imported Indian iron, and steel (σίδηρος 'Ινδικὸς, καὶ στόμωμα), and Indian cotton cloth,' § 6, p. 24. Though it is not so stated, the axes, adzes, and swords must at this time have been of iron. In § 8, p. 25, we find that into Malao (Berberah) there is imported '... iron, and gold and silver coin not much,' and in § 10, p. 26, the author says that at Mosyllum (Ras Hantarah) the people are willing to import '. . . a very little iron, and glass.'

Evidently the superiority of iron weapons over more primitive ones had been impressed upon the natives in the neighbourhood of Adulis. No doubt the same lesson had been learned to some extent by the natives of the other places up and down the coast at which the Ptolemies had established hunting stations. But, as it happens, it is only at Berberah and Ras Hantarah that we hear of iron being wanted, and even then at the latter place only 'a very little.'

Trade round these coasts was still just as international as it had been two hundred years before. The author of the Periplus says that there was a trading community established on the Island of Socotra (Dioscorida), and that it consisted of Arabs, and Indians, and Greeks (8: p. 34 § 30, p. 133).

Three hundred years later than the Periplus, about A.D. 350, we hear of iron once more. This time it comes from the west; from the Island of Meroe. Eizana, the then king of Aksum, has left a long inscription in Ethipoic recording his conquests. He says that he conquered the Noba (Nubians) and 'burned their cities of masonry and of straw and [my people] plundered their corn, and their bronze (*birti*), and their iron (*hasin*), and their . . . .' Eizana says that he set up his throne at the junction of the Nile (Seda) and the Atbara (Takazze) (12).[4] This is north of Meroe, so a fragmentary inscription which comes from Meroe itself is almost certainly a tangible record of his expedition. This one is written in Greek as are some of Eizana's inscriptions, and treats of the conquest by a '[king of the Aksu] mites and Homerites,' whose name is lost (13).

Some one hundred and seventy years later again, in the year A.D. 522, Cosmas Indicopleustes was travelling down the Red Sea, and he has left us the account of the iron trade in exchange for gold which has been reproduced in the companion article (14). Cosmas' relevant remarks are extracted here for ease in reference. He says that the caravan of 'upwards, say, of five hundred' merchants accompanying the king's agents start out from the country of Agau. 'They take along with them to the mining district oxen, lumps of salt, and iron, and when they reach its neighbourhood they make a halt at a certain spot and form an encampment, which they fence round with a great hedge of thorns.' Then ensues the dumb trade, the merchants laying out their wares and the natives coming and putting their nuggets of gold on whatever pleases them. As was shown in the companion article the information about the gold makes it certain that it was the country of Fazoqli that imported the iron in this way. Further, we note that the demand was sufficient to make it worth while for the merchants to undertake a journey of six months.

In the latter part of the eighteenth century A.D. iron was still one of the commodities that the natives of Fazoqli bought with their 'gold in small pellets' from the Agaus (3: ii, p. 432, iii, p. 737).[5] At this time they were also getting iron from the direction of the Sudan, for at Guba there was a market where the Shangalla (natives of Fazoqli) sold gold and slaves to the Muslims in return for iron and coarse cotton cloth (3: ii, pp. 438, 439). This iron probably came from Sennaar, for Guba is on the way there from Fazoqli. In that case it probably originated in Kordofan, whence Sennaar was importing iron in the opening years of the nineteenth century A.D. (15: ii, p. 295).

At that time iron was still a sufficient rarity in Fazoqli for the natives to save it for making splitting tools or ornaments. They did not waste it on ordinary tools for digging which would have worn it away, but for this they used hoes of wood (15: iii, p. 10).

The natives of Fazoqli were no doubt entirely dependent for iron on their imports. It is unlikely that they were able to smelt it for themselves, seeing that in the nineteenth century they did not even know how to melt their native gold (15: iii, p. 19). But it seems likely that they knew how to smith the iron they imported. Whether in the sixth or the eighteenth centuries there is no mention of the import of iron tools or utensils, but merely of iron, which implies that it was only in the unworked form of bars or pigs.

The history of the iron for gold trade in Fazoqli is not the only testimony that we have to the permanence of conditions in East Africa, for we find it again in Somaliland. In the early nineteenth century the natives at Berberah (16: ii, p. 369) were buying iron and other things from the *banians* (Indian traders especially those from Gujerat), just as in the first century A.D., 'from the district of Ariaca (Cutch, Kathiawar, and Gujerat) across the sea there are imported Indian iron, and steel, and Indian cotton cloth' into Adulis near the modern Massawa.

On the River Toumat in Fazoqli, where the natives imported it in Cosmas' day, iron is called *d'ong* by the present inhabitants (17: xxxi, p. 206). It is evidently the same word as the *dogn, dun* of the Berta dialects which are spoken along the Abyssinian border from the River Yabus to Roseires (17: xxxii, p. 23) (18: pp. 49, 53). The Uduk who live nearby call iron *tongkutur* (18: p. 33). Is it possible that this form includes the word also? The Uduk language is unrelated, at least to the neighbouring Burun languages, and the people are said to have come from Abyssinia five days beyond Arwa on the far side of the Galla country (18: p. 32). But I have not found anything like this in any of the languages of the Abyssinian world. At the end of the fifteenth century A.D. (19: pp. li-liv)[6] there was a migration of Shilluks into these parts. Yet neither Shilluk nor any of the Nilotic languages that I have been able to find call iron by any word the least like *d'ong*. Yet again, in the eighteenth century there were many 'Nubians' in the country, who came from Gebels Tagale and Eliri in south-eastern Kordofan (19: p. liv), but in the same way the words for iron in those countries bear no resemblance to *d'ong*. Neither is the word anything like those used for iron on the *gebels* near Fazoqli (18: pp. 11, 29, 39, 52), with the exception of those just mentioned. Can *d'ong* be, therefore, some ancient word which has come through to the present day?

NOTES

1. See Wainwright in *Man*, 1940, No. 192.
2. Kempthorne describes the tree, the gathering of incense, and its export to the markets on the opposite coast of South Arabia in the nineteenth century. Paulitschke, *Ethnographie Nordost-Afrikas*, p. 219 says that Somaliland exports as much as 100 to 200 tons of incense annually.
3. For other details of the chief huntsmen and the hunts, see Rostovtzeff in *Archiv für Papyrusforschung*, iv, 1908, pp. 302, 303.
4. The last word is damaged and can be restored as *nahis* 'copper', as Littman does, or as *feso* 'strips of dried meat', as Nöldeke does in *Zeitschrift der deutschen morgenländischen Gesellschaft*, lxvii, p. 701. Seeing that bronze has just been named Nöldeke's restoration seems the more probable, but fortunately neither of the possibilities concerns us here. For a study of Aeizana's reign, see pp. 48ff.
5. Their other purchases were copper, beads, and skins, but salt is not mentioned, though it was wanted in the sixth century, is so greatly in demand in Africa as a rule, and in Abyssinia even has a currency value.
6. The information is derived from 3: iv, pp. 463ff; 15: ii, pp.255ff.

REFERENCES

(1) Strabo, XVI, iv.
(2) McCrindle, J. W., *The Christian Topography of Cosmas, an Egyptian monk*, (London, Hakluyt Society, 1897), pp. 57-59.
(3) Bruce, J., *Travels to Discover the Sources of the Nile*, (1790), 4°.
(4) Wilcken in *Zeitschrift für Aegyptische Sprache und Altertumskunde*, lx, pp. 96-98.
(5) Otto and Stratmann in *Anthropos*, (1909), iv, pp. 168, 169.
(6) Ingrams in *Man*, (1925), No. 86, p. 140.
(7) Wainwright in *Man*, (1940), No. 192.
(8) Schoff, W. H., *The Periplus of the Erythraean Sea*.
(9) Harris, W. C., *The Highlands of Aethiopia*.
(10) Hall in *Classical Review*, xii, (1898), p. 276.
(11) Polybius, *Histories*, xviii, 55.
(12) Littman, E., *Deutsche Aksum-Expedition*, iv, pp. 33, 34, 11, 19, 29, 39, 40.
(13) Sayce in *Proceedings of the Society of Biblical Archaeology*, 1909, pp. 189, 190 and Pl. XXIV.
(14) 'Cosmas and the Gold Trade of Fazoqli' in *Man*, 1942, 30.
(15) Cailliaud.
(16) Wellsted, J. R., *Travels in Arabia*, ii, p. 369.
(17) Heepe in *Mitt. des Seminars für or. Spr.*
(18) Evans Pritchard in *Sudan Notes and Records*, xv.
(19) Westermann, D., *The Shilluk People*.

10

ESSAY ON THE HISTORY OF METALS IN WEST AFRICA*

Raymond Mauny

When, how, through whom, and from where did West Africa come to know metals? Who were the ones that got to know them first, and who did not? Which of the people became the first metallurgists, and which of them persisted in the old ways?

There are so many basic questions to solve which are linked intimately with the history of the country itself, to the development of its civilisation, to its economy, its arts and beliefs. We have little data available to enable us to solve these questions due to the present state of our knowledge of archaeology, ethnology, linguistics, anthropology and other disciplines. But it is important to broach the subject in the light of work and research done for the past 50 years (however incomplete it may be), and to attempt to consider these problems from a new point of view, or to direct new research towards new solutions. As a result, it was too simple and too tempting to say that the Stone Age had lasted until our era and as a result the country has come to know of the metals from the Arabs, or even the Europeans. Another easy explanation would suggest that the metals and techniques of working them were brought by the Phoenician navigators, Carthaginians, Romans, or Egyptian traders who reached the coast, or even penetrated the interior.

The authors writing at the beginning of this century were permitted to make and to offer such working hypotheses. The penetration of West Africa took place during the preceding twenty years. Half-a-century later it had to be realised that things were not that simple. We know from the Arab writers (El Bekri in particular) and by archaeology that in black West Africa the Neolithic Age was replaced

*Translated by the editors. This article, 'Essai sur l'histoire des métaux en Afrique occidentale', first appeared in *Bulletin de l'Institut Français d'Afrique Noire*, Vol. 14. No. 2, April 1952, and has been brought up to date by the author (1971).

by the Iron Age at least a thousand years previously, except for a few little isolated tribes which remained primitive.[1] But, as we shall see, recent discoveries tend to make us inclined to move this date back considerably.

It can be assumed that the Neolithic Age had ended in a given region when the tools, and more particularly the weapons, began to be made of metal. On account of the scarcity of the metals and the difficulty of working them, they were primarily used to satisfy the most urgent needs of the society such as weapons for the warriors and hunters, agricultural implements for the cultivator (confined only to the cutting tools), etc. Stone continued to be used and it fulfilled its old function of satisfying other needs.

The abundance of iron ore and wood in West Africa assured the Negroes, once they became metal workers, a regular supply of metal and a gradual extension of its use. On the other hand, the scarcity of copper resulted in the absence of both the Copper Age and Bronze Age in black West Africa. With regard to gold the hypothesis concerning the Punic and other navigations of the antiquity around the West African Coast, should be abandoned.

As to the Egyptian influence, particularly with regard to Nigeria, where certain authors tried to link the Yoruba centres directly with Egypt (Talbot, Lucas, etc.) and even to a pre-Hellenic Mediterranean civilisation (Frobenius), this approach, in spite of some recent writings, should be viewed with great caution.

We shall study the most important metals: gold, copper and iron, giving some general historical information and indicating the ancient mines known in the country, texts which mentioned them and archaeological discoveries concerning these metals.[2]

Gold

Gold in its original form and copper were the first metals that were known: its lustre and its permanence attracted the attention of the primitive man. It has been recorded for the first time in Africa in Egypt, during the Amratian Epoch (4500 to 4000 B.C.). The first remark, of real interest, can be found in Herodotus (IV, 196), who described the silent barter in gold on the Atlantic coast of Libya, where Carthaginians used to go to exchange various goods for precious metals.

Where did this traffic take place exactly? There is disagreement amongst writers, but the majority of them, particularly Carcopino, who devoted a part of his excellent work to 'Morocco as a gold market of the Carthaginians' made them go to the shores of tropical Africa in search of gold, as far as the estuary of the Niger. This hypothesis, according to some authors, is linked to Hanno's Periplus. From this confusing work they worked out the distance covered by the Carthaginian navigators, by estimating the number of days of navigation. Also, they identified the sole active volcano on the coast of Cameroons with the mountain which poured forth the flames and was called the Chariot of the Gods.

On many occasions I have dealt with the question of ancient voyages along the Atlantic coast of Africa and I came to the conclusion that the local conditions (nearly constant north-eastern winds on the coast of the Sahara, absence of fresh water, hostile populations etc.) limited those navigations to the zone situated to the north of the Cape Juby or Bojador (1a-b, 2: pp. 78-112). Also the unseaworthiness of the ancient vessels prevented the ancients from sailing against the wind thus making the return voyage impossible.

It was on these shores, particularly in the area between the rivers Sous and Draa, that I place the spot where the silent barter in gold took place. In my opinion the Chariot of the Gods is the Anti-Atlas.

Where did gold come from then? There are some gold mines in the Sous mountains and the thing to remember is, that Berbers had an overland contact with the southern fringe of the Sahara and this trade was done by means of oxen, donkeys, horses, camels, and carts. It is not surprising, therefore, that they searched for it in the Sahara, which was under their economic control, and that they obtained it from the black population who lived to the south of them where gold was abundant (Bambuk, Galam, Boure etc.).

One of the first comments made by the Arab authors on the Sudan referred to gold. Historian Iban Abd Al Hakam referred to an expedition undertaken in 734, when Habib ben Abi Ubaida brought back in his booty from Sous and the Sudan an abundance of gold (2: p. 119).

Less than twenty years later a regular connection was established between Sous and the Sudan when wells were bored along the route (3: pp. 296-8). Prior to the year 800 astronomer Al-Fazari referred to Ghana as the land of gold.

During the whole of the middle ages the Sudan was described by the Arabs as the true land of gold. It would be superfluous to mention all the authors who wrote about it. We shall only take note of the most interesting references. Al-Husayn (950) mentioned that at Djarmi (Djerma, Fezzan) gold could be bought in exchange for copper; El-Bekri (1067) spoke of purchases of gold dust and wire made of refined gold manufactured in Audaghost. Mention was also made of jewellery and bells made of gold in Ghana, as well as coins without any inscriptions from Tademekket. Idrisi (1154), Yakout (1229), Iban Said (1280), Al Dimaschki (1327), Ibn Batuta (1354), Ibn Khaldun (end of fourteenth century) (4) all of them made references to trade in gold.

The arrival of the Portuguese on the West African coast, after 1434, diverted a considerable part of the flow of gold toward Arguin and Gáambia. The main Portuguese trading post, Elmina on the Gold Coast, owed its name to the brisk trade in gold which took place there. Ca da Mosto (1455) described gold trade in the interior of Africa. One can safely say, that the Sudan was during the whole of the Middle Ages, till the discovery of America, one of the main suppliers of gold to the Mediterranean area.

There were numerous gold mines in West Africa. The most important ones were those in the West of Gold Coast, which were in operation at the time of the arrival of the Europeans (XV c.). Also, there were mines in the Ivory Coast to the east of Bandama, in Boure (Siguiri region), on the upper Faleme River (Satadougou) and in the Upper Gambia (Kedougou). There were many abandoned ancient mines in the Lobi country (Upper Volta), in the valley of Geba (Portuguese Guinea) and elsewhere.

Craftsmanship in gold, particularly the filigree work, flourished in the Sahel. Till recent decades figurines, masks and pendants (amulets) were made of gold, of which Bosman already spoke in 1705[3] (5).

Copper

Copper is much more of a necessity to man than the precious metals. In its original form it was used, just like gold, for adornment. Copper beads were the only objects made of this metal in Egypt, during the Badarian Era (5000-4500 B.C.). The Amratian culture (4500-4000 B.C.) had some small hammered objects: sharply pointed tools, chisels, needles, arrow heads, ringlets, and beads. The proto-dynastic era (3500?-3200 B.C.) had bowls, basins, etc.(6: p. 360, et seq.).

Between the years 3000 and 2800 B.C. bronze (85% copper and 15% tin) was discovered in the Middle East (Egypt, Sumeria, Iran, India).

In the year 2400 B.C. approximately, it is found in the Aegean Archipelago, and about 2000 B.C., in Western Europe. We do not know anything about the history of North Africa during that period. However, Atlantic navigators possessing copper and bronze objects and weapons sailed along its coast and it is certain that they called and perhaps even established themselves at various places where commercial activities were taking place.

Maghreb must have also known this metal, which was imported there in the second millenium B.C. This was before the arrival of the

Phoenicians, which the historians, relying on ancient writings, generally assume to have taken place in 1100 B.C. This date could be moved back if one based oneself solely on archaeological findings.

Mauritania has experienced from the first millenium B.C. a copper age, proved by the discovery of many copper tools and weapons, and of a copper mine, which gave Carbon 14 dates of the fifth century B.C.(7).

As to West Africa, south of Mauritania, the first reference to copper was made during the Arab era. Al Husayn (A.D. 950), told us that in Djarmi (Fezzan) pure gold was exchanged for copper, the latter being undoubtedly destined for the Negro countries, where the gold came from. El Bekri (A.D. 1068) mentioned that copper smelted at Igli (Sous) was exported to the countries of the Infidels, that is to the Sudan. This he corroborated by mentioning that in Silla (Tucolor country) ringlets of copper were used as money, and in Ghana a duty had to be paid to the sovereign for the importation of this metal (3: pp. 306, 325, 331). Idrisi (A.D. 1154), noted that in Tekrur (Tucolor country) gold was exported and copper was imported. Al Umari (A.D. 1349), said that in Kanem pieces of copper were used as money and in the states of the king of Mandigoes Musa Mansa there was a copper mine at Dkra (4: p. 1236) (5: p. 310). From Ibn Batuta (A.D. 1354), we had the description of Takedda[4], a town famous for its copper mines. The ore was locally smelted and converted into bars which eventually served as a medium of exchange. Copper was exported to the South, to the countries of the 'Black Infidels' and to Bornu, as archaeology has proved by the discovery in the Sahara of hundreds of copper ingots from a 'wrecked' caravan dated from the twelfth century.

. El Bakouwi (A.D. 1413) mentioned that amongst other commodities brought to the Sudan by the merchants from Maghreb, there were ringlets made of copper. Several decades later (A.D. 1447), a Genoese named Malfante, who resided at Tuat, in his famous letter reported that trade with the black countries was based on two main products: copper and bars of salt. Copper came from the Greek Empire by way of Alexandria, and was sent to the Sudan. 'What do they do out of it? I have often asked this question but no one was able to give a definite answer' (8).

From the middle of the fifteenth century, copper continued to flow from North Africa to the Sudan. It was carried by the caravans (Leo Africanus, 1526). However, to the countries inhabited by the blacks it arrived primarily from the coast where the Portuguese and other Europeans acted as intermediaries.

We learned about the price of copper from E. de la Fosse (1479-80). On the Malagueta Coast (present-day Liberia) one could purchase a slave woman and her child for a barber's washbasin and three or four ringlets of brass. During the subsequent centuries, copper continued to be in great demand. Above all it was sold in the form of bracelets.

The copper mines were more numerous in North-West Africa: Tenes (Algeria); Tadla, Agadir, Aguememu, Sous (Morocco); Ougarta, Adrar (Southern Algeria); Akjoujt (Mauritania). There were also many sites around Nioro (Mali); Azelick, Air, InGall (Niger); Gaoua (Upper Volta) and Cameroons. All these mines had been worked since ancient times. It is not possible to establish their age, but none of them is now of any importance. In many instances the deposits were rapidly exhausted.[5]

Archaeological discoveries of objects made of copper or brass were quite numerous. It seems that bronze was never known in West Africa, except as an imported alloy.

Craftsmanship in copper is still practised in West Africa in the Lobi and Mossi countries, Dahomey, Yoruba country[6] and Bamoun (Cameroun). Unfortunately the general tendency is to manufacture objects of the so-called 'Negro art' which are destined for European buyers. In earlier times copper craftsmen worked primarily for their chiefs.

Until the twentieth century, in countries such as Bawle and Ashanti weights for weighing gold were still in use. These were made of copper, bronze and brass and were manufactured by the lost wax casting technique. They represented animal or human forms or were made in the form of stylised objects. It seems that this form of art reached its peak in the seventeenth century (Kjersmeier).

Abundant literature exists on this subject and important collections have been made. A. J. Arkell (9) described two lamps made of 'bronze' (?) found in the ancient graves of Attabubu, in the Bron country to the north of Kumasi (Gold Coast). One of them was in the shape of a bird suspended by chains, and the other is a lamp on a stand with a ringed stem and with bent legs. They strikingly resemble the lamps of the Christian East, and in particular those of Egypt of the fifth to seventh century A.D. There is no doubt that the lamps of the Gold Coast were inferior imitations of the eastern lamps. It is unknown how their prototypes came to the banks of the Gulf of Guinea. Was it by way of Fezzan, Nubia or Tchad?

The inhabitants of the Gold Coast were always very fond of copper and bronze objects. Lamps of this type were followed by prototypes of elegant containers called 'Kuduo', which were often decorated with ornaments, but seldom with human or animal figures. The earliest such containers were supposed to have been imported from Moslem Spain (10: p. 15), and bore inscriptions in Arabic. There were also oil lamps decorated with birds, possibly from the same source. Objects of copper and brasswares were brought to the Mine during the fifteenth century (11) and even later.

These objects (prototypes of lamps, Kuduo, etc.,) could have come by way of the Arab trans-Saharan trade rather than through Nubia, which only achieved some measure of stability much later, i.e. after the downfall of the Christian Kingdom of Nubia (fourteenth century).

The famous Ife heads, from the Yoruba country, belonged to a distinct group and were dated back to about the thirteenth and fourteenth centuries. The Benin 'bronzes' which in reality were made of brass, similarly as the heads from Ife,[7] stemmed from the art of the religious capital of the Yoruba, an absolutely unique centre in black Africa. These magnificent heads, of natural size, made with the lost wax technique, were discovered in 1910 and in 1938 respectively. They reveal to us the naturalistic art which equalled in beauty that of any ancient art.

To conclude, it seems that copper, apart from the Mauritanian exception, was introduced in sub-Saharan Africa later than iron, and nearly exclusively by way of importation. It was mainly due to the commercial activities of the Arabs that the use of copper was extended to black Africa.

Iron

This metal, difficult to extract and to work, was discovered much later than other metals, with the exception of the use, everywhere in the world, of meteoric iron[8] before man was able to extract iron from the ore.

Nearly all the authors agree that iron smelting and working was discovered towards the middle of the second millenium, in the region situated between the Caucasus and Cappadocia. According to our knowledge, the oldest iron industry was dated to about 1400 B.C. It was that of the Hittites of Asia Minor. We learn this from a letter sent by a Hittite king to Ramses II, in which he explained the delay in the delivery of this metal[9]. But Egypt, always traditional in its attitude, seemed to have accepted with reticence this foreign metal. Iron was used since 1100 B.C. on the coast of Syria, however it appeared only infrequently in Egypt between the XXIInd and XXVth dynasties (950-715 B.C.), the first iron tools found in that country, date back to the Assyrian invasion (Assurbanipal, 666 B.C.). Even in the seventh and sixth centuries iron was so scarce that the bands on the chariot wheels were made of copper (12).

An important question was whether Egypt obtained the knowledge of iron from the North (Asia Minor, Syria), or from the South (black Africa, Nubia). Some authors (F. von Luschan, 1909; G. Maspero,

1891; G. de Mortillet, 1903; A. Reinach, 1913; D. de Pedrals, 1950), thought that iron was discovered by the Blacks and its knowledge was passed on to the Egyptians. All these authors, with the exception of D. de Pedrals (13)[10] wrote prior to the great excavations of the twentieth century and the subsequent researches in the field. Belck, 1910, Flinders Petrie, 1915; Daryll Forde, 1946; and above all Wainwright, 1944, who specialised in this matter, refuted this hypothesis.

There is much less information with regard to North Africa. Around the sixth century, when iron became common in North Africa, the knowledge of its extraction and working must have been transmitted to the Berbers by the Carthaginians. The bilingual inscription of Dougga, which dates back to the middle of the second century, mentioned iron smelters in the indigenous kingdom of Numidia (14: p. 78). Gradually all the Berbers learned how to smelt and work iron. Both the iron ore and wood (the latter used for smelting) were abundant in the Maghreb.

Pre-Roman graves of Fezzan (hence earlier than the first century (15: p. 416) and the pre-Islamic funerary monuments of North Africa and Abalessa (fourth century A.D. at least), have provided us with objects and jewellery made of iron (16: pp. 7, 14, 16, 37, 98).

In my opinion, it was improbable that the Southern Berbers, who were in constant contact with their Northern compatriots and were inveterate warriors, did not introduce iron as soon as they could in order to manufacture weapons. They must have been anxious to improve their quality. It can be assumed that in that era, as well as in the fairly recent past, the Berbers of Southern Sahara possessed numerous black slaves whom they used for more exacting kinds of work[11]. Thus, without even realising it, the Libyco-Berbers of the south must have taught the Blacks how to work iron. Some of these slaves may have escaped and returned to their country of origin. Alternatively they were even sent there purposely to obtain this metal. It was difficult to establish an exact date when this source of supply became available, but I feel that it may have taken place since about 300 B.C. During the preceding centuries the Berbers of the South knew only iron which was imported from the North. Soon thereafter the Negroes of the Sahel and of the savanna learned to use and manufacture iron.

The most obvious proof of the ancient use of iron by the Negroes of West Africa was provided by the discoveries made by B.E.B. Fagg, on the plateau of Bauchi (Nigeria), and above all in the tin mines of Nok. Magnificent earthenware statuettes were found (17: p. 21-22), deep in the ground, in the stratum which geologists attributed to a wet phase and which could have been contemporary with that of Nakuru (Kenya), i.e. approximately between the fifth century B.C. and our

Christian Era. He excavated later on an iron metallurgy site in Taruga and the Carbon-14 dates ranged from 440 to 280 B.C. (18: p. 152). In the region which we have just discussed, that period was close in time to our era.

The ancient writings were of little use to us, but with the arrival of the Arabs (VII c.) important written sources of information referring to Southern Sahara and the Negro countries were available. Though the Arabs had reached Sudan in the eighth century, it was as late as 1068 that El Bekri provided the first interesting remarks: firstly, about an iron mountain (Adrar nr. Ouzzal) in the desert on the way from Draa to Ghana[12], and secondly about the short javelins of iron used by the Negroes of Silla (the Tucolor country) for killing hippopotamuses (3: p. 325).

Al-Zouhri (before 1150) mentioned Ghanaian expeditions to pagan tribes living close to the Ocean and west of their territory, 'who have no knowledge of iron and fight with sticks made of ebony; the people of Ghana could defeat them as they fought with swords and spears.' (4: iii, p. 801)

Iron was known all along the coast at the time of the arrival of the Europeans in the middle of the fifteenth century. The Cronica de Guiné (about 1453) described the spikes, arrow heads, and native harpoons of Cap Vert (19). Ca da Mosto (1455) provided some more details such as: assegais with scimitar shaped crampons were 'forged without any steel'. The natives obtain their iron from a Negro kingdom 'which is situated far away' (20). Also we learn from V. Fernandes (about 1506) that iron was brought to Gambia from the interior by merchants, by way of a river (fol. 110v.).

From the beginning of the seventeenth century iron was imported in large quantities from Europe along the Senegal River, and iron bars became the means of barter trade.

NOTES

1. The Bambuti (Pygmies) of Central Africa, the Bushmen of Southern Africa, the Guanches of the Canary Islands, the Tonga of Mozambique, and the inhabitants of the Fernando Poo Island are the only peoples of Africa, who at the time of the arrival of the Europeans, were still in the true Stone Age and had no knowledge of metals.

2. The ample linguistic evidence provided in this article is omitted from this abridged version [Editors].

3. On the question of gold and other metals in West Africa, see more recent information in (5).

4. It is believed that the site of the famous town was at Azelick west of Air. See Brouin, G., 'Du nouveau au sujet de la question de Takkeda', (*Notes Afr.*, No. 47, avril 1950), pp. 90-91 and (5: pp. 308-311).

5. See more recent information in (5: pp. 306-313).

6. It is to be noted that in the Yoruba country, the smelters of copper use a blowing apparatus in the form of a pouch with a clapper operated by hand, which came from the North, whereas the iron workers use a blowing apparatus of a West African type, with two valves and without a clapper (Frobenius, *Mythologie de l'Atlantide*, 1949, p. 90). The working of copper appears, therefore, of more recent origin than that of iron, and is of North African provenance, most likely Arabo-Berber.

7. See (21: p. 78). Considerable literature exists on heads of Ife and the Benin 'bronzes'. However, it would be desirable to analyse some of the heads of Ife in order to establish their origin, if not their approximate age. See, in particular, (21: p. 2); according to Fagg the heads of Ife were made of brass.

8. The objects made of this iron are easy to identify, as they contain a considerable proportion of nickel (5 to 26%), whereas nickel-bearing minerals, even after treatment which increases nickel-content, do not contain more than 2.5% of nickel.

9. On the coming of iron to Africa and its earliest appearance in Egypt see Leclant, J., 'Le fer dans l'Egypte ancienne, le Soudan et l'Afrique' in *Actes du colloque internat.* 'Le fer à travers les ages', Nancy, 1955, published in *Annales de l'Est*, Mein. No. 16, (Nancy, 1956), pp. 83-91; summary in (2: pp. 67-77).

10. Pedrals considers the fact that Arkell has found iron arrowheads in 'the graves of Meriotic type' contradicts the views of Wainwright, according to whom iron did not make appearance in those regions before the sixth century B.C. This may be due to misunderstanding on the part of Pedrals. Correctly the Meriotic period extended from 540 B.C. to A.D. 350.

11. At that time the Sahara was more humid than it is now, but all the same it was a desert. The black agriculturalists had to withdraw gradually toward the South, and the areas turning into a desert were passing to Libyco-Berber hunters and nomads. The ancestors of the Fulani (racial mixture of the Western Negroes and Libyco-Berbers) had, therefore, to occupy the pastures of Sahel which extended a little more to the North than today. To be correct the Ethiopians (burnt faces) of the North of the Sahara, described as such by the ancient authors, were the Southern Berbers and not the Negroes.

12. Could correspond to Kedia of Idjii, where iron is abundant; see (3: p. 310).

REFERENCES

(1) Mauny R.: (a) 'Note sur le périple d'Hannon' (C.R. l-re Conf. Internat. Afr. Ouest, Dakar, 1945 Paris Maisonneuve, 1951), pp. 509-530; (b) 'Un problème de géographie historique: les origines lointaines de la découverte du Cap Vert' (C.R. 2e C.I.A.O. Bissau, 1947, Lisboa, 1950, pp. 297-307); (c) 'L'Ouest Africain chez Ptolemée' (C.R. 2e C.I.A.O., Bissau, 1947, Lisboa, 1950), pp. 241-293; (d) 'Autour d'un texte bien controverse: le "périple" de Polybe' (Hesperis, Rabat, 1949/1951), p. 47-67; (e) 'Protohistoire et histoire ancienne' (de L'A.O.F.), Encyclopédie Mar. et Colo. Vol. A.O.F., t I, p. 35-42; (f) 'Les Puniques et l'Afrique Noire occidentale', Actes 70e Congrès Assoc. fr. Av. Sc. Tunis, 1951 (Tunis, Bascone & Muscat, T. III, 1953), p. 53-62. *Les siècles obscurs de l'Afrique noire. Histoire et archéologie.* (Paris, Fayard, 1971).

(2) Al-Hakam, Ibn Abd, *Conquête de l'Afrique du Nord et de l'Espagne.* Transl. A. Gateau, Alger, Carbonel, (1942).

(3) El-Bekri, *Description de l'Afrique septentrionale*, Transl. by Slane, Alger, Jourdan, (1913).

(4) Citations from Arab authors: *Monumenta Cartographica Africae et Aegypti* by Kamal, Y. Le Caire, Vol. 4, (1926-1938).

(5)   Mauny, R. *Tableau géographique de l'Ouest africaine au Moyen Age*, Dakar, Mem. I.F.A.N. 61, 1961, pp. 293 sq. (Amsterdam, Swets & Zeitlinger, 1967).
(6)   Furon, R., *Manuel de préhistoire générale*, (Paris, Payot, 1951).
(7)   Lambert, N., 'Les industries sur cuivre dans l'Ouest saharien', *West African Journal of Archaeology*, I, (1971).
(8)   Roncière, Ch., de la, *La Découverte de l'Afrique au Moyen Age*, (Le Caire, 1925, Vol. I, p. 151 et seq.).
(9)   Arkell, A. J., *Antiquity*, March, 1950, p. 38-40, 4 fig.
(10)   Kjersmeier, C., *Centres de style de la sculpture nègre africaine* (Paris, Morance, 1935, 2 t.).
(11)   Fosse, E., de la, *Voyage à la côte occidentale d'Afrique* (1479-1480), publ. by Foulché-Delbosc, R., (1897) and Mauny R., (1949).
(12)   Rickard, T. A., *L'Homme et les métaux*, (Paris, 1938, p. 343).
(13)   Pedrals, D. de, *Archéologie de l'Afrique Noire* (Paris, Payot, 1950, pp. 22-24).
(14)   Gsell, S., *Histoire ancienne de l'Afrique du Nord*, (Paris, 1913-30), VI, p. 78.
(15)   Caputo, G., *Scavi archeologici nel Sahara libico* (Ann. Instit. Orient. di Napoli, 1949, p. 416).
(16)   Reygasse, M., *Monuments funéraires pré-islamiques de l'Afrique du Nord*, (Paris, 1950), pp. 7, 14, 16, 37, 98.
(17)   Fagg, B. E. B. 'A preliminary note on a series of pottery figures from Northern Nigeria' (*Africa*, January 1945, pp. 21-22, and 1946, p. 52).
(18)   Fagan, B. 'Radiocarbon dates for sub-Saharan Africa',: VI, *Journal of African History*, X, No. 1, 1969, p. 152.
(19)   *Chronica das Feitos de Guine*, Lisboa, Agencia das Col. 1949, Vol. II, p. 285.
(20)   *Ca da Mosto*, transl. J. Temporal, publ. Ch. Schefer, Paris, 1895, p. 84.
(21)   Cline, W., 'Mining and Metallurgy in Negro Africa' (General Series in *Anthrop.* No. 5, Menasha, Wisc., U.S.A., 1937, pp. 166).
(22)   Fagg, W. and Underwood, L., 'An examination of the so-called "Olokun" head of Ife, Nigeria', (*Man*, Jan. 1949, pp. 1-7).

PART IV

Some Economic and Technological Aspects of the Iron Age

11

THE IRON AGE OF ZAMBIA*

Brian Fagan

The Earliest Agriculturalists

The earliest agricultural peoples apparently spread into Zambia from the north or northwest and are known to us only from their highly characteristic pottery. We have no proof whether they were farmers, although it is probable that they were, on the argument that pottery elsewhere in Africa is almost invariably synonymous with the introduction of agriculture. Sheep were kept by the earliest pottery makers in Rhodesia (18) and there is no reason to suppose that their contemporaries north of the Zambesi did not have domestic stock.

Posnansky (1961a), Clark and Fagan (1964), and others have compared Zambian Channel-decoráted pottery to the Dimple-based Ware of East Africa, and it is generally agreed that the connections between these two pottery types are only of a rather general nature.[1] The elaborate channelled scroll decoration and dimple bases of the East African material are totally absent south of Tanzania. The Zambian industries are perhaps a form of devolved Dimple-based Ware, from which the more elaborate features are absent.

It is also generally accepted, admittedly on not particularly strong evidence, that the first potters in Zambia entered from the north or northwest. The earliest farming population in the Southern Province was probably very small, to judge from the low number of sites known to us. Such as have been discovered have yielded only scanty cultural material.

*This paper, revised by the author in 1971, was originally part of a symposium, followed by comments (Current Anthropology, Vol. 7, No. 4, 1966, pp.469-478) from: J. H. Chaplin, Elizabeth Colson, Oliver Davies, Jean Hiernaux, Jacques Nenquin, Richard Pittioni, Merrick Posnansky, K. R. Robinson, J. Rudner, H. v. Sickard, and R. Raymond Wood. The comments are followed by replies from the authors (pp.478-481). The original version of this paper was written before the introduction of the nomenclative changes proposed by the Wenner-Gren Symposium on African Terminology in July, 1965.

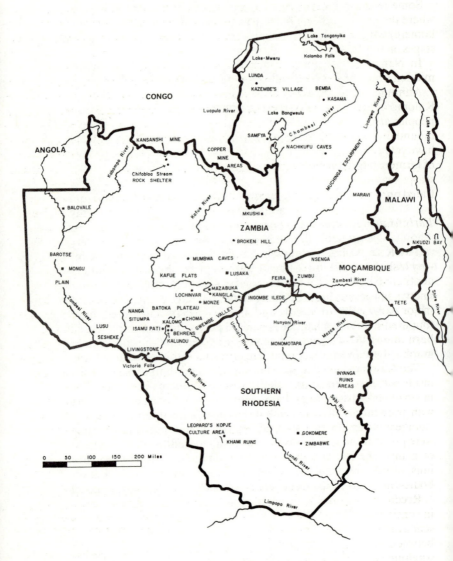

Outline Map of Zambia, Malawi and Rhodesia
Shown are the sites referred to in the text. No chronological significance is
intended for the distributions.

Some of these farmers moved over the Zambesi into Rhodesia, where the earliest pottery belongs to the Zimbabwe Class One (Gokomere) type, carbon-dated to A.D. 330 + 150 (M-913) for its closing stages on the Acropolis at Zimbabwe (19).

In Nanga Forest, near Machili Forest Station, is an Iron Age midden which has yielded pottery of the earlier Kalomo culture type.

Although no date is yet available for the lowest levels of the Kalomo culture, it would seem that the Channel-decorated pottery peoples arrived perhaps about 600 years before the more advanced mound dwellers of the plateau. No sites belonging to the early period have yet been discovered on the plateau, though the small population of farmers may have lived along the banks of the Zambesi or on sand scarps overlooking open clearings or streams, and only rarely penetrated onto the highlands.[2]

Early Mound Dwellers and Others

Two Kalomo culture sites have been excavated, the one – Kalundu – by Inskeep (1962) in 1957 and myself in 1962. I have also excavated another 10 miles on the Livingstone side of Kalomo. This latter site, known as Isamu Pati, has been excavated on a large scale and the major part of our knowledge of the Kalomo people is based on the four months' work done here. The excavation of the Kalundu site has been undertaken to amplify Inskeep's results and to obtain a stratigraphical check on the Isamu Pati sequence.[3]

The Kalomo people lived in round pole and mud huts, with the inside of the walls plastered. These were grouped on top of the mound in small clusters, perhaps with a cattle kraal in the middle, together with grain bins built on stones to keep them off the ground, and small storage pits dug into the body of the midden. Many of their structures were probably flimsy affairs of grass. In accordance with the customs of many other Bantu peoples, they buried their dead amongst the huts, in the case of the Isamu Pati site in the central area, with the bodies tightly contracted and associated with very scanty grave goods.

Recent excavations have enabled us to reconstruct their economy in considerable detail. Although only preliminary results are at present available, it is clear that their way of life was a delicate balance between hunting, agriculture, and stock-breeding. They cultivated sorghum and collected wild fruit and seeds, among them the wild fig, to supplement their meat diet. Their stock-breeding was based on small Sanga-type shorthorn cattle, some with humps, to judge from clay figurines, and small goats. Dogs were kept, and appear to have been lightly built, long-nosed beasts.

In the earliest stages of the Kalomo culture, hunting was much more common, with particular preference for duiker, klipspringer, impala, kudu, buffalo, and occasionally zebra.

During the later phases of occupation, domestic stock was much more plentiful, and hunting became correspondingly less popular. This increase in domestic animals can perhaps be correlated with a sudden rise in the number of globular (liquid-holding) pots, which is certainly suggestive of a greater role for milk in their diet. Various small rodents were also consumed at all stages, including cane rats (*Thryonomys swinderianus*) and perhaps pouched mice (*Saccostomus campestris*).

Kalomo culture pottery has certain peculiar features of its own, but in general belongs to a widely spread basic continuum of early Iron Age pottery distributed over much of Southern Africa. One might call it a very distant cousin of the Leopard's Kopje ware of Rhodesia (17), although there is no doubt that the two cultures were in no way in close contact with each other. In both cultures, clay vessels are small, with economical use of comb-stamped and incised decoration. Although the evidence from Rhodesia is confined to a fairly brief description in Robinson (1959), it would appear that the economy of the two cultures is basically the same, with dependence on pastoralism and hunting, especially in the earlier stages. Unfortunately, no C-14 dates are yet available for the Leopard's Kopje culture, which could establish the degree of contemporaneity between the two peoples. But we are beginning to obtain a picture of a basic cultural continuum over much of Southern Africa at this time.

In the lowest levels of the Kalundu mound (11), grooved decoration in well-defined bands is common; in the middle stages this becomes less important, and there is a gradual change to globular vessels and rather shapeless pots. The same sequence of pottery is found at Isamu Pati, although it would seem that the site was originally occupied and abandoned later than Kalundu.

Iron tools are comparatively rare in these middens, being confined to simple barbed arrowheads and razors. Only one hoe was recovered, the blade of which was completely worn down, indicating the great value of iron at this period. Several bored stones show that weighted digging sticks were in use.

If the C-14 dates from the uppermost levels of the Kalomo sites are correct, these people either died out, were assimilated, or moved from Batoka plateau at a date later than A.D. 1250. At the north end of the plateau, however, recent excavations on a small site at Kangila Farm, 15 miles southeast of Mazabuka, have revealed an Iron Age culture which has some similarities in economy with the Isamu Pati people, although their pottery is different. Mound-dwelling in its strict sense of traditional village sites occupied over many generations, resulting in the accumulation of deep ash middens, is not a characteristic of these people, for the midden deposit is normally little more than three feet deep. The Kangila people, whose sites are found at Lochinvar Ranch, near the Kafue Flats, and elsewhere in the Mazabuka District, had a preference for shallow bowls with lightly grooved decoration. No evidence of seeds or fruit-gathering was found in our excavations. Agriculture was practised, but the preponderance of cattle bones in the midden shows that stock was an important feature of their economy. The plateau highlands upon which the sites are situated are famous for both African and European stock-breeding today. Duiker were also hunted. A peculiar feature of this site was the complete absence of charcoal from the deposits, as if firewood were scarce and cattle dung used for fuel for the tree cover in the area today is very poor.[4]

Early Trade in the Zambesi Valley

The Iron Age cultures of Zambia flourished in the interior with, for the most part, only sporadic contacts with the main trade routes of the Zambesi valley and Monomotapa's empire.

Isolated finds of cowrie shells, in the base of the Kalundu mound, show that the Kalomo culture people were able to acquire certain trade objects from their earliest period of settlement. That their trading contacts were only sporadic is shown by the small number of glass beads and other imported items which are found in their villages.

Traders visited the Middle Zambesi valley from an early date. Written records of Zambesi trade go back as far as 1514, when Antonio Fernandes visited the interior; but there is little doubt that traders were active in the valley as a whole at very much earlier dates.

Ivory seems to have been the principal commodity that attracted visitors; gold, copper, and perhaps iron ore were also traded down the river, being obtained from the mines on the plateau. In Zambia the Batoka plateau with its few useful economic resources was little visited, for it is probable that the trade routes into the northern interior were well defined and almost invariably adhered to.

There was also extensive trade up the Luangwa valley and perhaps overland to Kilwa, although it is more likely that most of the trade was channelled through the Zambesi outlet.

Recent excavations in the Middle Zambesi valley near Lusitu, 32 miles downstream of Kariba, have given us a clear idea of the type of trade practised in the Middle Zambesi valley during the late 1st millenium. An ash capped ridge known as Ingombe Ilede (Tonga – 'the place where the cow sleeps') lies some 32 miles downstream of the

Kariba Dam Wall on the north bank of the Zambesi. In 1960 the foundations for a water tank were dug into the top of the hill in connection with the Kariba Resettlement Scheme. The labourers exposed a burial with rich grave goods. Subsequent rescue excavations by Chaplin (1962) and further work in 1961 and 1962 by the present writer have given us a clear picture of a village engaged in sporadic trading activity.

No less than 46 skeletons were found during the course of the various seasons of excavation. In the centre of the site lay 11 extended male skeletons, several of which were buried with gold and glass beads, *conus* sea shells, copper cross ingots and trade wire, pottery, and wire drawing tools. Copper bangles or bracelets adorned the legs and arms of certain of these skeletons. In places the oxidising effect of the copper had preserved fabrics, and several different varieties of imported and indigenous cloth have been recognised. The richness of these burials strongly suggests that they are the bodies of a chief and his retinue. The trade which made these people rich was presumably based on copper, ivory, gold, and perhaps slaves, in exchange for cloth, beads, and other luxuries from the coast. The Livingstone brothers (1865) recorded that the Lusitu stream was famous for its salt, and this local commodity may well have been a basis for trade. The copper and gold must have been obtained from the interior either north or south of the Zambesi, but at present the problem of the origin of the Lusitu raw materials remains unsolved.

Stratigraphical evidence suggests that the settlement originally started as the result of elephant-hunting. The pottery from the lowest levels vaguely recalls that from the Kangila mound on the plateau. In the last occupation phases, however, the pottery is finer, and trade goods are more common, suggesting that the volume of trade increased in the later stages of the settlement. The pottery from the upper levels is probably in part a direct evolution from the basal ware, although new features in the form of very fine vessels have been added to the industry. The Ingombe Ilede vessels certainly in no way resemble modern Valley Tonga pottery, but do display certain Shona features.

In addition to cultivating sorghum and keeping cattle, goats, and dogs, the inhabitants hunted a wide variety of game including duiker, impala, waterbuck, zebra, and buffalo. The elephant was also killed for its economically valuable ivory, and fragments of tusks were frequently found in our trenches. The huts were flimsy affairs, traces of mud floors were seldom found in the deposit. Some form of building with a substantial floor had been erected over the central burials. Unfortunately this was destroyed by workmen digging into the foundations before scientific investigations had begun. It is likely that most of their dwellings were built of wood and sticks or stood on stilts. Most of the life in the Gwembe valley is spent in the open air (8), owing to the great heat and small diurnal temperature range. The later investigations also yielded the remains of 35 skeletons, many of them infants less than a year old, indicating a very high death rate. Obviously these were the remains of either the common people or slaves, since virtually no decorations adorned the bodies, and the corpses had been deposited both at the edge of the site and haphazardly in the body of the midden. The same, somewhat unusual, extended burial position was used.

Radiocarbon dates for the site have been processed by a variety of laboratories. The date of the gold beads is thought to be around the fifteenth century, whilst the site was first occupied in the seventh century A.D.

The Ingombe Ilede thus belongs to the earliest period of Zambesi trade, although its roots probably lie in the early Iron Age tradition of the Batoka plateau region.

Copper Mining and Trade

Undoubtedly one of the most interesting features of the Iron Age period in Zambia is the copper trade. Although Clark (1957) has published a general account of pre-European copper-working in Zambia, no specific research on the techniques and development of copper mining and trade has yet been undertaken.[5] It is unlikely that much will be learnt, because the early workings in Katanga and on the Copperbelt have been destroyed by modern mining. The earliest records of copper mining in Central Africa are found in Pigafetta's (1591) account of Africa in which he refers to the copper mines of Bembe, which were probably situated in Angola, but may well have been as far northeast as Katanga, for 'Bembe' is an old Bemba name for Lake Bangweulu. In the last decade of the sixteenth century an Englishman called Andrew Battell of Leigh in Essex spent several years in Angola as a Portuguese prisoner. He mentions trade in copper in the coastal and central regions of Angola, the metal being derived from the far interior. Again it is not improbable that this refers to the Katanga and Copperbelt mines. In 1810, two Portuguese traders visited the Katanga copper areas and saw mining operations in progress (5) and referred to the copper trade with the Bisa at Kazembe's court (9).

In the earlier centuries of the Iron Age, the working of copper was probably on a very small scale, for only rare fragments of wound copper strip bangles are known from Kalomo culture sites in an eleventh century context, and these isolated specimens evidently predate the considerable expansion of the copper trade in the seventeenth century or thereabouts. During that century, however, it appears that the Copperbelt became a centre for copper trade; this was probably the result of the arrival of new immigrants from the Congo Basin, who appeared in Zambia in successive migrations from perhaps the sixteenth century onwards and also as a result of the gradual fragmentation and diaspora of the elements of the great Lunda kingdom of Chief Mwata Yamvo, whose relation Kazembe crossed the Luapula into Zambia in the mid-eighteenth century. The copper from these mines found its way over much of South Central Africa, perhaps to the Rhodesian ruins; it also went to the Portuguese settlements in Mozambique, and later to the Tanzania coast with Arab traders. Copper from Katanga also reached the west coast. Although the copper trade was widespread, little work has yet been done on the spectographic analysis of copper objects in archaeological deposits to establish the origin of the raw materials. This would probably be a profitable field of research if sufficient analyses could be made. Virtually nothing is known about pre-European gold trade in Zambia, but it was probably insignificant when compared to copper.

The techniques of copper mining were not elaborate, for operations were confined to outcrops of malachite or rotten copper ore, usually found on the slopes and tops of small hills. The ores were recovered by means of circular shafts sunk into the kopje, or by deep trenches such as can be seen today at Kansanshi Mine near Solwezi, which followed the outcrops into the ground. Quarrying tools consisted of iron-headed picks, and hard rocks were removed by fire and water. Baskets and ropes transported the ore to the surface.

Chaplin (1961) has recently described the processes of smelting, and it is not intended to describe them at length here.

The copper was smelted in small, temporary furnaces made up of a circle of small anthills plastered together with clay. Another anthill was used as a nozzle for a set of goat-skin bellows, which provided an artificial draught. An earth-filled clay pot was set into the ground below the furnace as a receptacle for the liquid metal which trickled down on to the top of the earth filling. Upon completion of the smelting process the furnace was destroyed and the liquid copper poured from the top of the pot into a mould.

The whole business of mining and refining was in the hands of a few families, who camped on the site of their outcrop in temporary shelters and guarded their secrets closely. The molten copper was cast in moulds to form copper 'cross' or bar ingots or drawn to form wire for bangles, which were traded over enormous distances.

The Later Migrations

As stated above, this increase in copper mining can probably be associated with the arrival of various tribes of Congo origin who moved eastward and southward into Zambia in successive waves from earlier than A.D. 1500 (13). Today the majority of the tribes in the more northerly parts of Zambia are of Congo origin. One of the earliest groups seems to have been the 'Maravi', a term applied by early travellers to the tribes living between the Luangwa River and Lake Nyasa, who are said to have settled in that area from the west before Portuguese settlements were founded on the Zambesi. The Chewa are one of the tribes belonging to the Maravi group (13). The first known written record of the Maravi is that by Gaspar Bocarro in 1616, during his overland journey from Tete to Mozambique (20, III:416), so presumably their migration antedated Bocarro's journey. In the eighteenth century many of the present tribes arrived, the Lunda 40 years or so before Lacerda visited Kazembe's capital in 1798, the Bemba, the Bisa, who became active traders in ivory, copper, and slaves, the Kaonde, the Soli, and many other groups. Many of the movements were connected with the diaspora of the Lunda peoples of Mwata Yamvo's kingdom in the eighteenth century. Mwata Yamvo's area was a great centre of iron-working (10), and the new migrants brought a knowledge of advanced ironworking methods which seem to have resulted in the standardisation of smelting and smithing techniques over much of northeastern and northwestern Zambia. The present writer has recently described some of the work of nineteenth century Soli smiths (10) and summarised the relevant literature, and Chaplin (1961) has published an account of the techniques of iron smelting amongst a tribe of Congo origin.

Several types of iron smelting furnace are found in Zambia. In the northern parts of the territory the kilns are tall, conical structures made of a wooden framework plastered with anthill clay. This type, fired by natural draught, is thought to have been introduced by the skilful iron workers of the Congo Basin perhaps as late as the eighteenth century. In the North Western Province, a more elaborate furnace with 'legs', representing a woman giving birth, is used, while in the south a low, conical form of kiln is found. Both these furnace types are fired by artificial draught using goat-skin bellows.

These migrations led to a considerable increase in the population of Zambia, resulting in greater pressure on agricultural land and the eventual extinction of the remaining Later Stone Age communities in the Northern and Eastern provinces (4). The earlier agricultural communities were easily overrun, for they appear to have had little political organisation or cohesion compared with the new immigrants. The more southerly tribes such as the Ila/Tonga group are of unknown origin, for their oral tradition was largely forgotten during the nineteenth century, under the stress of marauding Kololo, Lozi, and Ndebele raiders (8) and such problems as these cannot be solved with facility by purely archaeological methods. The Lozi, who are probably of northwestern origin, are omitted from this summary, but an account of their recent history can be found in Jalla (1961).

Arabs and Portuguese

Written records of the pre-European tribes north of the Zambesi are scanty principally because the energies of both Arab and Portuguese colonists and trades were, in the main, concerned with the fabled wealth of the kingdom of Monomotapa, in present-day Rhodesia. It was only incidentally that they came in touch with the tribes who lived in the interior north of the Zambesi. Antonio Fernandes recorded well-established Arab trade in what Abraham (personal communication) regards as the Middle Zambesi valley in 1511-1514 (21), for the Arabs had been trading with the Mashonaland gold mines from the region of Sofala for at least four and one-half centuries before the expedition of Vasco da Gama in 1497-98. Abraham (1961) suggests that the Arab population of Rhodesia in the early sixteenth century A.D. was probably a large one, and although south of the Zambesi, presumably had sporadic contacts with tribes north of the river.

The Portuguese began to operate in the Lower Zambesi in the sixteenth century, founding settlements at Tete and Sena to act as bases for trade with the kingdom of Monomotapa. From the written records, however, it appears that they traded far up into the Middle Zambesi, as well as operating in the Chirundu/Kariba area by 1600 at the latest. Perhaps there were also other sporadic contacts with the interior.

In 1798 Dr. Francisco José de Lacerda e Almeida made a journey from Tete to Kazembe's capital, passing through Maravi and Bisa territory on the way, in an attempt to cross the continent to Angola. He also hoped to open up trade with Kazembe as a result of the Lundas' sporadic contacts via the Bisa with Manuel Pereira, a trader well known in Tete (9). Lacerda himself died at Kazembe's capital, and the expedition was forced to return to Tete without establishing any really worthwhile trading relationship. The brothers Pombeiro crossed the continent via Kazembe's territory in 1802-11; they were detained for four years by tribal warfare, and also by Kazembe's anxiety to curtail the brothers' exploration. Another, final journey by

Monteiro and Gamitto in 1831 was an abysmal failure, for Kazembe was not interested in serious trade with Tete; his needs were more than satisfied by Mwata Yamvo's west coast contacts and by Arab-inspired Bantu middlemen trading in his country from the coast of Tanzania (9). The primary objective of Portuguese penetration to Kazembe's country was the establishment of a transcontinental route between her two coastal dependencies, and trade was a means to this end. Expeditions operating in the far interior were dependent on the goodwill of the local chiefs and their people, but the various Portuguese expeditions did not succeed in cultivating this. In the nineteenth century, Arab slave-traders from Tanzania succeeded where the Portuguese failed, presumably because their methods made it easier for them to adapt themselves to the tortuous ways of Central African society, which rendered them free of the whims of chiefs.

In comparison with Southern Rhodesia, very few permanent trading posts were set up by the Portuguese in Zambia. Although there had been some form of trading centre at Zumbu for many years, it was not until the early eighteenth century that a permanent settlement was established at Feira, at the confluence of the Zambesi and Luangwa rivers. After a brief period of prosperity lasting some 50 to 100 years, the place declined owing to poor trade facilities and the unhealthy climate, and fell into disuse. Its ruins were visited by Livingstone in 1856 and 1860. Clark (1962) has recently surveyed the ruins of the settlement, and has made a plan of the fort. It was a square, stone-walled area with bastions and a gate, and the foundations of the houses which stood inside the fortifications are still clearly visible today when the grass is low. Imported china picked up on the surface of the old settlement was dated to the eighteenth century by the Victoria and Albert Museum.

NOTES

1.   The typology of pottery of the Central African Iron Age has changed considerably since this paper was written. The importance previously attached to the Channel-decorated pottery is not borne out by the latest discoveries (see: Phillipson, D. W. 'The Early Iron Age in Zambia – Regional Variations and Some Tentative Conclusions'. *Journal of African History*, IX, 2, 1968, pp. 191-211).

2.   The lowest levels of the Kalomo culture have been recently carbon-dated to circa A.D. 300 ± 90 years, and it is likely that the aforementioned gap was less than 600 years. Evidence has also been accumulated for the existence of settlements along the banks of the Zambesi.

3.   Since then many other sites have been discovered.

4.   This culture dates to A.D. 1200-1500.

5.   A more recent study has been undertaken by Phillipson, D. W. and others.

REFERENCES

(1)   Abraham, D. P. 'Maramuca: An exercise in the combined use of Portuguese records and oral traditions'. *Journal of African History* (1961), 11:212.

(2)   Chaplin, J. H. 'Notes on traditional smelting in Northern Rhodesia'. *South African Archaeological Bulletin* (1961), 16:53-60, 62.

(3)   Chaplin, J. H. 'A preliminary account of Iron Age burials with gold in the Gwembe Valley, Northern Rhodesia'. *Proceedings of the First Federal Science Congress*, 1960, pp.397-406.

(4)   Clark, J. D. 'A note on the pre-Bantu inhabitants of Northern Rhodesia and Nyasaland'. *South African Journal of Science* (1950b), 47:80-85.

(5)   Clark, J. D. 'Pre-European copper mining in South Africa'. *Roan Antelope,* May 1957, pp. 12-16.

(6)   Clark, J. D. (1962), 'Feira'. *Northern Rhodesia Journal.*

(7)   Clark, J. D. and Fagan, B. M. 'Charcoals, sands, and Channel-decorated pottery from Northern Rhodesia'. *American Anthropologist* (1964), 67:354-71.

(8)   Colson, E. *The social organisation of the Gwembe Tonga.* Manchester: Manchester University Press (1960).

(9)   Cunnison, I. 'Kazembe and the Portuguese, 1798-1832'. *Journal of African History* (1961), 2:61-78.

(10)   Fagan, B. M. 'A collection of nineteenth century Soli ironwork from the Lusaka area, Northern Rhodesia'. *Journal of the Royal Anthropological Institute* (1961), 91:228-43.

(11)   Inskeep, R. R. 'Some Iron Age sites in Northern Rhodesia'. *South African Archaeological Bulletin* (1962), 17:136-80.

(12)   Jalla, A. *The story of the Barotse nation.* Lusaka: Publications Bureau (1961).

(13)   Lane Poole, E. H. *The native tribes of the Eastern Province of Northern Rhodesia.* Lusaka: Government Printer (1938).

(14)   Livingstone, C. and Livingstone, D. *Narrative of an expedition to the Zambesi and its tributaries.* London: John Murray (1865).

(15)   Pigafetta, F. (1591), *Relatione del reame di Congo et dell circonvincine contrade tratta delli scritti ragionamenti di Odorado Lopez, Portoghese;* First English translation, *A Report of the Kingdom of Congo and of the Surrounding Countries,* 1881; reprinted Frank Cass, London, 1970.

(16)   Posnansky, M. 'Pottery types from archaeological sites in East Africa'. *Journal of African History* (1961), 2:177-98.

(17)   Robinson, K. R. *Khami ruins.* London: Cambridge University Press (1959).

(18)   Robinson, K. R. 'An early Iron Age site from the Chibi District, Southern Rhodesia'. *South African Archaeological Bulletin* (1961a), 16:63, 75-102.

(19)   Robinson, K. R. 'Excavations on the Acropolis Hill (Zimbabwe)'. *Occasional Papers of the National Museum of Southern Rhodesia* (1961b), 3, No. 23A:159-92.

(20)   Theal, G. M. *Records of South-Eastern Africa.* London (1898-1901).

(21)   Tracey, H. *Antonio Fernandes descobridor do Monomotapa, 1514-1515.* Lourenco Marques: Arquivo Historico de Mocambique (1940).

12

ASPECTS OF THE USHI IRON INDUSTRY*

G. Kay and D. M. Wright

Throughout the Fort Rosebery District of Northern Rhodesia, the homeland of the Ushi, one may find evidence of a former iron industry. Slag, which is virtually indestructible, is the most common evidence and is easily seen on many inter-village paths. Investigations in the surrounding bush often lead to the remains of kilns and, though a circle of crumbled clay and broken ventilation pipes is all that one usually encounters, it is quite possible to find an almost complete specimen. Samples of early iron work are less common. We have seen several arrow heads, spears and ceremonial bow-rests, but very few implements and no utensils. The indigenous products were rapidly ousted by imported goods and iron of European manufacture when these became available and all but valued items of local origin would then be discarded. It is probable that most are lost for ever, and any search is hindered by the custom of cultivating abandoned village sites and by the rapid oxidisation of iron in acid soils (1).

Production and Trade

Without a detailed and comprehensive survey of the Ushi country it is impossible to provide even a semi-quantitative account of the production and trade but we can outline some of the main features.

In 1906 H. T. Harrington noted that 'the Wa-Usi are celebrated as iron workers and the hoes, axes, knives, spears, etc., made by them are much sought after from all parts of the country, but as usual with these people the supply is not nearly equal to the demand'(2). It is possible that their iron goods were celebrated because of their durability, but it is unlikely that the Ushi were ever important producers, exporting goods on a large scale. In this they were overshadowed by their northern neighbours, the Chishinga (now subdivided into the Chi-

*Reprinted from the *Northern Rhodesian Journal*, Vol. 5, No. 1, 1962.

shinga and the Mukulu) who were 'formerly widely reputed for their iron working' (3) and carried on extensive trade with the Bemba, the lakeside-Bisa and the Unga (4). None of our informants remembered an export trade of importance, though the exchange of iron for salt in the Katanga was mentioned, and it is not impossible that the Ushi were importing iron before the European traders came to their country. Chief Kalaba's spontaneous reply when asked 'Where did you get iron from before the Europeans came?' was 'Nyasaland'. This proved to be a reference to the Arab-organised slave trade based on Lake Nyasa. The slavers brought iron goods, probably from the great, N'goni(?) (5) iron-producing area west of the lake noted by Livingstone (6), and exchanged them for ivory and slaves. We have, however, discovered no other evidence of an early import trade and it must be assumed, particularly since the slave trade did not penetrate to this region until late in the nineteenth century (7), that the Ushi were generally self-sufficient in iron goods.

Whilst, as we have noted, there is evidence of a widespread industry, certain localities were undoubtedly dominant, and intra-tribal trade, as distinct from local sales, was well developed.

There seem to have been two main sources of ironstone. *Bog-iron,* 'found extensively round the edges of swampy depressions or dambos' (1:p.307) in many parts of southern Africa, was mined from shallow diggings throughout the country. The most extensive of these pits discovered are around dambos in Chief Mibenge's area. This bog-iron is of low quality but, occasionally supplemented by imported supplies of ore, it supported small, dispersed groups of smelters. However, there is ample evidence that these small groups did not produce sufficient iron to satisfy their localities' requirements and there was a general demand for the products of the major industrial centres.

These centres were based on the more valuable ironstone, an ore excavated from the plateau surface rather than the dambo margins and limited to areas within the country of Chiefs Chimese, Kalasa Lukangaba and, possibly, Chisunka. The Chofoshi Valley, where kiln sites are most prolific and twenty-five were located along some 350 yards of the river banks, and Kundamfumu's domain were the two most important centres of both mining and smelting. The iron produced there was exceptionally hard, probably because of the traces of manganese in the ore, and perhaps for this reason it gained a wide reputation. Certainly there stemmed from these centres a considerable trade in iron goods and also in ore, but this trade was conducted predominantly within the tribal group.

Dried fish, goats, sheep, salt, ivory, cloth and slaves were accepted in exchange for high-class weapons and implements, and occasionally for ore. Kundamfumu described how he and his people had been wealthy because of this local trade, and had been highly esteemed amongst the Ushi. He complained bitterly that the European immigration was responsible for the decline and eventual death of the industry and thus for his people's poverty. He referred to the B.S.A.C. obtaining all mineral rights and imposing a levy on all mining, though he could not recall anyone paying it, and to the traders who brought cheaper and, perhaps, better goods than those produced locally. That the tribe as a whole benefited from the cheap supply of imported goods is but cold comfort to him.

The Smelting Process

Thus we have a picture of at least two separate industrial centres whose output supplemented that of numerous smaller producing areas scattered throughout the Ushi country. A similar method of smelting occurred everywhere but, as is to be expected amongst widely scattered groups of workers, local variations in detail were common. For instance, we have seen nine almost complete kilns at six widely separated places, three at Mwanasasa, one at Chimese, one at Kalaba, one at Mibenge and two at Milambo, and slight variations in form were noted at each place. (A tenth kiln, in Chimese's Area, has been reported to us). The following account of the industry has been built up from a variety of sources and is generally applicable to the whole area; where possible we have noted regional differences, but we do not claim to be exhaustive in this respect.

Smelting was a seasonal activity carried on largely during the months of April, May and June; after the rains had ceased and before July, *chikangala pepo* – when it is very cold. Favourable weather conditions were important to men spending four to eight weeks in temporary grass shelters, but this was also a season of little agricultural work. The women could complete the harvesting, and tree cutting for the next year's gardens was spread over several months. Also the rain-softened ground facilitated mining for both clay and iron.

First a suitable site was selected for the kilns and a variety of factors affected this choice. Proximity to the ore pits was not of paramount importance, though generally the kilns were not far removed from them, particularly where bog-iron was mined. However, Barnes noted that the ore might be 'brought from the hills where it is quarried'; Kundamfumu described its transport on machila-type stretchers from the *musunda* hills west of his villages, and parts of Matanda's area also were supplied from these hills. We have noted above that trade in ore was occasionally carried on, and we have reports of ore being carried in long, oval-shaped baskets. Thus it is apparent that other factors received due consideration before the kilns were built. Woodland where suitable trees for fuel were available was necessary, and a nearby stream or dambo was essential to supply water for both industrial and domestic purposes. The site should be reasonably near the villages so that the men might be warned of any event requiring their presence, and beer and food might be obtained occasionally, though most parties were usually self-sufficient in the latter. And yet it should not be too close, for the kilns had to be guarded against the eyes of certain people and the men worked naked when the kilns were fired.

Within any general situation satisfying the above requirements large anthills were the most important localising factor. They supplied clay for the kilns and ventilation pipes, though dambo clays might also be used. Equally important they provided sloping ground which permitted slag to run freely away from the base of the kiln, and perhaps the elevated position benefited from a more vigorous circulation of air. Certainly the vast majority of the sites observed have been on the slopes of anthills. Some, like the Kundamfumu kiln, were placed on the summit of the mound despite obvious difficulties of working on the surrounding steep slopes. The few kiln sites seen that were not on anthills were all on sloping ground.

Having selected the site, which was usually in the vicinity of those of previous years, the various materials were collected together. Both charcoal and wood were burned in the kilns and particular trees, such as *mutondo, mubanga, kapanga, kayimbi*, and *sase* (8) were selected because their hard timber provided excellent fuel. Charcoal was made in much the same way as it is today, and this has been described elsewhere (9). The firewood was cut into logs varying from one to three feet in length and these were stacked until required.

The ironstone had to be broken into pieces about the size of walnuts, though bog-iron often occurs in small nuggets. Whilst there is general agreement on this size one former kiln owner explained that he broke the ore into several grades ranging from the size of walnuts to the size of kaffir corn; this finest grade he termed *bunga bwa lubwe* – ironstone flour. Barnes describes an interesting use of boiling water in this ore-crushing process (a method commonly employed in stone breaking in road construction) but we heard no mention of this. We were told of the use of iron hammers (*nondo*) and of heavy, stone sledge-hammers (*nkama*).

The clay was dug and mixed with water into a stiff but malleable matrix and then the expert builders created the kilns and the air pipes. The latter were skilfully moulded around smooth poles; they were about two feet in length and slightly tapered towards the end to be inserted in the kiln. Barnes provides a detailed description of the manufacture of these pipes, a process he obviously saw, and we can do no better than refer the reader to his work on this subject.

It is obvious from the kilns we have inspected that there were various methods of construction. Some, like the Mwanasasa kilns, were built in three sections, and are characterised by a very definite waist and a broad base in relation to their height. The lower part of the kiln was built first and when this was dry the upper, narrower section was added. Finally the kiln was given a distinctive crown of clay from small, tower-like termitaries known as *mafwesa*; what significance, if any other than as decoration, this crown had, we cannot say. In contrast, others, like the Mibenge kiln, consist of a uniform edifice which tapers irregularly towards the top; the waist is not particularly well marked and the base is relatively narrow. The Mibenge kiln has the suggestion of a crown of distinctive clay, but this detail does not appear on the Kundamfumu kiln.

Further differences were observed in the sizes and shapes of the arches built into the bases of the kilns. In all instances we found eight holes (Barnes noted nine) arranged at compass points in relation to one another, and with the largest hole always facing downslope. This was where the iron was withdrawn and is invariably referred to as the *cabwilo*, from the verb to extract. The sizes of the other holes vary from place to place, as does the names they are known by. For example, all seven are equal in the Kalaba kiln and they are referred to as *manchilo*. In the Mibenge kiln, if the *cabwilo* is regarded as the south point, the other cardinal points are occupied by slightly smaller holes, and the intermediate points by the smallest holes. The one at the north point is known as the *n'ganga*, those at the east and west as *kambowa* and the others as *cimbusa*. The same arrangement of sizes occurs in the Kundamfumu kiln but the terminology is slightly different; the *n'ganga* still occupies the north point in relation to the *cabwilo* at the south, but the east and west arches are called *cimbusa*, the south-east and south-west are *kambowa* and the north-east and north-west are *mukowa n'ganga*. These names are nicknames rather than functional terms and were provided at the whim of each team of workers. Together with the variations in structure of the kilns they demonstrate the insulated character of each working group even within one tribe. The origins of the names have not been satisfactorily explained, either they have been forgotten or are being kept secret, probably the former. (The *cimbusa* refers to the mid-wife and the *n'ganga* to the witch-doctor).

One other local difference in the structure of the kilns is worth noting though we have little evidence on this point. In all areas except Kalaba it was reported that at no time were the kilns capped over. A

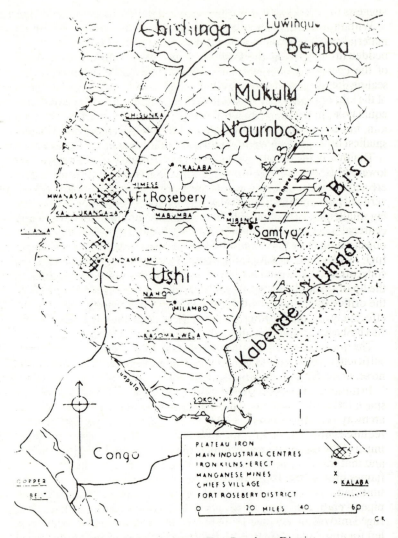

The Ushi Iron Industry, Fort Rosebery District

former kiln owner at Kalaba, however, described how a cap of clay enclosed the packed kiln and a single air pipe was inserted as a chimney. Through this the flames and gases escaped. He referred to this chimney pipe as the *ngala,* the long feathers from the wings or tail of a bird and hence a plume. Furthermore he declared that amongst some other groups in that locality it was known as the *cimbusa,* which suggests that the chimney was not merely a personal idiosyncrasy.

With the kiln and ventilation pipes sun-dried and all the necessary material at hand the actual smelting began. First, tiers of pipes were bedded in clay in all the holes at the base of the kiln with the exception of the *cabwilo*. Each pipe was plugged with clay thus effectively sealing the whole archway. The pipes were pointed towards the centre of the kiln but did not meet. Six pipes were placed in each of the seven equal holes in the Kalaba kiln. We have no total figures for any other kiln, but a vertical bank of three has been seen *in situ* in one of the smallest holes of the Milambo kilns.

The owner of the kiln then either crawled through the *cabwilo* or lowered himself into the bowels of the kiln from a platform of poles erected at one side. There he was handed long logs which he stacked vertically between the batteries of pipes. Above these he alternatively lay smaller logs and charcoal. Some informants suggested very little charcoal was used, others said it was more important than wood. The object was to pack the lower third of the kiln as solidly as possible with fuel, to place the crushed ore above this where the blast would be concentrated by the narrowing of the waist, and to pack more fuel to the lip of the kiln. As already noted it was common practice to leave the orifice open. Undoubtedly it required experience to pack a kiln effectively and each owner probably had his own ideas as to how this was best accomplished.

The question of a flux has been raised, and we can only assume that sufficient calcareous material was available in the ore, for apparently no separate flux was added.

In the late afternoon, when the air was calm, the kiln was fired in the space left at the *cabwilo*. This was then blocked with logs and the archway sealed with clay. For several hours slow combustion was required, hence the need for still, evening air. During this period much of the timber in the lower part of the kiln must have carbonised, and that in the upper part charred and thoroughly dried. Eventually flames broke forth from the top of the kiln, or the chimney, and the time had come to provide a blast. The clay plugs in the ventilation pipes were poked and raked out and the air was drawn in; the fire raged into an inferno and flames lit the sky (4, p. 279). The kilns were left for about two days to burn themselves out and the only attention given during this period was to ensure that the slag which flowed from the pipes did not unduly obstruct the intake of air.

As soon as the heat was no longer intolerable the *cabwilo* was broken open and the lump of smelted iron withdrawn from the floor of the kiln. Apparently this consisted of two grades, the outer parts were a mixture of iron and dross whilst the core, produced when the temperature was at its peak, was of relatively pure iron. These could be separated and broken up by use of the sledge hammer.

When the kiln was cool enough to handle the owner inspected it thoroughly. If it appeared to be sound any necessary minor repairs were made, inefficient ventilation pipes were replaced and the kiln was fired for a second time. A good kiln might be used several times in a season, but it was dangerous to fire a weakened structure because it was likely to collapse when the blast of air entered. One owner said he never used a kiln more than once because of this danger, and no kilns were used for a second season.

Barnes has described how the smelted iron was further reduced and purified in a smaller furnace 'like a closed forge having bellows on the higher side . . .' at the same site and, apparently, immediately after the smelting process. We are given to understand that this re-working fell into the smith's field of operations rather than the smelter's, and we have made no intensive enquiries about their work. The methods commonly seen in use today were practised a century ago. A small clay forge, burning only charcoal, is fitted with a pair of hand-operated goat-skin bellows and is capable of producing the intense heat required. The forge is called *ncelo*, the same name as the ventilation pipes fitted into the kiln (which is a *mucelo*).

It seems possible that the smelters were also smiths, or alternatively they handed their iron to other smiths to be worked into a variety of goods and then paid for this service with a share of the products. Certainly the smelters' rewards came with the disposal of iron goods and not from pig-iron. However, some knowledge of the social organisation of the industry is essential to understand the distribution of the profits.

Social Organisation and Rituals

So far we have deliberately avoided all discussion of the social organisation of the industry and of rituals, in order to maintain the continuity of the main theme. Below we outline the main features of these aspects, but, particularly in respect of rituals and medicines, we are unable to provide detailed accounts.

The 'owner' of the kiln was known as *n'ganga wa kaposa micelo* – the doctor for throwing kilns. He inherited the necessary medicines and charms for smelting iron, and no doubt the skill, from his ancestors who had previously been kiln owners. These he jealously guarded, for on them, and on his ability to enlist the valuable assistance of his predecessors' spirits, depended his position and wealth. However, as we shall demonstrate, he was effectively insulated against blame for failures and thus his reputation was, to some extent, safeguarded and his power assured.

He was in charge of all operations but his active participation was limited. He formally called upon his ancestors' spirits on three occasions: before mining operations began, to assist in finding good ore; before the kiln was built, to make the clay strong and the structure sound; and before he personally fired the kiln, to provide much, good iron. Our informants said that no shrines were erected to these spirits but Barnes noted that 'at an early stage in the proceedings a small shrine or spirit-house (was) made' and circumstantial evidence suggests that this was so. The owner also killed a chicken and sprinkled its blood on the newly made kiln to make it strong; the chicken was then eaten by the workers. The main work of the owner, however, was packing the kiln, an operation which involved considerable use of medicines, though we have no details of these.

The owner was organiser of a group of experienced workers on whom he depended and they on him. They need not be his relatives, and apparently the only qualification required was an apprenticeship. These were the *bashimicelo* – the fathers of kilns – and they were responsible for all the skilled work as well as the heavy burden of menial tasks. No woman was permitted to assist in any of the operations and no doubt the apprentices and young boys brought by their relatives had tiring and uninspiring employment.

The main body of rituals, or rather taboos, pivoted on the personification of the kiln as the wife of all the workers, and on her pregnancy during the actual smelting process. All the workers had to undergo a cleansing ceremony before commencing work and had to abstain from all sexual contacts until the work was completed; any such association would be regarded as adultery by the kiln. No unclean persons, adûlterers, menstruating women, or those married unlawfully according to Ushi custom, were allowed to visit the kiln. If any of these taboos was broken, then as a woman would be in danger of a miscarriage or a still-birth, so the kiln would not produce good iron.

The owner supervised the behaviour of his workers, and he usually prohibited all women from the camp and all strangers from the site of the kiln during the smelting process. Any worker transgressing the rules was either dismissed or cleansed. However, should the kiln fail to produce acceptable iron the owner would attribute this to a breach of the taboos. The blame might or might not be allocated to an individual, but clearly the owner's reputation as a powerful agent in the industry was assured unless he was unfortunate enough to suffer repeated failures with different personnel.

The kiln owner, by virtue of his ritual position and his skill, theoretically was owner of all the iron produced, but in fact he held it only in trust for the workers and he was obliged by custom to share it.

He was responsible for sending part of the final produce as tribute to the chief in whose area he worked, and then he selected the lion's share of the better goods for himself; this was his due. He supervised the allocation of the remainder amongst the various workers, including the smiths, according to the contribution of each to the industry and to his social position. Anyone who had been dismissed and, of course, the apprentices, received nothing. Each individual was free to dispose of his share of goods as he wished, though traditionally he was •expected to let his wife choose any implements she required for use.

The iron industry we have attempted to describe represents what was probably the most advanced technology practised by the Ushi. Less than sixty years ago it flourished and though it rapidly declined after the introduction of *pax Britannica* and the European trader, it lingered on throughout the first quarter of this century. Yet already it is difficult to collect reliable information about it, and with the passing of another generation the main sources will disappear. We feel, therefore, that this paper may serve some useful purpose in making available the data we have collected. We hope it might encourage others to make similar enquiries in other parts of central Africa in an attempt to increase the body of comparative material on what was an industry of prime importance to the indigenous peoples.

REFERENCES

(1)   Desmond Clark, J. *The Prehistory of Southern Africa* (1959), p.284
(2)   Desmond Clark, J. *The Fort Rosebery District Notebook.*
(3)   Whiteley, W. *The Bemba and Related Peoples of Northern Rhodesia.* International African Inst. (1951); p.15.
(4)   Brelsford, W. V. 'Rituals and Medicines of Chishinga Iron-workers', *Man,* Vol. XLIX (1949).
       Brelsford, W. V. *Fishermen of the Bangweulu Swamps.* Rhodes-Livingstone Paper No. 12, 1946, p.47.
       Gouldsbery, C. and Sheane, H. *The Great Plateau of Northern Rhodesia.* London (1911), pp.279 and 289.
(5)   Stannus, S. N. 'Nyasaland: Angoni Smelting Furnace', *Man* (1914).
(6)   Debenham, F. *The Way to Ilala* (1955), p. 233.
(7)   Gann, L. 'The End of the Slave Trade in British Central Africa', *Rhodes-Livingstone Journal,* No. 16 (1954).
(8)   Bands, D. P. *Fort Rosebery Forestry Management Book* (1956-). *Mutondo* – Cordyla africana/Isoberlinia paniculata. *Mubanga* – Afrormosia angolensis. *Kapanga* – Burkea africana. *Kayimbi* – Erythrophloeum africanum. *Sase* – Albizzia antunesiana.
(9)   Kay, G. *A Social and Economic Study of Fort Rosebery.* Pt. II, p.49, Rhodes-Livingstone Comm., No. 21 (1961).

PART V

Patterns of Trade

13

TRANS-SAHARAN TRADE IN THE MIDDLE AGES*

S. Daniel Neumark

In the Middle Ages the interest of the western world was excited by stories of gold carried by caravans from a land beyond the Sahara. It was also these stories of gold-laden caravans which later inspired Prince Henry the Navigator to explore the coast of Africa and to gain access to the gold of Guinea by way of the sea.

The source of this gold was believed to be the ancient kingdom of Ghana, the approximate frontiers of which were the Niger on the east, the Senegal and its tributary the Baoulé on the south, and the desert to the north and west, though the gold actually originated in Wangara, an area outside the political control of Ghana. The kingdom of Ghana, the earliest state of the western Sudan, was distinct from successive Sudanese states in that it enjoyed a long period of stable and orderly government.

There has been a great deal of controversy as to the origins of Ghana and its kings.[1] The existence of Ghana as a great state in the western Sudan was first mentioned by Arab authors at the end of the eighth century. Mauny, who rejects Delafosse's hypothesis that the founding dynasty of Ghana was Jewish and Syrian in origin (1: p. 204), insists that 'all that can be said of the history of Ghana before the coming of the Arabs in the eighth century must, in the present state of our knowledge of West Africa, be merely speculation' (1: p. 207). On the other hand, it has long been known that there were early infiltrations if not invasions into the western Sudan from North Africa. Indeed, Fage has summarised the available evidence as follows (2: pp. 89-90):

*Reprinted from *Foreign Trade and Economic Development in Africa: An Historical Perspective* by S. Daniel Neumark, with the permission of the publishers, Food Research Institute, Stanford University, © 1964 by the Board of Trustees of the Leland Stanford Junior University.

There is a good deal of evidence to show that following the adoption of the camel by the peoples of North Africa about the fourth century A.D., some of their tribes were enabled to conquer or to push back Negro peoples who had hitherto occupied the Sahara, to develop and control the trade routes between North Africa and the Sudan, and even to some extent to infiltrate into the Sudan themselves. There is some evidence to suggest that this revolution may have been inspired to some extent by emigrants from Cyrenaica, whose original home was in the region of Palestine and Syria, and that the Sanhaja and Lemta tribes, whose expansion brought them across the Sahara towards the western Sudan, and who are the ancestors of the modern Tuareg, the *muleththemin*, the people of the veil, who are basically of Berber stock, may have something of a Palestinian or Syrian strain in them.

Whatever the uncertainties of the origins of ancient Ghana, there is little doubt as to the important part played by Ghana in the gold trade of the Middle Ages. Indeed, as Mauny puts it (1: p. 209):

> The repute of the Ghana empire in the Middle Ages was remarkable. It was, for the Arab writers especially, the legendary country whence came a great part of the gold circulating in the Muslim world. Today, knowing the mines of the Transvaal, California, Alaska, Siberia, and Australia, with their high annual output, we forget that, in antiquity and during the Middle Ages, what we should now consider as very poor mines were then held to be first rate. The Western Sudan was, from the eighth century until the discovery of America, the chief supplier of gold for the western world; the trade commercialised first by Ghana, came under that name to the Mediterranean and enhanced the prestige of the kings who owned such a source of wealth.

Ghana was succeeded by the kingdom of Mali, whose renown spread through Europe and the Middle East during the reign of Mansa Musa who, in 1324, surprised the world by his prodigal display of gold. However, after Mansa Musa, the Mali empire began to decline, and by the middle of the sixteenth century it finally ceased to exist.

The next great state was the Songhai empire of Gao, which began its rise to power by plundering parts of the Mali empire. Thus, in 1468, the King of Songhai, Sonni Ali, under the pretext of helping the Muslims of Timbuktu against the pagan Tuareg, captured and pillaged the town. About five years later he captured the town of Jenné. At that time both Timbuktu and Jenné were well established centres of trade and culture. Songhai reached the peak of its power under Askia Mohammed I (1493-1528), who established an efficient administration, replaced the plundering levies by a regular army, and accorded men of letters a status they had never before enjoyed. 'With the revival of learning,' Bovill says, 'went, as always in the Sudan, a great stimulus to foreign trade which brought added wealth to Gao and Timbuktu' (3: p. 105).

By the end of the sixteenth century the vast empire of the Songhai stretched from the Hausa states in the east almost to the Atlantic in the west and into the Sahara in the north and northeast, including Taghaza and Agades which were wrested from the Berbers. The Songhai empire controlled the chief sources of supply of gold and the salt mines and possessed an inexhaustible supply of slaves. With this surplus wealth the Songhai rulers had no difficulty in providing themselves with all the luxuries of the Mediterranean. 'Never before,' says Bovill, 'had the gold and slaves so much needed in the north been in such abundant supply. Consequently the caravan routes of the Sahara were carrying more traffic than ever before' (3: p. 135).

In spite of all this wealth and the military victories over its non-Muslim neighbours, the empire of the Songhai had only a comparatively brief existence. The prosperous gold trade had long provoked the envy of Moroccan rulers who now tried to secure that trade for themselves. When this attempt failed, El Mansur, the powerful Sultan of Morocco, sent an army, equipped with firearms, across the Sahara to conquer the gold mines. The defeat of the Songhai army in 1591 marks the end of the Songhai empire. But the Moroccan military victory over the Songhai failed to give them control over the gold mines. For the collapse of the Songhai administration also meant the interruption of the existing trade with the gold-producing regions where gold could only be secured by peaceful exchange.

The economic prosperity of the early states of the Western Sudan seems to have derived from their strategic commercial position on the fringes of the Sahara.[2] Like the sea, the Sahara, instead of remaining an insuperable barrier to human intercourse, served as a highway for trade and culture. The camel, the proverbial 'ship of the desert,' and the camel-owning nomad, both comparatively late arrivals from the eastern Mediterranean or Southern Arabia (3: p. 53), made possible the development of trade on both sides of the desert.

Among the important commodities exported from the Sudan to Morocco were, in the first place, gold and slaves. In addition, there were exports of ivory, rhinoceros horns, ostrich feathers, skins, ebony, civet, malaguetta pepper, semi-precious stones, cloth and leather goods from Hausaland, and kolanuts from the forest. Apart from salt, imports from North Africa comprised a great variety of linen, silk and cotton cloth, copper utensils and tools of all kinds, iron work, paper, Islamic books, weapons, especially firearms, cowrie shells (which were used as money), a wide variety of beads, mainly from Venice, mirrors, dates, figs, sugar, cattle and North African horses.

In North Africa, the trade with the Sudan was controlled by white merchants who 'provided the capital and organised the camel caravans that regularly crossed the desert along recognised routes' (4: p. 10). Similarly, in the Sudan, white merchants, and later their descendants of mixed blood, controlled the export trade to Morocco, though Negro merchants brought out the commodities from the interior. A network of trade-routes ran from the cities of North Africa – Fez and Marrakech in Morocco, Constantine in Algeria and Kairwan or Tunis in Tunisia – via oases, to the commercial centres of the Sudan – Ghana, Mali, Jenné, Gao, Timbuktu, and Kano. Of these trade-routes the principal ones were the following: 1) the western route from Morocco via Sijilmasa (in the oasis of Tafilelt) and the salt mines of Taghaza, Taodeni, and Arawan, to Timbuktu on the Niger and to places lying to the west of it; 2) the central route from Tunisia via Ghadames, Ghat, Air-Agades to Katsina and Kano; and 3) the eastern or Bornu route from Tripoli via Murzuk, Kawar-Bilma and the region around Lake Chad to Bornu. Of these three major trade routes the western one was the most important,'not only economically but also politically and culturally (5: pp. 58-60). There was also a fourth trade-route from the Nile at Aswan by the *Derib el Arba'in* ('Forty Days Road') from Asyut in Egypt to El Fasher, a road which had probably been in use since the days of Harkhuf, the greatest of the caravan leaders of the Sixth Dynasty (c. 2423-2242 B.C.) (6: pp. 41-43, 214), and from El Fasher to Lake Chad and Bornu (5: p. 60).

As was mentioned earlier, the principal source of gold was in Wangara, a territory between the Senegal and the Falémé rivers. Ancient Ghana obtained the gold mainly in exchange for salt which was brought from the Taghaza and other salt mines along the western trade-route as it was not practicable to carry sea-salt for long distances through the forest. As a result, the people inhabiting the country north of the forest had to secure the bulk of their salt from the deposits of rock-salt in the Sahara. Among these people were the gold diggers of Wangara, 'who sometimes would not part with their gold for anything but salt' (3: p. 68).

NOTES

1.   For most recent discussions of the problem, see R. A. Mauny, 'The Question of Ghana,' *Africa*, Vol. XXIV, 1954, and J. D. Fage, 'Ancient Ghana: A Review of the Evidence,' *Transactions of the Historical Society of Ghana*, Vol. III, Part 2, Achimota, 1957.

2.   For an excellent discussion of the role of the trans-Saharan trade routes in the rise and fall of these states, see Mauny, R., *Tableau géographique de l'ouest Africain au moyen âge, d'après sources écrites, la tradition et l'archéologie*, Mémoires de l'Institut d'Afrique Noire, No. 61. IFAN-Dakar, 1961, especially pp. 439-41.

REFERENCES

(1) Mauny, R. A., 'The Question of Ghana', *Africa*, (July 1954).
(2) Fage, J. D., 'Ancient Ghana. A Review of the Evidence', *Transactions of the Historical Society of Ghana*, Vol. III, Part 2, Achimota, (1957).
(3) Bovill, E. W., *The Golden Trade of the Moors*, London: Oxford University Press, (1958).
(4) Fage, J. D., *An Introduction to the History of West Africa*, Cambridge University Press, (1955).
(5) Westermann, D., *Geschichte Afrikas*, Greven-Verlag, Köln, (1952).
(6) Arkell, A. J., *A History of Sudan*, University of London, (1955).

14

TRADE PATTERNS IN GHANA AT THE BEGINNING OF THE EIGHTEENTH CENTURY*

K. B. Dickson

The end of the seventeenth century is especially important in the historical geography of Ghana; for many of the features of the country's present human geography appeared or began to evolve at that time. The fundamental tribal structure had been formed, and the population was engaged in a number of economic activities whose basic organisational characteristics have persisted into the twentieth century. Politically, Ghana was a medley of independent states, and whatever coherence it possessed it owed to the intricate network of major and minor routes along which men from all parts of the country travelled to trade. In the same way Ghana was drawn closer to other West African countries and to Europe through trade. Trading, a major source of income, was a carefully organised economic activity and was conducted at three levels: local, regional, and international.

Local Trade

Local trade is here defined in the broad sense of trade in the markets within a single state. The markets in Ghana were held daily or at other frequent intervals and were governed by a code of laws drawn up to protect trade and to ensure orderly activity. Any infringement was heavily punished. For example, it was forbidden to carry weapons to a market, and traders from distant parts who necessarily carried weapons to protect themselves along the way normally deposited them in the village nearest the market. Barbot tells of a village chief who derived a regular income by charging one shilling a head for looking after traders' weapons (1, 1744: p. 275).

The daily market was commonly held in the open space, without sheds or stalls, around the village shade tree and was mainly resorted

*Reprinted by permission from the *Geographical Review*, Vol. 56, 1966, copyrighted by the American Geographical Society of New York.

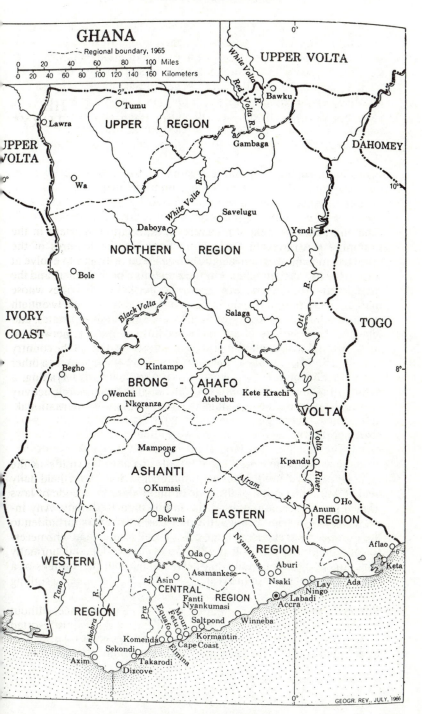

Fig. 1 – Location Map

to by women traders. The commodities offered for sale included foodstuffs, which varied with the locality, and craft products; there were also some European and western Sudan goods, the prices of which increased with distance from the coastal ports of the Sudan. Cape Coast market was typical: it began about sunrise, when large numbers of women, carrying their trade goods on their heads, arrived from the nearby villages, ,and it ended about sunset. The daily markets were also patronised by the local European residents, who purchased 'negro provisions' for the slave ships bound for the New World.

In addition to the daily markets were the markets held weekly or at eight-day intervals. They were fewer in number but drew traders from greater distances; they were characterised by bulk purchases and exchange of commodities not often sold in the daily markets. Still other markets were held at intervals between daily and weekly. An example was Aburi market, which functioned three times a week and attracted merchants from neighbouring Asin, Akwapim, and Akwamu towns; the merchants traded mainly for European goods brought up from Accra. Such periodic markets, unlike the daily markets, were normally held in large open spaces not necessarily in the towns but in a locality central to the surrounding major settlements. The markets often developed into important settlement sites. Ajumako Kwantanum (literally 'the meeting point of five roads') in Southern Ghana, and Bole, Wa, and Savelugu in Northern Ghana, are examples of settlements that owed their early importance to their function as focal points of trade for large regions.

Periodic markets included fairs that were held once or twice a year and attracted merchants from still greater distances. The fairs were also important social occasions and were attended by all non-resident members of the state. The large annual eight-day fair at Abrambo, for example, was a major social event for all citizens of the state of Fetu (1, 1744: p. 172). Another famous annual fair in Southern Ghana was held at Asin, the capital of the state of that name; to it Asin traders, who before 1698 monopolised the middleman trade between the coast and the interior, brought the precious iron bars obtained from the European warehouses on the coast to sell to merchants from the surrounding states (1, 1744: p. 188). To avoid overlap and competition, fairs and other periodic markets in neighbouring regions were held at different times of the year.

Regional Trade

As applied to Ghana at the beginning of the eighteenth century the term 'interstate trade' is perhaps more meaningful than the term 'regional trade.' First, the boundaries of the numerous states were real enough to make the term 'local' inapplicable once they had been crossed. Second, by considering trade between states it is possible to bring out the patterns of commodity movements both within and between the broad regions.

Agricultural Products and Livestock

The kinds of agricultural products traded and the patterns of their movements depended on the physical environment and on regional specialisation, which in turn depended on both physical and economic factors. The movements followed several directions. There were east-west and west-east movements along the coast, which reflected mainly the differences in the physical environment. Rice, for example, moved from west to east because, with the minor exception of the mouth of the Volta, only Axim, with its regularly distributed heavy annual rainfall and its wet soils, produced rice. On the other hand, Axim's physical environment did not permit the successful cultivation of many other crops, so that corn, sweet potatoes, and yams, for example, moved from east to west to Axim (2: Letter 1). Fantiland, centrally situated on the coast, was a major producer of corn, thanks to its suitable physical environment and its long-standing tradition of agriculture, and supplied minor coastal corn-producing areas such as Elmina.

Agricultural products also moved from the coast to the immediate interior, mainly in response to differences in livelihood. The principal alternatives to agriculture were gold mining and middleman trade, and areas devoted to these depended on their agricultural neighbours for foodstuffs. The Akim, who concentrated on gold mining to the virtual exclusion of farming, purchased food supplies from the agricultural areas between Winneba and Acca. Similarly, the people of Asin, famed throughout the country as traders or middlemen, apparently did not bring their land under adequate cultivation and therefore had to trade with their neighbours to the south, the Asebu, for provisions.

The pattern of agricultural-commodity movements in Ashanti is not clear, but it is unlikely that food crops were transported over long distances in view of the rational organisation of economic activities in Ashanti, which provided for the assignment of a number of agricultural villages to each major town in the member states. Ashanti settlements were arranged in a strict hierarchy based on the political status of the chiefs, and each settlement was surrounded by minor settlements tributary to it both politically and economically. At the bottom of the ladder was the purely farming village, inhabited entirely by slaves in the service of an overlord who resided in the town.

Although food crops may not generally have moved over long distances in Ashanti, agricultural products of restricted distribution, such as kola nuts and palm oil, the former the basis of Ashanti's foreign trade and the latter an indispensable part of the diet, crossed individual state boundaries in Ashanti and travelled long distances. Ashanti as a whole was fairly self-sufficient in food supplies. There is no indication anywhere that Ashanti trading caravans returned with food crops from the coast or from Northern Ghana, with the single exception of shea butter, which, although consumed as food in Northern Ghana, was used in Ashanti as an unguent.

The pattern of movements of agricultural products in Northern Ghana at the beginning of the eighteenth century is obscure, but it may perhaps be surmised from a later known situation within a similar social and economic context. Trade was the basis of wealth in Northern Ghana at that time, and agriculture was merely for subsistence. It is thus unlikely that agricultural products (except perhaps cotton and tobacco, which were confined to certain well-defined areas in the country but were in great demand) travelled long distances to reach their markets.

Northern Ghana also raised cattle, but again the place of livestock in the trade pattern within the region is not easily defined. The situation is much clearer for Southern Ghana, where the animals were traded laterally along the coast. The principal source of cattle in Southern Ghana was the coastal plains of the southeast, especially the extensive stretch of grassland behind and within the states of Labadi and Ningo. Herdsmen from the two states usually bought the animals in the neighbouring state of Lay, fattened them in the home pasture grounds, and then transported them to the cattle market at Accra and places farther west (1, 1732: pp. 185-186).

The prices of agricultural products and livestock in Ghana were determined simply by the law of supply and demand. Bullocks from Ningo and Labadi, which were always in great demand, were normally sold at thirty crowns each (1, 1732: p. 186). Similarly, maize, a relatively scarce commodity, commanded a high price in Southern Ghana, the only place where it was cultivated, whereas millet and Guinea corn, produced in much larger quantities and nationwide in distribution, generally fetched a lower price. In wartime the prices of all agricultural commodities rose because of the necessary suspension of farm work; then on the coast a thousand stalks of millet or sorghum, which usually sold for as little as about 2/6d., cost an ounce of gold, worth about £4 at the time (2: Letter 16). The price of millet also rose, though not as high, in the lean period between harvests, since storage facilities were inadequate.

Fishing and Hunting Products

The trade pattern for fish was uncomplicated, since the fishing communities on the coast supplied the rest of the country. The predominant pattern of movement was thus from south to north, and it was not greatly disturbed by supplies of fish from the inland rivers. Fishing was not traditionally an important occupation in the inland states, even in Northern Ghana, where splendid opportunities for fishing existed. The fish were transported dried or smoked from the coast to Ashanti, and possibly along the Volta River from Ada on the coast to Northern Ghana. This was certainly the pattern in the second half of the eighteenth century. It is unlikely that Ashanti transmitted any of the fish to Northern Ghana; for its kola-nut trade with Northern Ghana completely overshadowed everything else.

Neither tradition nor contemporary literature has much to say on the distributive trade in products of the chase, but it may be assumed that since hunting was a countrywide occupation, its products did not generally travel over long distances to markets. On the other hand, in those areas in Northern Ghana where cultivation seems to have been unimportant as compared with hunting, as in the poor lands of central Gonja or in the Desert of Ghofan, food supplies may have been assured by the selling of game to the neighbouring agricultural areas. One of the earliest and most definite references to game as an important article in interstate trade was made by the Danish botanist Isert, who wrote in 1786 that hunting, a major occupation in Akwapim, furnished the only products that the Akwapim could sell at Accra (3: pp. 259-60).

Salt

The two main salt-producing areas of Ghana, the coast and Daboya in Northern Ghana, had fairly well defined spheres of influence. The primary movement of sea salt was south-north in response to the insatiable demand from up country, and so important was the trade that a large body of middlemen functioned almost solely in connection with it. Ashanti, perhaps the largest inland consumer of salt from the coast, received its supplies mostly through Asin and Fanti middlemen. Salt from Ada may have reached Northern Ghana by the Volta, for such was the case in the second half of the eighteenth century.

Daboya, whose salt was extracted from the numerous saline 'soaks' in the area supplied the whole of Northern Ghana and also areas outside it. Caravans from Grunsi, Dagomba, Konkomba, Kabre in Togo, and elsewhere came to Daboya to trade for salt, but the Ashanti, preferring the variety from the coast, allowed none of the salt from Daboya to enter their territory (4: p. 18).

The salt trade was one of the major components of regional trade in the country and was highly profitable. 'It is not to be imagined,' wrote Bosman (8: Letter 16),

> what vast Riches the *Negroes* get by boiling of salt; and if they were always, or for the most part in Peace, those who follow that Employment would in a short time amass unweildy Sums; for all the Inland *Negroes* are obliged to fetch their Salt from the Shore, from whence it is easy to infer that it must cost them very dear: Wherefore the meaner Sort are obliged to make use of a certain saltish Herb instead of Salt, which their Purses will not reach.

In the inland areas of western Dahomey, Bosman added, and doubtless also of Togo and the Volta Region, a handful of salt was exchanged for one or two slaves.

Gold and Slaves

Like that of salt, the pattern of gold movements was straightforward. The major producers in Ashanti and Southern Ghana sent their gold down to the coastal ports; the smaller quantities from alluvial sources around Bole in Northern Ghana were transmitted to the western Sudan by Mande middlemen. Within Ghana gold probably circulated in regional (as well as in local) trade in the form of trinkets, but usually as gold dust where it was used as currency. On the whole, gold featured more prominently in the country's external trade.

Slaves were also more important for export than for internal trade. Two kinds of slaves must be distinguished: the *donko* and the domestic slaves. The latter, who as his name implies was engaged in household service within the country, was generally someone given away by the family in payment for a debt or as security for a loan; the *donko*, a prisoner of war or a panyarred victim, was exported. Slave marts for *ndonko* existed throughout the country; among the more famous were those at Salaga, at Mansu in Asin, and at Aflao.

European and Craft Industrial Goods

European goods moved primarily from the coast inland, but not all of them reached their destinations after passing through a number of regional or local markets. For strategic and political reasons, guns and ammunition, for example, were transported directly from the coastal ports to inland states by official trading caravans, and the Ashanti did not permit them to be transported through their territory to Northern Ghana. The Ashanti, indeed, maintained the embargo on the sale of guns to Northern Ghana until the late nineteenth century.

The taste for European goods was well established in Southern Ghana by the beginning of the eighteenth century, and Fanti middle-men made huge profits out of distributing commodities such as linen, knives, hats, bugles, and mirrors. The goods were expensive because of their scarcity in relation to demand, so that a regular practice among the middlemen was to stock them against the rainy season, when few ships were in the roads and prices rose even more steeply (1, 1732: p. 259).

Much less expensive were the products of craft industries – metal goods (gold, silver, iron, and brass), carved wooden articles, cloth, leather goods, and earthenware vessels. Metalworking and pottery were countrywide in distribution, but although most settlements had their metalworkers and potters, certain areas specialised in manufacturing particular products and distributed them over wide areas. The Shai, for example, were famous for their earthenware vessels, which they sold in neighbouring areas, including Accra (5: pp. 127-145). Leatherworking was confined to Northern Ghana, and the products of woodworking were exchanged mainly in Ashanti-Brong Ahafo and Southern Ghana. One product of the woodworking industry whose trade pattern was exceptionally uncomplicated was the dugout canoe. The distribution of canoe manufacture depended mainly on the distribution of the fishing industry: it was most important on the coast, where fishing was a major occupation. On the coast itself the distribution was uneven, depending on the availability of suitable trees, including the silk cotton, and the presence or absence of more remunerative craft industries. Takoradi and Axim apparently specialised in the making of large transport canoes; Butri, Ekon, Komenda, Kormantin, and Winneba produced large numbers of smaller craft (1, 1732: p. 266). The canoes were also purchased on the coast by European merchants, who used them with hired Ghanaian oarsmen to transfer goods to and from their ships when trading on the difficult surf-bound coast of the Volta Region and beyond (1, 1732: p. 266). The cost of a large transport canoe was between £40 and £50 (1, 1732: p. 152).

The cloth industry had two branches, the older of which produced bark cloth from the tree *Antiaris toxicaria*. A long, narrow strip of bark softened in water and beaten with wooden mallets became a single piece of cloth, supple and several times the original width of the bark. This branch of the industry was found mainly in the forest areas of Southern Ghana and Ashanti-Brong Ahafo, since the tree supplying the raw material is a forest species. Northern Ghana, covered with wooden savanna, has never been known to produce bark cloth.

The younger branch of the cloth industry was weaving on a simple loom worked with both hands and feet, and it apparently began to spread, in Ashanti at any rate, in the late seventeenth century, as tradition affirms (6: p. 220). Weaving may also have been known in Northern Ghana at the beginning of the eighteenth century, since the region was in uninterrupted contact with the culturally advanced centres of ancient civilisation in the western Sudan, but no evidence exists. Nevertheless, woven cloth, called *kente* by the Akan, was in short supply and expensive as compared with imported cloth; this situation also held true a century later, when weaving was certainly a countrywide occupation.

International Trade

Ghana's external trade at the beginning of the eighteenth century followed three directions: toward the sea and across to Europe and the New World; overland toward the Sahara; and overland or by sea along the coast as far as Nigeria and possibly beyond. Barbot even went so far as to declare that the people of Elmina were particularly skilled in canoe navigation and often sailed in large canoes as far as Angola (1, 1732: p. 266). The observant Bosman, who knew the coast well and was aware of the relatively short coastwise canoe voyages, does not mention the more ambitious trips to Angola. It will be recalled that European merchant ships regularly took on board canoemen from Elmina and other coastal settlements when trading on or beyond the coast of the Volta Region, and that these canoemen crossed the surf in their smaller craft to load or unload the ships. Some of the canoemen may have returned home with easily misinterpreted stories of how they had rowed their canoes to distant foreign shores. This probably explains Barbot's statement.

Export Trade

The principal overseas exports were gold, slaves, and ivory; the numerous minor exports included 'negro provisions,' guinea grains (*Aframomum* sp.), wax, and lime juice produced on the Dutch lime plantation at Mouri near Cape Coast (2: Letter 16). Another major export was the kola nut, which went overland to the western Sudan and eventually across the Sahara to North Africa. The exact quantities exported are not ascertainable, but all the evidence – especially the fact that Ashanti's immense commercial power rested mainly on its possession of the kola tree – points to the conclusion that exports must have been very large.

It is gold, the most precious object of European trade, for which most information is available. It was estimated that as much as seven thousand marks' worth of gold was exported annually, but only if the country was at peace and all the trade routes open (2: Letter 7). The export figure referred only to gold sent overseas through the coastal ports. A breakdown showed how much was exported by each of the major European trading companies and others (2: Letter 7): Dutch West India Company, 1500 marks; English African Company, 1200; Dutch interlopers, 1500; English interlopers, 1000; Brandenburgers and Danes, 1000; Portuguese and French, 800.

The gold trade was plagued with numerous problems, one of which was the increasingly large quantities of adulterated gold offered to the European merchants. Unwary merchants were liable to transport whole cargoes of false gold to Europe. Consequently, the Dutch in 1702 offered to pay the chiefs of seven major coastal states one benda, or an ounce, of gold for each local offender brought to their head-quarters at Elmina dead or alive (7).[1] The growth of the practice of falsifying gold was due in no small measure to the encouragement given Ghanaians by European merchants to sell adulterated gold to trade rivals, and it was not long before the instigators themselves began to suffer by it. Denkera merchants, when they controlled much of the gold trade at the Western Region ports, were particularly notorious for the large quantities of adulterated gold they black-mailed the European merchants into accepting. Bosman remarked that the Dutch fort at Butri, christened Batenstein because of the brisk gold trade there, should be rechristened Schadenstein, since Euro-pean merchants there were more likely to lose than to gain on the gold transactions (2: Letter 2). Nevertheless, not all the local merchants were that notorious; the Asin, for example, brought so much pure gold to the Central Region ports that the best gold from Southern Ghana came to be referred to as 'Accany sica' or Asin gold.

The export trade in slaves was uncomplicated. The main problem was the ensuring of regular supplies, but this depended at any given moment on the country's political climate: supplies were plentiful in times of intertribal war and meagre when there was peace. For example, sometime in 1682 a slave ship remained for days at the port of Lay without obtaining a single slave, yet only two months earlier, when there had been a serious war between the Akwamu and the Gã, a French man-of-war had collected three hundred slaves at the same port within a matter of days (1, 1732: p. 186). However, the interludes of peace were not long enough or frequent enough to discourage the flow of slaves to the coastal ports. The period about the beginning of the eighteenth century was one of numerous wars; besides, a regular occupation among the inhabitants of some parts of Southern Ghana – for example, of Ada and Keta Districts (referred to by Bosman as Coto) – was to travel inland and abduct men for sale at the ports.

Information about the third major article of export, ivory, is not as detailed as that for gold or slaves. The supply of ivory was plentiful because of the proliferation of elephants not only in the forest of Ashanti-Brong Ahafo but also in Southern Ghana, including the coast. About the beginning of the eighteenth century elephants were not an uncommon sight at Elmina (2: Letter 14). It is likely that the quantity of ivory exported was much smaller than the quantity produced, since ivory was in great demand locally for the manufacture of ornaments and musical instruments (trumpets). This was true also of the minor export commodity of wax, which was used in the country for lighting (1, 1732: p. 261).

Import Trade

Imports consisted of a wide range of goods of European manufacture, which typically included linens, silks, brocades, guns and ammunition, iron and silver bars, copperware and brassware, and alcoholic drinks. The Dutch also imported large quantities of cowries, which were used locally as currency. From the western Sudan came a wide variety of goods, including fabrics of all kinds, brassware, leather goods, and books. All these articles except firearms were distributed through the local or regional markets. The nature and origin of one import are surrounded by a thick fog of mystery. This was the 'aggry bead.' The beads were apparently imported from Benin in Nigeria until roughly the end of the seventeenth century, when importation practically ceased, partly as a result of competition in the markets in Ghana with cheap glass substitutes (8).

Several factors determined the prices of overseas imports. European goods were never available in large enough quantities to satisfy the avid demand for them, particularly in Southern Ghana; they therefore, other things being equal, commanded high prices. This imbalance between supply and demand was reinforced in certain localities on the coast where the European merchants, supported by superior firing power from their forts, prevented the neighbouring Africans from trading with rival European trading companies. The Dutch were especially brutal to Africans living close to their forts who were caught trading with other European nationals and in all the coastal areas controlled by the Dutch their merchants sold imported goods at prices fixed by the director-general (1, 1732: p. 274). Where the Dutch were not in control, they and other Europeans deliberately undercut trade rivals by selling almost at cost. Also adding to the complexity of price determinants was the activity of interlopers, who undercut everyone and disturbed the established patterns of trade. Ships of the interlopers, which were seized by the established European merchants whenever possible, were referred to as 'ten per cent ships,' since they disposed of their goods at heavy discounts and purchased slaves at inflated prices at those ports which were not efficiently patrolled by ships of the Dutch West India Company or the English African Company.

Organisation of Trade

The regulations governing trade in the local markets have already been referred to; and indeed they applied to the running of regional markets as well. But more important to trade at all levels, particularly the regional and the international, were the activities of middlemen. In Southern Ghana and Ashanti-Brong Ahafo, and possibly in Northern Ghana too, much of the middleman trade was in the hands of royalty, nobles, and rich citizens. The reason was probably purely economic: trading in distant markets in those times of general insecurity of life required a great deal of organisation, which in turn demanded a heavy outlay that only wealthy citizens could afford. Numerous porters had to be employed to headload the goods, and armed men hired to protect them; taxes for right of passage had to be paid to the many chiefs through whose territories the trading caravans passed. The poorer sections of the population were thus effectively barred from participating to any extent in the middleman trade. Nevertheless, it was possible for common people and even slaves to acquire wealth through trading, and this possibility society fully recognised and consequently prescribed (in Southern Ghana) elaborate ceremonies to be performed as a means of notifying the public of the change of status (2: Letter 9).

States also engaged in middleman trade. The main source of their importance in this function lay in their location with respect to the European trading posts on the coast, to which the complicated cross-currents of trade in Southern Ghana and Ashanti-Brong Ahafo eventually drained. Many of the expansionist policies adopted by states in Southern Ghana or Ashanti about the beginning of the eighteenth century or before can be understood in terms of jockeying for the position with the greatest advantage for middleman trade.

The states conducted their long-distance trade through trading caravans that were generally longer than those employed by individual merchants (the carriers forming the caravan marched in Indian file because of the narrowness of the trade routes). They were also better protected and were led by a court official carrying an emblem of state – a 'linguist's staff.' The Ashanti were known to send runners or messengers ahead to announce the arrival of their caravans in the settlements through which the trade route passed. State caravans, like the private ones, paid taxes to chiefs on their routes, and although the payment of these taxes was supposed to ensure them free passage everywhere, the caravans were sometimes plundered. The Twifo in the Western Region were notorious for plundering state trading caravans, and one of the objects of the Dutch diplomatic mission to Kumasi, capital of Ashanti, in 1701 was to assure Osei Tutu, king of Ashanti, that the Dutch would stop the Twifo from interfering with his trading caravans (9).

Trading states and middlemen possessed an additional source of income in the duties the European merchants had to pay them on imports and exports. All exports were dutiable except slaves, though it was not unusual for powerful brokers to demand duty on them as well. There was yet another convention, according to which European merchants were expected to give presents, called 'dassy' (Akan word for thanks), to brokers who undertook to sell their goods. This convention, which the European merchants found irksome but had to follow for fear of losing their trade, was originally instituted by the Dutch in the seventeenth century when they were trying to undermine Portuguese supremacy in the coastal trade (1, 1732: p. 260).

The great trading nations or states that functioned as middlemen at one time or another in the closing decades of the seventeenth century were Asin, Denkera, Fanti, Akwamu, and Ashanti. The Asin, who for most of the seventeenth century were renowned as a nation of traders, had achieved that distinction early in the sixteenth century after subjugating the Etsi (10), who until then had traded extensively with the Europeans. By the early years of the seventeenth century colonies of Asin traders, ruled by governors appointed by the paramount chief of Asin, were established in the major trading centres on the coast, and the Asin soon came to monopolise the middleman trade between Ashanti and all the European trading stations between about Elmina and Winneba (11, 2: Letter 6). Asin merchants traded as far as the Mande trading settlement of Begho in Brong Ahafo (1, 1732: pp. 190-1), but it is not certain whether they went as far as Northern Ghana.

In 1698 the Denkera crushed the power of the Asin in a major engagement and forever destroyed their pre-eminence in the country's trade. By the beginning of the eighteenth century the Fanti, who also had centuries of trading experience behind them, had effectively succeeded the Asin, and when Bosman wrote about them in 1701, they were powerful enough to close the trade routes to the Central Region ports and to suspend trade if they so wished. The Fanti had been able to climb to that eminence because of their position between the Central Region ports and Ashanti. They were to remain on that eminence for another century or so and to bring the fierce wrath of the Ashanti on themselves by unscrupulously exploiting their position.

Meanwhile the Denkera, who had defeated the Asin, controlled the middleman trade between the coast and the interior of the Western Region. They acquired vast riches, as all accounts of them attest, and were strong enough to intimidate European merchants into tolerating their sharp trading practices, such as falsification of gold.

The most powerful trading nation in the Eastern Region at the beginning of the eighteenth century was Akwamu, which controlled the long stretch of coastline from about Apam in the Central Region to Ouidah in Dahomey, together with a large expanse of inland territory. Merchants from inland states were not allowed to trade directly with the European trading posts at and near Accra but were directed to the thrice-weekly market at Aburi in Akwapim, where Akwamu merchants sold European goods at more than 100 per cent profit. The market was presided over by an overseer appointed by the king of Akwamu and empowered to fix the prices of goods (1, 1732: pp. 190-1).

Ashanti, the most illustrious empire of all time in the country, took the first long step toward gaining absolute control of the country's external trade when it inflicted a crushing defeat on Denkera in 1701. Ashanti, between Northern Ghana and the western Sudan on the one hand and the rest of Ghana on the other, was admirably situated for large-scale middleman or entrepôt trade, and it became a vast clearinghouse for European, western Sudan, and Northern Ghanaian goods. The importance of this middleman trade to the Ashanti was reflected in the care with which they drew up regulations to ensure its preservation and maximum success (12).

The economic geography of Ghana took a new turn with the rise of Ashanti after 1701. The Ashanti brought their organising genius to bear on trade, and throughout the eighteenth century and up to the last two or three decades of the nineteenth, Ashanti was the nerve centre and focal point of the country's trade and trade-route network. In spite of deliberate efforts by the British in the 1880s and 1890s to realign the major trade routes linking Northern and Southern Ghana in such a way as to isolate Kumasi (13),[2] the present-day network of major roads in the country is still basically the same as in the period of Ashanti political and economic supremacy.

NOTES

1.   The company's records on Ghana form part of the Furley Collection in the Balme Library, University of Ghana, Legon.

2. This is a series of official letters, referred to as 'Papers', from and to Ghana. Enclosure in Paper No. 2, dated 29 March 1883, Christiansborg Castle, refers to Ashanti's grip on the country's trade. The policy of economic strangulation of Kumasi is stated in 'Further Correspondence Respecting the Affairs of the Gold Coast', [*British Command Paper*] C. 4477, Colonial Office, London, 1885, Paper No. 37.

REFERENCES

(1) Barbot, John, *A Description of the Coasts of North and South Guinea* . . . (*A Collection of Voyages and Travels* [3rd edit.; 6 Vols. 'Printed by Assignment from Messrs Churchill', London, 1744 – 46] Vol. 5). Earlier edition printed in Paris, 1732.
(2) Bosman, William, *A New and Accurate Description of the Coast of Guinea* (London, 1705; 1907; new edition with a new introduction and notes, Frank Cass, London, 1967). Written as a series of letters.
(3) Isert, Paul Erdman, *Voyages en Guinée*, (Paris, 1793).
(4) El-Wakkad, Mahmoud, transl., 'Qissatu Salga Tarikhu Gonja', *Ghana Notes and Queries*, No. 3, (1961).
(5) Saxton, S. W., 'Historical Survey of the Shai People', *Gold Coast Rev.*, Vol. 1, (1925).
(6) Rattray, R. S., *Religion and Art in Ashanti*, (Oxford, 1927).
(7) W.I.C. 98: West India Company letter, 25 September 1702, from Elmina to Amsterdam.
(8) Fage, J. D., 'Some Remarks on Beads and Trade in Lower Guinea in the Sixteenth and Seventeenth Centuries', *Journal of African History*, Vol. 3, (1962); pp. 343-7.
(9) W.I.C. 97 (Guinea 1), 1702: Minutes of Council at Elmina, 5 June 1702.
(10) The Ati of Pacheco Pereira (Duarte Pacheco Pereira: *Esmeraldo de situ orbis*). [trans. and edited by George H. T. Kimble], *Hakluyt Soc.* [Publs.], Ser. 2, No. 79, London, (1937), p. 120.
(11) W.I.C. oc. 11: Letter dated 12 June 1645, from Elmina to Amsterdam.
(12) Rattray, R. S., *Ashanti Law and Constitution*, (Oxford, 1929), p. 111.
(13) 'Further Correspondence Regarding Affairs of the Gold Coast', *Africa No. 268.*, Colonial Office, London, (1884).

15

NINETEENTH-CENTURY TRADE IN THE BAMENDA GRASSFIELDS, SOUTHERN CAMEROONS*

E. M. Chilver

The Setting

The Bamenda uplands, in the present administrative divisions of Wum, Nkambe and Bamenda offered some defensible sites for resistance to the mounted slave-raids directed by the vassals of the emirates of Adamawa, Muri and Bauchi, and were protected from them to some degree by the strong state of Bamum on their eastern flank. Their soils, not so fertile as is generally supposed, produce enough maize (and formerly guinea corn and finger millet) root crops and legumes to support a fairly dense population; the present population (1953 Census) is 429,000 at a density of 67 per sq. mile. Edible melon seeds (*egunsi*) are still an important article of diet. The older root-crops appear to be trifoliate and white yams and rizga. Sweet potatoes and cocoyams are said to be early introductions. Cassava, *makabo*, Ogoja yams and potatoes – the last introduced in 1889 together with white beans by Zintgraff – are more recent introductions. The oil palm grows in the lower lands in the West and North-East of the province and in sheltered valleys. The other main tree crops are the raffia palm, providing wine and building and basketry materials, the banana, and the kola. Tobacco is a pre-colonial crop. Small stock – goats, smooth haired sheep, pigs along the forest edge, and fowls – are plentiful. Dwarf cattle were kept by chiefs in the past and a few humped cattle were kept in at least one chiefdom, Bali-Kumbad, before regular German administration started.

The domestic building, crafts and industries of the Bamenda peoples commanded the respect of early travellers, who were struck by their relatively high standard of living. Zintgraff could compare Bafut favourably with Yola; von Stetten, traversing the Tikar towns outside our area, but evidently similar in construction and layout to the larger

*Reprinted by permission from *Afrika und Ubersee*, Band 45. Heft 4. 1962.

settlements in Bamenda, considered Ngambe the most interesting and attractive town he had so far seen. The construction of some of the ceremonial buildings, sometimes perched on high platforms of dressed stones, with patterned pebble floors, and lined with raffia mats, split canes or batiks, evidently called for a fair degree of craft specialisation and exchange. Some centres of specialisation in carving, such as the Babanki villages in metal-work such as Ngo and Oku (1), in pottery such as Bamesi, and in woven bags, such as Nsei, exported their products widely. The cire-perdue specialities of Bamum and Bagam and their beadwork and featherwork were widely diffused. Oral tradition asserts that the indigo-dyed cloth of the Adamawa and Benue trade replaced bark-cloth in some chiefdoms, and undyed narrow-loom strips in others. The evidence for the age of cotton cultivation and local narrow-loom weaving is contradictory; they were certainly practised before the arrival of the earliest European travellers. During the period we are concerned with, the 'eighties and 'nineties of last century, cotton seems to have been cultivated mainly for the manufacture of the baldrics and caps associated with the membership of societies and the enjoyment of honours. The elaborate styles of dress reported by Zintgraff and Hutter, from the embroidered gowns or *tóyù* of the Bali notables to the voluminous loincloths and beaded shirts of Bafut (*Bufă*) made use of imported goods. The armament of the Bamenda peoples, flintlock, spear and cutlass, seems in some areas to have superseded the bow and ancillary weapons: their most impressive military development was, however, their system of defensive earthworks.

The chiefdoms of the Bamenda Grassfields ranged in size from the small village chiefdoms of Widekum to the expanding conquest-states of Nso and Bafut, with populations estimated at 20-25,000 by their German conquerors. The Widekum villages to the West and South-West varied greatly in political organisation: in Ngi they were organised round village heads assisted by a council of heads of local kin-groups, whilst in Müta and among the Ngömba-speaking groups some of the features of Bamenda-Tikar chiefship have been adopted. Among the Ngömba chiefdoms Mankon is the largest, and is organised along much the same lines as its neighbour Bafut. The Bamenda-Tikar chiefdoms, and we include in this category some whose dynasties do not claim Tikar origin, are characterised by sacred kingship, a priesthood concerned with the royal ancestors and God, state councillorships vested in particular lineages, princes' societies, war and hunting societies (*mánjÌ*) open to the adult males of a particular locality and a regulating society (*kwifòn, ngwéròn, ngumba, nwose, no, tifo* etc.), recruited from particular social categories. The majority have patrilineal descent and succession. Certain of these features are found in the neighbouring Bamileke chiefdoms which are culturally slightly distinct in their proliferation of state-societies, *nkap* marriage, and a skull-cult associated with a system of double unilineal descent (2). The composite Bali chiefdoms, consisting of a Chamba core with Tikar, Wute, Bamileke and Widekum accretions, are marked by a special development of war societies under princely leadership, a more secular kingship, and state-rituals of Adamawa origin. Wum in the North-West is a federation of ward-chiefs with a ritual primus: though it claims 'Munshi' origin neither its language nor its institutions are of the Tiv type. Small refugee groups of Mambila of virtually unknown but seemingly northern origin lie along the border with Tigon and Adamawa.

The Approaches to the Bamenda Grassfields

Zintgraff stumbled out of the forest into this world in 1889. It has previously been quite closely approached. Becroft and King took the steamer Ethiope as far as the rapids of the Cross River below Mamfe in 1842 in a search for a route connecting Calabar and the Benue lands. Thereafter until Flegel ventured to Banyo and Berabe in 1884 only rumour or hearsay reached the outside world. This is recorded in Clarke's Specimens of Dialects (1849) and his evidence before Parliamentary Committees, Koelle's Polyglotta Africana (1854), the itineraries set down by Barth (v.ii, App. IV), and odds and ends recorded from traders and captives by Baikie (1856), Hutchinson (1853, 1861), Rohlfs (1872) and von Bary (1880). Seen from the north and east the area seems to have been included in the inland districts called 'Tikar', 'Mbafu' and 'Bahun'; from the south and west in 'Bayong', 'Mbrikum' or 'Mbudikum'. Koelle's classification of some of the Grassfields languages as Moko reflects the vocabulary of the slave-trade from the point of view of the coast-handlers, drawing their slaves from the hinterland of Rio del Rey.[1]

The existence of a long-distance slave-trade with an outlet in Ambas Bay is first recorded by Samuel Braun, c. 1614. At the end of the eighteenth century some 7,000 slaves a year for the Atlantic trade were exported from Old Calabar and Cameroons. Even after the establishment of anti-slavery naval patrols a clandestine slave trade for the Cuban and Brazilian markets continued; how far this was fed from the Grassfields is unknown, though some names in the registers of captured slaves cargoes – Nyamsi, Mombonfon, Kuinso – have a Grassfields ring. Koelle's Grassfield informants were mostly shipped in the late eighteen 'twenties and 'thirties, a few from Duala, more from Calabar; many were victims of slave-raids into the Grassfields by mounted warriors who may have been either Chamba or Fulani.

But to judge from the evidence of early travellers, the southern slave-trade from the Grassfields had mainly been directed. from perhaps the 'twenties onwards. to the domestic rather than to the export trade. The palm-oil hinterland of Old Calabar which included Balundu. Bakundu. the Ekoi areas and Banyang. were dotted with 'Bayong' slave-villages. settled. according to Hutter. for generations. The spectacular growth of the West African palm-oil trade encouraged the exploitation of new inland areas and demanded the services of collectors, processors and carriers. The ramifications of the commercial activity generated in Old Calabar reached the south-western edges of the Bamenda Grassfields. chiefly mediated by the Ekoi peoples and the Banyang. with lesser groups. such as the Biteku and Ambele. playing a part. 'Bayong' slaves were present in Duala: from Duala the Bell traders had penetrated up the Mungo Valley. the Abo and S. Balong being important intermediaries. According to Asmis (1907) the Bell and Akwa trading chiefdoms concentrated on the Mungo and Wuri routes respectively after the growth of competition between them: our material on 'tied' markets and trade alliances for the Duala traders is slender however. The evidence for the conversion of their commercial interests to palm-oil. and later palm-kernel supply is stronger. Capt. Lilley who had already accompanied Allen some way up the Wuri in 1841 told a Parliamentary Committee in 1847 that the palm oil trade in the Cameroons Rivers had practically ousted the Atlantic slave trade. though it continued on a small scale at Bimbia. The growth of the palm oil trade had its effects inland: though we cannot trace developments over time we know. for example. that the Bakoko increased their production of palm oil products. traded through Duala. Malimba. and Ngumba canoemen (Y. Nicol. 1929. 132ff.). Further south. along the Batanga coast. the export trade mainly directed from the Gaboon trading houses remained concentrated on ivory.

The European imported goods provided through the coastal and Niger-Benue trade and their middlemen are too familiar to be worth recording in detail: the main goods reaching the Grassfields were flintlocks and gunpowder. salt. brass and copper. cloth. beads and cowries. European cloths. as we shall see. faced competition from the products of the Hausa and Benue looms. trade salt from the local products of Mamfe and Akwana.

If the western part of the Bamenda Grassfields were linked with Old Calabar. its eastern ones are likely to have been in closer touch with the Duala and Batanga trade. Bamum's routes to the coast in later times. when it was still heavily engaged in the domestic slave trade, went according to Conrau (1898) across the highlands between the Mbam and the Mungo to the Bakossi mountains. A trade route between Bagam and Fontem is reported by early German patrols.

Some of the trade salt reaching Bamum came through Bafusam from Yabasi or from the coast via Bangangte and some of its slaves reached the coast via Bandem. Bamum had also been in touch with Hausa traders since Fon Nsaangu's reign in the 'seventies or 'eighties and perhaps earlier. This trade, according to Dubié (1957), had been pioneered by the royal merchants of Kano. Rumours of it reached Grenfell and Harry Johnston on the coast.

Before considering the northern trade routes into the Bamenda Grassfields the effects of the jihad on trade must be taken into account. Modibbo Adama on his return from Sokoto in 1806 was accompanied by Toronkawa soldiery and Hausa who came to take advantage of the trading and slave-dealing opportunities opening up. To judge by Yola sarki titles Kano was by no means the only centre from which Hausa traders came. The emirs of Yola never succeeded in establishing secure conditions on the southern marches of Adamawa, partly because of the internecine wars of the southern lamidats and their offshoots, but chiefly because of the nature of Fulani exploitation of the border areas, which were, by and large, treated as a pagan slave-march. According to Barth (ii, 502-4) Yola received a tribute of 5,000 slaves a year from its subordinate lamidats at the time of his visit, seemingly a modest proportion of captures and acquisitions, to judge from his other evidence. Adamawa's 'sole exports' were then slaves and ivory. Apart from the slaves disposed of by way of tribute and trade or embodied in slave-armies, some were settled in agricultural or pastoral slave settlements. But this productive use of slaves does not seem to have been systematic except around Yola itself. Barth records that the great men of the Chamba-Tibati and Koncha-Banyo lamidats held slaves on an immense scale but drew their provisions from the conquered rather than by forming slave settlements.

The southern lamidos, after a period of competition, perhaps most intense c. 1840-60, concentrated their slaving expeditions as follows: Banyo and its rebellious Gashaka colony along the northern borders of Bamenda with occasional deeper raids especially after a war-camp had been established at Ndu, c. 1870, and at Berabe, before 1883; Tibati, south and south-east of its base towards the Sanaga and possibly beyond, with occasional westward raids across the Mbam such as that recorded by Barth for 1848/9; Ngaundere, once the Mbum had been reduced, east and south-east of its base against the Lakka, Yangere, Dek and other Shari peoples. The ivory and slaves of the Shari lands had, we may infer from El Tounsy's accounts of long-distance licensed slaving expeditions from Baghirmi and Wadai, already been exploited in the early nineteenth century. It is conceivable that Bornu expeditions may have, before Rei Buba was established, reached some of the areas later exploited by the Fulani. Barth received information from a Kanuri trading from Ngaundere and Vogel in 1854 (apud Benton, 1911, 284-6) reports Bornu-protected slave raiders in the western marches of Adamawa. During the second half of the nineteenth century raids mounted by the dependents of the Muri and Bauchi emirates reached the north-western borders of Bamdenda. They had been preceded here by the Chamba whose Benue settlements were visited by Baikie in 1854. In the last decades of the nineteenth century the south-western borders of the Yola emirate and the southern marches of Tibati remained unsafe but the profits of the trade were sufficient to attract Hausa enterprise to the areas south and south-west of Banyo. A few years before Zintgraff's arrival light-skinned traders had been in Bafut and were murdered when they left it. In 1891 a Hausa was trading in Bafreng, where Hutter met him.

The Bamenda Grassfields had been visited by Jukun or Jukunised traders before the Hausa reached it, to judge from traditional accounts. Clarke records, from a 'Bendov' (possibly Tamu-speaking) informant the presence of traders called Battok, bringing salt, cotton cloth and palm-oil to exchange for ivory and slaves – the Battok are perhaps connected with the market of Patoku between Bandam and the Tikar areas of Bamum. Perhaps these are Hausa traders, perhaps the Wukari and Akwana traders who, according to Meek (1931, p.38 and 1928 MSS), had traditional salt-trade connections with the Wute and Tikarized Chamba of Banyo before it became the centre of Haman Gabdo Dandi's kingdom.

The Chamba-led raids and subsequent 'Bali' settlement in Bamenda itself in the 'thirties and 'forties led as we saw to the capture of refugees by other tribes to the south of them and, if Clarke's information is to be trusted, they involved the sale of slaves to northern markets as well.

Local Organisation of Trade and Gift-exchange

The material we collected on pre-European trade in Bamenda can be referred largely to the 'eighties and 'nineties. We shall expand it wherever possible by reference to contemporary information. We discuss first the organisation of trade and gift-exchange, secondly the main commodities imported and exported from the area and the routes along which they travelled.

In the areas characterised by centralised chiefdoms, large or small, some degree of royal regulation of trade existed. This was expressed most frequently in the control of markets which were policed by royal retainers or the maskers of the regulating society. In Bafut, for example, the main market is still opened with a recital of the names of the Fon's ancestors by the leading men of *kwifòn,* accompanied by the masker *mugbu* carrying a jingle-spear and emitting the bird-like chirrup associated with *kwifòn*'s punitive night-walks. In Bali the market is controlled by the *kôm mfon,* royal councillors, assisted by *bàgwè,* picked warriors who acted as spies in war and peace. The main eight-day market at the chiefdom capitals, which took place on a rest-day, was the centre of a system of communication between palace and people. Announcements were made at it by designated officers, public tasks assigned and criminals admonished, trade with hostile groups forbidden, and new market sites and days declared. The market site might also contain sacrificial monoliths and the summoning drums of societies and it provided the festal centre of the chiefdom. Apart from minor markets there were, also, a few markets with other characteristics at the edge of a trading territory such as Fonfukka in Bum, Widekum and Ntem; these acted as inland ports, neutral areas to which long-distance traders repaired, protected by a local chief and individual trade-friendships.

Competitive exchanges between persons of the type recorded among the Pangwe and Ndiki do not seem to have occurred. Competitive accumulation and distribution of wealth was associated with membership of state-societies, entry into princes' fraternities such as the *ygarensi* of Bafut, mortuary ceremonies involving the dead man's fraternity, or presentations to a chief by men seeking honour. The chief himself might accord insignia of honour (*mbu'mi,* Nso, *ku'u,* Wiya) to prominent men; these often took the form of tufted caps, blue and white cloth, ivory armlets, brass hatpins and beads. Chiefs engaged on their own behalf in gift-exchanges with their peers. These exchanges were effected by emissaries carrying cowrie-decorated raffia bags (*abanto,* Bafut, *ku'nka,* Bamunka; *kibam ke-fon,* NSO) marked with peace emblems which contained such articles of value as camwood, ivory armlets, carved drinking horns, brass pipes or stencilled cloth. These royal exchanges had diplomatic connotations; they might follow the settlement of boundaries and be succeeded by the return of captives and runaway wives and the opening of regular trade. Such alliances, for example, existed between Bali-Nyonga and Ngo, Nso and Bum, Nso and the Nsungli chiefdom of Mbot, Bamunka and the Bamileke chiefdom of Balim, Nsei and Wum. The small but strategically placed chiefdom of Bamesi exchanged bags with Nso, Kom, Bafut and Baba (Papiakum); Mankon exchanged bags with Nso, Kom and Nsei. These exchanges are distinct from individual blood-friendships, the blood-pacts recorded from the Widekum, Banyang and Mbem districts, or the rituals associated with peace-making.

In Nso there existed a system of royal trade. Here a man of substance could buy the Fon's market bag (*kibam ke-wai ke-fon*) with prestige goods or supplies of food and wine. He received war-captives or ivory to sell from the royal stock: occasionally a bag might be given on credit. Profits above fair average prices (in terms of cloth, cowries or 'important' beads) were kept by the entrepreneur and the balance taken to the palace when the next supply was sought. In Oku the palace bag (*kibam ntok*) was entrusted to royal retainers who, besides trading war-captives and ivory, disposed of the wares made by the chief's own blacksmiths. Trade in valuables by royal retainers is recorded also from Bafut and Bali-Nyonga.

Institutions for debt-collection and price-control do not seem to have developed to the extent they did among the Cross River peoples or in Bamum. In Bum traders defaulting on advances were tried by *kwifon* and fettered in wooden ankle-blocks. In the last resort persistent debtors were, to judge by Clarke's informants, taken and enslaved by the creditor chiefdoms. *Kwifon-a-Bum* controlled prices of some commodities; in Nso evidence for the degree of price-control is conflicting, but the price of wine and fowls required for sacrifices and fines were fixed by market announcements of royal stewards (*atanto*). One of these stewards acted as *sá'wái* or market-announcer.

Trade in valuable goods might be reserved. In Bum trade in slaves was restricted to members of *ntul*, one of the two governing institutions. In Bali-Nyonga ivory-trading was a royal monopoly, elsewhere a virtual monopoly which excluded collected or traded ivory. Trade in dyed cloth was, before it entered the area in quantity, undertaken on behalf of chiefs and men of rank only, since only they had the right to wear it. In the Wiya chiefdom of Ndu profits on the sale of war-captives were divided between the chief (*nkfu*) and his hereditary councillors (*ta'la sigogor*) in fixed proportions.

We turn now to some of the main items of trade.

Guns and Gunpowder

The flintlocks reaching the Grassfields from the coast and, in the 'nineties, from the Benue factories seem to have been of the types known in the trade as Danish Black Guns and Buccaneers: firing mechanisms of the 'Tower' type appear to have been imitated in conversion jobs by local smiths. Cap guns had penetrated inland and the value of breech-loaders (English Sniders, Albini Marbutts and Winchesters are mentioned by Büchner among the coastal peoples) was recognised. The 2,000 guns of the Bali-Nyonga are described by Zintgraff as flintlocks in 1889; by 1891, according to an official report, they had acquired breech-loaders; some, no doubt, were issues to the

'Balitruppe' under training. By the end of the century some were in
the hands of the Bamundum (Ramsay, 1904). Our authorities are
silent about ammunition supplies for the more advanced weapons,
apart from pilfering or caputre. The Bali-Nyonga say that their
breech-loaders became useless for lack of ammunition, but that the
gun-barrels were converted to flintlock use.

Three main routes of flintlock and gunpowder supply can be
discerned: from the direction of Mamfe and the Banyang markets,
from the Benue lands via Takum and from the Bamileke markets,
especially Bagam. Flintlocks had, according to Becroft and King,
reached the Mamfe area by 1842. The Banen, according to Dugast
(1955, p.221) had acquired them before 1850.

The eastern Tikar had no guns but the neighbouring 'Jetem' had,
according to Barth's informants, in 1848/9. The Bali-Nyonga claim to
have had some guns on their first entry into the Bamenda Grassfields,
possibly in the late 'twenties or 'thirties, and their leader Gawolbe had
a famous 'short gun', perhaps a pistol or musketoon.[2] So far as we
could judge from chiefly genealogies, the entry of guns can be dated
in other chiefdoms to the 'forties and 'fifties, but they were few.

Guns were an objective of Bali-Nyonga raiding parties for the
captor might retain them; *mânjòn* membership was conditional on
possession of a gun, captured, given to a man by a father or patron, or
presented to him by the king (*mfon*) after an act of bravery. In Nso and
Bamunka also, guns were the royal reward for bravery: a man
bringing in war-captives to the palace might be given a gun or two. In
Ngo young retainers at the end of their period of palace service were
given guns. Apart from the royal stock of guns there were also royal
stocks of gunpowder in charge of palace stewards and retainers. In
Bali-Nyonga the male population was divided into sectors for gunpowder distribution which was in the hands of designated titleholders.

Slaves

We have already referred to the southward drift of penal slaves and
captives through the Upper Cross markets and those of Bamileke and
suggested that a substantial southward movement from some areas
followed Chamba and possibly Fulani raids. A northward drain
followed the subjection of Ntem, the establishment of a Banyo
war-camp at Ndu, c. 1870 and an equivocal alliance between the
Fulani and the Wiya people. Traditions assert that captives were sold
to Banyo by Wiya chiefs even earlier.

The slaves who reached the external markets from the Bamenda
Grassfields were mainly adult males. This preponderance reflected

the local division of labour and the workings of the redistributive system centred on the palace. Women had an obvious value as wives and workers in societies where the bulk of food-farming was done by them. Boys had some value as servants and were assimilated as pages, royal wine tappers and firewood carriers: in Bali-Nyonga a more open and competitive society offered them good prospects in royal service or as trading agents of their masters: but men were of greater value as a means of exchange for valuables with those who had need of their services. Guns were among the valued goods which could be exchanged for male slaves and were the most usual reward to captors, who in most chiefdoms presented their booty through their lineage-heads. Some women were distributed soon after capture and some were kept at the palace for eventual distribution to notables, retainers, outstanding warriors, as complimentary gifts to fellow-chiefs and for exchange against some especially prized article denied to commoners.

The nature of the trade can be illustrated from a few cases. Nso in the 'eighties and 'nineties was expanding north and north-east and selling its northern captives to its southern neighbours in the Ndob plain at 5,000 cowries a man and 7,000 cowries or more a woman. A small scale two way trade with surrounding chiefdoms went on. Slaves were bought in Bamum at small markets near the Nso border and sold in the direction of Bum. Some slaves were also sold by the king's bag holders at an unidentified market across the Donga, and some at Ntem. Bali-Nyonga sold its captives mainly through Tuka market (Babudjang) and Widekum towards Mamfe, and to the Bangwa and northern Banyang markets. It also handled slaves sent down from Wum through Mubadji. The opening of the Bali-Mundame road enabled sales to be made to Kumba via Ikiliwindi market. Bum, exchanging slaves with surrounding chiefdoms, sent some up to Takum for salt. From Kom, captives and traded slaves valued at 30-50 goats, were sent to the Ndob plain towns among which the refugee Bamum chiefdom of Baba stands out as an active slave-handler. From the Ndob plain there were sales south to Bagam. Our informants agree that slaves were always sold at the greatest possible distance from their place of origin. Captive women frequently accompanied a king's bag or were offered when news was spread that a chief had valuables to exchange. Thus two Müta girls taken in a well-remembered Bafut raid were sent down with royal messengers to Bapinyi where some fine cloth had been spotted.

Zintgraff's and Hutter's impression that the Bamenda slave trade was on a modest scale in comparison with that of Adamawa is certainly correct. Most transactions we recorded were of small numbers and most took place outside the markets. The only internal

open slave markets we were able to record with certainty, other than
the border markets mentioned, were in Nso, Ndu and Bali-Nyonga.
There were minor collecting points in the Ndob plain feeding the
Bamileke markets.

The numbers of 'Bayong' slaves routed to the upper palm-oil areas
and Old Calabar, where they were highly prized according to Ander-
son (writing in 1856) might have been expected to level off after 1855,
when the palm-oil trade had ceased to expand at the phenomenal rate
of the 'thirties and 'forties. Yet Burton, giving evidence before a
Parliamentary Committee in 1865, was convinced that the domestic
trade directed to the Oil Rivers had increased; that the price of slaves
had fallen, and that, because of the high cost of provisions, slaves were
worked to death and replaced. By the 'eighties, however, the prices
paid for slaves to Ekoi middlemen had risen, and their conditions
were less harsh. The part played by the ex-slave Yellow Duke
(Namete) from the 'seventies onwards, in the organisation of the
palm-oil and kernel traffic to Old Calabar was clearly important (vide
Langhans, 1902), but its long distance effects and that of the
movements of trading factories up the Cross River remain obscure.

Cloth

Most of our informants agree that the first cotton cloth to supersede
bark-cloth or undyed strips, came from the north or north-west. The
Bali say that their first clothing was made of narrow strips of undyed
woven cloth, of the type described by Thorbecke for the eastern Tikar,
and that they first acquired blue and blue and white cloth during their
settlement in 'Banyong' from traders behind them. These indigo-
dyed cloths are most commonly known among traders as Bali-Nyonga.

Undyed cloth strips, sold for manufacture into gowns and society
hoods, loin cloths or tails were also traded; some of them were said to
be the products of local looms. Other white cloths in circulation were
the 'Munshi' blankets (the *gudu* and *batai* of Wum) entering from the
north-west, and finely woven cloth (the *gan* of Wum) said to come
from Ibi, some of it perhaps of European manufacture. White or
undyed cloths were frequently stained with camwood. Red cloth, to
judge by Zintgraff's account of Fon Bo'mbi's dress, had reached
Bafut: local legend has it that the uncertain attitude of Bafut towards
his expedition was the result of coveting the red sailor-blouses of his
carriers for dance outfits. Some quantity of red cloth had evidently
reached Bali-Nyonga, for Hutter illustrates a typical short gown of
'Wukari' blue cloth with an insertion bearing the dorsal red 'moon'
which signifies the high status of the wearer.

The Hausa and Benue cloths entered the Grassfields through Takum, through Gayama also, and from the southern Adamawa markets through Mbembe and Ntem. Bagam is also mentioned as a source of cloth but we have no information about the types distributed. 'English cloths' are reported by Zintgraff from the Metcham valley, possibly of the same provenance as the closewoven cloths brought by occasional Benue traders to Wum and its neighbourhood. European cloth was also handled by the Hausa traders camped between Banyo and Ntem at the end of the century.

The stencilled Benue cloths seem to have been regarded as having more prestige and beauty than most European cloths. Their use was *dòmà* or in common usage as Wukari, Bikom or Munshi cloth[3] originally restricted to persons of high status; they were also used in the burial of chiefs, or to line their residences and arbours on festal occasions. They played a considerable part in gift-exchanges. Quite small strips for use as belts, baldrics or scabbard-cloths were given out as royal favours, or decorated the sacra of the chiefdom. Three or four *vilanlan* (of 3 fathoms) could purchase a woman slave in Nso; European cottons fetched little over a quarter of the equivalent price.

Salt

The two main sources of imported native salt in the Bamenda Grassfields (apart from vegetable salt) were the salt springs of the upper Cross districts, in particular those near Nsanakang and Osidinge, and the Akwana salt. The salt of the upper Cross was traded in balls of about 1 kg or in small palm-leaf bags; at the turn of the century five small bags were valued at one 'brass' or 25 pf. It reached the western Grassfields through the Banyang and Bangwa markets. The Akwana salt-trade seems to have been a long-established one. According to Meek (MSS.1928), the Jidu-Wute of Banyo before their flight to Takum were in touch with Jukun salt-traders; the leader of the combined Chamba, Tikar, and Wute group which established itself at Takum was traditionally the son of an Akwana princess with whose father trade-friendship has been established. The early pastoral Fulani settlers near Banyo had, after disease had wiped out their herds before the jihad, taken to the salt-trade and claim to have penetrated some way into the Bamenda Grassfields (Brackenbury, 1924). There were, of course, other sources for the salt circulating in the Adamawa trade, but the compressed bagged salt – the *mbamfuk-wana* of Bum – appears to have been in great demand over a wide area. The Bum occasionally exchanged a slave for a couple of large bags, some measure of its value. The Jukun trade seems to have waned by the time of Zintgraff's passage and to have been taken over by Hausa traders, whom he found settled at Ashakum and Takum, and their increasing entry brought the Grassfields, particularly through the Bum centre of distribution, in touch with other sources of salt supply – the Bilma as well as the European trade salt of the Royal Niger Company factories. The trade-salt of the European coastal factories also found its way up the Calabar – Cross routes and the Mungo and Wuri routes, perhaps replacing the evaporated salt of the coastal peoples which had, according to Esser, penetrated inland. Evaporated salt in sticks was found by early German patrols in the Nun Valley and they traced its route back to Bafu-Fondong and Fotomena; the description leaves one in doubt about its nature. Trade salt, to judge from Adams' careful account of the Cameroons trade (1786-1800) was in strong demand at the end of the eighteenth century and an essential article of exchange in the ivory trade, representing £55 worth of the articles valued at £240 exchanged for a ton of ivory. Its importance, as an element in the market-to-market network connecting coast and hinterland never abated. Bamum, according to Egerton, exchanged tobacco with Bangangte for salt obtained from the coastal peoples, and salt came up the Wuri route to Yabasi and Bandem for further distribution. The Duala traders mixed the trade salt with plant-ash and other ingredients and sold it in greyish-black cones.

Beads

We shall deal here only with highly-valued beads imported for ceremonial dress, hoarded and redistributed, and used as a medium in the slave-trade or trade in valuables. There were, apart from these, bugles of all colours in circulation, principally dark-blue and white in older beadwork pieces. Cut canes of glass, translucent or opaque, were also used in the beadwork decoration of stools, carved figures, fly-whisk handles, shirts, masks and calabashes; they are most often dark-blue, white or red-brown. Bead-work decoration was, in some chiefdoms, the occupation of the women of the palace. In addition to those types we describe, and we describe them from the user's viewpoint, numerous other types — Bida wound beads, millefiori and imitation leopards' teeth for example — were in circulation.

Chevron Beads (sa'nkonti, Ntem, buf , Bamunka, siba , Nso).

These are of several types, mainly red, white and blue ellipsoids or rounded barrels, usually with a greenish transparent core and up to 3″ in length. The matt blue glass sections show striations in some pieces when held up to the light. They are said to have been brought from

Kano and Sokoto by Hausa and Fulani traders. Some smaller glossy modern imitations are current and less valued: these are similar if not identical with the "finest cut Rosetta beads" from a modern trade card illustrated by Mauny in Notes Africaines, 74, 1957.

Large Chevron beads are frequently worn with beads of *sakinci* or *sintem* type (v.i.) by chiefs and councillors and necklaces including them are among the heirlooms of chiefs and titleholders. In Bali-Nyonga chevron beads were used for marriage-payments, 1-5 necklaces being exchanged.[4]

Sakinci (*sakinci*, Nso, *sa'nci*, Ntem, *we*, Ngo)

These are the most highly-valued beads, and their wear is restricted to chiefs and persons licensed by them; they are worn on public occasions only. They range in shape from rather irregular oblates to finely-shaped, slender, long barrels. Associated with them are cylinder beads with a wide perforation (*sintem*, Nso and Ntem) of various lengths but usually ¼" to ½", often with irregular ends: *sintem* are often used as stoppers with *sakinci*. Both *sakinci* and *sintem* are translucent often with a creamy white tinge with lighter slightly irregular longitudinal stripes in the glass. About twenty *sakinci* would purchase a male slave. *Sakinci* beads were collected one by one to make necklaces or anklets.

Both types are said to have come from the direction of Ntem or Banyo or to be brought by traders from 'Nsungli'. In Bangangte also they are said to come from the north. They formed part of the buried royal treasure of Nkar which was driven out of its capital by Nso before 1850.

Black and White Slave-beads (*sinji* in Nso and elsewhere)

The term *sinji* is applied to black and white striped beads usually of long barrel form used in slave-purchases as well as to various types of barrel and circular black beads with painted-on white spots, sometimes with a red 'eye'. Some of these are in the Pitt-Rivers Museum collection of trade-beads, presented by Levin of London.

Cylinder Beads

Deep-blue cylinder beads, c ½" long, c ⅛" diameter, were also used for slave-purchases; about 100 or 3 necklaces would buy a slave. In Nso these, *nfwaya-nso*, might only be worn by the chief. Narrow, tubular, opaque, pale blue beads (*nsamnsam* in Nso), paler and longer than the *akori* beads illustrated by Krieger (1943, Fig. 4 of

Table), were also highly valued. Other types in use in Nso were *mban-a-cecer*, dull red cylinder beads, up to ½" diameter, used as spacers; *kiyon*, white cylinders of various sizes, and *konfem*, tubular beads, striped, with contrasting cores: the last are said to have come from the direction of the eastern Tikar, and resemble Venetian 'rosettas'; one type is identical with 'Rosetta 791' of a Società Veneziana trade-card of 1907.

The deep blue cylinders resemble the Bákki described by Passarge (1895, p.433) as being brought to Kuka by the Teda. White, short cylinder beads of small size (c ⅛" long) called *fusawa* in Bum were used in headbands to distinguish royal wives and palace serving women: these are said to come from the Benue lands.

Other Types

Atam (Bum) are pale blue, ellipsoid, opaque beads with red and white arrow-markings at the poles, ⅞" long. Nyemba (Bum) are black ebony or hardwood beads with blue inlays, 1/6" long, radius 3/32". These two types were brought in from the Benue lands. *finennen* (Nso) are dark blue, opaque, circular beads 1/6" in diameter across the perforation, and well-finished.

Imported Media of Exchange

There is general agreement that both types of cowries, Molucca whites and Zanzibar blues, were in circulation, and that white cowries were in use before the brass-rods of the Calabar and Cross River trade were widely diffused. White cowries are said to have been brought in in quantity by Jukun traders: presumably these were in touch with the southern Benue or northern markets since the main media of exchange in Wukari were conventional hoes (*akika*) and packaged salt.

Brass manilas were in use in small quantities in the southern Widekum areas for ceremonial payments, but were only more widely diffused as a currency after the German pax had encouraged the entry of larger numbers of Hausa traders, according to our informants. Besides the chevron beads used for marriage-payments in Bali-Nyonga, small 'money-beads', such as the red beads described by Hutter, were used for minor market purchases in the south-west.

Cowries appear to have entered the Bamenda Grassfields from four directions, Bum, Bagam, Bamum and Banyo. They circulated in strings of 80-100, and in Nso royal trade were issued in bags of about 10,000. Their ritual and decorative use has been described by Jeffreys.(3)[5]

Ivory

The Jantzen & Thormählen trading expedition which accompanied Zintgraff's second and larger official expedition to the Bali lands in 1890/1 hoped to find in them one of the important sources of the Adamawa ivory reaching the world market. Its hope does not seem to have been well-founded. At the time it reached the area elephants were by no means common. The main hunting grounds seem to have been the Mbokam uplands on the Nso-Bamum border (where Nso and Bamum competed), the lower lands between the northern borderlands of Bafut and Kentu, the Tikar plain, the corrugated lands between the Nkambe uplands and Mambila, and the southern forest-edge of the Western Grassfields. The eastern Tikar plain ivory was already exploited by ivory-hunters based on the stranger-settlement of Patoku. Some of this ivory and ivory drawn from the Wute-dominated areas in the Mbam-Sanaga triangle was passing through the independent Tikar city state of Ngambe, Bamkin and Bandam to the Banyo-controlled ivory entrepôt at Maharba. More of the southern ivory seems to have been reaching Tibati, via Yoko; at the end of the century this was added to by the booty won in Amalamu's wars. Another rich ivory area lay between the Donga valley and Gashaka; Hausa ivory-hunters and European poachers from this reach were penetrating the northern borderlands of the Bamenda Grassfields at the end of the century. In 1898 Moseley reported that elephant herds were being driven to migrate from Bafum towards the Dama country. By 1905 Glauning could report that elephant hunting in the Bamenda Grassfields was then conducted predominantly by the peoples of the Nkambe plateau, and to some extent by the Nso, with the help of pit-traps, while Hausa hunters were camped in Kentu. Earlier reports mention the use of pit-traps in the upper Ndob plain, but no organised ivory trade is recorded for this area.

Strophanthus-poisoned harpoons fired from flintlocks by immigrant Hausa hunters to the Upper Cross areas are reported for the late 'nineties; to judge from Thorbecke's account of Tikar armament, there were harpoon-guns in use in the Tikar plain also; strophanthus-poison is also reported by Glauning (in 1905) in the eastern Donga country. Hutter is positive, however, that this improved hunting technique was not in use in the Bali lands. There is no record of strophanthus in the Bamenda highlands, though S. Barteri has recently been reported from the vicinity of Fang in Fungom in a low-lying area with a savannah-type flora.[6] The relations between hunting-techniques, herd-movements, ecology and human settlement, and the dates of entry of professional ivory-hunters need further investigation without which nothing very positive can be said

about the relative or changing importance of the Bamenda Grassfields as a source of ivory.

Ivory in the Bamenda Grassfields was a royal monopoly. It seems
that by the turn of the century, Mbembe villages and possibly some
Bafum ones had ivory sharing agreements with Hausa hunters, but
we found no evidence of this in the large chiefdoms: our Nso informants, for example, were positive that no Hausa hunters had reached
their hunting grounds. Much of the ivory stored in the larger chiefdoms derived from the annual hunts on behalf of the king. The
withholding of ivory from a king was a declaration of rebellion; a
demand for it a demand for submission. Ivory transactions were
therefore in the main gift-exchanges or royal favours, and a large
store of ivory implied the ability to extend a ruler's area of influence.
Some ivory – gift ivory, ivory acquired in exchanges for goods of high
value, or ivory traded by royal agents – might enter into trade. The
ivory armlets worn by men of rank also seem to have been traded: Nso
informants state that these were valued at 10,000 cowries.

Such trade as existed in the eastern Bamenda area seems to have
passed through Bum, Ndu and Ntem, and some of the ivory reaching
these markets derived from Bamum and Bagam. Its passage through
Nso to these destinations accounts, perhaps, for the later importance
of Kumbo as an ivory entrepôt. The supplies of the south-western
Grassfields and Upper Cross area were fed into the routes reaching
Calabar. Bagam, at the end of the century, was an ivory-market
intermediate between Bamum and the Bamileke chiefdoms: a trade
route joined in to the Bangwa markets.

Kola

To judge from Barth's traders' itineraries it had become known at
least by 1848/9 that in the 'more south-westerly districts' of the
country of the Tikar, two kinds of kola, including the *honoruwa*
relished in Bornu, were to be found in plenty. By 1879 Flegel's
informants were well-acquainted with the routes into the country
south-west of Banyo. Von Stetten learnt at Ngambe and Bamkin that
kola grown in 'Bali' was preferred to local kola and considered as tasty
as Gonja kola, and that kola traders at Maharba knew the kola
markets of Bafut (Bafum?). Zintgraff on his return to Bali from
Takum via Bum – to which he was guided in mistake for Bafut – met a
large Hausa caravan loaded with kolas and ivory. At Guanase, near
Bum, he met more Hausa and noted that every compound had its kola
trees. Moseley could describe Takum in 1898 as the kola-market for
all the Benue states from which kola-traders descended to Bum or
'Great Bafum'. The position of Bum as a kola-centre had evidently

extended its influence, for the Fon of Bum's 'passport' was respected over a wide area. Bum itself, despite Zintgraff's impressions, was not a large kola producer. Its supplies came largely from nearby chiefdoms. Nso appears to have been the largest producer originally, marketing its kola through an intermediate market at Nkor and insisting on *dòmà* and salt in exchange. Ndu appears also to have been quite an important collecting centre; Oku and Kom also. From Nso kolas also went to the Ntem market where they were sold for cowries, and into Bamum and across the Donga. Bagam and nearby markets attracted kola from some of the Ngömba villages. Bamum, both a large consumer and exporter, drew on the Bamileke chiefdoms. Bali-Nyonga had a reputation as a producer of high-quality kolas, but the best of these may be the products of Zintgraff's plantings in 1896 with varieties from the Victoria Botanic Gardens.

Our informants agree that the deliberate expansion of kola planting was a relatively late phenomenon associated with the increasing entry of Hausa traders into the border areas of Bamenda. We may perhaps date it from the 'sixties or 'seventies of last century. Unlike the restricted ivory and slave trade it enriched all kin-heads who controlled tree-crops, drew some of them and their agents into the 'port' markets and encouraged new entrants into general trading.

Some Conclusions

At the end of the nineteenth century the Bamenda Grassfields exported no commodity in quantity except kola; their trade in ivory and slaves in exchange for guns, salt and luxury articles was relatively modest. They were not rich in wild rubber. Their access to European goods from the coast depended considerably on an indirect market-to-market trade in which small stock, dogs, tobacco, small surpluses of well-prepared palm-oil, and local manufactures, such as ironware, mats, bags, and baskets, played an important part. The palm-oil production of the Bamenda Grassfields themselves was largely consumed locally. Hausa traders, who found it worthwhile to bulk and carry the palm-oil of the Tikar plain to Bakundi, found no local oil supplies large enough to claim their attention except possibly in the Mbembe area. The profits of slave-trading had to be balanced against the attraction of retaining captives as wives, or as servants who might, as in Bali, undertake arduous trading journeys on behalf of their masters. The local prestige value of ivory often outweighed its commercial value, and indirect economic benefits could be secured by its local distribution, or by gifts to foreign concerns – such as Bali gifts to the West-afrikanische Pflanzungsgesellschaft Victoria and Bum gifts to the Royal Niger Company. Superior armament or military skill could induce a flow of palm-oil, kolas, smoked fish, livestock, wine and other consumable goods for redistribution, and encouraged additions to a chiefdom's capital in the form of gifts of women and ivory by surrounding small chiefdoms anxious to purchase peace. The immediate returns to be got from opening direct trade in European goods with the Bamenda Grassfields was too small to make a station viable, as Esser calculated. It was only after their major resource, labour, had been exploited for some years that regular administration began, in 1902. It was followed by the rapid advance of the Hausa trading frontier.

NOTES

1. The supposed location of some of these districts is shown, for example, in Petermann's and Hassenstein's map illustrating their article, 'Inner-Afrika nach dem Stande der geographischen Kenntnis', *Petermanns Mitt. Ergbd.* 2, 1862/3, and in a map prepared by the Gesellschaft für Erdkunde zu Berlin to illustrate Flegel's routes, Verhandlungen II, Heft 8. The meaning of Bayong is explained by Joh. Ittmann, 'Religiöse und Volkskundliche Begriffe im nördlichen Waldland von Kamerun', *Afr. und Ubersee,* Beiheft 26, 1953, p.3. References to Bayong by Rogozinsky (1884), Büchner (1887, p.68ff), and Zintgraff (1888) indicate that Bamum and some Bamileke chiefdoms were meant by their informants. Hutchinson's list of Mbrikum chiefdoms (1861, p.326-7) includes Bamum and 'Bansok', perhaps Nso.

2. The dating of the Bali settlement is discussed in an article by M. D. W. Jeffreys. I am also much indebted to him for access to his MS. on Wiya history, and other help.

3. This is quite distinct from the narrow embroidered cloth known as *kwashe* in Wukari but the *bu sese* method of stencilling (C. K. Meek, *A Sudanese Kingdom,* 1931, p.433) is still employed there.

4. For illustrations of chevron beads similar to those found in Bamenda see Fourneau, J., 'Sur des perles anciennes de pâte de verre provenant de Zanaga', *Bull. IFAN,* 14, 1952, 956-969; and Egerton, 1938, pl.103, for a necklace combining chevron and *sakinci* beads.

5. We are not concerned in this paper with locally manufactured currencies, such as iron rings, hoes and shovels.

6. Personal communication, Dr. G. Taylor, Royal Botanic Gardens, Kew, 1961.

REFERENCES

(1) Jeffreys, M. D. W., 'Oku Blacksmiths', *Nigerian Field,* 26, (1961), pp.137-144.
(2) Tardits, C., *Les Bamileke de l'Ouest Cameroun,* (Paris 1960), pp.18-51.
(3) 'The Cowry Shell and the Lozenge in African Decorative Art', S.A.M.A.B., 6, 4, (1955).

16

SLAVERY AND THE SLAVE TRADE IN THE CONTEXT OF WEST AFRICAN HISTORY*

J. D. Fage

There have been at least three widely held and influential views about slavery and the slave trade in West Africa, and also about their relation to its society in respect both of their origins and of their effects on it.

The first is that the institution of slavery was natural and endemic in West African society, so that the coming of foreign traders with a demand for labour, whether from Muslim North Africa or from the countries of maritime Europe, led swiftly and automatically to the development by West Africans of an organised trade in slaves for export.

The second is a contrary view, that it was rather these external demands for labour which led to a great growth of both slavery and slave-trading in West Africa, and so corrupted its indigenous society.

The third view, which may or may not be associated with the second, is that the external demand for West African labour, especially in the period *ca.* 1650 to *ca.* 1850, was so great that the export of slaves to meet it had a disastrous effect on the peoples of West Africa, disrupting not only their natural demographic development but their social and moral development as well.

In this paper it is proposed to examine and reassess these views in the light of recent research and thinking, and, as a result, to offer an interpretation of the roles of slavery and the slave trade in the history of West Africa which may be more in accord with its economic and social realities.

The first view, namely that the export slave trade was possible because both slavery and trading in slaves were already deeply rooted in West African society, was of course a view propagated by the European slave-traders, especially perhaps when the morality of their

*Reprinted by permission of Cambridge University Press from the *Journal of African History*, Vol. X, No. 3, 1969.

business was being questioned. Norris's and Dalzel's books on Dahomey towards the close of the eighteenth century are developed examples of this attitude (1); Dalzel, for example, quite seriously argues that greater good was done by exporting slaves to American plantations than by leaving them in West Africa, where they were likely to become victims of the practice of human sacrifice. But the slave-traders' view in effect persisted into the abolitionist atmosphere of the nineteenth century and was, in fact, put forward as a principal moral justification for European colonisation. To stamp out the evils of slavery and slave-trading in West Africa, occupation of its territories was thought essential; indeed, it was specifically imposed as a duty on the European powers following the Brussels Act of 1890. The view that West Africans left to themselves were inherently prone to own and trade in slaves became in fact one of the received myths of the conquering colonisers.

Analysis and criticism of this view are complicated by the problem of deciding what institution or institutions in West African societies corresponded to the European idea of slavery. Many people will be familiar with Rattray's analysis of slavery in Ashanti society, in which he defined at least five separate terms to describe the various conditions or degrees of voluntary or involuntary servitude in Ashanti (2). Only two of these, *odonko*, a foreigner who had been purchased with the express purpose of making him or her a slave, and *domum*, a man or woman received in tribute from a subjugated foreign state, might seem to correspond more or less to what an eighteenth century European or white American might understand by 'slave'. But Rattray then goes on to consider the rights of such slaves in Ashanti society, and these were far in advance of the rights of any slaves in any colony in the Americas. He concludes that the rights of an Ashanti slave were not so very different from 'the ordinary privileges of any Ashanti free man, with whom, in these respects, his position did not seem to compare so unfavourably'. He also states that 'a condition of voluntary servitude was, in a very literal sense, the heritage of every Ashanti', and that to be masterless in that society was an open invitation to involuntary servitude. Similarly, Dalzel reports of the neighbouring, somewhat more authoritarian society of eighteenth century Dahomey, which he knew at first hand, that its inhabitants were '*all* slaves to the king' (3).

But it is not necessary here to enter into the arguments as to whether various forms of unfreedom in various West African societies should be called by the name of 'slave', or by such other terms as 'subject', 'servant', 'serf' or 'pawn'. It would seem possible to produce a straightforward definition of slavery that is perfectly adequate for the purposes of this present enquiry: namely that a slave was a man or woman who was owned by some other person, whose labour was regarded as having economic value, and whose person had a commercial value.

It is obvious enough that slaves as so defined existed in many West African societies during the heyday of the Atlantic slave trade from the seventeenth to the nineteenth century, though possibly not in stateless societies or in societies that were little or not touched by the major routes of trade. The question is, then, whether such slavery existed in West African societies before the impingement on them of external trade.

It is impossible to answer this question with respect to those parts of West Africa in the Sudan to which external trade came across the Sahara. The only considerable body of evidence which is really relevant is the accounts of the Arabic writers who were the first to describe the West African Sudan either from their personal knowledge or on the basis of others' first-hand experience, together with early local written histories such as the Timbuctu *Tarikhs* or the Kano *Chronicle*. This evidence has been reviewed by Mauny (4). It may be said that both its quantity and its quality are disappointing. The Arab authors take the existence of both slavery and trading in slaves very much for granted, and neither seems to them to call for very much comment. It is thus apparent that both institutions were well established in the major states and empires of the West African Sudan from the eleventh to the sixteenth century. We cannot tell whether these institutions were indigenous, or whether they had evolved following the growth of trans-Saharan trade, because, of course, Arab traders had preceded Arabic scholarship across the Sahara by about four centuries. Furthermore, traffic of some kind across the Sahara between North and West Africa had been in existence for something like a thousand years at least before the Arab conquests began in the seventh century A.D. It has been shown, in fact, that a trans-Saharan trade in Negro slaves must have existed though perhaps in little volume, as early as about the second century A.D.(5). However, we have no means of knowing what relation this may have had to slavery and the slave trade within West Africa itself.

In default of evidence of the relation between the existence of an external demand for slaves and of slavery and an internal trade in slaves for the West African Sudan, we must turn to the Guinea area, where commonly the first truly external traders were the European sea-traders, who first arrived on the coasts in the fifteenth century. The evidence for Upper Guinea, from the Gambia to modern Liberia, has been analysed by Dr. Walter Rodney (6).

The ethnographic picture that can be built up for this part of the coastlands from sixteenth and seventeenth century European, especially Portuguese, accounts would seem to be good and detailed, but the references to slaves are few and far between. They indicate little more, Rodney says, than that the kings and chiefs of the area had a small number of 'political clients' in their households. There is no evidence for the existence of 'chattel slaves, agricultural serfs, or even household servants' in any numbers, or in any condition to differentiate them from ordinary citizens. He concludes, therefore, that there was no sizeable class of men, and no indigenous trade in men, which could serve as a launching-pad for the Atlantic slave trade. In this part of West Africa at least, a class society involving slaves and trade in them was a consequence of the European demand for slaves for the Americas, and not an indigenous feature upon which an export trade could be built up.

Rodney contrasts this picture, not only with the eighteenth and nineteenth century situation in his area, when specialised traders, mainly Mandingo and Fula, possessed and dealt in large numbers of slaves, but also with the sixteenth and seventeenth century situation farther north, in the Senegal, and also farther east, in Lower Guinea. In the latter case, he does not do very much more than refer to the fact that, as early as about 1500, the Portuguese were *selling* slaves on the Gold Coast, which of course presupposes a society knowing of the value of slaves and having a demand for them[1]. But the whole context in which the Portuguese first traded in Lower Guinea seems to have been very different from that in which they sought to trade in Upper Guinea.

We might begin by remarking that the ethnographic picture that can be built up from early Portuguese accounts of Lower Guinea is slighter, less complete and less detailed than that which can be built up for Upper Guinea. It is sometimes suggested that this is so because, after the Portuguese Crown had asserted its control over the Gold Coast trade in the 1480s, it required that its own and its subjects' doings in Guinea should be kept as secret as possible to place their foreign competitors in the Guinea trade at a disadvantage. But in fact most of the information used by Rodney is later than 1500, and it seems possible that the relative dearth of Portuguese ethnographic material for Lower Guinea may have other explanations. It seems possible that one of these may be that on the coasts of Lower Guinea, especially on the Gold Coast and in and around Benin, the Portuguese were in contact with organised kingdoms which had developed trading systems of their own and which were already engaged in long-distance trade or in trading with long-distance traders (like the Mande merchants on the Gold Coast). Whereas in the Upper Guinea coastlands the Portuguese had to deal with societies which were politically and commercially less well developed, and which therefore had to be thoroughly examined to see what prospects of profitable trade they might offer, no such exploration was necessary for the kingdoms of Lower Guinea, which already knew what commodities they had to offer to strangers and on what terms they would deal in them.

In these circumstances, for Lower Guinea it is necessary to infer local attitudes to slavery and trading in slaves from the trade which the Portuguese conducted there. It is immediately apparent not only that there was a market for slaves on the Gold Coast, but that there were communities farther east which both had slaves and knew the conditions on which they could be offered for sale. Thus as early as *ca.* 1500, Pacheco Pereira could write of Benin that the kingdom was 'usually at war with its neighbours and takes many captives, whom we buy at 12 or 15 brass bracelets each, or for copper bracelets which they prize more; from there slaves are taken to [the Gold Coast] where they are sold for gold' (7). It is interesting that Pacheco says nothing about the royal ban on the export from Benin of male slaves which Professor Ryder says was 'imposed at the beginning of the sixteenth century'. Presumably it was not yet in force when Pacheco wrote. Conceivably it may have been instituted in the belief that it was more beneficial to the kingdom to maintain than to export its manpower.. Conversely, and more probably perhaps, the subsequent decline of European trade at Benin as the trans-Atlantic slave trade developed, and the need to reverse this decline when neighbouring kingdoms were gaining strength through growing trade with Europeans, may well explain why the ban was rescinded in the 1690s (8).[2]

In general, we can be confident that what the Portuguese sought to do in Lower Guinea from about 1480 was to profit by imposing themselves (as later they were to do in East África and Asia) on already existing patterns of trade, and that they found their organised kingdoms in which the idea of foreign trade, carried on under royal control and in accordance with state policy by established merchant classes or guilds, was already well established. Such a system involved the use of slaves – and an appreciation of their economic value – in a number of ways: as cultivators of crops for market on the estates of kings or nobles; as miners, or as artisans in craft workshops; as carriers. on the trade roads, and even as traders themselves; as soldiers, retainers, servants, officials even, in the employ of kings or principal men in the kingdom. A similar but, one suspects, less well developed pattern was evident, as Rodney admits, in the Senegal region on the western fringes of the Sudan, and it was undoubtedly from the Western and Central Sudan that it had spread into Lower Guinea some time before the arrival of the Portuguese. In this sense the area of Upper Guinea, where in the sixteenth and seventeenth centuries there was no organised slavery, was an economically little developed and backward region.

There seems in fact to be a close correlation in West Africa between economic development (and political development, because indigenous commercial activity was largely king or state-directed) and the growth of the institution of slavery as here defined. This growth was already well advanced before European sea trade with West Africa began in the fifteenth century, and certainly before the main commercial demand of Europeans on West Africa was one for slaves – which was not really until the middle or the second half of the seventeenth century. Neither the first nor the second of the commonly held views about the relationship between the Atlantic slave trade and slavery and slave-trading within West African society is really satisfactory. Slavery and the commercial valuation of slaves were not natural features of West African society, nor was their development and growth simply a consequence of the European demand for slaves for American plantations. This last may well have been the case in Upper Guinea, but elsewhere, e.g. in Lower Guinea, all the coming of European slave-buyers meant in principle was that African kings and merchants were increasingly presented with a new element of choice – fundamentally, it would seem, an economic choice: whether it was more advantageous to them to keep their slave labourers at home, as farmers, artisans, porters, retainers, soldiers, etc., or to exchange them or some of them for other forms of wealth (or of power, e.g. guns and powder).

We arrive then at a first conclusion, that slavery and the making, buying and selling of slaves were means by which certain privileged individuals in West African society, or persons who wished to gain or to extend positions of privilege in that society, sought to mobilise the wealth inherent in the land and the people on it, and that this process had already gone some distance before the Europeans arrived. In so far as it seems to have started in the Sudan, rather than in Guinea, it is of course still possible, even perhaps likely, that the process was sparked off by the demands of visitors coming to West Africa from across the Sahara, from North Africa. On the other hand, such evidence as there is suggests that it is *un*likely that these first external demands were primarily or even essentially demands for labour. The prime North African demand was probably for gold and exotic produce, and the first basis of the trans-Saharan trade the exchange of salt for gold. It would thus be a demand for *commodities* which provoked the vital change by which some West Africans began to view some others not as kin or non-kin but as a means by which to obtain wealth and power.

We are still left, however, with the questions whether, and, if so, to what extent, the external demands for West African labour, especially the great European demands for labour for the Americas, may have distorted the natural economic development of West Africa, and have produced socially, economically, and even politically disastrous consequences.

Clearly we should begin by assessing, first, the actual size of this demand for labour exports and, secondly, its possible demographic effects in West Africa. Thanks to the recent researches of Professor Philip D. Curtin (9), it is now possible to do this with rather more confidence than before in respect of the export of slaves to the Americas. The numbers of slaves reaching the Americas and so, allowing for losses *en route*, the numbers leaving Africa seem likely to have been appreciably smaller than has been commonly supposed. For the whole four centuries of the trade, Curtin's evaluation of the evidence available points to the conclusion that the number of slaves reaching the Americas cannot have been more than about nine millions, and may well have been rather less. Furthermore, he doubts whether it would have been technically possible for the shipping resources available to Europe to have transported more. He also has evidence that suggests, too, that the losses *en route* from sickness, starvation and revolt, not more than 16 per cent on average, were significantly less than the figures commonly accepted, which derive – like the earlier estimates for total volume – from the exaggerated pleadings of the abolitionist campaigners. On this basis, the total number of men and women exported from Africa during the whole period of the slave trade is unlikely to have been much more than about 11 millions. Of these, a considerable and growing proportion came from south of the Cameroons, and so from outside West Africa as commonly understood. The *West* African contribution to the Atlantic slave trade is in fact unlikely to have been much more than about six millions.

It would be helpful if we could compare this estimate with a figure for the number of slaves exported northwards from West Africa across the Sahara. This, frankly, is impossible: the available data are exiguous and unreliable in the extreme, as is admitted by Mauny, who, however, offers a guess of a minimum of 20,000 a year, or two million a century (10).[3] Something like the first of these figures might be reasonable for the annual capacity of the trans-Saharan caravan roads, but it would seem totally unreasonable to suppose that anything like this number crossed the Sahara every year during the seventeen centuries in which we know the northern slave trade to have existed, or even during the twelve centuries following the Arab conquest of North Africa. Thirty-four or twenty-four million Negroes would have made an impact on the population of North Africa and the Middle East quite as great as nine million Negroes on that of the Americas, and really there is little evidence of this. It seems safer to conclude that, extending over a very much longer period, the trans-Saharan trade removed fewer Negroes than the Atlantic trade, and that its effect on the West African population during the time the Atlantic trade was operating was relatively minor.

Prior to the middle of the seventeenth century, the Atlantic slave trade was on a small scale; Curtin's figures suggest a loss of population to West Africa before 1600 of only about 200,000. The seventeenth century figure would be nearly a million, but it was in the years from 1701 to 1810, when something like four-and-a-half million slaves were removed, that the effect of the trade was most serious, averaging a loss of 41,000 men and women a year. The nineteenth century loss, in so far as West Africa was concerned, was much lighter, probably of the order of only about 11,000 a year on average.

We do not, of course, know the size of West Africa's population in the eighteenth century. But extrapolation backwards from twentieth century censuses and estimates and rates of increase suggests that the population of West Africa may have been at least 25 million at the beginning of the eighteenth century, with a rate of natural increase of about 15 per 1,000 at the beginning of the century and of about 19 per 1,000 at the end. If these estimates are anything like right, then at first sight the effect of the export slave trade in the eighteenth century may have been more or less to check population growth, the rates of slave exports and of natural increase being of the same order. For other centuries, the effect of the slave trade would have been slight.

Various refinements can be made to such a crude calculation. For example, some allowance should be made for deaths caused directly or indirectly by the operations of the slave trade within West Africa itself. On the other hand, such a factor might be more than offset by the fact that only a third of the slaves exported were women, so that in a polygynous society the rate of natural increase by new births may not have been as much affected as would otherwise have been the case.

It is probably more important to appreciate that the incidence of the slave trade, both in time and space, was by no means even. Thus in the 1780s, for instance, about 80% of all slaves exported from West Africa (and nearly half of the slaves taken from *all* Africa) were taken from the coast from the Gold Coast to the Cameroons inclusive. Thus if there were serious depopulation and other destructive effects caused by the Atlantic slave trade, they might be expected to show most clearly in this region. In point of fact, they do not appear to show at all. This, by and large, remains the most densely populated part of West Africa, and the Ibo country is as thickly settled as any part of the whole continent. Moreover, this was the part of Guinea, including the Akan states, Dahomey, the Yoruba and Benin kingdoms, which was politically and economically best organised.

The conclusion to which one is led, therefore, is that whereas in East and Central Africa the slave trade, sometimes conducted in the interior by raiding and warring strangers, could be extremely destructive of economic, political and social life, in West Africa it was part of a sustained process of economic and political development. Probably because, by and large, in West Africa land was always more abundant than labour[4], the institution of slavery played an essential role in this development; without it there were really few effective means of mobilising labour for the economic and political needs of the state. (One may recall Charles Monteil's dictum that 'a Sudanic empire is in essence an association of individuals aiming to dominate the generality for profit' (11). But in this process the *trade* in slaves, certainly the export trade, was essentially incidental, only one of a number of ways of increasing a kingdom's wealth and power, and in the Guinea coastlands only during the eighteenth century the most important way. Whether or not to export slaves and, if so, in what quantities, seems to have been increasingly an economic choice.

It has already been suggested that this choice was exercised at Benin. Here, shortly after 1500, the authorities seem to have concluded that the kingdom and its economy would be weakened if the export of male labour were permitted. Later on, the view seems to have been taken that the resultant loss of trade with Europeans (*inter alia* the vendors of firearms), and the consequent gain to the trade and strength of neighbouring African rivals, was more dangerous than the loss of manpower. Dr Akinjogbin has suggested a similar argument in eighteenth century Dahomey: first a refusal to export slaves (lest the kingdom be weakened), then a realisation that it was only through selling slaves that the kingdom could buy the guns and powder necessary to maintain its power (12). It may also be significant that, although the European demand for slaves for the Americas was continually growing and the price of slaves steadily increasing from about 1650 to about 1810, the numbers of slaves exported from the well-organised Gold Coast states remained more or less constant throughout the period, never really exceeding about 10,000 a year. It may be argued, then, that economic and political logic had in effect persuaded the Gold Coast authorities that this was about the number of slaves they could afford to export, in order to obtain the guns and other imports their states required, without weakening their societies. The numbers of slaves exported through the Niger delta ports did greatly increase during this period, but this too could also have been a more or less conscious economic response to a different set of circumstances. In the Ibo hinterland of the delta, where, although political authority was diffuse, economic life seems to have been well developed, it may well have been that there was already an unusual growth of population in relation to the productivity of the land, so that men of enterprise may have concluded that it was becoming more profitable to export labour for sale than to employ it at home.

But the balance should not be struck exclusively in economic terms (even if it may be suggested that at the time the economic arguments were becoming increasingly important in the minds of the ruling segments in West African societies). There is not space here to enter into a discussion of the host of moral and social issues involved in the slave trade, but there is one politico-social point that should be briefly touched upon. It has been seen that European slave-traders like Dalzel justified their activities on the ground that they were rescuing Africans from oppression and exploitation by their own rulers, and that likewise the abolitionists argued that their campaigning was needed to redeem African society from the degradations brought by the slave trade. It is therefore worth asking whether the ever-increasing American demand for slaves from West Africa from the middle of the seventeenth to the beginning of the nineteenth century led to increased slave-raiding and to more wars being fought for the expressed purpose of securing slaves, and so to a growing political instability which was destructive of economic and social progress.

This is a very large question, and one to which there may well be no single answer applicable to all parts of West Africa and to all kinds of West African societies. It might, however, be argued – as, for example, Professor Flint has argued (13) – that the stereotyping of such polities as the emirates of Nupe and Ilorin as 'slave-raiding' was part of the apologetics by which the European colonisers justified their conquests. For one area, and for one type of West African society, namely the kingdoms of Lower Guinea, there is, however, some interesting evidence on record. Both King Kpengla of Dahomey (1774-89) and King Osei Bonsu of Ashanti (*ca.* 1801-24) were specifically asked by European visitors whether they engaged in warfare with the express purpose of capturing slaves for trade (14, 15). Both are reported as saying that they did not, that their wars were fought for political reasons, to protect, maintain or promote the power and prestige of their nations relative to their neighbours.

If it is argued that their replies may not have been properly reported by their inquisitors, who may well have had their own motives for distorting them, then attention should be drawn to the strong similarities between their reported arguments, and to the fact that their reporters had opposing biases, Absom and Dalzel (in the case of Kpengla) being partisans of the slave trade, and Dupuis (in the case of

Osei Bonsu) being an opponent of it. In these circumstances, Kpengla's and Osei Bonsu's statements have the ring of truth: their own opinion was that their wars were not fought to secure slaves for sale to the Atlantic slave-traders. But the existence of the Atlantic trade did give such kings a new choice: whether it was more profitable for them to sell their war captives abroad, or to keep them at home, employed as soldiers, or as labourers on their and their generals' estates or on their trading enterprises, or, perhaps, whether they might best be used for the traditional sacrifices to their and the nation's ancestors (sacrifices whose scale may have been growing as the scale of royal and national power was itself growing). A similar choice was also intruding into more domestic spheres, whether criminal and civil malefactors should be punished by such traditional penalties as fines or execution, or whether they might best be dealt with by selling them to the Atlantic traders – in effect, by deportation. Here analogies from seventeenth and eighteenth century English history might suggest that the latter remedy was on the increase (but this might be thought a social good rather than an evil).

On the whole it is probably true to say that the operation of the slave trade may have tended to integrate, strengthen and develop unitary, territorial and political authority, but to weaken or destroy more segmentary societies. Whether this was good or evil may be a nice point; historically it may be seen as purposive and perhaps as more or less inevitable.

One may perhaps conclude with the reflection that, in the context of the times in West Africa, by stopping the slave trade and by attacking slavery, Europeans did much to improverish and weaken its monarchies. This was so because, on the African side, the slave trade was conducted on a large scale by a relatively small number of major entrepreneurs under state patronage or, indeed, direction. Thus, when the export slave trade was ended, the African monarchies lost a major source of revenue and a large part of the economic structure which supported them. This might not have been the case had the slaves available been put to plantation production for export – an expedient which certainly seems to have been considered, for example by King Gezo of Dahomey in the 1850s (16). But in practice the so-called 'legitimate' trades which replaced the slave trade as the staple of West African foreign commerce tended to be based rather on production by large numbers of small-scale 'peasant' farmers. The major kingdoms found difficulty in adapting their fiscal, economic and political systems so as to profit from this change in the economic structure. For this reason, as the nineteenth century progressed, they seem to have become at once less efficient in securing revenue from, and less able to provide the order needed by, their peoples' producers and traders.[5]

The steps taken by Europeans against the slave trade and slavery therefore hastened the day when, in their own economic interest, they thought it necessary first to conquer the West African kingdoms, and then to continue the process, initiated by African kings and entrepreneurs, of conquering the segmentary societies and absorbing them into unitary political structures.

NOTES

1. Barbot in 1682 also reported that the Dutch sometimes *sold* slaves on the Gaboon (Churchill's *Voyages*, V, p. 390).
2. To Professor Ryder, the Benin refusal to supply male slaves to the Portuguese seems to be associated with the Portuguese refusal to sell firearms to the pagan Benin kingdom. But this does not seem to invalidate the argument about the economic, and therefore (in a state-directed economy) the political, appreciation of the value of slaves. By the later seventeenth century, with the growing and competitive European arms trade, Benin's rulers must have concluded that the acquisition of firearms was more vital to the strength and wealth of the kingdom than the conservation of its manpower.
3. A. Adu Boahen estimates the volume for the first half of the nineteenth century at about 10,000 slaves a year: *Britain, the Sahara and the Western Sudan, 1788-1861*, (1967), 127.
4. As was pointed out to me by my colleagues Mr D. Rimmer and Dr A. G. Hopkins.
5. The only place in which this argument seems to have been developed is, with reference to Yombaland, in an article by Hopkins, A. G., 'Economic imperialism in West Africa: Lagos, 1886-92', *Econ. Hist. Rev.* XXI, No. 3 (1968), 587-92.

REFERENCES

(1) Norris, Robert, *Memoirs of the Reign of Bossa Ahadee, King of Dahomy* (1789), and Dalzel, Archibald, *A History of Dahomy* (1793), 2nd ed. with a new introduction by Frank Cass, London, 1967.
(2) Rattray, R. S., *Ashanti Law and Constitution* (1929), ch. 5.
(3) Dalzel, *History of Dahomy*, 124.
(4) Mauny, Raymond, *Tableau géographique de l'ouest africain* (1961), 336-43, 377-9, 422-4.
(5) Law, R. C. C., 'The Garamantes and trans-Saharan enterprise in classical times', *J. Afr. Hist.* VIII, No. 2 (1967), 196.
(6) Rodney, Walter, 'African slavery and other forms of social oppression on the Upper Guinea Coast in the context of the Atlantic slave-trade', *J. Afr. Hist.* VII, No. 3 (1966), 431-43.
(7) Pereira, D. Pacheco, *Esmeraldo de Situ Orbis,* ed. Mauny Raymond (1956), 134.

(8)   Ryder, A. F. C., 'The Benin missions', *J. Hist. Soc. Nigeria*, II, No. 2 (1961), p. 237 and 'Dutch trade on the Nigerian coast during the seventeenth century', *J.H.S.N.*, III, No. 2 (1965), p. 203.

(9)   *The Dimensions of the Atlantic Slave Trade* (Madison, Wisconsin, 1969).

(10) Mauny, R., *Tableau géographique*, p. 379.

(11) Monteil, Charles, 'Les empires du Mali', *Bull. Com. et Sc. de l'A.O.F.* XII (1929), p. 312 (p. 22 in the separate 1968 reprint).

(12) Akinjogbin, I. A., *Dahomey and its Neighbours*, 1708-1818 (1967), pp. 73-80, 90-5.

(13) Flint, John E., *Sir George Goldie and the Making of Nigeria* (1960), 246.

(14) Dalzel, *History of Dahomy*, 217-21.

(15) Dupuis, Joseph, *Journal of a Residence in Ashantee* (1824), 2nd ed., with a new introduction and notes by Ward, W. E. F., Frank Cass, London, 1966, 163-4.

(16) Ross, D. A., 'The autonomous kingdom of Dahomey, 1818-94' (unpublished London Ph. D. thesis, 1967), Chapter 2.

17

EARLY TRADE AND RAW MATERIALS IN SOUTH CENTRAL AFRICA*

Brian M. Fagan

Some years ago Professor Vansina (1: pp. 375-90) published a lucid analysis of long-distance trade in Africa in which he argued that the regional trading net-works already in existence in the far interior played a critical part in the later development of the ivory and slave trade. Ultimately, however, the expansion of trade in later centuries has its roots in the early development of inter-village traffic in raw materials during the first millennium A.D. The archaeological evidence for early trade in Central and South Central Africa is both limited and unsatisfactory; this paper is an attempt to place the evidence into a theoretical context.[1]

The fundamental economic changes which took place at the beginning of the African Iron Age led to major alterations in population distribution, settlement patterns, trading practices, and social organisation over much of the subcontinent. Nowhere were these more dramatic than in South Central Africa, where the transition from food gathering to food production coincided with the introduction by metallurgy into the region.

Later Stone Age hunter/gatherers lived in small camps of several families, exploiting the natural environment within a comparatively small distance of their home bases (2). The critical factor in hunter/ gatherer subsistence is the distribution of water relative to game and vegetable resources, so that the amount of territory covered by one camp varies from area to area. The degree of contact, and hence presumably of trading and social intercourse, varies with the density of population relative to natural resources, as well as with the range of each camp's food gathering activities. Among some !Kung bands today, the amount of visiting and trading contact between camps varies with the availability of food.

*Reprinted by permission of Cambridge University Press from the *Journal of African History*, Vol. X, No. 1, 1969.

Most hunter/gatherer groups in Southern Africa before the period of Bantu and European contact were largely self-sufficient in raw materials. Although cases are known of trade in such commodities as ochre and some other raw materials, most of life's requirements were obtained from local sources, and the amount of regional trade was much smaller than it is under similar conditions today (3). Rock paintings depict a wide range of economic activities, while abundant evidence from archaeological sites indicates that the camp of Later Stone Age times was very self-contained (4), (5). Wood and bone were combined with stone to furnish the essentials of material culture, while water could be carried in antelope-stomach bags and other such containers, made from materials readily available to the hunter.

With the new food-producing economies, however, trade became far more important, for many requirements of a more complex economy and material culture had to be met from other sources than those available locally. While such items as skins, grains, hut poles, and other commodities were frequently a significant part of inter-village trade (6), three basic raw materials were of vital importance to the Iron Age farmer. Iron, copper and salt were responsible above all for the development of complex inter-regional bartering networks which were based on a comparatively steady, but informally structured, demand for raw materials.

Iron

Iron ore and iron implements were essential to the functioning of an Iron Age, agricultural economy. Cultivation on any scale required hoes and axes; these were made from iron ore obtained from ferricrete layers, bog iron deposits, and sometimes mines (7). Supplies of iron ore are comparatively plentiful in many areas, but not in others, where there is limited archaeological evidence for the importation of the raw material. The Machili site, in Southern Zambia, dated to A.D. 96 $\pm$ 212 (C-829), yielded a few lumps of a foreign substance identified tentatively as ferricrete (8: pp. 354-71). The site lies in a sandy area, and the ferricrete was imported by man, presumably for iron smelting. In later centuries there are numerous historical records for the trading of iron tools from areas where the people were skilful metallurgists.[2]

During the Early Iron Age, iron tools were confined to small, functional artifacts such as arrowheads, spearheads, razors, and occasional axes and hoes (9: pp. 199-210). Such artifacts are fairly common in the deposits of the Kalomo mounds, as are iron rings and strip bangles (10: pp. 88-91). Unfortunately, preservation conditions at early sites preclude the discovery of many iron artifacts, but a few iron tools of similar types to those found with Kalomo-type occupation are known from the Dambwa site, dating to the eighth century, and also from the lower levels of the Gundu mound near Batoka, dating to the fifth century, as well as from sites in Central Zambia (11: pp. 34, 12: pp. 191-121).

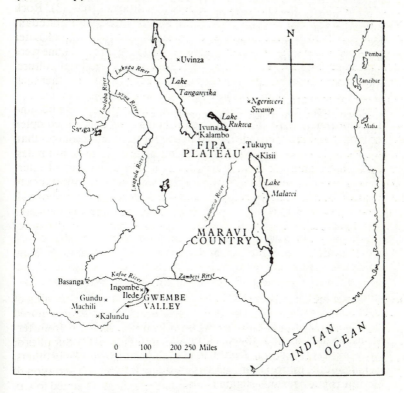

Fig. I. Iron Age sites in South Central Africa mentioned in the text.

The simple iron artifacts made during the Early Iron Age did not require extensive metallurgical activity, resulting in a small demand for ore compared with that in latter centuries, when ironworking was both widespread and an important attribute of political and commercial power. But the existence of trade in iron ore and finished artifacts was probably a factor in the development of a standardised but simple metallurgy over much of South Central Africa during the earlier Iron Age, although the limited range of technological skills available to the metalworkers also affected their products.

By the fourteenth century, the inhabitants of Ingombe Ilede in the Zambezi valley were in possession of iron tools of ceremonial type which were far more elaborate than the artifacts of the Early Iron Age farmer. Single bells, long-bladed hoes and wire-drawing tools were deposited in graves at the site (13). The hoes were unworn, whereas those found in the deposits of the village itself had been heavily utilised. Iron slag is rare at Ingombe Ilede; even in recent times, metallurgy was rarely practised in this area. One has the impression that the inhabitants of this site were manufacturing their own domestic artifacts, most of which were of similar design to Early Iron Age tools. Their ceremonial implements are more elaborate, and were almost certainly obtained by trade. It is as if the iron trade received a new dimension in later centuries with additional traffic in more elaborate artifacts which were passed to groups with lesser metallurgical skills, while domestic tools were made in most areas for local consumption. But many more discoveries will have to be made before this tentative hypothesis can be supported by firm evidence.

Salt

Salt was an important commodity for Iron Age peoples, and was widely traded during the first and second millennia. Deposits from which cake salt of comparatively good quality can be extracted are rare, and were the object of considerable trading activity in Iron Age times. Although salty water was sometimes obtained by boiling certain river grasses or reeds (14), much of the salt came from such localities as Uvinza (15 and Ivuna in Tanzania (16), the Kiburi and Mwashya pans in the Katanga (1: p. 386), and the extensive Basanga salt workings in Central Zambia.[3] The archaeological record so far includes little information on salt trading, for few of the known localities have been investigated.

The Ivuna salt pans, nine miles south-east of Lake Rukwa, were studied in a campaign of excavations in 1966 (16). A long sequence of Iron Age pottery associated with salt-making activity was recovered from dumps round the pans, and has been radiocarbon-dated to the period A.D. 1215 ± 110 to 1420 ± 110 (17: p. 520). Some of the salt-workers lived in villages built on dumps overlooking the salt lake; they cultivated sorghum, kept cattle and small stock, and buried their dead near the huts which were uncovered in the occupation levels in the dumps.

Broken pots, and much salt-flecked earth associated with them, are grounds for assuming that salt-working and, presumably, trade in cake salt were important activities. The pottery from the later levels of the dumps comes from several different cultural traditions, which may tentatively be assigned to one or other of the various tribal groups living in the area today.[4] Such a mingling of pottery types may imply that different peoples have collected salt from the pans at various times, or that the control of the trade changed hands from time to time. Alternatively, the archaeological record may reflect both cultural diversity in the Ivuna region and also regular visits by peoples from outside the immediate area who sought salt. Pots were an essential part of the salt-making process used at Ivuna until recent times, and may be taken as an accurate yardstick of the salt trade. When more is known of the archaeology of Southern Tanzania it may prove possible to plot the distribution of Ivuna pot types over a wide area, for Ivuna salt is traded as far east as Tukuyu at the present time, and the nearest alternative source of cake salt is about 150 miles away.[5] Sophisticated methods of trace element analysis are now being applied to pot clays and other materials (18), they are to be applied to the Kissi pot trade in Northern Malawi,[6] where pottery is traded over large areas from a single manufacturing source on the eastern shore of the lake. Once the association of salt-making and a particular type of pot is established,[7] such analyses might prove informative when applied to wares found at or near localities such as Ivuna.

Cake salt is produced by a process of boiling and evaporation, and is readily handled in containers of standard size, thereby providing a stable commodity of exchange (as does the copper ingot). Such a standardised unit of exchange would have been a basis for regional trade centred on Ivuna, the salt being handled from village to village by barter of other materials, such as iron tools from the Fipa plateau and also grain. While much of the trade may have proceeded on the basis of inter-village barter, other people may have travelled to the pans to collect salt themselves, a process that was certainly in progress at Ivuna in the nineteenth century[8] and also elsewhere – for example in Katanga and Malawi (14a). The result of the Ivuna trade in an essential commodity was a degree of direct and indirect contact between peoples living up to 150 miles away or more from each other, and also the creation of a network of regional trade.

Although the earlier levels at Ivuna contain a different type of pottery,[9] there is no reason to believe that the methods of salt-working changed in later centuries. We may expect to uncover evidence of Early Iron Age salt-working from other localities where the stratigraphy is more complete. But Ivuna is an indication of the type of evidence which the archaeologist may expect to find in future investigations of earlier sites.

Copper

Copper is another raw material which was highly prized during the Iron Age, especially for ornamentation and also as a trade commodity. The evidence for copper trade as opposed to that in salt is easier to reconstruct from the archaeological record as the results are more tangible, in the form of artifacts or by-products of metallurgical activity.

Early Iron Age sites in South Central Africa contain few copper fragments. An occasional ring or fragment of strip bangle is found in the deposits of early settlements, such as Dambwa, where the few copper ornaments can only have been imported from outcrops at least 200 miles away (13). By the seventh century the inhabitants of the Kalomo mounds possessed copper strip bangles, such ornaments occurring slightly earlier than the wire type with a fibre core, which was established by the eleventh century (17: p. 123). The quantity of copper is small enough at all the sites to indicate that the material had an ornamental significance, but that, as far as can be established from present evidence, copper had not acquired the great commercial significance which is associated with it in the later centuries of the Iron Age.

The early history of the African copper trade is still almost unknown, although important series of copper artifacts have been excavated at Sanga in Katanga, and at Ingombe Ilede in southern Zambia. Sanga has been radiocarbon-dated to the late seventh to ninth century (15), while the graves at Ingombe Ilede have been provisionally assigned to the fourteenth century (16).

Our knowledge of the owners of the Sanga cemetery near Lake Kisale is confined to a description of the contents of fifty-six graves, most of them containing more or less complete pots, together with a range of iron tools and copper ornaments and ingots, including some remarkable necklaces, and a very small number of glass beads and East Coast sea-shells (17). Jacques Nenquin has divided the burials into three distinct groups, whose stratigraphical relationships are somewhat problematical. The major group, the Kisalian, is represented by twenty-seven graves, and is dated to the seventh to ninth centuries. Copper ingots were found in only two graves of these people, although they are characteristic of the site as a whole; certain composite copper chains also belong to this culture.

Nenquin's second group, the Mulongo, is known from six graves, whose stratigraphical relationship to the Kisalian graves is not exactly established, although the distinctive Mulongo pottery shares some features both with the first group and with the Red Slip ware graves, which are demonstrably later than the Kisalian. Copper croisettes were found in all the Mulongo graves, but they were even more common in the Red Slip graves, over 360 ingots being found in the four graves of the group which have been excavated.

Although the stratigraphical and chronological relationships of the three Sanga pottery groups are still imperfectly known, the increase in copper ingots within three groups of graves is striking, and may perhaps indicate an increasing importance at the end of the first millennium for copper as a trade metal as opposed to an ornamental one.

Most of the copper objects from the Sanga necropolis are ornamental in concept, consisting of bangles, elaborate wire chains of sophisticated design, and also a number of minor artifacts such as needles. Copper croisettes are found in two forms – the so-called Handa type (18), and also a diminutive form, most of which were found in the later graves. Nenquin records that one group of Handas was tied together with strings (17: p. 194); they are of a type widely known from South Central Africa.

Sanga lies in the middle of an area where copper outcrops are abundant, as well as salt deposits. The archaeology of this mineral-rich region is almost unknown, but it is vital to our understanding of the Iron Age of South Central Africa. The site provides abundant evidence for sophisticated methods of copperworking in the Katanga area by the eighth century, reflected both in the ornaments of the inhabitants and in the large number of ingots found in later graves at Sanga.

A dual attitude to copper as a metal seems to be characteristic of the peoples of Sanga. On the one hand it has an important ornamental role, as evidenced by elaborate chains and bangles. On the other, standardised ingots are common possessions. Such objects have no ornamental significance, but may be interpreted as symbols of wealth and possibly as a form of rudimentary standardised currency, or units of exchange. The implications of this dual attitude are far-reaching; the scope of the copper trade is widened, and formalised by the use of standard units of exchange, whereas in earlier centuries, and away from the main centres of commerce, the traditional and informal methods of barter in essential commodities still continue, for the volume of trade in raw materials is insufficient to require any more regular form of exchange unit.

According to Vansina (19: p. 35), Sanga may have been involved in direct long-distance trade, but the archaeological evidence does not yet support this tempting hypothesis, for imports from coastal regions are rare, confined to a few East Coast sea-shells and glass beads, and may merely reflect the final process of long distance hand-to-hand trade as opposed to formal caravans. But the greater use of copper ingots may well indicate an increasing concern with larger-scale trade and the development of long-distance trade routes.

Somewhat later evidence of copper trade comes from Ingombe Ilede in the Middle Zambezi valley, far away from mineral outcrops. Several of the central burials, from fourteenth century horizons, were deposited with copper cruciform ingots of a type found from Rhodesia in the south to as far north as Katanga (18). Three skeletons were buried with complete sets of wire-drawing equipment, closely similar in form to Venda specimens described by Stayt many years ago (20). A typical outfit consists of a series of hammerheads, tongs, spikes, and the wire-drawing plates themselves. Lengths of rectangular cross-section trade wire were found at the heads of three burials, and had been bent around sticks to form standardised lengths of wire, presumably for trade purposes. One burial also contained a bundle of finer wire which had obviously been drawn from the trade lengths on the site, and was presumably made for eventual conversion into ornaments. The gauge of the finer wire is similar to that used to make the bangles which were fabricated by winding copper wire round a fibre core from the *Raphi* palm.[10] Numerous copper bangles, beads, needles, a razor, and fragments of wire complete the inventory of artifacts in this metal.

Ingombe Ilede lies in a flood-plain area where outcrops of copper are unknown; all supplies of the metal had to be imported. The artifacts suggest that the ornamental role of copper was very important, to the extent that the principal inhabitants were importing both ingots and trade wire, and then converting the latter into bangles for their own use. Whether or not they were re-exporting the finished bangles it is impossible to establish; but, with an important salt-trade outlet in the area (13), conditions would have been favourable for the handling of finished ornaments for local markets, as well as the standardised ingots favoured in the Zambezi trade.

The strictly commercial importance of copper is clearly seen at Ingombe Ilede. The cruciform ingots have remarkably similar weights; the trade wire is bent in standardised lengths, which obviously had an established value in long-distance trade circles. This is in contrast to the strictly ornamental functions of the metal, which were of regional and local concern to Iron Age traders. Perhaps we may glimpse in the Ingombe Ilede site the overlapping of two distinct trading patterns, the one based on local demands for salt, copper ornaments, and other prosaic commodities; the other on an increasing volume of long-distance traffic in ivory, copper, and other raw materials, a trade which may have depended on its standardisation of commercial units, and perhaps even on a form of rudimentary 'currency' in the form of copper bars, etc., to function effectively.

Such distinctions are hard to draw from the archaeological record, but the archaeologist will be able to learn much by carefully controlled studies of the distribution of ingots and other artifacts commonly handled in the more important centres of commercial activity such as Sanga and Ingombe Ilede. We may hope one day to learn more of the extent of the more sophisticated trade systems which flourished with the aid of a series of 'monetary units' which may have served as a means of storing wealth and also as a medium of exchange.

Long-Distance Trade

Although South Central Africa was basically self-sufficient in minerals and other essential raw materials during the first millennium, the tenuous trading patterns of the far interior absorbed a certain number of exotic commodities, such as glass beads and sea-shells, which may reflect a different type of trade.

The evidence for contact between the East Coast of Africa and the South Central African interior during the Early Iron Age is confined to a few finds of exotic imports in the deposits of early farming villages in Southern Zambia (21) and some isolated specimens from Malawi (22). The earliest dated imports yet recorded from Zambia are East Coast species of cowrie shell (*Cypraea annulus L.*) found in the lowest levels of two Early Iron Age mounds on the Batoka plateau in an area with no mineral outcrops or special economic importance. A shell found at the base of that Kalundu mound is dated to A.D. 455 ± 95 (GX-1114) (23). The associated occupation levels belong to the earliest Iron Age cultural tradition in Zambia.

Our limited archaeological finds of glass beads and sea-shells do not indicate a formalised trade in such commodities during the Early Iron Age. The copper and iron objects which survive in the archaeological record from this earliest period are functional or decorative in nature, and do not reflect any overriding concern with standard-sized ingots or exotic objects as a primary motive for trade. Copper ornaments are rare, and may indicate that Early Iron Age trade was essentially informal and concerned almost wholly with local raw materials. This is in contrast to the picture in later centuries, when copper at least appears to have had a comparatively formal role in long-distance trade.

Unquestionably imports were reaching the far interior via the Zambezi valley from the early centuries of the Iron Age, for it is most likely that the imports on the remote Batoka plateau arrived there from the Middle Zambezi area. The discoveries at Ingombe Ilede have, however, filled in many gaps in our knowledge of long distance and local trade at an early stage in its development. The site lies some 32 miles downstream of the Kariba Dam, on the floodplain of the Zambezi, in an area formerly rich in ivory and salt but not in minerals. Ingombe Ilede (13) was inhabited by Iron Age peoples who practised a mixed farming economy based on the cultivation of cereals (including sorghum), kept cattle, goats, chickens, and dogs, and also depended to a considerable extent on hunting and food gathering to supplement their diet. The so-called gold burials from the centre of the site, already mentioned, were associated with large numbers of imported objects.

The foreign imports from the central burials include sea-shells and glass beads – commodities known to have been widely handled during the Iron Age.[11] Three species of sea-shell were found with the skeletons and give an idea of the range handled in the trade. Two burials were associated with *conus* shells; all of them were cut off at the base, leaving only the basal disk for trading, the common form in which this species was handled. There is abundant evidence that *conus* shells were widely traded in the Iron Age (24). Cowrie shells were also common finds at Ingombe Ilede, being associated with several of the less-important burials. All the cowries had been split down the back, before being worn in the hair or on clothing. A third sea-shell species (*polynices mammilla*) was represented by a single group of shells deposited with a burial at the southern borders of the settlement. This East Coast species is known to have been traded during the Iron Age, although it was not as popular as the cowrie or *conus*.

Glass beads are the most commonly found import at Ingombe Ilede, as well as in many sites in the interior. An extensive literature, principally concerned with their use as dating evidence, has grown up in recent years (25), from which it seems that their principal value is as indicators of the extent of trading networks rather than for dating purposes. The Ingombe Ilede beads were found in long strings around the necks or waists of the central burials. Most of the cane beads were Indian reds, opaque dark blues, turquoise, and yellow forms. Less frequently found are wound green beads, a string of 'melon' specimens, three carnelians, and a series of flat green and white beads, which are similar in form to the freshwater shell types also found at the site. The trade in glass beads at this time seems to have been based on a comparatively limited number of shapes and colours, which had a very wide chronological range during the Iron Age. Only rarely does one find a large collection of glass beads outside important commercial settlements such as Zimbabwe and Mapungubwe. Beads were traded into the interior in large strings. Once imported, they were used for the adornment of important individuals, and disseminated in small numbers into regional trading networks.

The primary preoccupation of the coastal trade was with the export of raw materials, including gold, ivory, copper, and iron. Gold was mined even in the early centuries of the Iron Age (26), but the range of objects made from this metal was limited, being confined to beads of various shapes, metal sheet, and wire bangles. A gold sheet backing-plate, a considerable number of beads, and some bracelets were found at Ingombe Ilede. There were no signs of gold slag or of other by-products of goldworking, such as were found at Mapungubwe, for example (27). Frey (28) had demonstrated that the Ingombe Ilede beads were made with the same techniques as those used to manu-facture Rhodesian gold ornaments. Since there are no gold outcrops near Ingombe Ilede, all the metal must have been traded, perhaps either in the form of dust in porcupine quills or as finished objects(29). We cannot, of course, estimate how much gold passed through the hands of the chieftains of Ingombe Ilede, but they seem to have retained a proportion of the metal for their own adornment. Gold was apparently never an important metal for domestic use, for it is normally only found in contexts where long-distance trade was im-portant, and may, like copper, have been a monetary unit of fixed value.

We have argued elsewhere that ivory was the staple of the East Coast trade (21: p. 91), but its importance in the archaeological record has been underrated because it is rarely found or described by excavators. At Ingombe Ilede, ivory fragments are scattered throughout the deposits and elephants are abundant in the region; it appears likely that the inhabitants of the settlement recognised the economic value of elephant tusks. Fragments of ivory are sometimes found in Batoka plateau villages, but whether these were collected for local ornamentation or for trade we cannot tell.

Three out of the four raw materials found at Ingombe Ilede were imported by the inhabitants from outside the Gwembe valley. Gold, copper and ivory were attractive commodities to those who wished to exploit the trading networks of the Zambezi and receive exotic objects from downstream. Minerals were obtained from the plateau country on either side of the river, a commerical process in which the Lusitu salt deposits probably had a role. Livingstone (30) speaks of wide-spread salt trade in this area in the mid-nineteenth century, the flourishing regional trading networks of the last century resulting in constant interaction between the plateaux and the Gwembe. At the time when Ingombe Ilede was occupied, similar trade, also based on local demands for raw materials, carried minerals to the Zambezi trade-routes and resulted in the dissemination of exotic objects far into the interior.

The staples of the coastal trade are well defined in both archaeo-logical and documentary records. Undoubtedly, a great deal of the commerce was conducted initially by bartering, a process of trade which led to more formalised trade routes in later centuries, reflected in the ready Portuguese annexation of well-trodden roads to the goldfields and ivory grounds of the interior (31), and the increasing number of ingots and other artifacts of possible monetary sig-nificance in the archaeological record.   Ingombe Ilede demonstrates the critical importance of regional trade-routes in the development of Iron Age trade. The inevitable demands of metallurgist and farmer led to continued if irregular contact between communities living up to several hundred miles apart, which developed into complicated barter networks extending over enormous areas. Political and social considerations, as well as economic factors, prompted the evolution of many complex commercial relationships. The successive masters of the East Coast trade used local trading networks as a starting-point for their trade, stimulating demands for raw materials. The result was economic and political change, and the development of sophisticated centres of metallurgical and commercial activity in the far interior, reflected in such finds as Sanga and Ingombe Ilede.

In Early Iron Age sites and in settlements far away from the outcrops of copper and gold, we find scattered foreign imports in early middens, which are the earliest signs of one of the dominant historical processes of the last 2,000 years. The diffusion of more advanced metallurgical techniques and artifacts, more sophisticated agricultural methods, and the establishment of important chieftain-ships, could not have taken place without the greater mobility of products and people caused by the informal trading networks between countless Iron Age villages through South Central Africa. But the character of this type of trade in local materials is quite different to that of the long-distance commerce in raw materials and exotic luxuries which developed around such centres as Sanga or Ingombe Ilede. One of the big questions for future research is to plot and assess the influence and impact of the sophisticated commercial centres, whose locations were determined by many different factors, such as proximity to outcrops or to well-established trade-routes. How much interaction did they achieve with their less fortunate and humble neighbours with their less-advanced technologies, and agricultural methods? How much of a distinction can be drawn between the two types of commerce? Trading activities are as impor-tant an agent of social and political change as population movements and the sword, a point which the archaeologist and historian some-times tend to forget.

NOTES

1. This article has benefited from presentations and discussions at the 'East Africa and the Orient' conference held in Nairobi in March 1967, and at a seminar on Iron Age Africa held at the State University of New York, Binghamton, in April 1968. I am grateful to the Ford Foundation, the University of Illinois, Urbana, and the State University of New York, Binghamton, for financial support to attend these meetings. Dr. Bernard Riley kindly drew Fig. 1.

2. David Livingstone records trade between the Toka and Kololo in iron hoes, which were also given as a tribute.

3. The Bassanga salt-workings were described by the Rev. Arthur Baldwin in his diaries, and were examined briefly by the writer, Mr. T. N. Huffman and Mr. Robin Fielder in 1967.

4. A number of different groups live in the area, including the Namwanga, Siceela, Wanda, and others, whose pottery styles are distinctive enough for us to be able to distinguish them the one from another (B.M. Fagan and J. E. Tellen, 'The potmakers of Ivuna', in preparation).

5. Ngeriweri Swamp, Saja (Mr. H. Sassoon, personal communication). .

6. Professor J. Desmond Clark, personal communication.

7. Illustrations published by Gray, (14a), show pots in use for salt-making in Malawi of a very similar form to those commonly found at Ivuna (our classes I and II).

8. Mrs. Beverley Brock, personal communication.

9. The earlier Ivuna wares have no connection with either modern vessels or the Early Iron Age channel decorated pottery tradition found at Kalambo Falls.

10. Identification by Kew Botanical Gardens, London.

11. A few fragments of imported cotton cloth were found with one of the burials; the remaining fabric is thought to be of local manufacture, (13).

REFERENCES

(1)   Vansina, J., 'Long distance trade routes in Central Africa', *J. Afr. Hist.* III (1962).

(2)   Lee, R. B., 'The subsistence ecology of the !Kung Bushmen', Unpublished Ph.D. thesis, University of California, Berkeley (1965).

(3a) Clark, J. Desmond, *The Prehistory of Southern Africa* (London, 1959), 219,

(3b) Lee, R. B., personal communication.

(4)   Gabel, Creighton, *Stone Age Hunters of the Kafue* (Boston, 1965).

(5)   Fagan B. M., and Van Noten, F., *The Hunters of Gwisho* (Tervuren Musée de l'Afrique centrale, 1971).

(6)   Miracle, M. P. 'Plateau Tonga entrepreneurs in historical inter-regional trade', *Rhod-Liv. J.* XXVI (1959), pp. 34-50.

(7)   Schwellnous, C. M., 'Short notes on the Palabora smelting ovens', *S. Afr. J. Sci.* XXXIII (1937), pp. 904-12.

(8)   Clark, J. Desmond, and Fagan, B. M., 'Charcoals, sands, and channel-decorated pottery from Northern Rhodesia', *Amer. Anthrop.* LXVII (1965).

(9)   Fagan, B. M., 'Pre-European ironworking in Central Africa, with special reference to Northern Rhodesia', *J. Afr. Hist.* II (1961).

(10) Fagan, B. M., *Iron Age Cultures in Zambia*, (London, Chatto & Windus, 1967).

(11) Fagan, B. M., and Huffman, T. N., 'Excavations at Gundu and Ndonde, near Batoka', *Archaeologia Zambiana*, III (1967).

(12) Phillipson, D. W., 'The Early Iron Age in Zambia: regional variants and some tentative conclusions', *J. Afr. Hist.* IX (1968), 2.

(13) Fagan, B. M., and Phillipson, D. W., and Daniels, S. G. H., *Iron Age Cultures in Zambia*, II (in the press).

(14a)   Gray, Ernest, 'Notes on the salt-making industry of the Nyanja people near Lake Shirwa', *S. Afr. J. Sci.* XLI (1945), pp.459.

(14b)   Brock, Mrs. Beverley, personal communication.

(15)   Cameron, V., *Across Africa* (New York, 1877), p. 228.

(16)   Fagan, B. M., and Yellen, J. E., 'Ivuna: ancient salt-working in Southern Tanzania', *Azania*, III (1968, pp. 1-43).

(17)   Fagan, B. M., 'Radiocarbon dates for sub-Saharan Africa V', *J. Afr. Hist.* VIII (1967).

(18)   Perlman, L., and Asaro, F., 'Deduction of provenience of pottery from trace element analysis', *University of California Reprint*, No. UCLR-17937 (1967).

(19)   Nenquin, J., 'Two radiocarbon dates for the Kisalian', *Antiquity*, XXV (1960), pp. 140,132.

(20)   Fagan, B. M., 'The Iron Age peoples of Zambia and Malawi', in Bishop, W. W., and Clark, J. Desmond, *Background to African Evolution* (Chicago, 1967), pp. 659-86.

(21)   Nenquin, J., *Excavations at Sanga, 1957* (Tervuren, 1963).

(22)   Walton, James, 'Some features of the Monomotapa culture', *Proc. Third Pan-African Congress on Prehistory* (1955), pp. 336-56 (Livingstone, 1957).

(23)   Vansina, J., *Kingdoms of the Savannah* (Madison, 1966).

(24)   Stayt, H., *The BaVenda* (Oxford, 1931).

(25)   Fagan, B. M., *Southern Africa during the Iron Age* (London, 1966), 93.

(26)   Robinson, K. R., 'A preliminary report on the recent archaeology of Ngonde, Northern Malawi', *J. Afr. Hist.* VII (1965), pp. 169-88.

(27)   Fagan, B. M., 'Radiocarbon dates for sub-Saharan Africa, VI'. *J. Afr. Hist.* X. I, (1969), p. 162.

(28)   Harding, Joan R., 'Conus shell ornaments (*Vibangwa*) in Africa', *J. R. Anthrop. Inst.* XCI (1961), 91, pp. 52-66.

(29)   Schofield, J. F., 'Southern African beads and their relation to the beads of Inyanga', in Summers, R., *Inyanga* (Cambridge, 1958), pp. 180-229.

(30)   Summers, Roger, 'Iron Age industries of Southern Africa, with notes on their chronology, terminology, and economic status', in Bishop, W. W., and Clark, J. D. (eds.), *Background to African Evolution* (Chicago, 1967), pp. 687-700.

(31)   Fouché, L., *Mapungubwe* (Cambridge, 1937).

(32)   Frey, E., 'Goldworking at Ingombe Ilede', in (13).

(33)   Theal, G. M., *Records of South Eastern Africa*, IV (London, 1898), p. 43.

(34)   Livingstone, C. and D., *Narrative of an Expedition to the Zambezi and Its Tributaries* (London, 1865), p.225.

(35)   Axelson, Eric, *Portuguese in South-East Africa, 1600-1700* (Johannesburg, 1960).

18

THE EAST AFRICAN COAST

An Historical and Archaeological Review*

J. E. G. Sutton

Pre-Islamic Times

Some writers have speculated on the doings of Egyptians, Phoenicians, Assyrians and Israelites of Solomon's day on the East African
coast in the two thousand years before Christ. It is true that Ancient
Egypt and other countries of the Near East did trade with regions
bordering the Gulf of Aden (known to the Egyptians as Punt), and
from there as well as from the Persian Gulf they had contact with
various lands bordering the Indian Ocean. But as far as Africa south
of the Horn is concerned, one can only say that no evidence of contact
has come to light, and that the subject does not merit discussion.

Our first knowledge of the coast south of Cape Guardafui belongs
to the period of the Roman Empire and the commerce that it
stimulated far beyond its borders. At some time in the first three
centuries A.D. a Greek-Egyptian sailor compiled a handbook for
navigating the Indian Ocean. This text, known as the *Periplus of the
Erythraean Sea,* is mainly concerned with the ports of the Red Sea and
the Gulf of Aden and the voyage thence to India, relying on the
monsoon winds. The African coast round the Horn is, by contrast,
briefly treated: known as Azania, it is presented as a backwater of
which the writer probably had no personal experience. However the
Periplus, supplemented a century or two later by a few pages in
Ptolemy's *Geography,* tells of a number of harbours as far south as
Rhapta. The site of Rhapta, generally thought to be somewhere on
the Tanzania coast, remains unidentified. The trade was monopolised by Arabs from Mouza at the southern end of the Red Sea.
But the ivory, rhino-horn, tortoise-shell and coconut-oil that were

*Abridged by the editors by permission of the author, from *The East African Coast: an
historical and archaeological review* (Historical Association of Tanzania, Paper 1),
1966: Nairobi, East African Publishing House.

exported from East Africa are goods that may have been in greater demand in India and eastern countries – at least, so one would conclude from the analogy of later times. Neither gold nor slaves are mentioned at this period, though from the Horn, slaves were being exported to Egypt. Some of these could perhaps have been re-exports originating from further south.

While the *Periplus* implies that there was some regularity in the trade, Rhapta and the other places mentioned on the Azanian coast do not seem to have been highly developed centres: maybe they only functioned as seasonal harbours and markets. The local people are reported as placing little utilitarian value on the objects of glass and iron and other goods that they obtained in exchange from the Arabs. Such a picture is supported by the lack of archaeological relics of this period (in marked contrast to southern India where the account of the *Periplus* is supplemented by finds of Roman coins and pottery). It is true that Persian, Egyptian and Roman coins dating from the third century B.C. to the sixth century A.D. have been picked up or reported from several sites in southern Somalia and the coast and islands of Tanzania. But these should not be considered reliable evidence, for the circumstances of their discovery are most unsatisfactorily recorded (1), and it is strange that no more have come to light with the more intensive archaeological research of recent years.

The Indonesian Problem

Eastern connections with pre-Islamic East Africa are not merely indicated by the presumed destination of the ivory and other exports. It is well known that various cultural items and food-crops that are widespread in Africa originated in south-eastern Asia, and, of these coconuts and sewn boats are noted in the *Periplus*. It is not necessary to assume an actual migration to have brought them to Africa: they may have been passed on from place to place around the shores of the Ocean. Nevertheless, one is tempted to link these distant influences with the population of Madagascar, of which a considerable proportion can be shown on physical and linguistic grounds to be of Indonesian descent. Little is known of how this migration took place – whether directly along the south equatorial current, or, more likely, by stages via southern India or Ceylon and other coasts. Nor is it clear whether it was a single migration or a series of movements covering many centuries. Its date is generally reckoned to have been in the early centuries A.D., very likely later than the time of the *Periplus*. But it is possible that Indonesian pioneers or merchants were earlier reaching the Azanian coast, which (depending on how one prefers to interpret the *Periplus* and Ptolemy) could have extended as far south as Madagascar and the Mozambique Channel. This is arguable, but much later, in the tenth and following centuries, Arab geographers refer or seem to refer to contacts between the Indonesian islands and eastern or south-eastern Africa. Moreover, Maldive Islanders, themselves considerably influenced by Indonesians, were visiting East Africa still later, and it is probably they who are remembered as Wadiba in certain places.

This discussion of Indonesian influences remains unsatisfactory. But it may be in this wider Indian Ocean context that we should seek evidence of continuity in the trade and activity of the East African coast between pre-Islamic and Islamic times. There are indications of an eastern slave-trade that might support such a view, for slaves transported via Java and referred to by names resembling Zanj occur in Chinese documents of the early seventh century and onwards, while the ivory that al-Masudi reports being shipped to China and India in the early tenth century recalls the trade of the *Periplus'* time. It was during the eighth and succeeding centuries that the Hindu kingdom of Sri Vijaya centred on Sumatra became the dominant mercantile power in the Indian Ocean. But by the twelfth or thirteenth century, if not before, Indonesian seafaring in the western part of the Ocean seems to have been eclipsed by that of Arabs and Indians.

Early Islamic Period

Whether or not there was continuity in the East African trade, it is clear that when in the ninth and tenth centuries Arab writers began to show an interest in Zanj, the main direction and control of its trade shifted from south-western Arabia to Oman and the Persian Gulf. It has been suggested that this change in direction since the time of the *Periplus* was due to Persians, whose ascendancy in the middle centuries of the first millennium helped to bridge the gap between the Roman and Arab empires. But evidence of direct Persian effects on East Africa remains thin, in spite of arguments that have been advanced. Of more immediate importance was the attraction of the great city of Baghdad, the capital of the Caliphate, which was approached through the Persian Gulf, as well as the mingling with the eastern trade-routes in the ports of the Gulf. In the early tenth century al-Masudi recorded the export of gold from the Sofala coast. It was very likely the demands of Baghdad, of a short-lived mint at Oman, and of the Muslim world in general that had stimulated the opening-up of the Rhodesian gold-fields, at a time when the Asian gold-routes were closed. African leopard-skins, moreover, were being prized as saddles in Muslim countries, while the timber of the East

African coast and islands was another attraction to the merchant seamen of the treeless Arabian shore. But the other East African products that al-Masudi witnessed were mostly being shipped via Oman to India and China – ambergris, tortoise-shell, and especially ivory. In the Gulf too the African slave-trade may go back to pre-Islamic times. Zanj slaves, besides figuring in the *Thousand and one nights,* were required to work the saltpetre at Basra. They are best known for the famous revolt of the late ninth century, but there had been another revolt two centuries earlier. It is thought that many of these slaves were from East Africa.

The Height of the Coastal Civilisation, c.1200-1500

It was in the three centuries between the 'Shirazi colonisation' and the coming of the Portuguese – that is the thirteenth, fourteenth and fifteenth – that the Islamic civilisation of the East African coast enjoyed its greatest days. To these centuries belong most of the mosques and tombs, houses and palaces that dot the coastline in more or less ruined state; the coinages of the sultans of Kilwa, Zanzibar and Mogadishu; as well as much of the Islamic and Chinese pottery whose broken pieces litter several of the beaches. Each settlement and state had its ups and downs, but a general level of prosperity was maintained along the coast. While most of the sorghum, millet, bananas, rice and other everyday needs were doubtless locally produced or bought from neighbouring tribes, the wealth and indeed the whole existence of the coastal settlements depended on trade. Ivory, ambergris and slaves (for use by the wealthy townspeople as well as for export) might be obtained along most of the coastline or its immediate hinterland, and Portuguese in the sixteenth century again record ivory, as well as honey and wax, being brought from the mainland to Mombasa and Kilwa. But more important, especially for Kilwa and others of the more southerly towns, were the gold and copper of Rhodesia and probably Katanga which were carried by head or by canoe down the Zambezi to the Sofala coast and thence shipped northwards. The rise of Kilwa at the expense of Mogadishu in the thirteenth century is said to have been through her capture of the Sofala gold trade. There may be a direct connection here with the motives behind the presumed 'Shirazi' migration to Kilwa from the Banadir, perhaps from Mogadishu itself. Essentially it was a luxury trade to satisfy demands in Arabia and other lands bordering the Indian Ocean and beyond. One might note, however, a record of rice from Kilwa being imported at Aden (2).

We know very little about the organisation and ports of the Sofala coast. From Portuguese records it is clear that in the fifteenth century numbers of coastal or Arab traders had established posts at Sena and elsewhere up the Zambezi, were visiting parts of the kingdom of Monomutapa, and had vague reports of the famous stone buildings at Zimbabwe.[1] But the mines and most of the interior handling remained under local control, and proved a mainstay of the power of Monomutapa and the other kingdoms of the interior of southern Africa. There may have been more direct overland routes from the Zambezi to Kilwa, but such a journey is not recorded till 1616 when the Portuguese Gaspar Bocarro and his porters had reasons for approaching the coast that way. Northwards from Kilwa penetration of the interior appears to have been very shallow, and in Kenya would have been impeded by the dry *nyika* country. However, Kirkman has drawn attention to a passage in the mid-sixteenth century writer de Barros recording the memory of a single negro caravan that a century or so earlier descended the Sabaki river to exchange gold and ivory for cloth at Malindi. Ivory alone would sound more likely, for the Sabaki is well off the known gold routes, but it is not impossible that a caravan from Ethiopia had been intercepted or deflected. For, further north again, on the Banadir coast, trade routes did descend from Ethiopia through the fertile Juba and Shebelle valleys, especially at times when unrest between Christians and Muslims in the Ethiopian interior disturbed the routes to the ports of the Red Sea and the Gulf of Aden. It was probably such memories that later aroused Portuguese hopes of approaching Ethiopia from the Malindi coast: this was never realised.

Visitors and outsiders were more interested in the exports of East Africa than the imports. Nevertheless, some information on the latter can be gleaned from the Arab and the early Portuguese documents, and, as far as imperishable goods are concerned, from archaeology. A certain amount of grain was imported at places, but better attested are household utensils and standard trade-goods. By the fifteenth century the amount of Chinese porcelain in use had considerably increased at the expense of Islamic wares. There is, of course, no suggestion of direct trade between East Africa and China.[2] The porcelain was shipped by stages round the Indian Ocean, much of the distance in Indian bottoms, notably from Cambay (the region of Gujerat). Also from India came several of the types of glass beads that were used for exchange. They were also made locally at Kilwa and Mogadishu. Cowrie-shells, another form of currency collected on the East African coast and other shores of the Ocean, were also used, but they appear to have had wider circulation in the interior of Africa than on the East Coast. Cloth was the most important trade-good. It was from various lands as well as manufactured along the coast. Mogadishu cloth was particularly famous and prized in Egypt in the fourteenth century. The first sultan of Kilwa is said to have bought the island for coloured cloth, and thus earned the nick-name 'Nguo nyingi'. Silk was also imported and worn by the well-to-do. Foreign coins would not have circulated far, but there were the cheap copper coinages minted at times by three of the East African sultanates. Moreover, the products of the African hinterland and the Zambezi region – gold, copper and ivory – had always an exchange value besides an ornamental or utilitarian one.

While the trade with the East maintained a steady flow, and while that with Cambay in particular was increasing until the Portuguese intervention, contacts between East Africa and the Persian Gulf apparently decreased (at least relatively) in the thirteenth and subsequent centuries. With the decline of Baghdad and the increasing importance of Cairo and the demands of Europe beyond, there was a shift of emphasis in the Arabian trade back towards the Gulf of Aden and the Red Sea.

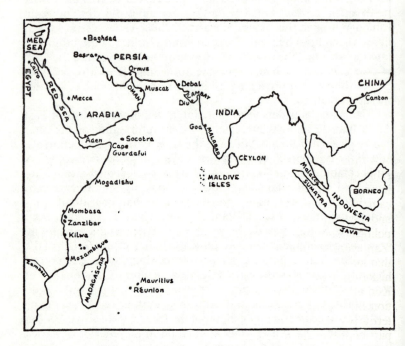

1. The Indian Ocean, showing places mentioned

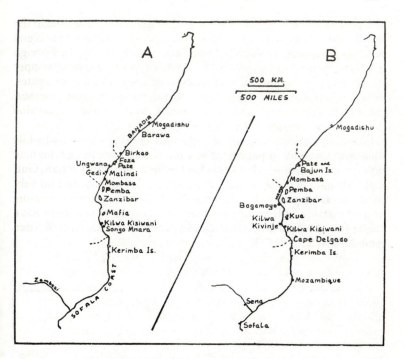

2. The East African coast, showing the main sites
A–to the sixteenth century
B–seventeenth to nineteenth centuries

Although the East African coastal settlements had commercial, religious and cultural connections with overseas territories, they were in no way politically subject to foreign powers until the Portuguese came. Moreover, the degree of religious and cultural uniformity up and down the coast should not be taken to imply that there was any political unity. As Freeman-Grenville adequately points out, the 'Zanj empire' that figures in certain books is quite mythical. It is true that many of the smaller settlements (from what we know of their histories) were tributary to larger ones, and that islands like the Kerimbas, rich in coir for ship-building, were an object of competition and exploitation. The fair town of Gedi was probably part of the territory of Malindi, while Kilwa and Mafia were long together. For part of the thirteenth century the latter was apparently the more important, and even the seat of the sultan. Kilwa, in the late thirteenth and early fourteenth centuries at least, had control over the Sofala trade. Her influence spread further afield, and ibn Battuta found her the principal town of the coast; yet de Barros' statement that she became mistress of the whole coast from Mombasa to Sofala is doubtless coloured by the bias of his indirect informants. In the mid and late fourteenth century Kilwa lost her pre-eminence. Wealth decreased, and the mint ceased operation. At some time the great mosque collapsed. One wonders whether the ostentatious living that the Abu'l-Mawahib dynasty brought to Kilwa about 1300 had not exhausted her resources. Ibn Battuta implies this when he contrasts the virtuous and generous sultan at the time of his visit (1331) with his mean successor, who (so the story went) could only complain, 'He who gave is dead and has left nothing behind to be given.' The early abandonment of the great palace of Husuni Kubwa may be a further indication of impoverishment following on extravagance. It has been argued that this decline in Kilwa's power and wealth coincided with a rise in that of Pate, whose chronicle claims the conquest of all the coast from Mogadishu to the Kerimbas in the late fourteenth century. This is unlikely: the Pate Chronicle as related by Bwana Kitini is highly suspect, and parts of it are patently wrong. At all events, whether Pate partly filled the vacuum or not, there was a revival at Kilwa in the fifteenth century. The extension to the great mosque was rebuilt about 1420-40 under a sultan remembered as 'the New Rain'. But political instability and many short reigns ensued, from which de Barros and Freeman-Grenville tell a sad tale of decline in the half-century before the arrival of the Portuguese. Yet the town itself, judging from the excavations and Portuguese accounts, may have been as wealthy and well-built as ever before. More remarkable in the fifteenth century was the rapid rise of Mombasa, which the Portuguese found bigger and more formidable than Kilwa. Further north, Mogadishu was an ancient settlement and always important, and the one town that the Portuguese found too powerful to overrun.

East Africa and the Portuguese, 1498-1698

The East African coast did not suffer an organised conquest, but a series of unpredictable visitations, all the way from the Zambezi mouth to the Banadir. A Portuguese fleet, small squadron, individual ship or free-lance adventurer would call at a convenient harbour demanding submission and tribute to the Portuguese crown. In the case of refusal or hesitation the threatened force might be used with devastating effect. Besides the storming and looting of Kilwa in 1505 and the more terrible sackings of Mombasa in 1505 and 1528, several smaller towns were destroyed or suffered tip-and-run raids or acts of piracy. But the prosperity of the coast was not immediately shattered; instead it slowly declined throughout the sixteenth century. Mombasa weathered its storms and continued to defy the Portuguese, and at several towns there is evidence of activity and prosperity during the early years of the Portuguese ascendancy. The low ebb was not reached till the end of the sixteenth century. It has been asserted that decline had already set in before the Portuguese arrived, but this is not substantiated (as explained above). In the late sixteenth century and after there were indeed other adverse factors besides the Portuguese presence; the wandering Galla and Segeju were menacing the northern towns, while the Zimba horde wrought havoc at Kilwa in 1587 and elsewhere. Santos' account of the atrocities of the Zimba may be exaggerated, but they were certainly a direct scourge as they worked northwards from the Zambezi to Malindi where the Segeju finally withstood them. There is some doubt as to whether the town of Kilwa was inhabited at all for some years after this.

There were other more fundamental causes for the impoverishment of coastal towns. Their failure to recover their former lustre after the impact of the Portuguese and these other calamities was due not merely to the suppression of much of their trade, but particularly to the loss of that which originated in the Zambezi region, especially the gold, now being shipped direct overseas from the Sofala and Mozambique coast. This was most keenly felt by Kilwa, which apparently declined more rapidly than most of her former rivals. But the African coast as a whole found itself increasingly a backwater on account of the changed directions of Indian Ocean and world trade (and nothing could illustrate better the extent to which the earlier coastal prosperity had been parasitic – that is, dependent on the production and demands of other parts of Africa and the world). To the Portuguese the reports of gold, silver and other metals in the kingdom of Monomutapa and adjacent regions were the principal attraction of the western shores of the Indian Ocean. They therefore established small stations both north and south of the Zambezi mouth, and in 1505 a fort was erected at Sofala (the name now adopted by a specific settlement a little way south of the Zambezi estuary). In time Mozambique island became much more important as a town of some size and the main port of call between Portugal and India. In 1558 a fort was begun there, though lack of energy and resources caused delay in its completion and neglect in its subsequent maintenance in the seventeenth century. The Captain of Mozambique was the highest-ranking Portuguese official in East Africa, and to him was generally granted the monopoly of the commerce of the interior. Not content with gradual exclusion of the Swahili and Arabs and with taking over the stations up the Zambezi, the Portuguese wanted to reach and work the mines themselves. These attempts to dispense with the middlemen in the metal trade did not have the desired results, but provoked the suspicion and opposition of the rulers and peoples of the interior. Relations, fortunes and the volume of trade fluctuated rapidly, but in general the Portuguese managed by fire-arms and alliances to maintain their trading-stations and defended posts on the rivers, and in the mid and late seventeenth century Monomutapa became little more than a Portuguese puppet. Certain Portuguese estate-owners prospered as virtually autonomous rulers, but plans that were periodically devised in Mozambique, Goa or Lisbon for systematic exploitation of the Zambezi region came to little. In fact, throughout the sixteenth and seventeenth centuries the Portuguese were constantly disappointed in their high hopes of obtaining great riches from this region, while from the close of the seventeenth century their influence was considerably reduced. The costs of maintaining Mozambique and the minor stations on the coast, as well as the incompetence and dishonesty of the successive captains and other officials, left little profit if not an actual loss for Goa and Portugal. There was little attempt to penetrate the northern part of the Mozambique interior or to exploit the coast itself, save for the Kerimba isles that supplied Mozambique fort and town.

All trade on the sea was to be conducted by licence from the Portuguese captains of Mozambique or Malindi (removed to Mombasa in 1593) and to pay customs dues at these places. At certain periods minor customs houses were established at Pate and elsewhere. Owing partly to inefficient or corrupt administration, trading-permits were not easily obtained by the coastal ship-owners, and evasion was often worth the risk. Muslim shipping between the Swahili coast, the Gulf of Aden and the Red Sea, as well as Cambay, though clearly much reduced especially in the years following the foundation of Fort Jesus, was never effectively suppressed by the Portuguese. Exemptions could sometimes be purchased. Excepting the absence of metals, the range of products and trade-goods was little different from that of earlier periods. Chinese porcelain, among other items, continued to reach Africa, while a notable product of this and later times was copal, used locally for caulking ships as well as overseas for the extraction of varnish. Moreover, certain southern Arabian families saw sufficient inducement to follow in the wake of their predecessors who had migrated to East Africa in its more prosperous days. The continued independence of Mogadishu, though it shared itself in the general economic decline, probably helped to maintain and encourage these links.

East Africa and the Rise of Oman, 1650-1840

Late in the sixteenth century Dutch and English ships began to invade the Indian Ocean, and early in the seventeenth the Dutch wrested the bulk of the eastern spice-trade, and established a much more effective monopoly than the Portuguese had before them. But the latter, though increasingly harassed and impoverished, remained the leading power in the western half of the Ocean. In 1650, however, Muscat was captured by the Omani Arabs, who thereupon challenged Portuguese supremacy in the north-western section. Very soon they were making common cause with the malcontents on the Swahili coast and despatching fleets to encourage revolt. Pate became the centre of opposition to the Portuguese, and in the last quarter of the seventeenth century was virtually lost. The Portuguese at Mombasa and Goa were too weak or otherwise committed to make speedy or effective reprisals, and when they managed to exert themselves even the sternest measures had no permanent effect. The oft-told fall of Fort Jesus in 1698 after a three-year-siege and defence, in which each side excelled itself in incompetence and irresolution, was merely the culmination of this gradual loss of grip.

The expulsion of the Portuguese from the Tanzania and Kenya coasts did not and could not entail a return to the trade patterns of the fifteenth century, but it did allow the East African ports to trade more freely with the Arabian shores and north-western India. The principal exports were ivory and slaves. Ivory, as well as gums and vegetable oils, was now finding a readier market in Europe, while slaves were in increasing demand in Omani and other Muslim lands. European dealers were also becoming interested. The effects of the slave-trade were not everywhere destructive or depopulating; nor were the caravan-routes dominated by the Swahili and Arabs till the middle of the nineteenth century. For perhaps as much as a hundred years before that, up-country traders, among whom Nyamwezi, Kamba and Yao figured prominently, journeyed to the coast with products from near and far. As a result various trade-goods – cloth, wire, iron-ware, copper, beads, cowries and in time fire-arms – began to penetrate the interior. From Mombasa and the several harbours of the Mrima coast the highland regions of Kenya and northern Tanzania were reached, while Pate and the Bajun islands thrived on the trade of the Tana valley. The routes through Unyamwezi went much deeper, round the lakes as far as Buganda in one direction and Katanga and its copper in another. Those from Kilwa extended to Lake Nyasa and beyond in the late eighteenth century. Caravans on southern routes went mainly in quest of ivory; it was the southerly routes that became notorious for slaves. The early history of these interior links and trade is poorly known; it is noteworthy, however, that in the eighteenth or even the seventeenth century some new coastal settlements were established or old ones taken over by families descending from the hinterland – a process that culminated in the mid-nineteenth century when Kim-weri of Usambara incorporated within his kingdom a stretch of the Mrima coast.

From the beginning of the nineteenth century Zanzibar was the main slave and ivory mart of East Africa, drawing particularly on the Nyamwezi routes through central Tanzania. Hence the rise of Bagamoyo and certain lesser towns as termini opposite Zanzibar. The trade of the Nyasa region began to abandon the old town and harbour of Kilwa Kisiwani, so admirably situated for the coastal trade of earlier times, and by mid-century her royal family had ceased to command any power or respect. The newer site of Kilwa Kivinje, on the mainland a few miles to the north, proved more convenient for the caravans. Slaves were shipped thence to Zanzibar and Mombasa. On the northern coast Mombasa remained the principal of several competing harbours. It is interesting to note that with the new commerce and communications of the twentieth century it is the old port of Mombasa that has retained its dominant position, whilst Bagamoyo and Kilwa Kivinje have become increasingly redundant – Bagamoyo particularly, now a sleepy town surviving as a monument to the height of the slave and ivory-trade and of the Zanzibari sultanate in the middle of the nineteenth century.

The increasing commercial attraction of East Africa moved the rulers of Oman to press their claims and assert their control over the coast. Kilwa and Zanzibar were brought to closer submission in the 1780s, and the duties paid on slaves, ivory and other goods proved highly profitable. Seyyid Said in the middle years of his long reign (1804-56) went further. After a series of expeditions, the Mazrui, who had for long been independent in Mombasa, were overthrown, and in 1840 Said made Zanzibar his residence. The coast was brought more nearly than ever before under a unified government. The political and economic life of East Africa was centred on Zanzibar and her 'merchant-prince', who enriched himself on the monopolies he reserved. Said's rule did not extend inland – despite what he and his successors tried to maintain before foreigners – but the commercial influence of Zanzibar was felt along the caravan routes.

Said's position was made tenable by external political and economic forces. First, the financing of the slave-trade and the connected shipping from Zanzibar was largely in the hands of Indians, many of whom began settling on Zanzibar and the coast. They claimed British protection, imported British goods, and paid a heavy tax to the Sultan. Further, European nations and even more American cotton-cloth manufacturers were finding an attractive market in East Africa by shipping the exchange-goods required by the caravans. But it was chiefly the British and their navy, attempting to use Seyyid Said as an

ally against the French and in their effort to suppress the slave trade –
vital though it was to his power and his subjects' wealth – who
projected him into the East African scene. This widening of European
interest – commercial, political and humanitarian – was the background for the opening of the later history of East Africa, both coast
and interior.

NOTES

1. There can be no suggestion that the buildings at Zimbabwe and other Rhode-
    sian sites are of Arab design or workmanship. They are of a style that evolved
    locally in Rhodesia, bearing no relationship to the Islamic architecture of the
    East Coast. This subject is best treated in (3) and (4).
2. The two Chinese expeditions that visited Somalia and perhaps Kenya in the
    early fifteenth century were not typical and probably unparalleled. See (5) or
    (6).

REFERENCES

(1)   Freeman-Grenville in *Journal of African History*, I, 1960. pp.32-4.
(2)   Serjeant, R. B., *The Portuguese off the South Arabian Coast*, p.10.
(3)   Summers, R., *Zimbabwe*, London (1963).
(4)   Fagan, B. M., *Southern Africa in the Iron Age*, London (1966).
(5)   Duyvendak, J. J. L., *China's Discovery of Africa*, London (1949).
(6)   Wheatley, *Geographers and the tropics*, (Steel and Prothero, eds., London,
      1964).

19

THE EAST AFRICAN SLAVE TRADE*

Edward A. Alpers

Historiographical Introduction

The East African slave trade has attracted much less attention from
both professional historians and popular writers than has its West
African counterpart. The reasons for this are not difficult to find.
Most of the people who have written about the slave trade have been
European, or American, or Afro-American, people whose relevant
historical traditions link them intimately and overwhelmingly with
West Africa. West Africa was the great reservoir for the Atlantic slave
trade; East Africa entered that story only as a single, final chapter.
Where the Atlantic Ocean provided the world setting for the West
African slave trade, the Indian Ocean was the stage for the East
African slave trade. Consequently, relatively few Western writers
have been concerned with the latter, as it only marginally forms part
of their heritage. Even more regrettable is the fact that the major work
which has been done to date on the East African slave trade is not at all
satisfactory.

Sir Reginald Coupland was a British imperial historian writing in
the 1930s. His pioneering studies, *East Africa and its Invaders* (Oxford: Clarendon Press, 1938, reprinted 1961), and *The Exploitation of
East Africa, 1856-1890* (London: Faber and Faber, 1939), are mas-
sively detailed histories of the East African coast and the western
Indian Ocean, but his interpretation of the genesis and nature of the
East African slave trade clearly reveals his bias and does not stand up
under close examination. Coupland argued that the slave trade in
East Africa began with the very first contacts with Asia, and that it was
from then on a theme which ran 'like a scarlet thread through all the
subsequent history of East Africa until our own day'. To the slave

*Reprinted by permission of the author from *The East African Slave Trade* (Historical
Association of Tanzania, Paper 3), 1967: Nairobi, East African Publishing House.

trade he attributed the small population of East Africa. He also subscribed to the view that long before there was a demand for slaves at the coast, slavery was a common institution among all Africans; that 'for ages past' the Arabs had struck far inland in order to trade with the Africans; and that almost all Africans made 'docile and dutiful' slaves and were characterised by their 'mute submission to their fate'. His final conclusion was that although the annual volume of the East African slave trade never rivalled the numbers involved during the heyday of the West African traffic, its operation over 'at least two thousand years' suggests that the total number of slaves exported over this period 'must have been prodigious', with the implication that it at least equalled the total for West Africa.

No historian of Africa will dispute the assertion that slaves have been exported from East Africa for as long as Coupland has stated. But just as we draw a distinction between the incidental trade in slaves which trickled across the Sahara from West to North Africa as long ago as the days of the Roman Empire, on the one hand, and the phenomenon which we call the West African slave trade, on the other, so we must draw a similar distinction for East Africa. Indeed, both Dr. G. S. P. Freeman-Grenville and Miss Alison Smith do so in their chapters (5 and 7) in the Oxford *History of East Africa* (Oxford: Clarendon Press, Vol. I, 1963, ed. Roland Oliver and Gervase Mathew). But these first steps towards the revision of Coupland's interpretation, which reads uncomfortably like a lame apologia for European exploitation of Africans in the Atlantic slave trade, have not received much attention outside of scholarly circles. Since it was first published in 1957, Zoe Marsh and G. W. Kingsnorth's *An Introduction to the History of East Africa* (Cambridge University Press), which is still the standard school textbook in East Africa, has doggedly repeated Coupland's colonial point of view through two new editions. Our task here is to destroy the myth of this erroneous interpretation and to present a more balanced, realistic picture of the East African slave trade.

The Rise and Decline of the Slave Trade: External Factors

It is very clear that the East African slave trade as a factor of continuing historical significance traces its roots back no further than the first half of the eighteenth century. Coupland's argument that it was of continuing importance from the earliest contacts with Asia simply cannot be substantiated. The slave trade as a factor in the modern history of East Africa does not trace its roots back thousands of years. The African slave revolts in ninth century Iraq, as well as in fifteenth century Bengal, which Coupland embraced as proof of his point, need to be considered more critically than he did. In fact, all the sources on which we rely for these accounts of slaves from East Africa need to be re-examined in the light of modern scholarship. For example, little is known of the precise origins of these slaves. There is certainly no evidence at all that East Africa was being depopulated by slaving during the centuries of this earlier trade. For the low population density of East Africa we must look instead to its frequently harsh ecology, to its great stretches of dry, highland plains which are unsuitable for large, settled agricultural communities. On the contrary, the greatest slaving province of East Africa — the Lake Malawi region — has long been one of the most densely populated areas of East Africa. In this respect the common myth of depopulation is no more valid for East Africa than it is for most of West Africa. The case of Angola stands out as the exception, rather than the rule. And Coupland's citation of the great revolts of African slaves in Asia, not to mention the great slave rising on Zanzibar in the late 1830s, is evidence that his low regard for their bravery and love of freedom is a flagrant distortion of the truth.

Further evidence that the slave trade was by no means prominent in East Africa before the eighteenth century comes from the Portuguese. Surely the Portuguese, as the pioneers of the Atlantic slave trade, would have tried to exploit the slave trade in East Africa had they found it to be already flourishing. But the early Portuguese chroniclers only mention the slave trade in passing. Much more important were the gold and ivory trades to Arabia and India. It is to these products that the Portuguese invaders turned their attention throughout the sixteenth and seventeenth centuries, not only along the coasts of Kenya and Tanzania, but also in Mozambique and Zimbabwe. Even wax and ambergris seem to have been more important than slaves during most of this period. For unlike the colonialists in the Americas, the Portuguese never developed any sort of plantation economy in India. The Portuguese slave trade from Mozambique to India rarely reached as many as one thousand individuals in any one year, and was usually less than half that number. That to Brazil was illegal until 1645 and was never seriously pursued until the beginning of the nineteenth century. As late as 1753, when the foundations of the new slave trade in East Africa were being laid, there was a grand total of only 4,399 African slaves in the whole of Portuguese India.

What were these foundations? Despite the long Arab contact with East Africa, and their notorious domination of the export trade in the nineteenth century, the Arab slave trade formed only one pillar upon which the degrading business was built. The other was the establishment of a typical colonial plantation economy, utterly dependent on slave labour, on the French island colonies of Mauritius and Réunion, in the middle of the Indian Ocean. This revolutionary development dates from 1735, when Bertrand François Mahé de la Bourdonnais became Governor-General of the Mascarene Islands, as they were known together. During the previous decade there had been isolated slave trading expeditions from the islands to Mozambique, which was by then the only Portuguese stronghold in East Africa, Mombasa having been finally lost in 1729. Madagascar, which had earlier been the only source of the few slaves then on the islands, was no longer considered to be a safe place for the French to trade because of the hostility of the chiefs with whom they had been doing business. So when La Bourdonnais began casting around for a source of slave labour to work on his newly planted sugar and coffee plantations, he turned to the nearest European colonial power which was in a position to help him. His choice was also influenced by the fact that he was an old friend of the incoming Governor of Mozambique, Nicolau Tolentino de Almeida, as corrupt an individual as ever graced the administration of the Portuguese colonial empire. Together they inaugurated the cruel, systematic exploitation of the people of Mozambique by selling them into slavery halfway across the Indian Ocean.

At first, the demands made for slaves by the French at Mozambique were very small. In the first five years of La Bourdonnais' administration of the Mascarene Islands only 1,000 to 2,000 were sold to them by the Portuguese. The whole business dragged to a virtual halt at Mozambique during the 1740s and 1750s because the Portuguese officials of the period were fairly attentive to the royal laws against allowing foreign powers to trade there. During these years, however, the French responded by shifting their attention to Ibo, the principal port of the Kerimba Islands, which lay just south of Cape Delgado and well outside any effective Portuguese administration. The French slave trade to the Mascarene Islands really got under way during the 1770s, when the new Governor-General did everything he could to encourage the slave trade with the French. According to official figures, more than 1,000 slaves were being exported each year. French smuggling, to avoid the taxes which were levied at Mozambique, probably raised the annual figure to at least 1,500. A similar figure was probably taken away from Ibo during this decade. Henceforth the Portuguese at Mozambique and Ibo (and later at Quelimane, near the mouth of the Zambezi River) were committed to a policy of slaving from which there was no turning back until abolition.

The trade became much brisker in the 'eighties, especially after the conclusion of the American War of Independence. During the 'seventies a few adventurous French slavers had taken cargoes from Mozambique to the West Indies, because they were finding it increasingly unprofitable to seek their chattels along the Guinea coast. Now, in peacetime, with greater competition for slaves in West Africa, the way was opened for a massive expansion of the American slave trade from East Africa. At the same time Portuguese vessels also began to take an active, though still secondary, part in the trade to the Mascarene Islands. Official figures from Mozambique alone show that from 1781 through 1794 a total of 46,461 slaves were embarked on Portuguese and foreign ships, nearly all of which were French. Allowing for a minimal amount of smuggling, at least 4,000 slaves annually must have been leaving the Mozambique area during this period. While the Kerimba Island trade was still important, it seems not to have kept pace with the Mozambique trade. At the end of the century Brazilian slavers began to make their presence felt at Mozambique. The Napoleonic Wars somewhat curtailed the slave trade at Mozambique until after 1810, although one observer estimated that 10,000 slaves were exported from there in that year. Furthermore, during the same era slaves replaced ivory as the single most important export of the Portuguese colony. For the next four decades the Portuguese imperialists, having antagonised legitimate African trade to Mozambique, were economically committed to slave trading in order to maintain the thinnest veneer of an administration in their East African colony.

To the north of Cape Delgado, beyond which the Portuguese no longer commanded any sort of authority, a similar situation was shaping up. After the Omani Arabs had responded to the call of some of the Swahili rulers of the coastal towns and with their help had in 1698 evicted the Portuguese from Mombasa and other outposts, they were themselves too weak to do more than disturb and rob the very people who had sought their aid. The ruling Yorubi dynasty of Oman was divided against itself and a series of civil wars made it impossible for the Omani to devote much attention to their claims in East Africa. But after the Busaidi family overthrew the Yorubi and established their rule in Oman in about 1744, they were able to begin effective economic exploitation of the people of East Africa. Like all previous merchants on the coast they were primarily interested in ivory; but from this point on we can also detect a steady increase in the slave trade.

There are not, however, any accurate statistics on the volume of the Arab slave trade in the eighteenth century. The first indication which exists comes from a French slaver named Jean-Vincent Morice, who traded at both Zanzibar and Kilwa, which was the most important slave port on the coast, in the 1770s. On 14 September 1776 Morice made a treaty with the Sultan of Kilwa for the annual purchase of at least 1,000 slaves. In three trips to Zanzibar and Kilwa before signing this treaty, he had bought 2,325 slaves for export. Morice does not tell us how many slaves the Arabs were taking away from the coast each year, but he clearly considered it to be big business by French standards. It seems reasonable to suggest that at least 2,000 slaves a year were involved in the Arab trade at this time. So although the French did not dominate the slave trade here as they did at Mozambique, they acted as an important stimulus to the demand for slaves at a period when the Arab trade was still outgrowing its infancy. French efforts continued through the 1780s, but by the end of the century these probably had become much less important than the Arab trade. In 1811 the captain of a visiting British ship estimated that at least 6,000 to 10,000 slaves annually passed through the Zanzibar market. Considerably more than half of these would have come from Kilwa.

It is only in the last two decades of the eighteenth century, then, that the East African slave trade began to reach the proportions of the sixteenth century trade in West Africa. By 1810 the total East African trade was barely two-thirds of the average annual number of slaves exported from West Africa throughout the seventeenth century. It was not until after 1810 that the East African slave trade became anywhere near as voracious as the West African trade at its height in the eighteenth and first half of the nineteenth centuries.

Several new factors gave rise to the increased demand for slaves from East Africa during the nineteenth century. In the Portuguese coastal sphere of influence there was a sharp upswing in the slave trade to Brazil. This was caused by the removal of the Portuguese royal family from Lisbon to Brazil during the Napoleonic Wars. Special concessions were granted to the Brazilians and soon a flourishing trade in slaves was being carried on around the Cape of Good Hope at Mozambique. This traffic was further stimulated in the 1820s by British pressure to limit Portuguese and Brazilian slaving to south of the equator. These measures were largely ineffectual until the abolition of the slave trade by the Brazilians themselves in 1850, at which time the trade was quickly choked off. What they did do, however, was to encourage the Brazilians to explore the possibilities of the Mozambique trade. By 1820 at least 10,000 slaves a year were legally embarked at Mozambique for Brazil alone. When we allow for smuggling and the still considerable French slave trade to Réunion (the British had taken possession of Mauritius in 1810), it seems reasonable to suggest that about 15,000 slaves were being carried away from Mozambique each year during the 1820s and 1830s. At the same time there was a great rise in the trade from the Zambezi port of Quelimane, as well as a marked increase of the trade from Ibo. Both of these areas were infamous as slaving ports and frequently are condemned as such in the writings of members of the British naval anti-slave patrol, which was provided for in the Moresby Treaty of 1822 between Great Britain and the Sultan of Oman. Although no accurate figures exist, both areas seem to have been exporting some 10,000 people annually during this period, with Quelimane perhaps providing up to 15,000 individuals in more active years. Ibo particularly was frequented by Arab and Swahili slavers, while the French and Brazilians gathered at Quelimane.

The Brazilian slave trade in East Africa came to a quick halt at mid-century, but the French remained active into the 1860s by resorting to a system of thinly disguised slave exportation which was called 'free labour emigration'. This arrangement had been initiated in 1843 at Kilwa and Zanzibar. In 1854 it was extended to Mozambique by virtue of an agreement with the Portuguese colonialists. Slaves were purchased at the coast by the French and then 'voluntarily' signed up on board ship to emigrate for as many as five years to Réunion, or to the recently acquired colonies of Mayotta, in the Comoro archipelago, or Nossi-Bé, off the north-west coast of Madagascar. This crude sham was only brought to an end in 1864, by which time the French were comfortably assured of a steady supply of cheap labour for their colonies in the only slightly more respectable form of 'coolies' from British India.

But this was not the end of the slave trade from the coast of Mozambique. In the many inlets and harbours away from the few points of Portuguese control, Arabs and Swahili continued to take on cargoes of slaves to be carried across the Mozambique Channel to the Sakalava chiefdoms of north-western Madagascar. In fact, there was an upswing in this trade during the mid-1870s, and it cannot be said to have been abolished until the beginnings of effective colonial rule in both Mozambique and Madagascar, in the 1890s. Eloquent testimony to this little known trade is found in the considerable number of culturally unassimilated Makua people who today live in north-western Madagascar.

Turning northwards again, we see that the great upswing of the slave trade in East Africa ultimately was due to the creation of a plantation economy on Zanzibar and Pemba Islands and to the establishment of an Omani Arab commercial empire in the north-western Indian Ocean. As we have already seen, the latter process as well underway by 1810. But the consolidation and business-like organisation of the commercial dominion, together with the encouragement given to Omani Arab penetration and settlement in East Africa, only came with the reign of Sayyid Said ibn Sultan, who ruled Oman and its possessions from 1806 to his death in 1856. Sayyid Said was a merchant-king, and he soon realised that a great fortune could be made in East Africa. He first came to East Africa in 1828, eager to consolidate his feeble hold on the coast and, in particular, to put down the long-standing challenge to Omani over-rule which was posed by the independent Mazrui leaders of Mombasa. The Mazrui were finally crushed in 1837, and their senior members deported to Oman. Three years later, in 1840, Sayyid Said moved his capital from Muscat to Zanzibar.

Now Zanzibar was more than the commercial centre of East Africa, it was the seat of a powerful Arab state. In his wake Sayyid Said brought many Arab immigrants to Zanzibar, certainly many more than had previously settled there. In no time at all they created a wholly new society, based on a colonial plantation economy in which they were the masters and Africans were the slaves. The staple product of this economy was cloves. Cloves were only introduced in about 1818, probably from the Mascarene Islands, but they were perfectly suited to conditions in Zanzibar and Pemba. Yet their cultivation was limited until Sayyid Said demanded that his Arab subjects grow them more extensively than any other crop. By the end of his reign cloves ranked behind only ivory and slaves in exports. Cloves are not a difficult crop to grow on the islands, but they thrive so successfully that they are harvested twice a year. Similarly, coconut palms, which are valued for their copra, do not require much care after they are planted, but they produce their fruit four times each year. So a lot of labour was required to work the new plantations on Zanzibar and Pemba. As the indigenous population of the two islands avoided working for the Arabs, the latter began to import large numbers of slaves to man their plantations. Throughout the nineteenth century well over half the population of the two islands (which was probably several hundred thousand people) were slaves. And like any slave labour plantation economy there was a constant demand for new hands.

Sayyid Said also spearheaded the Arab invasion of East Africa. Even before his final decision to settle in Zanzibar he had sent a large caravan up-country to Unyamwezi after ivory and slaves. Finally, Sayyid Said encouraged more Asian merchants to settle in East Africa because he wanted to make use of their commercial skills and capital in the expansion of his own enterprises. Asian traders became the economic backbone of the entire Zanzibar system financing virtually all the caravans which left the coast for the interior on credit which they alone could afford to give, and controlling the export-import trade. From this powerful economic base the Omani rulers of Zanzibar were able to exploit East Africa much more effectively than ever before. We have seen how the creation of a plantation economy on the islands was one major factor in increasing the demand for slaves from East Africa. There is no evidence of similar developments in Asia at this time, yet there was clearly a great increase in the number of slaves being exported across the Indian Ocean to the countries bordering on the Persian Gulf and Arabian Sea. It seems reasonable to suggest that this trade was able to grow not because there was an increased demand, but because there was now a more efficiently organised state in East Africa which had an active interest in promoting this trade.

The effects of these two developments were soon reflected in the increasing numbers of slaves who were being brought to the coast for sale. From an estimated 10,000 in 1811, one contemporary observer believed that there was a rise to perhaps 40,000 or 45,000 slaves being sold on the Zanzibar market in 1839. One modern historian has suggested that from 50,000 to 70,000 slaves annually were reaching the coast in the 'sixties. These are only intelligent guesses, because we do not possess official Omani records of the slave trade, but the famous explorer Richard Burton has preserved those from the Custom House of Kilwa Kivinje during the period 1862-1867. These show that a total of 97,203 slaves were exported legally from Kilwa in these years, with a rise from 18,500 in 1862 to about 22,000 in 1866-1867. There can be no doubt that several thousand more were smuggled away from Kilwa to avoid paying taxes to the Sultan's treasury. These unique official figures only too vividly support the estimates which we have already noted.

It should be clear, then, that when the export trade in slaves from East Africa became illegal in 1873, the trade was actually at its height. The Anglo-Zanzibar Treaty of 1873, which was the culmination of a half-century of British diplomatic efforts to stifle the East African slave trade from the sea, completely prohibited the export of slaves from the mainland and called for the immediate closure of all slave-markets in the Sultan's jurisdiction. Britain's motives in spear-heading the campaign to eradicate the East African slave trade were, as in West Africa, mixed. On the one hand, it was a logical extension of the humanitarian effort to combat the Atlantic slave trade. On the other hand, it reflected the increasingly aggressive role of both British capital and British imperialism in the Indian Ocean. As for the Sultan of Zanzibar, Bargash ibn Said, his reasons for agreeing to a treaty which clearly was damaging to his economic interests were that he owed his position to British support and was threatened with a British naval blockade if he did not sign.

Quite naturally, all kinds of attempts to evade the abolition were made by the slave traders. Slaves were driven overland from Kilwa to the coast opposite Zanzibar and smuggled across in canoes and small boats to the islands. In 1876, at British insistence, Sayyid Bargash issued two proclamations which prohibited both this sort of traffic and the bringing of slaves to the coast from the interior. A direct attack on the organisation of the trade at Kilwa Kivinje brought about the collapse of the most important slaving market on the East African coast. By about 1880 the slave trade from the East African dominions of the Sultan of Zanzibar was virtually ended. In almost no time at all the prosperity of these coastal towns was restored by the substitution of legitimate items of trade for slaves. Ivory continued to be an important export and its value actually increased in the late 1870s. But ivory was now surpassed in importance by both cloves and rubber, this last now becoming the most important East African export. A profitable trade also arose in gum-copal and sesamum, two other coastal products which had previously been neglected in favour of the slave trade. So long as the status of slavery itself remained legal, however, there was an incentive to bring slaves to the coast, where they could be bought by wealthy plantation owners. And although slavery was abolished on Zanzibar and Pemba in 1897, it persisted on the coast until 1907 in Kenya and until the beginning of the British mandate in Tanganyika, in 1921.

20

THE EAST AFRICAN IVORY TRADE IN THE NINETEENTH CENTURY*

R. W. Beachey

The East African ivory trade is an ancient one. It is mentioned in the first accounts of geographers and travellers, and they give it more prominence than the slave-trade. It may have been the search for ivory which brought the first ships around Cape Guardafui, and then southwards along the East African coast. By the second century A.D. the coast, as far as 10° S., was 'subject under some ancient right to the sovereignty of the power which held the primacy in Arabia', and Arab merchants were exporting ivory from it in great quantity.[1] Reference to the export of ivory from the East African coast continues throughout the early and later middle ages. Al Masudi, writing in the early tenth century says that elephants were extremely common in the land of Zinj, and that it was from this country that large elephant tusks were obtained: 'Most of the ivory is carried to Oman whence it is sent to India and China'. Marco Polo refers to the East African coast and states: 'They have elephants in plenty and drive a brisk trade in tusks'.[2] During the Portuguese domination of the coast from the sixteenth to the eighteenth century, ivory continued to be an important export; it receives more mention in Portuguese records than does the slave trade. In the sixteenth century 30,000 lb. of ivory passed through the port of Sofala yearly.

East African ivory is soft ivory and is ideal for carving. It was in keen demand in the Orient because of its superior quality and because it was less expensive than that from south-east Asia. But in addition to the markets of the East, East African ivory was much sought after in Europe for the large ivory carving centres which had grown up in southern Germany and in the Low Countries during the Middle Ages, and which supplied large numbers of religious reliquaries and artistic novelties for Christian Europe.

But it was in the nineteenth century that the great development of

*Reprinted by permission of Cambridge University Press from the *Journal of African History*, Vol. VIII, No. 2, 1967.

the East African ivory trade took place. An increased demand for ivory in America and Europe coincided with the opening up of East Africa by Arab traders and European explorers, and this led to the intensive exploitation of the ivory resources of the interior. Throughout the nineteenth century, East Africa ranked as the foremost source of ivory in the world; ivory over-topped all rivals, even slaves, in export value, and it retained this position right up until the end of the century. Until the early nineteenth century, ivory was obtained in sufficient quantity from the coast to meet demand, but, writing in the 1840s, the missionary Krapf observed that, although the elephant was still found in some areas near the coast, ivory caravans were now making regular trips into Usagara, Masailand and the Kikuyu countries. Krapf was surprised to see an elephant tusk from Kikuyuland so large that it required three stalwart Akamba tribesmen to carry it. The ivory trade was lucrative, and the Masai, despite their vaunted aloofness, were eager to share in it, and strove to drive the Waboni tribe from the southern bank of the Sabaki River, so that they could gain access to the port of Malindi with their ivory.[2]

It was the ivory trade which evoked from Krapf the cry: 'How many slaves, how many women, how much palm-wine, how many objects for the gratification of lust and vanity are purchased by the Galla, Wanika, Wakamba and Swahili with the ivory which they bring to the coast.'(3)

The onslaught on the ivory reserves of the East African interior in the nineteenth century took the form of a two-way thrust, that from the north by the Egyptians under Muhammad Ali, which penetrated southwards into the Sudan and Equatoria, and that from the east coast by the Arabs under Sultan Said of Zanzibar, following the transference of the seat of his authority from Muscat to Zanzibar in 1832. Within a decade of Said's move to Zanzibar and the Egyptian advance southwards, the ivory traders were out *en masse*. Khartoum, at the confluence of the White and Blue Nile, became an important centre at about the same time that Tabora, in central Tanganyika, came into prominence as a great meeting place for Arab ivory and slave hunters from the East Coast. Arabs reached Ujiji on Lake Tanganyika about the same time that Gondokoro on the Upper Nile became an outpost for Muhammad Ali's adventurers.

By mid-century there were well-defined caravan routes into the interior. The most northerly, and that still preferred by some missionaries in the latter part of the century, followed the present route of the railway from Tanga to Moshi and Arusha, then swung westward to the Masai country, and from here, after a journey of fifty-five days, Burgenej, near the south-west corner of Lake Victoria, was reached. A southerly route ran from Kilwa on the coast to Lake Nyasa and across to the Arab settlements on the west side of that lake; a variation of this route was by way of the Rovuma River as far as its sources, and from thence across to the lake. But the most frequented route into the interior, and that chosen by Burton, Speke and other European travellers, left the coast at Bagamoyo and, after crossing the dry, barren strip immediately behind the coast known as the 'Nyika', ran through the savannah and scrub bush country of what is now central Tanzania, where water holes were scarce but well known, following approximately the route of the present central railway from Dar es Salaam to Tabora. From Tabora it continued westward to Ujiji on Lake Tanganyika. The total travelling distance by this route from the coast to Ujiji, 'prolonged by the sinuosities of the road', was 955 statute miles; it took Burton and Speke some 7½ months to make the journey: 'Arabs seldom arrive at the Tanganyika Lake under a total of six months . . . those lightly laden may do it in four months.'

The two great inland markets for ivory were Unyanyembe (Tabora) in what is now central Tanzania, and Ujiji on the east coast of Lake Tanganyika.[4] From Tabora routes branched to the north, to Uganda, to the west, and to the south and Lake Rukwa. At Unyanyembe and Ujiji, Arab merchants had set themselves up in style surrounding themselves with the coconut palms of their Zanzibar home, and living in cool *tembes*, waited on by slaves, and comforted by concubines – reproducing the languid environment of the spice island. At Unyanyembe the Arab merchant from Zanzibar met his compatriot returning from the lake or Karagwe, and here much bartering and trade took place. Porters hired on the shores of Lake Tanganyika were paid off, and a fresh gang collected from those discharged by a previous caravan arriving from the coast, which in turn would take on the porters laid off by a down-going caravan.

Ujiji, lying in one of the few inlets on the eastern shore of Lake Tanganyika, was a centre of refreshment and supply: rice, grown in the nearby Luiche swamp, was an important article of food for the Asians who began residing here by the 1860s. Ujiji was a busy market for slaves and ivory. Cameron, arriving here in 1874, speaks of the 'special ornaments' here of 'beautifully white and wonderfully polished hippopotamus ivory'.(4) These ivory carvings at Ujiji were exceptional, for generally speaking there is no tradition of intricate ivory carving in East Africa, no counterpart to the wonderfully carved ivory tusks and masks found in West Africa, despite the fact that East African ivory is much superior to that of West Africa.

By the time Livingstone arrived in 1869, Arabs from Ujiji were trading to the west of Lake Tanganyika. Kasenga, on the west side of Lake Tanganyika, was an Arab trading centre by 1859, and when Livingstone and Cameron arrived a decade or so later, well-known trails already extended north-west to the Manyema country. In this region Livingstone met an Arab trader, Dugumbi, with a prize load of 18,000 lb. of ivory. A pretty woman could be purchased here for 300 cowries and a hundred strings of beads, and she could be traded again for much more in ivory. On the Lualaba, some 200 miles west of Lake Tanganyika, was Nyangwe, the capital of the Manyema country, 'well-chosen by the Zanzibar traders as a permanent settlement'. Some 2,000 people assembled daily at the market here.

As the century went on, caravans travelling into the interior became bigger and bigger, until by 1885 it was not unusual to have over 2,000 porters in a single caravan. The ivory caravans developed a life of their own, and the supply of their needs led to a system somewhat similar to that of ship chandlering. Information as to the condition of routes, the risk of native wars and the best seasons for travel were all available to the enterprising trader.

The assembling of the stock-in-trade in the right proportions and proper assortment, the packing of this into loads of 50 to 60 lb., required care and experience. The trade in beads was perhaps the most complex of the ivory traders' dealings; and for this an expert knowledge of changing fashions was essential. The caprices and vagaries in taste of African women in the interior might jeopardise a trader's profit. Cases are recorded where a trader made the mistake of assuming that because a blue bead sold well one year, it would do so the next, but found to his sorrow that fashion had changed. In 1886-87 Count Teleki discovered that the Dorobo no longer preferred the so-called Masai beads, and that the 45 cwt. of these which he carried were practically useless. Cloth was brought inland by the ivory traders in immense quantity; it was of various kinds: *merikani* (a white inexpensive cotton – first introduced from America in the early nineteenth century); *kaniki*, a blue cotton cloth manufactured in Surat and Gujerat especially for the East African market – some of it was said to be carried by the Portuguese to Brazil; and the more exotic cloths, *bandar assilia*, *barsati*, and the much desired *dobwani* from Muscat. There is a record of one caravan in the 1880s carrying 27,000 yards of *merikani* made up in loads of 30-40 yards each, and, in addition, thousands of yards of other kinds of cloth.

The popular measurement of cloth in East Africa was the 'piece' or *shukkah* which, although varying in breadth, was always four cubits in length. The cubit was supposedly a standard measurement, the length from the elbow to the tip of the outstretched fingers of a full-grown man. However, traders swore that the biggest man in the village, someone with a 'peculiarly long and simian forearm', was summoned when cloth was being measured. A double length of *shukkah* was called a dhoti.

In addition to beads and cloth, a great quantity of copper and brass was carried inland. In the 1870s iron wire became fashionable, especially in the Masai and Kikuyu country. Teleki took 100 loads of iron wire and 15 loads of brass and copper wire on his expedition to Lake Rudolf. Guns and powder were important items of trade. But the Arabs took care that effective arms did not fall into African hands, and usually disposed only of muskets of the flintlock type, surplus arms from the Crimean War, and well-nigh useless. European traders were less careful. Stokes, an ex-missionary turned ivory trader, sold Martini-Henry and Winchester repeaters to the ruler of Buganda at the rate of one firearm for two *frasilah* of ivory (about 75 lb.), and one Snider or four cap-guns for one *frasilah* of ivory. A great quantity of gun-powder passed into the interior, much of it American gun-powder; the first reference to American trade with the East African coast mentions this article. On the coast, gun-powder sold for $5-10 a keg; inland, in Unyamwezi, it was worth six times that amount. The British East Africa Company purchased ivory in Buganda at the rate of 35 lb. of ivory for two kegs of powder. The Berlin Act of 1885, the Brussels Act of 1890, and the Anglo-German agreements of 1886 and 1890, all attempted to deal with the arms and ammunition trade but with small success.

Other trade articles included scissors, looking-glasses, picture books, jointed jumping dolls, rings, daggers, naval and cavalry sabres, and cooking pots. In Buganda there was a special taste for parasols, and Lugard found here a demand for 'white donkeys and opera glasses . . . for which they would pay any price'.(5)

The packing of all this merchandise was an art in itself, and so important that the caravan leader began the task with 'prayers and incense burning'. In packing cloth, several pieces of coloured stuff were usually laid between two bales of white material, and the whole was then placed in cheap white *merikani* or calico, and this in turn was covered with coconut matting which, after being beaten into the smallest possible compass with strong sticks, was sewn tightly up into a hard firm ball. Beads were packed in common sacks, which sometimes burst on the journey, 'much to the delight of the carriers'. Coils of wire were tied together and sewn up in matting. Finally, every load was marked with a legible number which was then entered in a ledger.

The ivory trader had to know his ivory, which varies from hard to soft. On the whole, the ivory of East Africa is of the soft variety. The dividing line between soft and hard is the Congo border; west of this line it is hard, to the east it is soft, although there are variations within each region. Buyers maintained that soft ivory came from areas where water was scarce; for example coastal ivory from near Pangani and

Mombasa was never as good as that from the dry, upland regions of the interior. Soft ivory is white, opaque, and smooth, it is gently curved, and easily worked, and has what might be called 'spring'. Hard ivory, on the other hand, is translucent, glossy and of a heavier specific gravity than soft ivory; it is more subject to extremes of temperature and more difficult to carve.

Ivory tusks ranged in weight from the small tusks destined for the Indian market and weighing no more than a few pounds, to the huge tusks of 200 lb. and more which were regularly carried to the coast.[5] Small tusks of soft ivory – 'scrivellos' as they were called, under 20 lb. weight, 'very bluff, little bent, with girth of three fingers and with bamboo shallow', had a ready market in India for rings, armlets and bangles.[6] Female tusks, being softer and malleable, were highly prized for billiard balls for the American market.

It was difficult to find a perfect match of tusks. These are seldom alike, for 'just as a man uses his right hand in preference to his left, so an elephant works with a particular tusk'. One tusk is usually more worn and lighter than the other; and it is frequently broken owing to its use as a lever to tear up small trees, hence the term *el hamid* – 'the servant' – given to this tusk by the ivory traders. The task of obtaining perfect tusks was also complicated by their being buried in the elephant's head to a depth of 24 in. or more; a large one mentioned by Baker, was 7 ft. 8 in. long, and was buried nearly 3 ft. in the head. The task of removal was much facilitated by using a steel axe, which the Arabs usually possessed, but the natives rarely.

Bargaining for ivory required infinite patience. In some countries, such as Buganda, Bunyoro and Ankole, the ivory trade was largely controlled by the ruler, with whom negotiations were carried on; one tusk of every pair belonged *de jure* to the king, who also possessed the right to purchase the remaining one. Ivory also fell into the ruler's hands in the form of tribute from subject states.[7] The arrival of Basoga and Bakedi chiefs bearing rich presents of ivory was a common occurrence at Mutesa's court, as the first missionaries in Uganda observed. But in those tribes where the chiefly system was lacking, as among the Akamba, Akikuyu and Masai, the ivory, especially if it happened to be a very large tusk, was deemed to be the property of many, and the purchase of ivory was thus a long and tiresome process.

The value of ivory was calculated in different ways. The African estimated its value by its size and quality. The Arab carried his steel-yard scales which were simple and practical, and, all things being equal, he purchased ivory by weight, the unit being the *frasilah* (34-36 lb.)[8] In the southern Sudan and some parts of East Africa – for example, in Karagwe – ivory was valued in terms of cattle, and this was one of the causes of the cattle raids carried out by ivory dealers.

With the cattle they looted, they could trade for more ivory.

Ivory was a heavy article to transport. It was only its relatively high value which repaid carriage to the coast; the cost of transport from Ujiji to the Indian Ocean was generally reckoned at £50 per ton. Ivory was far more lucrative than slaves, suffering no loss in transit, and steadily increasing in value as the coast was approached. Ivory no doubt, when combined with free porterage in the form of slaves, was highly lucrative, for both could be sold at the coast, and the profit from slaves was in a sense *baksheesh*. But the view, summed up in the slogan 'black and white ivory', that slaves captured in the interior carried most of the ivory to the coast is much exaggerated.

Children and women, on the whole, comprised the bulk of slaves brought to the coast, and they did not make good carriers. Records indicate that the great ivory caravans going inland throughout the century consisted largely of professional porters hired at the coast and in Unyamwezi, or slaves hired out by their masters.[9] At Tabora half a million such porters were estimated to pass through yearly. Loads carried by porters were staggering in their weight, apart from their bulk and awkwardness in handling. Felkin and Wilson in 1879 said that the loads were usually 70 lb. Grant, in his *A Walk Across Africa*, notes that he was surprised to see porters in the southern Sudan carrying 50-60 lb. on their heads. Chanler states that his porters on the march carried 80 lb. weight on their heads.(7) Livingstone had a high estimate of the Banyamwezi as porters, and claimed that he knew of one who carried 200 lb. of ivory all the way from Tabora to the Indian Ocean. The usual weight carried by a porter was 50 lb., and this was the weight in which loads were usually made up.

Despite the rosy picture given by early European explorers of Arabs living in ease and luxury at Ujiji and Unyanyembe, large fortunes from the ivory trade were not common.[10] Burton stated: 'Arab merchants gain little beyond a livelihood in plenty and dignity by their expeditions to the interior.' An investment of $1,000 in trade goods rarely brought in more than 70 *frasilah* (2,450 lb.) of ivory, and assuming an average of $50 per *frasilah* at Zanzibar prices, this was worth $3,500, giving a gross profit of $2,500. But against there was the cost of porterage and rations, at least $5 per *frasilah*; and the enormous interest on borrowed capital, sometimes as high as 100%. There was, in addition, the risk of loss, and the wastage of time and outfit which upon the whole was excessive. 'Though time, toil, and sickness, not being matters of money, are rarely taken into consideration by the Eastern man.'

The business of ivory trading could only be rendered lucrative by constant extension and development, and this required more capital than the Arab possessed. The first Europeans to arrive on the East

African coast had found the ivory trade largely in the hands of the Indian merchants at Zanzibar. Colonel Hamerton, who arrived in Zanzibar in 1841 as British consul, remarked: 'The whole trade in ivory, slaves, and gum copal is carried on by the natives of India, the ivory is consigned to them from the interior'. Hamerton noted that even the Sultan's ivory and copal trade on the mainland was managed by an Indian agent. The Indian merchant, domiciled at Zanzibar or on the coast, was chary of letting his money out cheaply or of allowing it to slip out of his control. He gave credit to the Arab caravan leader in the form of trade goods, and this was repaid at enormous rates of interest in the form of ivory and slaves. The shady character of the business transactions of the Indians was notorious. As late as 1890 the British consul-general at Zanzibar, Euan-Smith, reported to Salisbury: 'The profits made by the Indian merchants, on the whole, have been enormous. They have produced a tendency to remain unsatisfied with the modest returns of ordinary commerce.(9)

The quest for ivory was never-ending. The price on the world market was remarkably free from fluctuations; no commodity retained such a stable price as did ivory in the nineteenth century. Fresh supplies tended to keep the price on the world market from rising, although in the interior the price might fluctuate in terms of trade goods. It rose from 10 lb. of ivory for 1 lb. of beads in 1848, to almost weight for weight in 1859; then at the time of the Franco-Prussian War there was another rise, and then the price levelled off. For the remainder of the century, there was little variation in price, either in the interior or on the world market. Up to the mid-eighties, the barter system was the usual method of purchase by the ivory traders, but increasing competition for ivory resulted in its being forcibly taken from the Africans. Stanley, marching through from the west coast in 1888, met the Arabs who, in their ever-increasing quest for ivory, had come to grips with the Belgians at Stanley Falls on the upper Congo, and here 'every month come Europeans in two or three boats and they took all the ivory on board, and often had to leave some behind'. Stanley noted that both Belgian and Arab were no longer trading for ivory, but plundering for it by use of force.

At the same time as the ivory reserves of East Africa were being tapped from the east coast, there was also taking place a substantial ivory trade to the north by the Nile route. The penetration of Muhammad Ali's expeditions as far south as Gondokoro in the earlier nineteenth century was the forerunner of the establishment of a wide network of ivory hunters' camps, often camouflaged under the name of Egyptian administrative posts.

Figures of ivory exports from East Africa during the early nineteenth century are not easy to obtain. Various estimates range as low as 40,000 lb. a year to as high as 200,000 lb., but no indication is given as to how these figures were arrived at. But from the arrival of Colonel Rigby as British consul at Zanzibar in 1858, customs returns are available. We get a definite figure based on customs returns for 1859, showing that 488,600 lbs. of ivory worth £146,666 were exported. The next most valuable export was cloves, worth £55,000. Although there was a rise in the price of ivory at the time of the Franco-Prussian War from £39 to £68 per cwt., ivory exports remained around 400,000 lb., despite the price rise, and continued at this level almost to the end of the century, except for a poor year in 1885, when they dropped to 260,000 lb. In 1890-91 they rose to 950,000 lb., the result of an accumulation of ivory in the interior during the blockade of the German East African coast in the previous year. By 1894 the figure of exports was back to 412,920 lb., and it remained around this mark until the late 1890s, when the effect of game laws and a closer administrative control began to be felt. In 1899 the figure was down to just over 100,000 lb.; it rose a little at the turn of the century, and then thenceforth continued around the figure of 150,000 lb.

Ivory exports from the Sudan nearly equalled those from the East African coast. As calculated at Khartoum, from figures supplied by the journal *Explorateur* (10), and also by H. A. Meyer, the largest ivory house in Europe, exports were 202,400 lb. in 1853, 440,000 lb. in 1858, 383,000 lb. in 1859, and 367,000 lb. in 1871, and then they averaged around the latter figure until the early 1880s, when the rise of the Mahdi practically ended the ivory trade in the southern Sudan.

Various figures have been put forth to show the number of elephants killed to supply the above ivory exports. Baker's estimate that 3,000 elephants were killed annually, to supply the ivory transported down the Nile during the 1860s, may not be far off the mark. Taking the annual exports of about 350,000 lb. and taking 100 lb. per pair of tusks as an average (this may be on the high side) would mean that at least some 3,500 elephants had died to provide this ivory. Livingstone estimated that 44,000 elephants were killed annually to supply the ivory imported into England alone in 1870, but using a similar method of calculation this would appear to be an exaggeration. In 1894 the annual mortality of elephants for all Africa was estimated at 65,000 elephants (11). This figure included elephants dying from natural causes.

What was the ultimate destination of the thousands of tusks of ivory shipped every year from East Africa? A vast quantity went to England where the Victorian love of ornate furnishing and décor was expressed in ivory inlay work in myriad forms, ranging from ivory-handled umbrellas to ivory snuff boxes and chessmen. There were also large imports for the great cutlery works of the Midlands;

William Rodgers of Sheffield used up to 20 tons of ivory a year in making handles for cutlery. In the Latin countries ivory was used in many articles, such as delicate ivory fans, ivory diamond-shaped inlays for the fingerboards of Spanish guitars, the keys of Italian accordions, and finely carved boudoir articles. A large number of tusks went to ivory-carving centres in Europe: Dieppe was famous for its miniature ornaments, statuettes, crucifixes, mathematical instruments, little book-covers, paper-cutters, combs, serviette-rings and *articles de Paris* generally. St Claude in the Jura, Geislingen in Wurtemberg, and Erbach in Hesse, were ivory-carving centres of long tradition. Ivory was used for false teeth until porcelain came into use for that purpose in the latter part of the nineteenth century. It was the common material for making buttons and clasps, although rivalled more and more by vegetable ivory and casein from milk. In the United States a demand came with the rapid increase in population, and ivory was used for piano and organ keys, musical instruments, billiard and bagatelle balls, not to mention the ivory inlaid butts of six-shooters for the American west. America was the market for 80% of the soft ivory exported from Zanzibar in 1894.

But the greatest market for ivory remained in the East. India and China supplied a multitude of toys, models, chess- and draughtsmen, puppets, work-box fittings, the tremendous range of carved figures and ornaments, and the thousand artistic forms both for the home market and for export abroad and for much of this work damaged and broken ivory could be used.[11] Rhino horn had a more exclusive use in the East, where it was, and still is ground into powder and sold for love potions and medicines.

The qualities possessed by ivory resulted in its use in unexpected forms. Ivory is elastic and flexible, and can be used to make excellent riding whips, these being cut longitudinally from whole tusks. Nothing was wasted from ivory, hundreds of sacks of cuttings and shavings, scraps returned by manufacturers, were used as ivory dust for polishing, in the preparation of Indian ink, and even for food in the form of ivory jelly. The scraps were valuable for inlay work and for minute objects. In many ways, ivory played the same part in the nineteenth century as do plastics in the mid-twentieth century, but it was much more expensive and was always considered a luxury article.

Ivory was shipped from Zanzibar in individual pieces, and in packets made up of small and broken tusks. In 1896 Bombay imported over 6,000 tusks from Zanzibar, and 1,900 packets were shipped to London, New York and Hamburg, the chief markets outside India and China. Ivory usually remained in Zanzibar for some time before being exported from that island; being mortgaged, it went the rounds of the merchants and was used as security for business transactions. It was almost a form of currency, often remaining in Zanzibar for two or three years before finding its way to the overseas markets and the ivory carvers of the East (12). That it would ultimately leave the island was most likely, for no ivory carving was carried on in Zanzibar. As late as 1961, when thousands of tourists were passing through Zanzibar and Mombasa, and buying numerous ivory novelties and souvenirs, there was only one professional ivory carver in East Africa — a Ceylonese (13).

Zanzibar as the ivory market for East Africa, supplying 75% of the world's total in 1891, began to lose ground by the end of the century. There had been for many years a substantial ivory export from the lesser dhow ports on the mainland, such as Malindi, Kipini, Lamu and Kismayu. From the latter port in the period 1891-93, £6,695 worth of ivory was exported (14). In the late 1890s, Mombasa and Dar es Salaam began to hold their own ivory auction sales. Mr Marsden, Chief Customs Officer at Mombasa in 1901, endeavoured to make that port the centre of the ivory trade. He circulated printed ca-talogues, advertised periodical sales, and persuaded the government to provide free passages on government steamers so that Zanzibar and coast merchants could attend. These efforts were more than successful in attracting buyers, chiefly Germans and Italians, to the ivory sales at Mombasa, which were now held under government auspices (15). Mombasa's position as the centre of the ivory trade has been well maintained in the twentieth century. In 1960-61 not only did the entire export of East Africa ivory — 150,000 lb. — pass through this port, but also 200,000 lb. from the Congo. In January 1961 the *Mombasa Times* could well remark: 'Mombasa is slowly taking over the role of the world's main ivory centre from London (16).

NOTES

1. Rhaphta, somewhere on the Tanganyika coast, possibly Kilwa, was an important centre of the ivory trade for Arab merchants: see (1).

2. The Masai obtained most of their ivory — some 1,000-1,500 tusks a year — from the Waboni, a tribe of hunters whose trade they strictly controlled.

3. Krapf states that 6,000 tusks were exported annually. M. Guillain. *Documents sur l'histoire, la géographie et le commerce de l'Afrique Orientale,* III (Paris, 1948), 310-11, puts the export of ivory from the whole east coast at 25,000 *frasilah* (approx. 850,000 lb.). Pangani alone exported 35,000 lb. in 1856.

4. In addition to the main centres of Ujiji and Tabora, there were lesser ones such as Zungomero, some 100 miles in from the east coast, which was a resting place after crossing the Nyika, and where a great army of touters preyed on down-going and up-coming caravans. Msene, about 100 miles north of Tabora, was the chief *bandari* (centre) of the western Nyamwezi country.

5. Jumbe Kimemata, an ivory trader, possessed a tusk weighing 264 lb. and three others of 220 lb. each. Teleki obtained a tusk weighing 228 lb. The Natural History Museum, Kensington, London, possesses a tusk 11 ft. 5½ in. long and

weighing 236 lb.
6. Tipu Tib, the well-known ivory trader, who, with his father, traded for ivory at Ujiji and west of Lake Tanganyika, on his first trading expedition concentrated on small tusks. They were cheaper and easier to transport, and if well selected had a special market.
7. There was a royal monopoly of ivory in Ethiopia; and the ruler of Harrar had his own agent at Berbera, the great ivory mart of Somaliland.
8. The rumour of a proposed new scale of *ad valorem* duties at the coast in 1886 caused a rush to get the higher class of ivory down before it came into effect; see (6). (F.O. (C.P.) 5370/7, Kirk to Rosebery, 5 June 1886).
9. Livingstone, who probably gave currency to the idea that 'black ivory carried white ivory', states: 'Those Arabs who despair of white ivory invest their remaining beads and cloth in slaves' (*Last Journals*, I (1867), 232). Cameron, Tipu Tib, Schweinfurth and Petherick all affirm that hired porters, not slaves, carried the ivory.
10. Tipu's account of the ease with which he made his profits was not the usual fortune attending ivory trading. For a *frasilah* of beads Tipu bought 5 *frasilah* of copper at Utetera; he gave ½ *frasilah* to Stanley on parting, and with the remaining 4½ *frasilah* he obtained 20 *frasilah* of ivory. A *frasilah* of beads cost $3 in Zanzibar. He could sell the ivory for at least $50 per *frasilah*. Thus his $3 had turned into $1,000 (H. Brode, *Tippoo Tib* (1907), 129). Stokes, ivory trader and gun runner, brought down to the coast in May 1891 £8,000 worth of ivory (8). (F.O. (C.P.) 6051/415, Euan-Smith to Salisbury, 21 May 1891).
11. No European artist quite succeeded in cutting concentric balls of ivory after the manner of the Chinese.

REFERENCES

(1) Frisk, H., *Periplus of the Erythrean Sea*, Goteburg (1927), p.17.
(2) Latham, R., (trans.), *The Travels of Marco Polo*, London (1959), p.276.
(3) Krapf, J. L., *Travels and Missionary Labours in East Africa*, (1860), p.185.
(4) Cameron, V., *Across Africa*, New York (1877), vol. 1, p.243.
(5) Lugard, Report no. 4 (March-August 1892), p.88.
(6) F.O. (C.P.) 5370/7. Kirk to Rosebery, 5 June 1886.
(7) Chanler, W. A., Through Jungle and Desert, London (1896), p.33.
(8) F.O. (C.P.) 6051/415, Euan-Smith to Salisbury, 21 May 1891.
(9) F.O. (C.P.) 6039/310, Euan-Smith to Salisbury, 24 February 1890.
(10) *Explorateur, Journal géographique et commercial*, nos. 1-4, Paris (1875-6).
(11) *Gazette of Zanzibar and East Africa*, 5 December 1894.
(12) F.O. (C.P.) 6538/235 Incl. 1, Piggott to the Imperial British East Africa Company, 7 February 1894.
(13) *East African Standard*, 13 January 1961.
(14) F.O. (C.P.) 6538/42, Crawford to Imperial British East Africa Company, 27 January 1894.
(15) F.O. (C.P.) 7823/162, Marsden to F.O., 12 June 1901.
(16) *Mombasa Times*, 3 January 1961.

PART VI

Trade Routes and Trade Centres

SOME REFLECTIONS ON AFRICAN TRADE ROUTES*

Gervase Mathew

There will be four main factors in the reconstruction of pre-European African history south of the Sahara; the recording of oral history, the study of anthropology, archaeological research and geographical analysis, all four must always be co-ordinated, in some instances they will blend.

There is none of the northern antithesis between tradition and the written source for normally the few chronicles are essentially segments of oral history recorded at different periods in documentary form as in the case of the chronicles of Kilwa and of Pate. The factual value of traditional history must always depend on the character of the social setting in which it has been preserved, adapted and at times created. In consequence the valid study of oral history is inseparable from scientific anthropology. But it is also interwoven with archaeological research whether the study of sites or of beads or of pottery forms; African tradition has often provided archaeology with its clues as in Uganda. Archaeology is providing the study of traditional history with a new technique for objective checking.

But geographical analysis combined with a perpetual awareness of economic factors must give the setting for any reconstruction of the African past. Perhaps the most immediate need is to apply the evidence of oral tradition, archaeology and geography to the re-discovery of pre-European trade routes. There are four main groupings of such routes to be investigated.

There are the lines of coastal traffic along the shores of the Indian Ocean and of the Atlantic, and perhaps along the deserts of the Sahara which formed an inland sea. There are the tracks by which exports from far into the interior reached the coast and were ultimately forwarded to foreign markets. There is the network of internal

*Reprinted from *Research Review* (Institute of African Studies, Legon, Accra), Vol. 3, No. 3, 1967.

trade within Africa brought into being by local needs for salt or iron or copper. Finally there is the possibility of transcontinen al trade routes. And in each case we are only at the beginning of any scientific study. In this paper I am tentatively making suggestions based primarily on personal experience.

The trade route of which most is known is that of the coastal traffic along the African shore of the Indian Ocean. It is relatively well documented by Graeco-Roman and Arab geographers. Its traditional history has been recorded fully. An archaeological survey from the coasts of Somalia to those of the Transkei was finally completed in the spring of 1963. Yet even here there are still some elementary questions unanswered.

How far south did this coastal traffic extend before the Portuguese rounded the Cape? Until the winter of 1962 I had assumed that it coincided, even if only roughly, with the area of the monsoon and that Sofala was the most southerly mainland calling-port to possess significance. But that November I worked on finds from the Mapungubwe site in the north Transvaal and they prove contact with Indian Ocean trade. Most of these are very difficult to date – 'trade-wind' beads and glass fragments – but they include some sherds of Chinese porcelain, Yuan ware celadon, which are clearly thirteenth century Mapungubwe is an obvious clearance centre for copper from the Messina workings and gold from the north Transvaal; and air photography shows that it is the most easterly of a line of sites which stretch into Bechuanaland. It seems likely therefore that there is a still undiscovered entrepot at the mouth of the Limpopo river.

But perhaps the Indian Ocean trade route went still farther south. I think that I found evidence of this in 1963 during an archaeological survey of the shores of the Transkei. It has long been known that sherds of Ming porcelain have been reported from Pondoland, now the Transkei coast. It was supposed that they had come ashore from sixteenth century Portuguese wrecks. It is clear from their surface texture that this is true of about thirty per cent of the sherds that I have examined. But at four sites in Pondoland, notably round at St. John and at Msicaba, and in the museum at East London there are fragments of Ming blue and white of the fifteenth or early sixteenth century which show no signs of being sea-tossed. More conclusively I have found numbers of Gujerati carnelian beads, characteristically fifteenth century types and carefully faceted, which show no mark of erosion; there were about eighty or ninety of them at Port St. John alone, and I have been told of others still brought in to up-country stores. It seems at last tenable that in the fifteenth century Pondoland was visited by Islamic traders from the north as the most southerly catchment area for ivory.

If in the fifteenth century there was a sea route from Somalia to the shores of South Africa were there transcontinental routes which would link this with the western coast? There are two possibilities; one leading from Kilwa in what is now Tanganyika to the old kingdom of the Congo and what was to be later San Salvador. The other from the Adan kingdom in what is now Somalia to northern Nigeria perhaps by way of Bornu. Traditions of the latter route are recorded by Burton. The first route is the only one that is yet documented. Ibn Battuta who visited Kilwa island in 1332 described an overland route that led from there to West Africa through the land of the Lam Lam. No geographer, except Sir Hamilton Gibb, took this account very seriously; but this year it has received a rather surprising corroboration from two eighteenth century French sources. Both were found by Dr. Freeman-Grenville and will be published in his forthcoming book *The French at Kilwa Island.* Morice writes in 1777 the fresh water sea of which I have spoken to you, is I estimate, a month's march from the ocean. This fresh water sea has a rise and fall of eight feet. It takes two days to cross it in a boat rowed by six oarsmen. On the other side lies a huge country which has been crossed by natives of the country, who, after two months' travelling, found the ocean and saw ships there manned by Europeans. There is every reason to believe that this is the coast of Angola. Cossigny added a few years later – an African caravan leaves Kilwa every year and proceeds to the west coast. There is a great lake which they say is a fresh water sea, in the middle of which there is a large island. They cross this lake on pieces of wood and make a halt at the island. The Africans assert that at the end of the journey there is a salt sea. They find there vessels like ours and Europeans to whom they sell their slaves. The agreement in their reports does not permit of any doubt as to the truth of the fact. The fresh water sea is presumably Lake Nyasa. It is tenable that the original route wound its way from Kilwa to the old kingdom of the Congo. There is still the tradition of a trade path from Kilwa to the southern end of Lake Nyasa. There was a nineteenth century report of a series of stone forts along it, but this has never been investigated by an archaeologist.

I once came across a possible clue to another transcontinental trade route. I never had the opportunity to follow it up, so it is perhaps worth recording in some detail in case some other archaeologist should have the chance to do so. In the winter of 1950 the government of the British Somaliland Protectorate invited me to make an archaeological survey. During it I worked on a group of twelve deserted towns along the frontier of British Somaliland and Ethiopia and carried out preliminary excavations at four of them. They are often of considerable extent; three of them, Amud, Abara and Gargesa, contain the remains of between 200 to 300 stone houses; in some cases the walls still rise to eighteen feet. It seems clear that they represent vanished cities of the late medieval kingdom of Adal. I examined twenty-six silver coins from them; the latest were struck at Cairo by Sultan Qait-Bey (1468-89); the earliest, also from Cairo, were struck by Sultan Barquq (1382-99). All were from mints either at Cairo or at Damascus. For the purpose of this essay there are three points worth noting. First, that these sites can be plotted in a pattern of a rather devious trade path of short marches. Secondly, that I was able to link them with an Indian Ocean terminus at Sa'ad-al-Din island, four miles north east of the modern port of Zeila. Thirdly, that during nearly twenty years field work throughout Africa I have never come across such evidence of late medieval wealth. There is the use of a silver coinage, unlike the copper which alone proliferates round Kilwa. There are the occasional gold coins; none have been reported elsewhere in East Africa. There is the quite exceptional quality of the porcelain. Fine celadon was predominant in each of the sites that I examined, found sometimes on the surface, sometimes beneath the surface to the depth of seven and a half inches, sometimes in the tight-packed middens that often rose to between four and five feet. There were sherds with a white crystalline body and green-white glaze without crackle, or glazed olive-brown; others with a grey granular body with a sea-green glaze or a blue-green glaze crackled all over. I also found a few fragments of Ming, red and white, and others of white porcelain with an opaque bluish tint. There was also a good quantity of early Ming blue-and-white; fragments of bowls ornamented with tendril scrolls on a slightly blued ground with black spotting at the end of the strokes, or of bowls with floral designs in strong outlines of grey or black-blue.

The most reasonable hypothesis would seem to be that I was working along a short segment of a wealthy trade path of the late fourteenth and fifteenth centuries that had one ultimate terminus in early Ming China and another northward, up the Red Sea, in Cairo. The signs of almost excessive wealth suggest that this track led far into the interior of Africa and even possibly tapped a gold supply; gold and ivory were two imports needed in late medieval China. Documentary evidence may yet be found to show that one pilgrim route from Mali to Mecca bent south of the Christian bastion of fifteenth century Ethiopia and followed some such path as this.

There is a third possibility of transcontinental traffic which should be mentioned even if, as I suspect, later research discards it. The great medieval port of Aidhab lies far up the Red Sea, to the north of Suakin. It was destroyed in 1426. The height of its prosperity would seem to have been in the late fifteenth century. I have never been able to visit the site but I have worked on objects from it both in the British Museum and in the museum at Khartoum. They were oddly similar to those from the Adal towns. It is not impossible that another pilgrim route from the west came to Aidhab by way of Darfur; traffic with medieval Nubia alone does not seem sufficient to explain its wealth.

Finally, late medieval Cairo was the apex of two trade paths, one leading to the kingdoms of the western Sudan, the other to the ports on the east coast. It may have been Cairene merchants who first popularised in the West trading techniques that they had become familiar with in East Africa – the use of cowries for barter, possibly systems of gold weights. The riches of fifteenth century Cairo were largely based on the African trade. But it seems probable that, while Cairo had trafficked with East Africa since the twelfth century Fatimids, effective Cairene penetration into the West Sudan did not begin till the accession in 1382 of the first of the Burji Mamluks, Sultan Saif al-Din Barquq.

Foreign merchants may have been active along all these routes. But this would not have been the normal pattern in pre-European African trade routes. It would now seem more likely that throughout Africa there were wide areas in the interior where trade goods circulated by barter, freely or sluggishly. At points near the circumference of such areas tracks came into existence leading, however deviously, to markets along the coast frequented by foreign merchants. But until well into the nineteenth century, both east and west, it was normally traders from the interior who penetrated to the coast, not coastal traders penetrating into the interior.

At least in East Africa the final section of such tracks will usually be found to follow rivers; for even when these were not navigable by raft, they provided a secure supply of drinking water. This will explain why so many of the medieval trading centres are by river mouths or opposite to them. In Kenya Malindi was by the old opening of the Sabaki which led down from the Kenya uplands; Kipini was at the mouth of the Tana, and goods could be shipped from there to Lamu and Pate. Mombasa was served by a system of creeks and streams. In Tanganyika the wealth of Kisimani Mafia in the thirteenth and fourteenth centuries was perhaps partly due to its position opposite the mouth of the Rufiji. There may always have been a track along the changing course of the Pangani and the streams that fed it. During a brief archaeological survey in Portuguese East Africa I noted how much the trade was dependent on the river systems of the Sabaki and the Buzi. Sofala was a river port.

But there were other routes that crossed rivers but did not follow them. Mr. Roger Summers has found traces of one which led from the gold-producing area round Penhalonga and the Ziwa people on the eastern border of southern Rhodesia to medieval Kilwa; this would seem to have crossed the Zambesi at Tete. But such routes may have been cut as wide as a swathe as the goods drifted from village to village in an un-organised traffic. It used to seem likely that most of the internal trade in pre-European Africa was after this fashion and that supply centres in southern central Africa were first stimulated in the twelfth century by the distant demand of Muslim traders on the eastern coast. Now I am not so certain. Dr. Brian Fagan has just discovered a new culture at Ingombe Ilede in Northern Rhodesia. It is reported to be well evolved, and a quantity of beads prove its contact with the Indian Ocean area. A radio-carbon dating gives A.D. 850, plus or minus. It was presumably a centre of copper diffusion, like Katanga in the Congo.

In the last months M. Mauny and Dr. Freeman-Grenville severally have worked on the references to the Wak-Wak peoples in the Book of the Marvels of India, the Kitab Ajaib al-Hind. They have established that there was an organised Indonesian penetration into East Africa during the tenth century. The demand for copper and for gold along the coast may have been pre-Muslim, created by Chola traders from south-east India and by the Sri Vijaya people from Sumatra and west Malaya. By the ninth century it may have been strong enough to have produced trade paths from Ingombe Ilede and Katanga and the entrepot that may have marked the earliest Zimbabwe. During the last two years the tendency in African archaeology has been to favour earlier rather than later datings.

Perhaps in the next few years it may become increasingly apparent that the diffusion centres radiated west as well as east and south. A pressing need is an archaeological survey in Angola. This might begin with the Kola complex to the south-west of Benguela. It seems probable that Angola will be found closely linked with Southern Rhodesia and with Katanga copper ingots common to both.

The skeleton of pre-European African history and archaeology will be reconstructed by the discovery of its trade routes. It now seems likely that the skeleton will prove to be pan-African.

22

LONG-DISTANCE TRADE-ROUTES IN CENTRAL AFRICA*

J. Vansina

The structure of indigenous trade in Central Africa makes it necessary to distinguish between three different types of trade. There is first the local trade from village to village within a given population. The goods exchanged are generally specialised products from local industry, and the exchange comes about because some villages possess supplies of raw materials which are not available to others, e.g. pottery clay, or because they are inhabited by specialists such as smiths or woodcarvers who are not available in others. This type of trade is conducted in local markets, and generally speaking, currency of some sort is in use. It is still alive today, and one can assume that it is very old, since such a system shows little dynamism. The necessities remain the same; the organisation is simple and efficient.

A second type of trade is conducted over greater distances either between culturally different peoples within a single state (25), or between neighbouring peoples. Transactions are made at market-places located close to the borders of the trading peoples, or at the capital of the state. They are held every fourth or every eighth day and are intimately connected with the week. On the other three days of a four-day week, local markets will be held. The fourth day is a day of rest and peace and is devoted to the regional trade. The organisation of the trade and the maintenance of peace is in the hands of the political authorities of the chiefdoms in which the market-place is located.[1] The goods exchanged are foodstuffs, specialised products from local industry, and products which come from markets specialised in the long-distance trade, such as European goods, salt or copper. The trade arises partly because some suitable raw materials exist only in some chiefdoms and not in others, and partly because of some special skills which are present only in some cultures. In

*Reprinted by permission of Cambridge University Press from the *Journal of African History*, Vol. III, No. 3, 1962.

Kubaland, the Pyaang are very skilled in iron-work, the Bushoong in the production of velvet-like cloth, the Shoowa in the manufacture of red and white embroidered cloth, etc.[2] The goods traded are not necessarily essential for all households. They may include luxury goods intended for the upper classes, in which fashion influences the markets more than if the goods were basic items such as pottery.[3] Standards of values and currencies are in general use. This trade survives only to a limited extent today. It shows more dynamism than the local trade.[4] It has connections with the political structure and, although the volume or the nature of the trade undoubtedly varied through time, it can reasonably be argued that the trade itself is at least as old as the state structures in the area.[5]

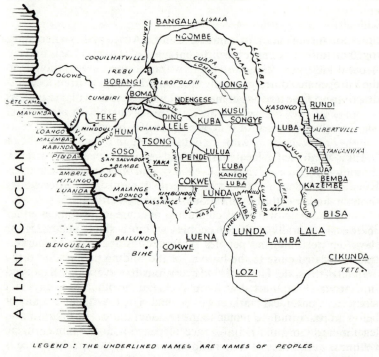

LEGEND : THE UNDERLINED NAMES ARE NAMES OF PEOPLES

SCALE 1 : 15,840,000

Long-distance trade, the third type of trade, was unknown in Central Africa before the arrival of the Europeans in the fifteenth century. It involves more than a passing on from market to market of goods coming from distant places; it is direct trade over long distances. It consisted mainly of the exchange of European goods – such as cloth, cowries, beads, fire-arms, powder, wine and, in some instances, iron or copper objects for slaves, ivory and copper, and, in the later seventeenth century, wax, and in the late nineteenth century, rubber. The trade was conducted by caravans, and currencies, standards of value, and means of payment for services were extensively used. The trade was based on coastal harbours where the African goods were shipped and the European stores unloaded. But in most cases the harbours were not themselves the places where caravans were fitted out and the bulk of goods were stored. These places, the 'staples', were in the interior at capitals such as San Salvador, Kassange, Bailundo, Bihe, and Kakonda. Only in the cases of Loango, Malemba, and Kabinda was the harbour the staple, and here the capitals of the African rulers were in the immediate vicinity. The entrepreneurs, who could afford to fit out caravans and supply them with goods, lived in the staples. They were European traders, sometimes local kings and African traders who would eventually come together to find the necessary capital (8: pp. 199-201, 20: pp. 8-9). Around 1900, with the administrative and economic organisation of the European colonies, this trade died out. This article is devoted to a description of the trade-routes along which it once flowed.

The Trade-Routes from the Coasts of Kongo and Loango

The Portuguese discovered Kongo in 1482 and trade started sometime after 1493 (11: p. 139). In 1512 Manuel I sent an ambassador to Kongo. It is clear that it was already known that copper occurred in the area, for the ambassador was asked to enquire into the possibility of trade especially with relation to ivory, copper, and slaves (21: pp. 387-8). Affonso I, the Kongo king, reacted favourably and a trade in slaves developed. But soon, in July 1526, Affonso complained that the traders were robbing the highways, kidnapping citizens, nobles, and even relatives of the king of Kongo, and he decided to close the trade. In October of the same year, however, he reversed his decision and instituted a three-man commission which would inspect all slaves before embarkation to make sure that they had been obtained by legal means (36: pp. 53-4). The trade grew. In 1536, 4,000 persons were exported and in 1648 the number had risen to about 6,000 (36: pp. 67, 84-90). Most of the slaves were exported to San Tome, and most of the European traders were inhabitants of that island. In 1547 a treaty was signed with Diogo I by the terms of which Portuguese traders were to be allowed to trade everywhere in the kingdom, but it was not enforced before the 1550s (1: pp. 52, 75). Before 1526 the Portuguese had been allowed to trade everywhere and some of them had founded factories at the residences of governors or district chiefs, but Affonso had charged that they instigated these to rebel against the king, and he apparently had forbidden them access to the interior except for San Salvador, his capital (36: pp. 53-4, 135).

After 1550 a through·trade-route from San Salvador to Stanley Pool seems to have come into existence. European traders called *pombeiros* (12: pp. 152-4)[6] directed caravans towards the Pool and bought slaves from the Hum, the Teke and prisoners-of-war originating from countries beyond the Teke kingdom, far to the north or the north-west of the pool (38: p. 38; 24). But soon they were no longer going out themselves; they were entrusting the direction of the caravans to slaves who were also called *pombeiros*. Later the name came to be applied throughout Kongo and Angola to these African caravan leaders alone.

By 1580 the caravans were also bringing ivory and raphia cloth from the Teke at the Pool in exchange for salt, which came from salt-pans in Ambriz and Pinda, *nzimbu* shells, and probably cowries (38: p. 38; 13: p. 192). *Nzimbu* shells were used as currency in the kingdom of Kongo and in most of the areas lying to the east of it, whilst raphia cloth was the unit of currency in Angola. This explains why the Portuguese were so eager to buy up raphia cloth, and the Teke or others so willing to take *nzimbu* shells (11: pp. 306-12).

At the Pool the trade-route touched on a number of regional networks. This is evidenced not only by the fact that slaves from beyond Tekeland are mentioned, but by the knowledge some authors have of kingdoms and rivers farther away. Dapper mentions for the period around 1640 the kingdom of Boma to the west of Lake Leopold II, the Mfinu, and the Hum (13: pp. 217-20). Garcia Mendes in 1603 mentioned *Ybare* and *Bozanga*. There was a small kingdom of the *Nsese la Bosanga* to the east of Lake Leopold II, and *Ibare* is a word which can be applied to any great river. Here it refers probably to the Fimi, the Lower Kasai, or to the Congo upstream of Stanley Pool, since the use of the term is not in vogue to the south of that area (51: pp. 4, 10-12, 41-50; 24)[7] A text of 1702 mentions that upstream of the Pool, the Dongo receives a mighty affluent, the 'Giordano' (data from 1696), which can be either the Kwa or the Ubanghi, probably the former (27: p. 432).

Another through route, apparently arising at the same time as the route to the Pool, led from San Salvador to and over the Kwango river, towards a place called Kundi in the country of Okanga. The name Okanga is not mentioned before 1595, but on Pigafetta's map, elaborated on data received before 1583, one finds the rivers Wamba and Bakari, which are tributaries of the Kwango, running *east* of that river (38: map, pp. 40-2, 79; 12: pp. 186, 195, 311-12).[8] Pigafetta goes on to say that the peoples of the Wamba have a wonderful gift of weaving different sorts of embroidered or velvet raphia cloth, the best cloth being known as *incorimba (nkudimba?)* (38: pp. 40-2). Now the market of Okanga became famous during the first forty years of the seventeenth century for this export of embroidered and velvet raphia cloth, which fetched very high prices in Angola, so that the traders enriched themselves rapidly.[9] Here too there was a link with regional networks. Around 1623 a text mentions that the cloth of Okanga was used as currency in Luanda, and that the traders had contact with the Tsong (Songo), who said that their neighbours bordered on a great water called Muu. This is probably the Lower Kasai, although it might be the Lower Kwilu (21: p. 375; 11: p. 9).

These trade-routes probably continued throughout the seventeenth century and San Salvador remained the staple for the whole trade. After the foundation of Luanda, a route ran from there to San Salvador, and the Angolan traders participated heavily in the trade to the Pool and to the Kwango. The influence of the trade must have been felt over large areas, not only over the land lying between Lake Leopold II and the rivers Congo and Kwa, the country between the Pool and the Kwango for which the names of the people are given, but also further afield, for European goods certainly trickled through the regional networks and, at least in the Teke area, slaves came from beyond the borders. Although it is admittedly difficult to prove such an assumption, it seems probable that the whole area between the Kwilu and Kwango rivers was directly affected by the trade and that after 1650 trade contacts went up the Lower Kasai into the Kuba country, although curiously enough, the main objects transmitted were not European goods, but copper from the Mindouli mines in Tekeland. This whole system of trade broke down with the breakdown of the Kongo kingdom after 1667. By 1700 a completely different pattern was taking its place.

In the sixteenth century the Portuguese also landed in Loango and began trading there. But they did not gain a good foothold in the area, since its main export was ivory, and ivory was a Portuguese royal monopoly. When the Dutch appeared in the Atlantic, soon after 1600, they at once began to trade with Loango for ivory, whilst the Portuguese bought slaves, raphia cloth, copper, and redwood.[10]

Dapper gives us the clearest description of the trade-routes and he is confirmed in almost every detail by Battell's earlier account. The trade was almost entirely in the hands of the Vili, the people of Loango, who manned the caravans and directed them (21: p. 275; 11: p. 9). The few Portuguese traders used to send their *pombeiros* inland. The main trade-route went from Loango to Stanley Pool, to the Teke town of Monsol. The Teke exported slaves and ivory. Copper came from the Mindouli mines, which first belonged to the Teke and were taken later by Kongo from Nsundi (45: pp. 50, 16, 22), and ivory from the Jaga who obtained it from Bokkemeale, a country to the north-east of Mayombe, where pygmies hunted it. The Vili brought European goods and salt inland as well as big iron knives which they bought in Mayumbe to sell them to the Jaga just east of that area.[11] The slaves were used as carriers and thus the entrepreneurs did not have to pay for the carriage of copper and ivory.

A more local network linked Loango with Mayumba (to the north), from which ivory, redwood, and edible oysters were exported, and with Sete Cama, still farther north, where there was also a great supply of ivory and redwood. With the ivory some elephants' hair was also exported to Loango and sold to the Portuguese, who carried it to Luanda.[12] Moreover the Portuguese had established a regional network between San Tome, Benin, Calabar, and the Rio del Rey, Loango and Pinda and Luanda. From Loango they exported to Luanda, elephants' hair, redwood, and raphia cloth. This raphia cloth was also used as currency in Angola. Copper from Loango and Pinda was exported to Luanda and turned into manillas which were exported to Benin, Calabar, and the Rio del Rey, where blue cloth would be bought to be sold again Loango and Pinda.[13]

The main road to the Pool followed the River Congo on its north side, or went along the Kwilu Nyari to Kimbede and thence to Brazzaville (45: p. 68). The area touched by the trade of Loango was considerable, extending from Cape Lopez to the mouth of the River Congo, covering the whole area between Kongo and Kwilu Nyari, the whole basin of the latter river, and large parts of the mountains and forests of Gabon (18: pp. 27, 30, 38, 47, 53, 54, 62). The trade never died out, although during the late eighteenth and nineteenth centuries more slaves were sold in the harbours of Kabinda, Malemba, and Boma, which though they had existed since 1600, gained in importance after the fall of the kingdom of Kongo. Part of the former trade with Kongo then went through these harbours instead of going through Pinda. In 1787 there is evidence that Teke and Hum were still exported as slaves and that some Bobangi were also available, although in small numbers. This meant that by that time the slave-trade was influencing the lower reaches of the Ubanghi river (15: pp. 10-146).[14] After 1800 the conjunction of several internal networks at Stanley Pool had become important enough for the Bobangi and the Teke to fight several wars to break or maintain the Teke monopoly on the Pool (14: pp. 61-2). When Stanley descended the river he found European goods as far as Lisala and the networks were linked in the following manner. The Ngala traded from the vicinity of Lisala down to Irebu, where the Bobangi took over to Cumbiri and Bolobo. The Teke then took the trade from these posts to the pool (47: pp. 301-2; 358-9). The farthest European goods had then penetrated to some 965·

miles from the mouth of the Kongo. On the Fimi, goods reached Lake Leopold II. These were carried from the Pool by the Nunu (48: pp. 36-42), while on the Lower Kasai some goods were traded by Teke and Yey (Yanzi) over a relatively short distance, the river being blocked at one point by Nkutu (54: pp. 380-1). In that area the trade linked up with regional networks extending all over the Kwango and parts of Kasai.

After the destruction of the kingdom of Kongo a new line of trade sprang up. Some ships would put in at Ambriz or Kitungo, near the River Loje, and trade in ivory and slaves from the county of Mosul of which this area was a part. The European goods travelled along the coast and could be found in Loanda itself, where they competed with Portuguese goods because they were cheaper and better in quality. Towards the interior, the trade went from chiefdom to chiefdom along the River Loje, and one branch went as far as the Soso, the inhabitants of the old province of Mbata (43: I, pp. 159-62, II, pp. 9, 15-21, 34-5, 41-3, 141-7, 171-3, 177-233; 35: pp. 554-5, 558; 31: pp. 21-4). The Soso traded with the Yaka and brought European goods to the Yaka capital (6: II, pp. 125-6). From here they went to Sukuland, and thence to the Mbala and the peoples of the Lower Kasai and Kwilu valleys. But a main route went from the Yaka capital due east to Mwata Kumbana in Pende country and to Mai Munene on the Kasai near Cikapa.[15] From here there was a connection with the Kuba[16] and also with the Ding on the Lower Kasai (54: pp. 343-4, 343, 356-7, 362, 374). From Kubaland a trade-route ran to the Ndengese, while another went to the Songye from Lusambo[17] and thence to Songye villages on the Lomami (5: pp. 270, 278). All the regional trade networks of the whole Kwango and the Kasai as far east as the Songye were linked to each other, although the more immediate hinterland of the Yaka country ended at Mwata Kumbana's in the east and near the Lower Kasai in the north. The trade was never very important; at least that part of it which went to Ambriz (15: II, p. 41-3). But some of it also went from the Soso to the harbours north of the Zaire. The links between Kongo and Yaka and between all the other peoples mentioned are attested only for the nineteenth century. This situation may however be projected backwards and presented as being in existence certainly by 1800.

II The Trade-Routes from Luanda and Kassange

The trade with Angola is older than the foundation of Luanda. The first trade document known dates from 1546, and is a grant of the exploitation of the Rio Longa, its ivory and its potential slaves (16: I, pp. 187-90). But before the foundation of the town in 1575-6 and the beginnings of the *conquista*, the trade was carried on on a small scale and consisted mainly in the buying of slaves from the Ngola or king of the country lying between the Kwanza and the Dande. From 1576 to 1604 a period of wars followed in which many slaves were captured and exported, or many were bought from the Jaga hordes who roamed over the Angolan territory from Kongo to Benguella and the Ovimbundu highlands.[18] Gradually, however, with the establishment of the first captaincies along the Kwanza and the opening of market-places (*feiras*) near the forts, some internal trade began to manifest itself.

The oldest trade-route led from Luanda to San Salvador, and was in use practically immediately after the foundation of the town.[19] Thus the town tapped some of the trade of the Stanley Pool and the Kwango markets. No great changes came about in this pattern until the 1650s, when a number of traders went to live at Kassange, the capital of the kingdom of the Imbangala near the Upper Kwango. There they bought slaves and sold goods to the Imbangala, who organised caravans to the capital of the Lunda king, Mwaat Yaav, bringing him European goods and asking for ivory and slaves. The Mwaat Yaav himself sent caravans to Kassange to carry on the trade (19: p. 84; 4: III, pp. 219-20).[20] After 1740 this trade-route was extended to the court of Kazembe and connected with trade-routes from the east coast. This route has been described by Cunnison (10: pp. 61-76), and little needs to be added to his article. It must be kept in mind that only the vast territories of the Lunda empire had connections between them, and that tribute caravans came in from the regional capitals and carried some of the foreign goods home.[21] The route ran also through the salt- and copper-producing districts of Katanga, and linked up there with the regional networks of the Luba area.

By 1795 or earlier, the Imbangala also had close relations with the Luena of the Upper Zambezi, and probably traded with them also. In 1797 the Jaga of Kassange had just sent his daughter to be married by Kinyama, the Luena ruler, so as to strengthen the ties existing between them (10a: p. 81). One may suppose that these ties were also commercial. But the Imbangala did not keep the Luena trade, for the Ovimbundu and Cokwe took it over, apparently before 1800.

Despite their efforts to preserve it, the Imbangala lost their monopoly over the Lunda route around 1850. After Graça's breakthrough in 1843, more and more Ovimbundu and Portuguese went from Bihe to the Lunda.[22] But about the same time the Imbangala started a trade-route farther to the north, towards Mwata Kumbana and Mai Munene, thus linking up with the regional networks of the Kwango and Kasai basin and sharing in the profits of the profitable ivory trade in the latter area (54: pp. 48-53). Before that time their influence in the Upper Kwango and Kwilu valleys had been to raid the populations for slaves (37: p. 25; 39: pp. 78-83). A note of Livingstone's shows that the Imbangala were in contact with Mai in 1853, but via an indirect route.[23]

Although the *feira* of Kassange was abandoned by the Portuguese after 1860 as a sequel to the Portuguese-Imbangala wars, the Imbangala kept on trading and now brought their products to the new staple, Malange, which was connected by road to Dongo on the Kwanza and from their with Luanda (42: pp. 4, 14-15, 81-3).

III Trade-Routes from the Ovimbundu of Bihe

During the seventeenth and eighteenth centuries the Ovimbundu peoples of the Angolan plateau organised themselves in several kingdoms. Before 1769 a number of European convicts or deserters had gone to live and trade with them, and the same year the governor-general of Angola proposed to lift the formal ban for Portuguese to trade in the interior outside of the *feiras*. The ban was not respected, and it was thought better to organise the *diaspora* around several posts in the interior where parish-priests and 'exterior judges' could be provided. A year later the first judge of Bihe, the most easterly kingdom, was appointed. The traders who lived there were vassals to the local kings, or, if they were unable to start a settlement on their own, they merged with the local population and communicated to it the taste for long-distance trade and for wealth for its own sake. But it was only after the 1774-6 war against the Ovimbundu that regular trade connections were established between these kingdoms and Benguela. Very soon Bihe became the most important staple in the interior. Not only was it located on the far eastern borders of the Ovimbundu area, but it had special connections with Luanda after the baptism of the Bihe king in 1778. The Biheans reached an agreement with their powerful neighbours of Bailundo, to the west, by which the caravans of Bihe would take the goods – slaves, wax, and some ivory – to Bailundo, from where they would be carried to Benguela by the Bailundo (8: pp. 195-9, 224-31).

Before 1795 a pattern of long-distance trade was well established and the traders had reached beyond Cokweland and made contact with the Luena (22: pp. 30-1).[24] Before 1835 they had reached Loziland (30: p. 218). By 1850 they were on the Middle Kubango, in Loziland, in the southern Lunda states, and in Katanga.[25] The farthest point to the east at which they were reported around 1850 was with the Lamba of Northern Rhodesia. There Bihe and Luena caravans met Bisa and Swahili traders who exported Lamba ivory and slaves to the east coast (44: p. 113).[26] The whole of eastern Angola and western Rhodesia was now open to the Ovimbundu trade. Ten to fifteen years later the whole of Katanga and Kasai had also been drawn into the orbit of Bihe. In Katanga, a Nyamwezi trader, Msiri, established a kingdom around 1856 and made contact with the Ovimbundu, whilst himself sending caravans of his people to both the east and the west coasts. By 1874 the Ovimbundu were on very good terms with the Luba king Kasongo Kalombo, whom they helped to raid his own subjects, and from whose capital they sent parties to the north of Lunda, the land of Kaniok, where ivory was plentiful (5: pp. 298-9, 331-4, 352-3).[27] At about the same time the Ovimbundu appeared on the Lulua and on the Kuba market of Kabao. But here the Cokwe preceded them just as the Luena had preceded them in the trade with Northern Rhodesia.

The Cokwe did not organise their caravans in the way the Ovimbundu did. They went out in smaller parties and for longer periods of time. They would hunt their way through, tracking down elephants and collecting wax. Frequently they would start small settlements in the areas they had penetrated, and then attack the local inhabitants. These would be defeated by the greater number of Cokwe guns. Slaves would be gathered by *razzias* of this kind or by trade, and were often not sold but incorporated into the Cokwe groups themselves, so that in a very short period from about 1852 to 1887 they had overrun all the Lunda groups everywhere, and had infiltrated into Luba, Kaniok, Lulua, and even Lele areas (33: pp. 28-35, map; 40: pp. 45-51). The main axis of expansion was the Cikapa valley, where a trade-route had been opened by Imbangala traders before their arrival, a route which led to the richest territory in ivory then known (30: p. 456).[28] By 1860 Cokwe were hunting between the Kasai and Lulua. One of them met a Lulua headman, Mukenge Kalamba, and entered into trade relations with him; Kalamba eventually became a major chief and sent his Lulua to trade in Kimbundo and even farther, to Bihe itself. They offered ivory and slaves and were very keen on rifles (30: pp. 131, 140-6).[29] Once the Kasai was opened to trade in this fashion, Cokwe Ovimbundu, Imbangala, and Ambaquistas found their way also to the Kuba, the Kaniok, the Luba Kasai, and the western Songye, where, by 1880, they met chiefs allied with Tippu Tip who sent their slaves and ivory eastwards. The whole of Central Africa south of the tropical forest was then drawn into the pattern of long-distance trade.

The character of this trade had changed somewhat since the beginning of the nineteenth century. The years 1832-5 had been the golden age for the slave-trade. But during the same years new products were exploited, such as gum copal and orchilia, and, more important, Portugal abandoned her royal monopoly over ivory. This meant that trade in ivory was becoming much more worth while than it had ever been before, and most caravans concentrated on this product more than on the buying of slaves, especially since slavery had been abolished in Angola in 1836. Slaves however were still in demand as carriers for ivory or for export to African peoples such as the Kuba (54: pp. 219, 248) or Lozi (5: p. 353), who would buy them in exchange for ivory. Many were still sent to Angola, where they were put to work on the local plantations after a prize court in Luanda started in 1844 to block the export to South America. Beeswax, which had been an export article since the seventeenth century, became also more important. It was collected by the elephant hunters, and in some ways it can be considered to be a by-product of ivory.

Then, from 1870 onwards, rubber became increasingly important. The rubber was tapped from creepers and trees, and was available only in the forest-galleries of northern Angola and in the Kasai area, which were also the main exporters of ivory. This helps to explain why Cokwe expansion took that direction. But after 1886 rubber from lianas (red rubber) became increasingly exploited, and this was available in central and eastern Angola. After 1893 the only trade left was in red rubber, ivory and beeswax having been ousted from the market. But by 1905 the rubber boom and the days of the long-distance trade itself were over.[30]

IV The Trade in Copper and Salt from Katanga

Katanga possessed two valuable raw materials which were always in strong demand all over Central Africa: salt and copper. The salt-pans were located all around the Katanga lakes, and at Kiburi on the Upper Lualaba and Mwashya on the Upper Lufira. Salt was so valuable that it seems to have played a role in the Lunda expansion to the east (10b: p. 225), where the Mwaat Yaav first and the Kazembe later controlled the Kiburi and Mwashya pans. The mines north of the lakes were in the hands of the Luba kings (53: pp. 56-9, 66, 86-7; 5: p. 296; 3: p. 234). Salt deposits were visited by numerous small parties, and salt found its way from regional market to regional market to places as far north as the Kuba kingdom (53: pp. 52-66).[31] The line of trade seems to have been from the Kibuli mines through Sambaland to Kaniok, and thence along the Lulua to the Kuba. The Mwashya and lake salt-pans apparently exported their salt to eastern Katanga.[32]

But copper was valued even more than salt. The main deposits were located at Mwilu near the salt-pans of the Upper Lualaba, in the region between the Lufira and the Lualaba, and east of the Lufira, where the principal mines belonged to the Katanga chief (34: pp. 107-29).[33] It was cast mostly in the form of bars or of small St. Andrew's crosses. In this form the copper from Mwilu was traded to the southern Lunda states (30: p. 362), and via the Samba-Kaniok-Lulua or Kasai routes to the Kuba and the Ding.[34] The copper from the central and eastern mines went to Kazembe (53: pp. 75, 95),[35] and northwards through eastern Katanga to the site of the present Albertville (5: p. 223).[36] It is even suspected that the copper used in Buha, Burundi, and possibly Ruanda, came originally from Katanga. To the north, copper from this area reached the Songye and the Kusu as well as the Tetela and Jonga.[37] From there it may well have been traded, along with Jonga ironware and pottery, down the Cuapa and the Lomela to as far afield as the site of the present-day Coquilhatville. On the Lower Kasai, in the former kingdom of Kongo, on the Kongo river upstream of the Stanley Pool, in the Lake Leopold II area, and upstream of the Lukenye, most copper came from Mindouli or Bembe. For these were the only other sources of copper in the area. The data suggest that copper and salt were traded from regional market to regional market, but the fact that copper was in use everywhere in the whole area suggests strongly that all of Central Africa between the Kasai, the Zambezi and the great lakes had a single net of interlocking regional trade systems. Although they did not conform to a long-distance trade pattern, these regional networks cannot be left out of the picture in any discussion of central African trade-routes without creating great distortion of our understanding of the trade in this area.

NOTES

1. W. Froehlich analyses this type of trade. It was spread over the whole Congo basin north of a line from Luanda to Lake Moeru (23: pp. 239-40).
2. Field-notes.
3. But fashion influences also the market for essential goods. In the late nineteenth century, the Kuba imported Pende pottery, but after 1900 this went out of fashion, to be replaced by similar Lulua, Shoowa or Songo Meno wares.
4. This type of trade dies out because it is competing with trade conducted in the framework of the modern market system.
5. W. Froehlich, 283, 288, stresses the connections with the political structures. That this type of trade is old is borne out by the use of a four-day week connected with the market system in sixteenth-century Kongo. Cf. (12: p. 122) [data from 1584 to 1587].
6. The text says that the Portuguese *pombeiros* trade as well with the heathens (non-Kongo people) as with the Kongo. They send them to *associates* in San Salvador or Pinda (the harbour), who forward them to San Tome. The custom of sending Africans as *pombeiros* is just beginning. *Pombeiro* comes from *Mpumbu*, the name applied by the Kongo to Stanley Pool (K. Laman, 588). The name is derived in Kongo from the Kikongo name for the Hum or Wumbu,

living on the south bank of the Pool. The use of the term in 1584 as a generic name for trader in the interior indicates then that the trade had been in existence for some time and that caravans were frequent.

7. It is likely to be *Ibari Nkutu*, the Kwa River.
8. Okanga was a kingdom ruled by a queen, independent, but allied with Kongo. In 1610 there was a permanent mission-station there, apparently already for some time.
9. Cf. (13: pp. 188, 203-4, 217-18) and especially (4: III, pp. 273-7). It is possible that the ubiquitous Battell, traded on this road at least as far as the town of Batta (cf. 41: pp. 38-9) which lay on the road.
10. Cf. (41: pp. 43-4; 50) where Battell mentions copper, raphia, cloth, redwood, and ivory. (38: pp. 34-5; 77-97) mentions the same products, adding that they are very cheap since iron is very highly priced. This particularity seems to have disappeared later on, since around 1600 Battell mentions abundance of iron in one of the inland provinces (41: p. 52).
11. These are probably the Jaga who destroyed Bungu in Mayombe. They may be now either Sundi, Manyanga, or Yaa. Cf. map in M. Soret. Pigafetta's statement about the high value of iron is even more puzzling after this information from Dapper, 217.
12. Cf. (41: p. 58). 'Here I was with my two negro boys to buy elephants' hairs and tails. And in a month I bought twenty thousand, which I sold to the Portugals for thirty slaves and all my charges borne', says Battell.
13. For the Loango trade see (41: pp. 52-9; 13: pp. 143-7, 157-9, 184, 197-8, 203, 210, 216-17, 219-20).
14. One-sixth of slaves offered were Bobangi.
15. Cf. (28: pp. 16-18); (50: p. 283 'Hungaan are middlemen in trade Yans and Mbala'); L. van Naemen, 194-5 (Yaka and Yey on Lower Kwango); O. Schuett, 171 (Suku and country of Mwata Kumbana); H. von Wissmann, 53 (Mwata Kumbana and Mai Munene).
16. Kuba traditions; field-notes.
17. Field-notes.
18. Cf. (41: pp. 19-35). Battell met the Jagas with a party who wanted to buy slaves from them.
19. G. de Sousa Dias, 105-11, shows that the route existed before 1580. For evidence of trade: (41: p. 58; 13: p. 220).
20. This source mentions Lunda caravans and the Kasai river, 1681. The Africans of the Ambaca fort participated heavily in the caravan trade of Kassange as well. They were allowed by the Imbangala to go inland. They are known as Ambaquistas.
21. Cunnison, p. 65, gives the example of Kazembe before 1798; A. Verbeken, M. Walraet, 40, that of a caravan from Kanongesha (southern Lunda) in 1806.
22. For the monopoly see (35: p. 557). L. Magyar, 446, relates that around 1850 the Biheans had been temporarily discouraged in trade with Lunda because their caravans were attacked by the bigger Imbangala parties on the route. For Graça, M. Ferreira Ribeiro, p. 14, also L. Magyar, p. 108.
23. D. Livingstone, p. 456. The route went to the Upper Cikapa and Luajima rivers, east of Kimbundo and then due north to Mai. It was used by all the later explorers of the Kasai (Schuett, Pogge, von Wissmann, da Silva Porto).
24. Jose d'Assumpcao e Mello of Bahia went to the Luena at the instigation of an African from those parts. The trade was so successful that he took Alexandre da Silva of Santarem with him on his third trip in 1795. The latter wrote a report about it.
25. L. Magyar, p. 298, note 20 mentions all these places. Confirmation comes from

A. da Silva Porto, pp. 17-19. Arab travellers on their way from Kazembe to Benguella met the major of Bihe in Katanga (1851). D. Livingstone, p. 289 mentions two traders at Shinte's (southern Lunda).

26.   Silva Porto's *pombeiros* provoked a riot in a Lamba chiefdom because the local people thought they were Luena or Swahili. Luena (Lovale) is also the name they give to Biheans, which shows that the Luena preceded the Biheans in the trade of this area (data December 1853).

27.   He claims that in 1874 the Ovimbundu had had contact with Msiri for about twenty years, but with Kasongo only for a few years.

28.   But by 1875, an important part of the population in that area was Cokwe. Chief Kimbundo was not a Lunda but a Luena, who had arrived there around 1855 and ousted the true Lunda chief. Cf. P. Pogge, 45-51 who describes Kimbundo as an old man who had known three Lunda kings. O. Schuett, 131-2, says that the Cokwe arrived some twenty years before.

29.   This dates the rise of Kalamba around 1865.

30.   For the description of evolution in the trade, cf. (8: pp. 199-215, 224-31).

31.   The *pombeiros* of 1806 constantly met traders in salt from the Lubudi eastwards. The salt from Lubaland had a special name on the Kuba market, and was brought there from Luba of South Kasai (according to Kuba traditions). But there were also salt-pans in the Kasai itself. Cf. P. Denolf, 162-3.

32.   But the people of the area of Albertville had their salt from Uvinza on the other side of the lake; Cf. (15: p. 226). There were also salt-pans on the Luvua; Cf. (9: p. 789).

33.   Katanga was the 'perpetual' name of the chief.

34.   For the Kuba traditions and presence of copper crosses; for the Dzing (54: p. 362). For Kasai (17: pp. 327-8, 141, 77, 37-8). They came to the South Kasai from the Kaniok.

35.   Chief Mwilu of the western mines is mentioned on 55-6 and 85-6. He paid tribute in copper bars to the Mwaat Yaav and to Kazembe.

36.   The copper from the Lualaba north of Kasongo came from the Lomami. Cf. (5: p. 273). Also (9: p. 740). For the area east of the Lumua, he says (790) that there are no markets, but that there are small caravans which go sometimes very far. See also (49: p. 28), for copper in the Tabwa region.

37.   Copper crosses are found everywhere. They are melted into rings by Songye smiths. Information for Tetela and Jonga from personal communication by Professor L. de Heusch.

REFERENCES

(1)   Baesten, V. *Les anciens Jésuites au Congo – Précis Historiques*, 1893-6 (extrait).

(2)   Bastian, A. *San Salvador*. Berlin (1859).

(3)   Burton, W. F. B. 'The Country of the Baluba in Central Katanga', *Geographical Journal* (1927), LXX, 321-42.

(4)   Cadornega, O. de (ed. Delgado, J. M.), *História géral das guerras angolanas*. Lisbon (1940-2), 3 Vols.

(5)   Cameron, V. *Across Africa*. New York (1877).

(6)   Capello, H., Ivens, R. *From Benguella to the Territory of the Yacca*. London (1882), 2 Vols.

(7)   Cavazzi de Montecucollo, G. A. *Historische beschreibung der in dem untern occidentalischen Mohrenland ligenden drey Königreichen, Congo, Matamba und Angola*. Munich (1694) (original in Italian. Bologna, 1687).

(8)   Childs, G. *Umbundu Kinship and Character*. London (1949).

(9)   Colle, R. *Les Baluba* in Overbergh, C. Van (ed.) *Collection de Monographies*

Ethnographiques, X, XI. Brussels (1913).

(10a) Cunnison, I. 'Kazembe and the Portuguese, 1798-1832', *Journal of African History* (1961), II, No. 1, 61-76.

(10b) 'Kazembe's Charter', *Northern Rhodesia Journal* (1957), III, 3, 220-32.

(11) Cuvelier, J. *L'ancien royaume de Congo.* Brussels (1946).

(12) Cuvelier, J., Jadin, L. *L'ancien Congo d'après les archives romaines (1518-1640)*, MIRCB, XXXVI, 2. Brussels (1954).

(13) Dapper, O. *Naukeurige Beschryvinghe der Afrikaensche Gewesten.* Amsterdam, 1676.

(14) Decazes, E. 'Chez les Batekés', *Revue d'Ethnographie*, 1885, IV, 160-8.

(15) Degrandpré, L. *Voyage à la côte occidentale d'Afrique fait dans les années 1786 et 1787.* Paris (1801), 2 Vols.

(16) Delgado, R. *História de Angola.* Benguella and Lobito (1948-54), 5 Vols.

(17) Denolf, P. *Aan den rand der Dibese*, in MIRCB, XXXIV. Brussels (1954).

(18) Deschamps, H. *Traditions orales et archives au Gabon.* Paris (1962).

(19) Duysters, L. 'Histoire des Aluunda', *Problèmes d'Afrique Centrale* (1958), XII, 75-98.

(20) Edwards, A. *The Ovimbundu under two Sovereignties.* London (1962).

(21) Felner, A. de Albuquerque. *Angola.* Coimbra (1933).

(22) Ferreira Ribeiro, M. *Homenagem aos heröes que precederam Brito Capello e Roberto Ivens na exploração da Africa Austral.* 1484-1877. Lisbon (1885).

(23) Froehlich, W. 'Das Afrikanische Marktwesen', *Zeitschrift für Ethnologie* (1940). LXXII, 234-328.

(24) Garcia Mendes de Castello Branco. *Da Mina ao Cabo Negro segundo Garcia Mendes de Castello Branco (1574-1620)* in Cordeiro, L. (ed.), *Memórias do Ultramar.* Lisbon (1881).

(25) Gluckman, M. *Economy of the central Barotse plain.* Rhodes Livingstone Institute Papers, No. 10. Manchester (1943).

(26) Haveaux, G. L. *La tradition historique des Bapende orientaux.* In MIRCB, XXXVII, I. Brussels (1954).

(27) Jadin, L. 'Le Congo et la secte des Antoniens. Restauration du royaume sous Pedro IV et la Sainte Antoine congolaise, 1694-1718', *Bulletin de L'Institut historique belge de Rome* (1961), 411-609.

(28) Kopytof, I. *Suku Religion.* Ph.D. Dissertation. Northwestern University, 1960.

(29) Laman, K. *Dictionnaire Kikongo-Français.* In MIRCB, II. Brussels, 1936.

(30) Livingstone, D. *Missionary Travels and Researches in South Africa.* London, 1857.

(31) Lopes de Lima, J. J. *Ensaios sobre a Statistica das possessões Portuguezes.* Volume III. *Ensaio sobre a Statistica d'Angola e Benguella.* Lisbon, 1846.

(32) Magyar, L. *Reisen in Süd Afrika in den Jahren 1849-57.* Pest and Leipzig, 1859.

(33) McCulloch, M. *The Southern Lunda and Related Peoples. Ethnographic Survey of Africa. West Central Africa.* Part I. London, 1951.

(34) Mathieu, M. A. 'L'exploitation du cuivre par les indigènes du Katanga', *Congo*, 1925, V, II, 107-29.

(35) Mello, Dom Miguel Antonio de 'Angola no Começo do século (1802)', *Boletim da Sociedade de Geografia de Lisboa*, 1885. Series f a, 548-64.

(36) Paiva Manso, L. *História do Congo.* Lisbon, 1877.

(37) Pierpont, J. de 'Les Bambala', *Congo*, 1932, XII, I, 22-37; 185-199.

(38) Pigafetta, F. (Burssens, ed.) *De beschryvinghe vant groot ende vraemt Coninckrijck van Congo (1596)*, *Kongo Overzee*, 1941-42, VII-VIII, 1-86, 113-206. (Original in Italian 1596.) First English edition, *A Report of the kingdom of Congo*, 1881; reprinted Frank Cass, London, 1970.

(39) Plancquaert, M. *Les Jaga et les Bayaka du Kwango*, in MIRCB, III, I. Brussels,

1932.
(40)   Pogge, P. *Im Reiche des Muata Jamwo.* Berlin, 1880.
(41)   Ravenstein, E. G. *The Strange Adventures of Andrew Battell of Leigh in Angola and the Adjoining Regions.* London, 1901.
(42)   Schuett, O. *Reisen in Südwestlichen Becken des Congo.* Berlin, 1881.
(43)   Silva Correa, E. da. *História de Angola.* Lisbon, 1937. 2 Vols.
(44)   Silva Porto, A. da. (Sousa Dias G. ed.), *Silva Porto e a travessia do continente africano.* Lisbon, 1938.
(45)   Soret, M. *Les Kongo Nord-occidentaux,* in *Monographies Africaines.* Paris, 1959.
(46)   Sousa Dias, G. de. *Relações de Angola.* Coimbra, 1934.
(47)   Stanley, H. M. *Through the Dark Continent.* London, 1877.
(48)   Storme, M. *Ngankabe la prétendue reine des Baboma d'après H. M. Stanley.* In MARSC (1) 1956, NS, VII, 2.
(49)   Tippo Tip. *Maisha ya Hamed bin Mohammed el murjebi yauni Tippo Tip, Supplement to the East African Swahili Committee Journals,* July 1958, 28, 2; January 1959, 29, 1 (with translation in English by W. Whiteley).
(50)   Torday, E., Joyce, T. A. 'Notes ethnographiques sur des populations habitant les bassins du Kasai et du Kwango oriental', in *Annales du Musée du Congo Belge Ethnographie.* Série III, II, 2. Brussels, 1922.
(51)   Van Everbroeck, N. *Mbomb'lpoku. Le seigneur à l'abime,* in *Archives d'Ethnographie,* 3, *Musée Royal de l'Afrique Centrale.* Tervuren, 1961.
(52)   Van Naemen, L. 'Migration des Bayanzi (Bayeye)', *Congo,* 1934, XIV, I, 189-96.
(53)   Verbeken, A., Walraet, M. *La Première traversée du Katanga en 1806,* in MIRCB, XXX, 2. Brussels, 1953.
(53)   Von Wissmann, H., Wolf, L., Von François, C., Müller, H. *Im Innern Afrikas.* Leipzig, 1888.

MIRCB: *Mémoires de l'Institut Royal Colonial Belge. Section des sciences morales et politiques. Collection in 8º.*
MARSC: *Mémoires de l'Académie des Sciences Coloniales. Section des sciences morales et politiques. Collection in 8º.*

23

SOME COMMENTS ON THE ORIGINS OF TRADITIONAL MARKETS IN AFRICA SOUTH OF THE SAHARA*

B. W. Hodder

Over the last decade or so, a certain amount of work has been begun by social anthropologists, economists and geographers on the market institutions of Africa south of the Sahara. Markets, in the sense of public gatherings of buyers and sellers meeting at appointed places at regular intervals, have been found to be important elements of the social and economic landscape and their study essential to any real understanding of the life and work of many African communities. The study of markets, however, and in particular the description, understanding and explanation of their distributions and functions, raises a host of problems, most of which can be discussed in as yet only very tentative terms. The present paper focuses attention on one of the most difficult yet fundamental of such problems – the origins of markets in the region – and puts forward some suggestions as a basis for further discussion and field research. To simplify the present discussion, only traditional, indigenous markets, in existence before the arrival of the various European colonial administrations, will be considered.

There are two main theories about the origins of market institutions. The first, wholly orthodox theory starts from the individual's propensity to barter, perhaps involving silent barter; deduces from this the necessity for local exchange, the division of labour and local markets; and infers, finally, the necessity for long-distance or at least external exchange or trade (1). In other words, the starting point is seen to be in local exchange and local markets, only few of which, commonly because of certain fortuitous locational advantages, become important market centres associated with long-distance trading. To quote one source on this, 'barter exists among the most

*Reprinted from *Transactions of the Institute of British Geographers*, Vol. 36, 1965.

isolated and inaccessible societies; and the wordless exchange of goods made without witnesses in the furthermost recesses of the jungle, in Asia, America and Africa is evidence of an economic need. As confidence grows between individuals exchanging their respective goods, local markets spring up; and in the more advanced cultures wide use may be made of money in the more important markets or regional fairs' (2:p.65).

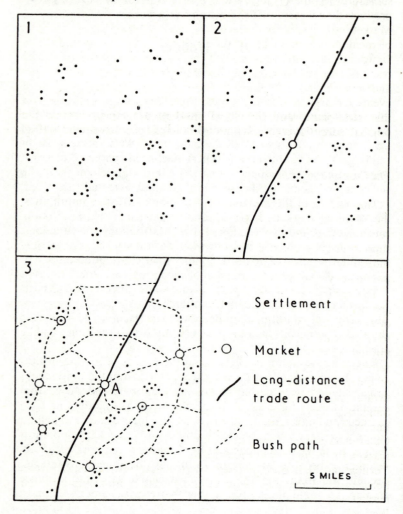

Figure 1 – The idealised sequence of events leading to the growth of markets.

An alternative theory about market origins reverses entirely this sequence of events, claiming that trade with its associated market phenomena can never arise within a community; for trade, it is contended, is an external affair involving different communities (3a; 3b; 3c: p.195; 3d: p.142). Markets can never arise out of the demands of purely individual or local exchange. As one writer puts it [in a substantive economy] 'local needs of exchange for foodstuffs or craft products do not seem sufficient to promote marketing activities . . . . Markets are primarily induced by external exchanges of complementary products with an alien population' (4). According to this viewpoint, then, markets are not the starting point but rather the result of long-distance trading, itself the result of division of labour and the variable geographical location of goods. The true sequence of events, it is argued, is thus: (i) trade route; (ii) market established on this trade route; and (iii) 'local' markets developing around the original 'parent' market as a network of tracks or roads develops (Fig. 1).

The Case of Yorubaland

The origins of market institutions have been examined carefully for the Yoruba country in West Africa, where traditional markets are very numerous indeed (5) and it must be admitted that the evidence in support of the second of these two theories appears overwhelming. Indeed, no positive evidence in support of the first, more orthodox notion has yet been discovered.

The earliest literary evidence of the first half of the nineteenth century (6a-f) shows clearly that markets were conspicuous features of Yorubaland long before the colonial period. Insofar as it is possible to reconstruct the distribution of markets in the Yoruba countryside through which these earliest observers passed, it is clear that markets were often located at junction zones, there being, for example, a line of old market towns along the contact zone between forest and savanna, where the products of each could be most easily exchanged. Similarly, the markets along the coastal lagoons and creeks were important contact points between agriculturalists and fishermen. Other markets were found at the junction of different peoples: Ketu market, for instance, was regarded as an important link between the Yoruba and Dahomey peoples; Iperu market was a contact point between the Egba and Ijebu groups of the Yoruba; and Mamu market was traditionally a frontier market between the Ijebu and Ibadan Yoruba. Even more important, markets of the early nineteenth century were often on or very near the chief trade routes of the day. Along these trade routes passed long-distance caravans, most of them connecting the coastal lagoon ports and markets of Porto Novo, Badagri, Ikorodu, Epe and Atijere with the Niger crossings farther north and forming but part of the great and ancient caravan trade linking Barbary, the Sahara and the forest lands along the Guinea coast. An important origin of many Yoruba markets, indeed, was that of a resting place: the Sapon market at Abeokuta, for example, took its name, which is a contraction of the Yoruba phrase meaning 'do favours to bachelors', from its origin as a place where hospitality – prepared food, soap, local beverages and shelter – could be offered to passing groups of traders (7: p.69). If such a resting place became popular, a market into which farmers brought their wares for sale soon sprang up; weekly markets were held; market sheds were built and the whole place became a sort of caravanserai for travellers (8: pp.90-1). While some of the caravans were quite small, others involved some 4,000-5,000 people; and there is in the literature of the 1820-50 period a number of descriptions of how these market centres on caravan routes greatly stimulated food production in their neighbourhood. R. Lander describes one such market, for instance, as 'a great thoroughfare for companies of merchants trading from Hausa, Borgoo and other countries to Gonja; and consequently a vast quantity of land is cultivated in its vicinity with corn and yams, to supply them with provisions' (6c: p.153).

A second relevant characteristic of these early markets as described by the first European observers refers to their commodity structure, which in every case included not only local food and craft products, but also many European and other non-Yoruba goods of a surprising variety. In Porto Novo at the end of the eighteenth century, J. Adams found an abundance of European-introduced goods – 'cloth, tobacco, iron, corals, cowries and beads alongside African cloth from Oyo and Ijebu' (9). H. Clapperton noted of Yorubaland that a considerable quantity of cloth was made and bartered with the people of the coast for rum, tobacco, European cloth and other articles; and at the market of Katunga (Old Oyo) the early travellers found an immense range of goods: local foodstuffs, the products of local craft industries and goods imported from neighbouring territories and from abroad, including Europe. Along the wayside Lander and Clapperton met many groups of slaves taking all kinds of goods – country cloth and indigo, for instance – to exchange for goods of European origin at the coast. There was also exchange with the areas north of Yorubaland: at Wow, the market was found to be well supplied with Indian corn and other commodities brought thither by wandering Arabs from the borders of the Sahara desert (6a: p.57).

Finally, it has been noted elsewhere that there is in Yorubaland a remarkable lack of correspondence between the location of tradi-

tional periodic markets on the one hand and the location and hierarchy of settlements on the other (10). Traditional markets here,
clearly, are not nuclei of settlement but foci of communications. This
phenomenon requires much closer study, but it is at least understan-
dable, even logical, in terms of the theory of market origins which sees
markets as being introduced from outside contacts (Fig. 1) rather than
arising naturally within an existing socio-economic framework.

Available evidence about markets in Yorubaland, then – their
location on long-distance trade routes, their commodity structure,
and their location in relation to the pattern and hierarchy of settlements – suggests that traditional markets in Yorubaland are related
genetically to external trading contacts.

Traditional Markets in Subsaharan Africa

Exactly how far the case of Yorubaland is typical of Africa south of
the Sahara it is as yet too early to say. Any comparative study of
market origins in the region has to depend upon inadequate, fragmentary and very uneven material. What evidence there is, however,
does seem to support entirely the conclusions reached for the Yoruba
country. This is particularly true of the majority of other West African
communities, such as the Ibo, Adja-Fon, Ewe, Ashanti and Mossi,
among whom markets are commonly traditional and, according to
the available evidence, similarly associated with external or long-
distance trading contacts. As M. G. Smith writes of the Hausa, 'the
record indicates that . . . the markets emerged with the large-scale
caravan traffic' (11: p.304).

In Ethiopia and the Horn of Africa, those societies with traditional
markets were similarly associated with external trading contacts.
Among the Somali, 'caravans laden with goods continually traverse
the country, especially in the season of the coastal fairs, when the
produce of the interior is traded for imports brought from Aden and
India. The modern towns of Somaliland . . . have developed from
market villages, established at the points of intersection of main
caravan routes. These were probably all originally founded by Arab
traders' (12: p.78). In Ethiopia the Galla have many traditional
markets which when first described were found to contain European
and other foreign goods as well as local produce; and the Galla are
known to have had 'direct contact with neighbouring kingdoms and
trade connections with the Somali coast' (13: p.111).

In East Africa, traditional markets are found among the more
southerly groups of the largest tribe, the Kikuyu. These southern
Kikuyu are known to have traded not only among their own tribal
groups and sub-groups but also with neighbouring tribes, notably the

Masai and Kamba, who in turn traded with Arab and Swahili caravans and acted as middlemen between the coastal and interior traders (14: pp.13, 20, 76). In Kenya, too, the Teita have traditional markets and have long been noted for their caravan trading to and from the coast (15: pp.109-16). The Buganda, Busoga and Swahili-speaking coastal peoples also have traditional markets; and all are known to have had important trading contacts with peoples and routes outside their own territorial boundaries (16a: p.49; 16b). Finally in East Africa, the coastal Digo tribe of the north-eastern Bantu are unlike their immediate Bantu neighbours in having traditional market institutions; and these Digo, significantly, have long enjoyed 'an influential position as middlemen in the ivory trade and traded with the Swahili, Arab and Indian merchants' (17: p.57).

Information on traditional markets in the Congo region is even more fragmentary and slender than for East Africa, but what evidence there is all points to the same conclusion. Among the Kongo people traditional markets are of very long standing and were clearly related to several important land and river trade routes through their territory (18: p.69). Among the Kuba, markets date back to at least the seventeenth century when the tribe are known to have been involved in trading activities with the Portuguese on the coast (19a: pp.190-210; 19b: p.17). Even among those peoples where traditional markets do not exist, a few isolated traditional markets may often be found around the periphery of the tribal lands where inter-tribal trade could take place: a few markets, for instance, seem for long to have existed along the Ubangi River where it forms the boundary between the Ngbandi and Banda peoples (20: p.87). Similar peripheral markets are to be found along the borders of the Ruandi and Urundi groups (21: pp.35, 130).

Though the positive evidence in favour of the second theory of market origins appears to be overwhelming in Subsaharan Africa, it should perhaps be pointed out that this is one of those situations where the nature of the evidence must almost inevitably tend to favour one theory rather than another. More particularly, the earliest literary evidence, given by Europeans in their earliest expeditions into the interior during the nineteenth century, refers almost entirely to journeys made along the major long-distance trade routes of the day. These earlier observers, therefore, were unable to comment at first hand on markets lying away from these routes. Lack of positive evidence to show the origin of markets in the needs of local or neighbourhood exchange is therefore to be expected and cannot reasonably be taken by itself to mean that no markets could originate independently of streams of long-distance trading (22: pp.510-11)[2] It is still clearly impossible to reconstruct the pre-contact trading patterns of most African societies.

Further evidence about market origins, however, relates to the geographical distribution of traditional markets in Subsaharan Africa. As a number of writers have observed, while traditional markets are the rule in most West African and north-eastern communities, such markets are often very scarce elsewhere in the region, especially in the south and east of Africa (23:x). In many parts of Subsaharan Africa, then, markets post-date European control; are frequently strictly European-introduced phenomena; and in some⸱ cases are operated by largely non-indigenous peoples.

Further, few of the Nilotic or Nilo-Hamitic tribes seem to have any traditional markets (24a; 24b: p.60); nor are indigenous markets characteristic of the Nuer, Nyoro, Toro, Amba, Konjo, Nyakore, Kiga, Haza, Zwina, Gisu or Ngoni (25a: p.88; 25b; 25c: p.20).

It is in southern and south-eastern Africa, however, that the absence of traditional markets is most striking. In Northern Rhodesia there is no evidence anywhere of traditional markets having existed. Here, on the contrary, markets are described quite clearly as 'of recent origin. Traditional trading was confined to small areas in the territory. There were no markets, in the sense of permanent places where buying and selling takes place' (26). In Southern Rhodesia the Shana and Ndebele have no past history of markets (27); and the same is true of the Herero of South-West Africa (28: p.618), the Basuto, the Swazi and the Sotho (29a: p.166; 29b; 29c). Among the Tswana of South Africa, too, there are no traditional markets: 'traditionally, whoever wished to sell or buy something inquired among his neighbours until he found a customer, and the transaction was then concluded directly between them' (30: p.29).

From the point of view of the present argument, the important thing to note is the reason for this areal differentiation in market origins. For if the orthodox notion about the rise of markets were correct, then markets would surely have arisen quite naturally among the indigenous tribal societies in all parts of the continent and not only in West Africa and a few other rather limited areas.

Lack of external trading contacts may help to explain the lack of traditional markets among those tribal societies who until very recently remained cut off from the main regional streams of trade and exhibited only the most primitive forms of subsistence economies. Among the Bulu of the Cameroons, for instance, the isolated, subsistence economy never gave rise to markets (31: pp.170-89). This is not to say that there was no internal exchange; but such internal exchange never gave rise to markets. As among most African communities, local exchange among the Bulu takes the form of reciprocal gift-giving based on kinship obligations or other socially obligatory payments; and this kind of exchange is often social in motivation and functions, though the goods exchanged may be economic goods in the sense that they are yams, rice, or stock. This kind of indigenous exchange, however, is not the same thing as trade and does not demand the existence of market institutions. Among the Amba of East Africa, too, 'as most families and villages were self-supporting, and most villages were composed of related persons, most distribution of goods and services in Bwamba was conducted along kinship principles and there was little foreign trade' (25b: p.84). Here again, then, there was no need for market institutions.

It can also be pointed out that one of the chief reasons for the great concentration of traditional markets in West Africa lies possibly in the geographical position of the region in relation to the Guinea coast in the south and the trans-Saharan routes to Barbary in the north. For centuries, parts of the West African coast were visited by European traders; and inland, important north-south caravan routes of great antiquity linked the trans-Saharan routes with the Guinea coastlands. Though it was not until the latter half of the nineteenth century that the interior parts of West Africa began to come under direct European administrative control, many parts of the region had long been associated with important long-distance, external trading interests. Even a poor area like that occupied by the Bororo of what is now the Republic of Niger could therefore support large numbers of markets before the period of French administration, since this was historically an important transit zone between the Sahara and the farming lands of the south (32: pp.335-62). Of the Mossi, too, it has been noted that 'the geographic position of Mossi country has much to do with its being an important trade and market centre . . . and . . . for several centuries caravans have passed through this region'.[3] It is also significant in West Africa that where societies were not so favourably located in relation to the major caravan routes, or suffered locally from difficult topographical barriers to trade, these societies commonly had no indigenous markets before the arrival of the European administrations. This is true, for instance, of most of the peoples of central Sierra Leone (33). In the case of the Kpe in the Cameroons, too, E. Ardener has correlated the lack of traditional markets in this mountainous territory with the absence of any important trade route passing through the country (34: p.48). Finally, among the Guro of the Ivory Coast it has been suggested that the chief reason for the existence of traditional markets in northern Guroland and their absence in the south lies in the comparative lack of a convenient medium of exchange and the absence of penetration by active trading agents in the south (4: p.288).

It is impossible, however, to establish any simple causal relationship between external or long-distance trading contacts on the one hand and traditional markets on the other. Though no examples have yet been found of traditional markets existing without such contacts, there are many instances of these contacts being present without their having given rise to market institutions. To some extent this may have been because the trading involved was never frequent, sustained or substantial enough to stimulate the growth of markets. On the other hand, not even vigorous trade has necessarily always resulted in the growth of market institutions. There are many examples of trade existing without markets. Among the Dorobo, for instance, inter-tribal trade has never given rise to special places for trade (35: p.60). In Northern Rhodesia, inter-regional and intra-regional trade was active and commerce vastly more complex in composition and in-volving far more tribes than is normally recognised. But though trade existed, as among the Lozi, there were no market places (36a: pp.39-40; 36b). Finally, among the Ovimbundu of Angola the car-avan trade was always a most important feature of tribal life; yet there is no evidence of any important pre-European market structure (37: p.16).

Long-distance, external trading contacts, then, are clearly not sufficient by themselves to generate market institutions. Though all traditional markets appear to occur only in societies with pre-colonial external trading contacts, there are many societies without traditional markets where precisely similar trading connections certainly existed. It is necessary, therefore, to examine other conditioning factors in the rise of traditional markets in Africa south of the Sahara. M. Hers-kovits sees the explanation largely in terms of economies: 'differences in the complexities of over-all systems and their technologies, between the economic organisation of the cattle-keeping peoples of East and South Africa and economies based on agriculture, are to be seen in clear outline in the presence or absence of markets in the pre-colonial epoch' (23). A. A. Nyirenda, on the other hand, puts the lack of traditional markets in Northern Rhodesia down to the fact that 'no urbanisation had developed among the indigenous people in pre-colonial Northern Rhodesia; nor are there any marked climatic zones leading to exchange of varying agricultural and pastoral produce' (26: p.63). Another writer has suggested that the savanna-forest milieu, but not the forest, creates a need for exchange between complementary areas (4: pp.283-5).

A review of existing evidence, however, suggests that the relative lack of pre-contact markets in certain parts of Africa may simply be due to the absence in these areas of two necessary conditions without which any opportunities presented by long-distance or external trad-ing contacts could never be grasped and channelled through market institutions.

First, it could be argued that market institutions cannot develop in areas of low population density. In Yorubaland it has been suggested that there is a critical figure of about fifty persons to the square mile below which markets do not occur (38: pp.48-58). It seems, in fact, reasonable to assume that only where the density of population is high enough does face-to-face contact of large numbers of people within ready walking distance of each other become possible; and furthermore, that a low density of population seriously limits the possibilities of economic diversification and any large degree of regional specialisation of production. Exactly how far this idea is valid in all parts of Africa, and if so, what past or present population density figures are critical, only further work can reveal; but in a number of cases – as among the southern Kikuyu and Burundi – the correlation between population density and the existence of traditional markets seems significant (14; 21). In West Africa, too, C. Meillassoux has commented in detail on the correlation of markets and population density in Guroland, examining the hypothesis that a high density of population promotes great trading activity (4: p.285).

Secondly, it appears that only where well-developed and highly organised political units existed could communities profit from what trading possibilities they had; for without this strong political organisation, the security of traders and the peace of the markets could not be assured. West Africa, significantly, had a very early and important development of highly organised kingdoms: notably the Ashanti, Dahomey and Yoruba kingdoms. In this respect, too, it is useful to compare the Kuba and Lele peoples of the Congo, only the former of which possesses traditional markets. Among the Kuba the political structure in pre-contact days was of a kind to guarantee the essential conditions of security and market peace, whereas among the Lele there was no such political organisation (39: p.191).

Conclusion

The ideas put forward in this paper can only be regarded as very tentative. Work on markets and trade in all parts of Africa is only just beginning, and the need for more detailed field studies and comparative work in other parts of the tropical underdeveloped world is clearly necessary. The need for a comparative study of traditional African and medieval European market is also indicated. The whole problem, however, is not simply a matter of collecting more and more data. It is also one of trying constantly to construct some general conceptual framework within which to consider such complex and little understood phenomena as market institutions. For without some such framework the study of these and similar features of the landscape can never develop beyond the presentation of a series of discrete descriptions.

As far as the origins of traditional markets in Africa south of the Sahara are concerned, no positive support has yet been found for the orthodox view that markets may arise quite naturally out of the demands of local exchange. While the nature of the evidence makes it impossible to state categorically that no traditional markets could have arisen in this way, it appears that the bulk of traditional markets in Subsaharan Africa received their initial stimulus from external, long-distance trading contacts. Yet while these trading contacts seem to have been necessary to the rise of indigenous markets, two other conditions – a sufficiently high density of population and a political structure powerful enough to secure and maintain the market peace – were necessary before a simple marketless society could develop naturally into an 'intermediate' society, in which there is evident all the formal structure of market institutions (40: p.14).

NOTES

1.   See also the invaluable records to be found in *Church Missionary Intell., Proc. Church Missionary Soc.,* and *Church Missionary Gleaner.*
2.   It can also be pointed out that pre-contact trade in many parts of West Africa, at least, was chiefly of two types: local petty trading in the hands of women; and long-distance trading by men. It is possible to associate 'large' markets, arising out of long-distance trade, with the latter type of trading; and to associate 'small' markets, arising out of purely local needs, with the former 'petty' trading by women. There seems to be no evidence for making this distinction in *origins,* however. See P. C. Lloyd, *A comparative study of the political institutions in some Yoruba kingdoms* (1953), unpublished B.Sc. thesis, University of Oxford. See also E. P. Skinner, 'Trade and markets among the Mossi people', in P. Bohannan and G. Dalton, op. cit. 254, who distinguishes between those markets specialising in external trading and markets specialising in internal commerce. Here, again, however, there is no evidence to show origins.
3.   E. P. Skinner; see note 2.

REFERENCES

(1)   Bohannan, P., *The Tiv Market Place* (1961), unpublished manuscript.
(2)   International Labour Organisation, 'Indian markets and fairs in Latin America', in *Indigenous People* (1953).
(3a)   Polanyi, K., *Origins of our Time* (1946).
(3b)   Polanyi, K., Arensberg, C. W. and Pearson, H. W. (eds.), *Trade and Market in the Early Empires* (1957).
(3c)   Weber, M., *General Economic History* (1930).
(3d)   Pirenne, N., *Medieval Cities* (1925).
(4)   Meillassoux, C., 'Social and economic factors affecting markets in Guro Land', Chapter 10 in Bohannan, P. and Dalton, G. (eds.), *Markets in Africa* (1962), 297.
(5)   Hodder, B. W., *Markets in Yorubaland,* unpublished Ph.D. thesis, University of London (1963).

(6a)   Clapperton, H. and Lander, R., *Journal of a Second Expedition into the Interior of Africa from the Bight of Benin to Seccattoo* (1829).
(6b)   Lander, R., *Records of Clapperton's Last Expedition to Africa* (1830); reprinted Frank Cass, London, 1967.
(6c)   Lander, R. and Lander, J., *Journal of an Expedition to Explore the Course and Termination of the Niger* (1832).
(6d)   Tucker, S., *Abeokuta: or Sunrise within the Tropics* (1853).
(6e)   Bowen, T. J., *Adventures and Missionary Labours in Several Countries in the Interior of Africa* (1857), 2nd ed., with a new introduction by E. A. Ayandele, Frank Cass, London, 1968.
(6f)   Townsend, G., *Memoir of the Reverend Henry Townsend* (1887).
(7)   Ajisafe, A., *History of Abeokuta* (1924).
(8)   Johnson, S., *History of the Yorubas* (1921), 90-1.
(9)   Adams, J., *Remarks on the Country extending from Cape Palmas to the River Congo* (1823); reprinted Frank Cass, London, 1966, 87.
(10)   Hodder, B. W., 'Rural periodic day markets in part of Yorubaland', *Trans. Inst. Br. Geogr.*, 29 (1961), 149.
(11)   Smith, M. G., 'Exchange and marketing among the Hausa', Chapter II in P. Bohannan and G. Dalton, op. cit.
(12)   Lewis, I. M., 'Peoples of the Horn of Africa', *Ethnographic Survey of Africa* (1955).
(13)   Huntingford, G. W. B., 'The Galla of Ethiopia', *Ethnographic Survey of Africa* (1955).
(14)   Middleton, J., 'The Kikuyu and Kamba of Kenya', *Ethnographic Survey of Africa* (1953).
(15)   Prins, A. H. J., 'The coastal tribes of the north-eastern Bantu', *Ethnographic Survey of Africa* (1952).
(16a) Fallers, M. C., 'The eastern lucustrine Bantu', *Ethnographic Survey of Africa* (1960), 49.
(16b) A. H. J. Prins, 'The Swahili-speaking peoples of Zanzibar and the East African coast', *Ethnographic Survey of Africa* (1961).
(17)   Prins, A. H. J., 'The coastal tribes of the north-eastern Bantu', *Ethnographic Survey of Africa* (1952).
(18)   Soret, M., 'Les Kongo nord-occidentaux', *Monogr. Ethnol. Afr.* (1959), 69.
(19a) Vansina, J., 'Trade and markets among the Kuba', Chapter 7 in P. Bohannan and G. Dalton, op. cit.
(19b) Vansina, J., 'Les tribus Ba-kuba', *Ethnographic Survey of Africa* (1954).
(20)   Burssens, H., 'Les peuplades de l'entre Congo-Ubangi', ibid. (1958).
(21)   D'Hertefelt, M., Trouwbrost, A., Scherer, J., 'Les anciens royaumes de la zone interlacustre meridionale', ibid. (1962), 35, 130.
(22)   Croix, G. E. M. De Ste, in *Econ. Hist. Rev.*, 12 (1960).
(23)   Herskovits, M., in P. Bohannan and G. Dalton, op. cit.
(24a) Butt, A., 'The Nilotes of the Anglo-Egyptian Sudan and Uganda', *Ethnographic Survey of Africa* (1952).
(24b) Huntingford, G. W. B., 'The southern Nilo-Hamites', *Ethnographic Survey of Africa* (1953).
(25a) Evans-Pritchard, E. E., *The Nuer* (1950), 88.
(25b) Taylor, B. K., 'The western lacustrine Bantu', ibid. *Ethnographic Survey of Africa* (1962).
(25c) La Fontaine, J. G., 'The Gisu of Uganda', *Ethnographic Survey of Africa* (1959).
(26)   Nyirenda, A. A., 'Africa market vendors in Lusaka, with a note on the recent boycott', *Rhodes-Livingstone J.*, 22 (1957), 37.
(27)   Kuper, H., Hughes, A. J. B., Van Velsen, J., 'The Shana and Ndebele of

Southern Rhodesia', *Ethnographic survey of Africa* (1955).

(28)   Gibson, G. D., 'Bridewealth and other forms of exchange among the Herero',
         Chapter 25 in P. Bohannan and G. Dalton, op. cit. 618.

(29a)   Ashton, H., *The Basuto* (1952), p.166.

(29b)   Kuper, H., 'The Swazi', *Ethnographic Survey of Africa* (1952).

(29c)   Sheddick, V. G. J., 'The Southern Sotho', ibid. (1953).

(30)   Schapera, I., 'The Tswana', *Ethnographic Survey of Africa* (1953).

(31)   Horner, G. R., 'The Bulu response to European economy', Chapter 6 in P.
         Bohannan and G. Dalton, op. cit.

(32)   Dufire, M., 'Trade and markets in the economy of the nomadic Fulani of Niger
         (Bororo)', Chapter 12 in P. Bohannan and G. Dalton, op. cit.

(33)   McCulloch, M., 'The peoples of Sierra Leone protectorate', *Ethnographic
         Survey of Africa* (1952).

(34)   Ardener, E., 'Coastal Bantu of the Cameroons', *Ethnographic Survey of Africa*
         (1956).

(35)   Huntingford, G. W. B., 'The southern Nilo-Hamites', *Ethnographic Survey of
         Africa* (1953), 60.

(36a)   Miracle, M. P., 'Plateau Tonga entrepreneurs in historical inter-regional trade',
         Rhodes-Livingstone J., 26 (1960), 39-40.

(36b)   Turner, V. W., 'The Lozi peoples of north-western Rhodesia', *Ethnographic
         Survey of Africa* (1952).

(37)   McCulloch, M., 'The Ovimbundu of Angola', *Ethnographic Survey of Africa*
         (1952).

(38)   Hodder, B. W., 'Distribution of markets in Yorubaland', *Scott. geogr. Mag.*, 81
         (1965) 48-58.

(39)   Vansina, J., 'Trade and markets among the Kuba', chapter seven in P. Bohan-
         nan and G. Dalton, op. cit.

(40)   Herskovits, M. J., *Economic Anthropology* (1952).

24

TRADE CENTRES IN THE NORTHERN
INTERLACUSTRINE REGION*

John Tosh

Salt and iron were two articles of trade which were essential to
everyday life. But there were other indigenous products which were
traded over considerable distances for their luxury value. The first of
these was bark-cloth. From at least the reign of Semakokiro onwards,
the making of bark-cloths was a vigorous domestic industry in
Buganda, and they had become standard clothing for the common
people by the late nineteenth century. Plain and dyed bark-cloths
were exported to Karagwe, Rwanda, Busoga, and Bunyoro, for none
of these countries produced cloth of comparable quality. Outside
Buganda, bark-cloth was generally worn only by the wealthy, but the
Baganda were assured a steady demand since bark-cloths were apparently worn out in a month (1: pp.403, 434; 2: pp.119-20; 3: II,
p.251).

Another well-established article of exchange was coffee. The cultivated plant was unknown, but wild coffee produced small beans
which were chewed as a stimulant. The traditions of the Haya states
show that in the eighteenth century traders from Kiziba were taking
coffee to the neighbouring states of Kiamtwara and Karagwe. In the
nineteenth century the coffee plant flourished in Bunyoro and
Buganda, and it was these countries which supplied Karagwe, where
it was customary for guests to be presented with a handful of beans.
European travellers found that the toasted beans made an excellent
beverage, and Emin remarked with considerable foresight on the
commercial potential of interlacustrine coffee (4: pp.75, 77; 5: p.482;
6: II, p.181; 7: pp.459-60; 2: p.118). But its place in the African
economy was small, as was the case with tobacco. Like coffee, tobacco

*Reprinted by permission from 'The Northern Interlacustrine Region' in *Pre-Colonial
African Trade,* edited by Richard Gray and David Birmingham, Oxford University
Press, 1970.

was a luxury with a long history; pottery tobacco pipes from the seventeenth century have been found at the Ankole capital site of Bweyorere. It was in Ankole that much of the best tobacco grew in Emin's day, and a surplus was exported to Karagwe and Bunyoro (8: p.193; 2: pp.78, 112; 9: pp.158-9).

Clearly, in a handful of commodities at least, quite a brisk trade affecting widely separated quarters of the interlacustrine region must have been carried on before the arrival of the coastal traders. But it is easier to record the existence of this trade than to describe the nature of the commercial process involved, for it was precisely at this level that the coastal traders made their greatest impact, especially as regards media of exchange. The subsequent European accounts may therefore be a most unreliable guide in this matter. They give very little evidence that the northern interlacustrine region was equipped with an indigenous form of currency. Roscoe claims that ivory discs were used as currency before either beads or cowrie-shells arrived from the coast, but this statement can hardly be accepted at face value without any indication of the economic context. Cows and probably also iron hoes served as units of account; the latter may conceivably have been a medium of exchange, though we have no direct evidence for thinking so. What is quite clear is that there was little or no means of hoarding currency as wealth and thus securing the economic services of others (1: pp.412-13; 10: p.78).

For the most part, it would therefore seem, trade was carried on by barter, and the lack of currency was partly offset by the existence of recognised markets where traders could rely on finding the fullest range of goods and customers. Later on, Arabs frequented these markets, but the European descriptions are of essentially African markets to which the coastmen came as outsiders. As Emin wrote when stressing the commercial bent of the Africans: 'whoever visits the markets of Werahanje [i.e. Bweranyange] in Karagwa [sic], Rubaga in Uganda, and Mpara Nyamoga in Unyoro will find convincing proofs of this fact', and he supported this assertion by giving a vivid detailed description of Mpara. Kibero was another such centre where in Emin's time ox-hides, skins, iron-ore, spear-heads, brass bars, and glass beads were brought in exchange for salt; on the other side of Bunyoro there were frontier markets to which the Baganda came with bark-cloths and plantains, and the Banyoro with hoes and salt, while further east in Lake Kyoga the islands of Namulumuka and Kaweri were established places for trade between the Banyoro and the Kumam (2: pp.112-13; 1: p.456; II). It is hard to tell whether these markets were seasonal or in session regularly throughout the year. Probably those which dealt mainly in salt and iron goods fell into the second category, since these commodities were worked by specialists who had no other livelihood and could practise their skills all the year round. As for the traders themselves, there is no evidence that they were professional entrepreneurs; rather, they were engaged in subsistence farming or one of the few specialised activities and took time off to barter their surpluses.

Yet if there were no professional traders and no one trading people before the arrival of the Arabs, some parts of the region seem to have been commercially more prominent than others. The available evidence strongly suggests that Bunyoro was the most important. Casati in the 1880s noted how the Banyoro 'exhibit their gifts in industries and commerce', and Samuel Baker had been equally impressed. It may be objected that these glowing reports merely reflect the tendency for Europeans to travel through Bunyoro, but the vital concentrations of salt and iron there lend substance to their accounts. Furthermore, Bunyoro derived substantial advantages from her strategic position as the northernmost interlacustrine kingdom: on two sides – the north and the east – her territory was contiguous with the non-Bantu areas inhabited by the Lango and the Acholi, with whom Bunyoro had ancient dynastic links. The initiative in trading with the Lango was apparently taken by the Jopalwo, a group of Lwo-speaking clans in north-east Bunyoro. In return for goats, cattle, butter, and later ivory, they traded metal hoes which the Lango needed both for agricultural use and for turning into spearheads. Neither the Lango nor their eastern neighbours, the Kumam and Iteso, knew the art of smelting, and in time the Banyoro established commercial links with these latter tribes as well. This traffic in ironware is the basis for D. A. Low's statement that the Banyoro dominated the trade round Lake Kyoga in the nineteenth century (12: II, p.54; 13: II, pp.54-5; 14: pp.30, 81; 5: pp.471, 479; 15: p.148; 16: p.327).

In two other areas – Buganda and Karagwe – the European accounts also give an impression of particularly vigorous commercial activity. But here it is more difficult to assess the place of indigenous trade, since these were the kingdoms most frequented by the Zanzibaris. Karagwe's dominance of the other Haya states may indeed have been due to her skilful handling of long-distance trade. The case of Buganda poses different problems; her eminence undoubtedly predated the arrival of the Arabs. Buganda's food supplies were the most plentiful in the region; they depended on a plantain economy which provided food all the year round with minimum human effort, thus freeing manpower for other activities. But this potential for entrepreneurial activity was not realised by the Baganda. Their dealings with the surrounding tribes were on a predatory rather than a commercial level, and this tendency was strongly encouraged by the

Kabaka in order to provide, at no cost to himself, rewards in the form of captured women and livestock for his chiefs and those Baganda who were anxious to better themselves. Iron and salt were obtained by plunder and tribute (tribute in the sense that no commercial exchange, however indirect, was involved, the transaction being essentially political), as well as by trade. According to their own traditions, the Baganda seldom travelled abroad to trade; instead, they waited for foreigners to come to them (18: p.452). Only on Lake Victoria is there any indication that they were involved in an extensive commercial network. Despite the piracy of the Buvuma islanders noted by Stanley in 1875, goods passed from one end of the lake to the other; the salt trade between the east side of the lake and Buganda has been mentioned already; in the late nineteenth century the Sukuma were supplying hoes and other iron goods to Busoga. Recent research there has shown that southern Busoga was traditionally an important centre of trade from the Sesse and Buvuma islands and the coastal parts of Buganda, dealing in white ants, dried fish and bananas, canoes, pots, hoes, livestock, and poultry. As the political influence of Buganda expanded along the lakeshore, her share in this trade probably increased; at any rate, Carl Peters believed that 'in estimating the political and commercial affairs of East Africa too little stress is laid on this internal trade among the tribes . . . . The barter trade of [B]Uganda along the coast defies all direct calculation' (18: I, p.223; 1: p.438; 19: pp.391-2; 20).

The centres of trade which attracted the notice of Europeans were probably not the only ones; indeed they may not have been the most important. But plainly such centres existed. To what extent were they under royal control? Here the evidence is particularly slender. Often important markets were sited at the royal residence: Mpara Nyamoga, for example, was Kabarega's capital in the 1870s. This suggests that the king was either a trader on his own account or else imposed some form of tax. In Buganda, market-places in and around the capital were supervised by a special chief who levied dues of 10% on all transactions for the Kabaka. More stringent controls must have operated at the Kibero salt-mines which Junker described as 'being largely in the hands of Kabarega'; in 1894 during the British campaign against Bunyoro, Colonel Colvile saw the mines as 'Kabarega's chief source of wealth and means of procuring arms and ammunition' (1: p.452; 5: p.524; 21). But it is hard to say whether this high degree of political control over trade was longstanding, or whether it was a reaction to the growth of long-distance trade which presented a more obvious challenge to the stability of the interlacustrine states.

The almost total lack of contemporary evidence renders any reconstruction of traditional trade distorted and incomplete, but some attempt must be made if the impact of the long-distance caravans is to be understood. Certainly, the apparatus of traditional trade was primitive enough. As far as can be seen, there was no currency nor professional trading, and the number of specialist producers was small. Nevertheless exchange seems to have been a highly significant feature of the interlacustrine economies, not only because it was the principal means of·distributing such essentials as salt and iron, but also because it transcended political divisions. The inhabitants, and especially their rulers, were familiar with a commercial system which was relatively advanced in scale, if not in methods. Without this experience Africans could not have exploited as they did the opportunities created by long-distance trade. The coastal traders provided an indispensable stimulus from the 1840s onwards, but they did not take control of the commercial life of the region. Instead, Africans dominated every stage of the commercial process save the actual transport of goods to and from the coast.

REFERENCES

(1)   Roscoe, J., *The Baganda*, 1911, reprinted with a new bibliographic note, Frank Cass, London (1965).
(2)   Schweinfurth, G. and others, *Emin Pasha in Central Africa*, London (1888).
(3)   Barker, S. W., *Ismailia*, 2 vols., London (1874).
(4)   Cory, H., *History of Bukoba District*, Mwanza, n.d.
(5)   Junker, W., *Travels in Africa during the Years, 1882-1886*, London (1892).
(6)   Burton, R. F., *The Lake Regions of Central Africa*, 2 vols., London (1860).
(7)   Parke, T. H., *My Personal Experiences in Equatorial Africa*, London (1891).
(8)   Posnansky, M., 'Pottery Types from Archeological Sites in East Africa', *J. African History*, 2 (1961).
(9)   Grant, J. W., *A Walk Across Africa*, London (1864).
(10)   Roscoe, J., *The Banyankole*, London (1923).
(11)   Kagwa, Paulo, 'Kakungulu Omuzira wa Uganda', 10 (MS. in Makerere College Library).
(12)   Casati, G., *Ten Years in Equatoria*, 2 vols., London (1891).
(13)   Baker, S. W., *Albert N'yanza*, 2 vols., London (1866).
(14)   Driberg, J. H., *The Lango*, London (1923).
(15)   Lawrance, J. C. D., *The Iteso*, London (1957).
(16)   Low, D. A., in *History of East Africa*, Oliver, R. and Mathew, G., (eds.), Oxford (1963).
(17)   Kiwanuka, M. S., 'The Traditional History of the Buganda Kingdom', London PdD. thesis (1965).
(18)   Stanley, H. M., *Through the Dark Continent*, 2 vols., London (1878).
(19)   Peters, C., *New Light on Dark Africa*, London (1891).
(20)   Cohen, D. W., personal communication.
(21)   F.O. (C.P.) 6557/147, Colvile to F.O. from Kibero, 5 February 1894.

PART VII

Media of Exchange and Standards of Value

NATIVE AND TRADE CURRENCIES IN SOUTHERN NIGERIA DURING THE EIGHTEENTH AND NINETEENTH CENTURIES*

G. I. Jones

Historical Survey

The earliest historical references to trading in the Bight of Biafra (the Eastern Nigerian and Cameroons Coast) is in the *Esmeraldo de Situ Orbis* of Pacheco Pereira which was written about 1508. Referring to the trade of the Rio Real (the common entrance to the New Calabar and Bonny rivers) he says, 'They come from a hundred leagues or more up this river bringing yams in large quantities; they also bring many slaves, cows, goats and sheep. Sheep they call "bozy". They sell all this to the natives of the village for salt, and our ships buy these things for copper bracelets, which are here greatly prized – more than those of brass; for eight or ten bracelets you can obtain one slave' (20: p.132). Unfortunately Pereira does not give the names either of the salt-making village at the mouth of the Rio Real or of the people who came down the river to trade there. Like the other Portuguese sources Pereira stops short at the Rio Real and does not refer to the Cross River estuary or to the Rio del Rey.

No other reference is made to the trade of the Rio Real until Dapper's *Description* first published in Flemish in 1676 and then in a French translation in 1686. Dapper incorporated all the information available to him up to the time when he wrote. During the intervening hundred and fifty years the Portuguese had been replaced by the Dutch as the principal traders in the Rio Real area, and the people with whom they did most of their business were the Kalaban. But, for reasons which are now unknown, the Dutch maps of the seventeenth century and later ones which followed them insisted on referring to the Efik settlements of the Cross River as Old Calabar and the

*Reprinted by permission of the International African Institute from *Africa*, Vol. XXVIII, No. 1, January 1958.

Kalabari of the Rio Real as New Calabar.

John Barbot's *Description of the Coast of North and South Guinea* was published in 1746 but it referred to the West Coast trade as he knew it from 1678 to 1682, and it included an abstract of his brother's, James Barbot's, later visit to the Rio Real in 1699 with additional information given by a Mr. Grazilhier who was visiting that river in 1704. John Barbot's account of the Rio Real area is a paraphrase of Dapper with amendments, interpolations, and expansions of his own. He refers to the trade as follows: 'Rings for Money. The principal thing that passes in Calabar, as current money among the natives, is brass rings, for the arms or legs, which they call *Bochie*; and they are so nice in the choice of them, that they will often turn over a whole cask before they find two to please their fancy. The English and Dutch import there a great deal of copper in small bars, round and equal, about three feet long, weighing about a pound and a quarter, which the Blacks of Calabary work with much art . . . to make what sorts of arm rings they please' (4: p.382).

Referring to the Cross River trade he has this to say: 'The Blacks there [Old Calabar River] reckon by copper bars reducing all sorts of goods to such bars; for example, one bar of iron, four copper bars; a man slave for thirty-eight, and a woman slave for thirty-seven or thirty-six copper bars.' This is confirmed in an appendix which gives details of trading by the ship *Dragon* which visited Old Calabar in 1698 (2: pp.383, 465).

James Barbot, however, shows that by 1699 the iron bar had replaced the 'Bracelet' on the Rio Real for the purposes of the European Trade; though 'Bracelets', which he calls copper rings, were still being imported. They were now so debased in value, however, that forty of them were reckoned as the price of one iron bar (2: p.460). Neither James nor his brother John Barbot makes any reference to collars or necklaces of polished copper and we can assume that this fashion had now ceased.

After Barbot no detailed reference is made to the trade of Southern Nigeria till the early nineteenth century in Captain John Adam's accounts which were presumably written about 1820.[1] Adams's account is corroborated by Captain Bold who collected his information about the same time. These two accounts show that the pattern of trade in the Cross River and in the Rio Real areas had changed little by comparison with that on the Slave Coast and in the Bight of Benin. Their information and that of Barbot and the previous authors are set out in the table on p.277. In this table Slave Coast includes Lagos; Western Delta refers to the Ports which served Benin and includes Warri; Eastern Delta represents the Rio Real area and the ports of New Calabar, Bonny, and Nembe, though none of these sources refers specifically to this last-named port; Cross River includes Old Calabar and the Rio del Rey.

It is clear from the details of the *Esmeraldo*, summarised in the first line of this table, that the Portuguese had a uniform system of trade throughout this area, that is from the Slave Coast eastwards, exchanging copper or brass manillas (bracelets) for slaves at the rate of twelve to fifteen of these manillas for a slave at the Rio De Laguo (Lagos area) and Huguatoo (Western Delta) and eight to ten copper manillas in the Rio Real. It is clear also that it was a different system from the one they employed on the Gold Coast. Whereas in the Nigerian area manillas alone are used, Pacheco mentions a number of different commodities which are exchanged at the Casa da Mina on the Gold Coast. The list includes 'Brass Bracelets' but the 'principal article of commerce' is said to be 'Lanbens' which are described as striped cloths or garments which are made in Barbary (20: pp.117, 120).

Dapper was careful to distinguish the local currency in different West African trading areas. Gold of different weights was used on the Gold Coast, cowries (Boesjes) on the Slave Coast and in the Western Delta, and bracelets of grey copper in the Eastern. He also referred to copper rods as a medium of trade on the Rio Real and the Cross River. His *Description* thus indicated three distinct currency areas. Firstly the Gold Coast with its gold currency; secondly the Slave Coast and Western Delta where the cowrie had replaced the manilla which was the former Portuguese medium of trade; thirdly the Eastern Delta where the copper manilla had been accepted as the local currency. To this third area can be attached the Cross River area where another more recently introduced form of copper – the thin copper bar or rod – has become the chief medium of trade. Dapper's account of the trade at Little Ardra on the Slave Coast also showed that the European trade was being conducted in terms of the Local currency. 'Un Esclave vaut cent livres de Boesjes [cowries] . . .' (11: p.305).

By the end of the century we find two different currency systems described in the case of the Slave Coast and also in the case of the Eastern Delta, one being the Native currency, the other the Trade currency. John Barbot showed that in the Eastern Delta the Native currency had become standardised and that people had begun to be particular about the form of their manillas. But by the time of James Barbot, although they were still trading in manillas, the Trade currency on which the Eastern Delta trade was based had become the iron bar. In addition to these two differing currencies Dapper and John Bosman who follows him referred to a further Native currency, that of Moko.[2] 'Dans la province de Moco, on bat une espèce de monnoie de fer dont chaque pièce est grande comme la paume de la main et a une queue d'un empan de long' (11: p.315). Dapper placed

Early Currencies of the Nigerian Coast

Period	Slave Coast	Western Delta	Eastern Delta	Cross River
Portuguese c. 1450-1560	Medium of trade Manillas (brass bracelets)	Medium of trade Manillas (brass and copper bracelets)	Medium of trade Manillas (copper bracelets)	Medium of trade Nil
c. 1600-1650 (Dapper)	Local Currency Cowries (Boejies)	Local currency Cowries (Boejies)	Local currency Manillas (bracelets of grey copper)	Local currency Copper rods
Late 17th and early 18th centuries (Barbot)	Native currency Cowries / Trade currency Iron bars	Native currency Cowries / Trade currency Not given	Native currency Manillas (copper rings) / Trade currency Iron bars	Copper rods
Late 18th and early 19th centuries	Cowries / Ounces and ackies (Gold)	Cowries / Unit of valuation Pawns	Manillas / Iron bars (bars)	Copper rods (coppers)
1850-1900	No details	No details	Local currency Puncheons of oil, iron bars, and manillas	Brass rods

Moko on the Western side of Okrika where the Ibo village Diobu now stands with its modern extension of Port Harcourt. Barbot located it, incorrectly, between Okrika and Bonny. I think we can accept Moko as an Ibo or Ogoni community bordering Okrika and assume that this iron currency derived from the hinterland; there are no iron deposits and with them iron workings farther south than the Okigwi-Arochuku ridge. If we do this we can connect the iron bar currency of the Rio Real with this iron currency and with a demand for iron in the hinterland, which was the area which produced most of the slaves exported from the Rio Real. Once introduced the iron bar remained the standard trade currency in the Eastern Delta until the middle and late nineteenth century, all articles of import or export being valued in terms of the bar.

The Portuguese apparently did not trade in the Cross River area and there is no record of trade there until Dapper's 'Description' where he says: 'Le grand négoce de cette rivière (Rio del Rey) est en esclaves qu'on échange contre de petites barres de cuivre, et on a 13 ou 14 qui pèsent 22 livres en tout pour un esclave bien conditionné' (11: p.316). These copper rods, the same as those traded at the Rio Real, remained the local currency of this area until the establishment of the British Protectorate.

Ethnographic data collected in the early twentieth century indicate three main Native currency areas where the unit of currency was, respectively, the cowrie, the manilla, and the brass rod. The cowrie area comprised the whole of the present Western Region of Nigeria (Yoruba, Benin) and adjacent areas of Dahomey, part of the Northern Region (Nupe, Hausa), and part of the Eastern Region including the Northern Ibo, the Isuama Ibo, and most of the Riverain Ibo. The manilla area comprised the Eastern Delta, the Southern Ibo, and most of the Ibibio. The Brass Rod area comprised the peoples adjoining the Cross River, that is the Efik, and some other Ibibio tribes, the Cross River Ibo, the North Eastern Ibo, the Ekoi, Yakö, Mbembe and other tribes of the present Obubra, Ogoja, and Mamfe divisions of the Eastern Region and the Cameroons.

All these currencies were obtained from elsewhere. Cowries, which are shells found in the Maldive islands, must originally have come overland through the Eastern Sudan and East Africa, but with the development of trade between Europe and India they were shipped from Indian to Western European ports whence they were brought by European traders to the Slave Coast in ever-increasing quantities during the seventeenth and eighteenth centuries. Manillas and rods were metal currency units originally made of copper and imported ·from Western Europe, the former as conventionalised bracelets, the latter in the form of very long and narrow rods bent double.

Besides these more recent native currencies ethnography and history suggest an earlier metal currency or currencies in which the unit was of iron and which preceded them, at least in Eastern Nigeria. The iron currency of Moko was in its general shape and size not unlike the iron currency called Akika in Idoma and Ibia in Mitshi (Tiv which Hutchinson saw on the Niger and described and illustrated in his *Impressions of Western Africa* (16: p.254). Iron was also used as late as 1930 in various more remote places in the Eastern region as subsidiary currency units; for example amongst the Nkumma Akajuk, and Ukelle tribes where it took the form of a flattened strip of metal shaped like a Y with a long tail, or amongst the Ibo tribes of the Eastern Highlands where it was made in the form of a small conventionalised arrow head.

We do not know what the original Portuguese copper bracelets or manillas looked like; none seems to have survived. The so-called Queen and Obo manillas which adorn Kalabari and other Delta shrines cannot easily be described as bracelets and resemble the torques ('colliers') which these peoples' ancestors made out of the copper they received from the Portuguese and the Dutch.[3] Manillas had by the eighteenth century, if not before, become conventionalised and relatively standardised in their modern reduced form. They were too small to encircle any human wrist and James Barbot describes them more accurately as 'rings'. He tells us they were imported in his day in strings, ten rings on a string and four such strings being valued at one iron bar. At the beginning of the nineteenth century English sources refer to them under their Portuguese name; their price remained the same – 'Forty Manilloes for one iron bar' – and they were made in Birmingham. There followed a period of minor variation and experiment in regard to their shape and size; various communities and special trading areas preferring manillas of slightly different design[4] By the end of the century one of these forms became the preferred one and was standardised over the whole area, and by this time manillas were no longer made of copper but of a baser alloy which coiners in the nineteen-thirties found very convenient for casting into counterfeit West African shillings.

The form of the rod currency seems to have undergone little variation. Rods changed from copper to brass during the nineteenth century and have remained so ever since. By the end of the century they had ceased to be used in Old Calabar as currency and had been replaced by lengths of copper or silver wire and by certain British silver coins.[5]

Trade Currencies

Manillas and rods, though by the end of the nineteenth century they had become the Native currencies of their respective areas, began as Trade currencies. Barbot makes it clear that the trade was not barter in the accepted sense of the term and though he and the Europeans who came after him frequently used the word, they confirm that everything that was bought or sold had a monetary value. From the late seventeenth century onward and probably for a considerable time before this, a ship could not trade in the Rio Real until the 'king and the principal men' of the port had met the captain and the supercargoes, assessed the capacity of the ship for trading, and from this assessment determined the value of the duties to be paid by it. At the same time the price of everything that was being traded was fixed in terms of the local currency unit. To quote from James Barbot, 'We adjusted with them the reduction of our merchandise into bars of iron, as the standard coin, viz. one bunch of beads, one bar. Four strings of rings, ten rings in each, one ditto. Four copper bars, one ditto. One piece of narrow Guinea stuff, one ditto. One piece broad Hamborough, one ditto. One piece Nicanees, three ditto. Brass rings, ditto and so pro rata for every other sort of goods.' The price of provisions and wood was also regulated. 'Sixty king's yams, one bar; one hundred and sixty slaves' yams, one bar. A butt of water, two rings. For the length of wood, seven bars, which is dear; but they were to deliver it ready cut into our boat. For a goat, one bar. A cow, ten or eight bars, according to its bigness. A hog, two bars. A calf, eight bars. A jar of palm oil, one bar and a quarter. We paid also the king's duties in goods; five hundred slaves to be purchased at two copper rings a head' (4: p.460). This was after a week of bargaining, mainly over the price of slaves, which was eventually settled at thirteen bars for a male and nine for a female.

But the foreign traders did not have to pay for the slaves they bought in this currency nor did the local African traders pay in this currency for European trade goods. Both were engaged in wholesale, not retail, transactions and there was therefore no need for any money to pass. Debits for goods bought were cancelled by credits for slaves sold. The usual procedure in the Eastern Delta and Old Calabar was for the European merchants to advance on credit to the African traders with whom he decided to deal, trade goods and, if asked for, currency as well, the whole advance being valued in terms of the trade currency. The African traders used the advance trading with it in the inland markets whence they returned with slaves and, in the nineteenth century, palm oil which they sold to the European merchants in settlement of their debts. To quote once more from James Barbot:

'We also advanced to the King by way of loan, the value of a hundred and fifty bars of iron, in sundry goods and to his principal men, and others, as much again, each in proportion of his quality and ability.' (4: p.460).

While the local demand for the currency was great, African traders received as advances both goods and currency, but even when there was a strong demand for the currency the foreign traders found it preferable to pay partly in currency and partly in goods. John Barbot writes, for example, of Fida on the Slave Coast: 'The most usual difference between the European and Fida merchants is when the factor will not give them such goods as they demand, especially cauries, which are the money of the country and what they are most fond of: but commonly this is adjusted by paying part in cauries and part in other goods; because slaves bought with cauries cost double the price as if purchased with other commodities especially when these shells are dear in Europe, the price being higher or lower according to the plenty or scarcity there is of them' (4: p.326). Similarly in Dapper's time at Little Ardra, 'Dans tous les achats, la troisième partie du payement se fait en boesjes, et les deux autres en marchandises' (11: p.305).

When the demand for the Trade currency was not great on either side, little and, in some cases, none of it changed hands and it eventually became purely fictional. For example, Adams records the Slave Coast Trade currency as being the same as that of the Gold Coast, the units being the ounce and the ackie of gold. Now the Slave Coast neither exported nor imported gold and its Native currency remained the cowrie. What appears to have happened there during the eighteenth century was that the European merchants sought to establish a Trade currency more satisfactory than cowries whose inflation could not be controlled and which indeed it paid them to inflate by selling as many of them as they could get from the Maldive Islands. They first tried the iron bar which they were then introducing into the Eastern Delta. It would appear that this proved unsatisfactory and so by Adams's time they had fallen back on the Gold Coast currency. But it is obvious that, as far as the foreign and native traders of the Slave Coast were concerned, the ounce or the ackie was little more than an accounting device. In the case of the Western Delta they went still farther and replaced the Trade currency by a fictional unit of valuation, the 'pawn'. Bold describing the Benin trade writes: 'They received ... the different articles mentioned hereafter every one of which has a stated valuation in pawns, a nominal mode of value whose origin is quite unknown' (7: p.66). To this can be added Adams's statement: 'The medium of exchange is salt; but accounts are kept in pawns, the value of one of which is equal to a bar in Bonny, averaging from two to three shillings sterling each' (1: p.243). By 1854, if we are to believe Baikie, the values of these various Trade currencies had depreciated and diverged from each other. 'Every river has its own mode of reckoning. Bonny counts in bars equal to about sevenpence each. Benin river employs prawns [sic] one being about fourpence. In Old Kalabar, coppers are used, one copper being about fourpence-halfpenny.'

On the Slave Coast and in the Western Delta the Trade and the Native currency systems remained distinct, neither the European nor the local traders being prepared to accept the other's currency unit. In the Eastern Delta and the Cross River, on the other hand, the Trade currency unit became the Native currency replacing, it can be presumed, one or more older but unknown units. When, as in the Eastern Delta, the unit of the Trade currency changed from manillas to iron bars there was no conflict. The manilla remained the basic unit of the Native currency system and a subsidiary unit of lower value in the Trade currency system.

NOTES

1. No publication date is given for his *Sketches*, the *Remarks* published in 1823 contain the same material as the *Sketches* and its appendix on the West Coast Trade is identical.
2. One spells it with a *c* the other with a *k*.
3. They are described by Talbot (23: p.235 and illustrated on p.238).
4. Talbot (23: p.284) gives a description of different varieties he met in Degema and Consul Hutchinson refers to different varieties in a consular report F.O. 2/16/1856 which is quoted in Talbot (22: iii, p.276).
5. I was unable to make a satisfactory study of Efik currency.

REFERENCES

(1) Adams, Captain John. *Sketches taken during ten Voyages to Africa, between the years 1786 and 1800*. No date of publication.
(2) ----- *Remarks on the Country extending from Cape Palmas to the River Congo*, London (1823).
(3) Baikie, W. B., *Narrative of an Exploring Voyage up the Rivers Kwora and Binue*, London (1856); reprinted Frank Cass, London (1966).
(4) Barbot, John, *A Description of the Coast of North and South Guinea*, London (1746).
(5) Blake, J. W., *Europeans in West Africa, 1450-1560*. Hakluyt Society (1942).
(6) Boteler, Captain Thomas, R. N., *Narrative Voyage of Discovery to Africa and Arabia from 1821-1826*, London (1835).
(7) Bold, Lieutenant Edward, R. N., *The Merchant and Mariners African Guide*, London (1822).
(8) Burton, Sir Richard, *Wanderings in West Africa from Liverpool to Fernando Po*. By a *F.R.G.S.* London (1863).
(9) Colonial Office Records. File C.O. 82/1-8. For the years 1828-35.
(10) Crow, Captain Hugh, of Liverpool, *Memoirs of the late Captain Hugh Crow*, Liverpool (1830); reprinted Frank Cass, London (1970)'

(11)   Dapper, O., *Description de l'Afrique*. Traduit du flamand. Amsterdam (1686).
(12)   Einzig, Paul, *Primitive Money*, London (1949).
(13)   De Cardi, M. Le Comte C. N., *A Short Description of the Natives of the Niger Coast Protectorate*. Appendix I in Mary Kingsley's *West African Studies*. First edition, London (1899).
(14)   Foreign Office Records in the Series F.O. 84/1-2111. Treaties in the files F.O. 93/6/3 and 8 and F.O. 97/432.
(15)   Hertslet, Lewis, *A Complete Collection of the Treaties and Conventions between Great Britain and Foreign Powers*, London, 1850 onwards.
(16)   Hutchinson, Thomas, J. *Impressions of Western Africa*, London, 1858; reprinted Frank Cass, London (1970).
(17)   ----- *Ten Years Wanderings among the Ethiopians*, London, 1861; reprinted Frank Cass, London (1967).
(18)   Jackson, R. M., *Journal of a Voyage to the Bonny River, 1826*, Letchworth (1934).
(19)   Owen, Captain, W. F. W., R.N., *Narrative of Voyages to Explore the Shores of Africa, Arabia and Madagascar*, London (1833).
(20)   Pereira, Duarte Pacheco, *Esmeraldo de Situ Orbis*. Edited G. H. T. Kimble, Hakluyt Society, 1937.
(21)   Smith, J., *Trade and Travels in the Gulph of Guinea*, London (1851).
(22)   Talbot, P. Amaury, *The Peoples of Southern Nigeria*, London (1926); reprinted Frank Cass, London (1969).
(23)   ----- *Tribes of the Niger Delta*, London (1932); reprinted Frank Cass, London (1967).   .
(24)   Waddell, The Rev. Hope Masterton, *Twenty-nine Years in the West Indies and Central Africa, 1829-1858*, London (1863); 2nd ed., with a new introduction by G. I. Jones, Frank Cass, London (1970).

26

COWRIE FROM NORTH
AND SOUTH

An Episode in the History of the
Dahomean Currency System

Karl Polanyi

Cowrie from North and South

Well before Dahomey came into being, black and white met in West Africa on two fronts. The story of cowrie in Africa should then reveal some of the modalities of that meeting, first on the Middle Niger and, a century later, on the Guinea Coast. When, where, and how did cowrie shells penetrate West Africa? And by what agency was cowrie established as a currency system?

Dahomey was situated between the Guinea Coast and the vast Niger Bend. On the beaches of the Bight of Benin and on the Middle Niger, respectively, cowrie was infused by two different sets of traders – Berber Tuareg and later Arab on the one hand, Portuguese on the other. Their zonal fronts were, however, separated by more than a thousand miles, the distance between Timbuktu and Gogo, where the Venetians were dispatching the Maldive cowrie by Tuareg caravans, and the Portuguese in the south in Benin and Ardra, those outposts of Yoruba culture.

The earliest date by which cowrie can be presumed to have reached West Africa from the north is the departure of Marco Polo from Venice for his voyage to the Far East, about 1290. The surprise he expressed in a detailed account describing his meeting with cowrie money in southwestern China's province of Yünnan was not feigned. Our sources name Venice, Marco Polo's home and the domicile of the family business, as the agency that transmitted the cowries from the Persian Sea to the Niger, in order to purchase its gold with those exotic shells. This narrows the time range from 1290 to the spring of 1352, when Ibn Batuta found cowrie money in use at Gogo, on the Middle

*Reprinted by permission from *Dahomey and the Slave Trade. An Analysis of an Archaic Economy*, by Karl Polanyi in collaboration with Abraham Rotstein, University of Washington Press, 1966.

Niger, where the river sharply turned south. By all indications, in the empire of Mali cowrie was, alongside of gold bars and copper wire, by that time a regular currency, the gold rate of which Ibn Batuta unhesitatingly quoted by tale. He had been, like Marco Polo before him in Yünnan, much astonished at meeting with cowrie in the Far East, though unlike Polo he was thoroughly conversant with it and its use for money. He was struck to find that its value was as high as 1,150 to a mitkhal, or gold ducat, which in the Maldives would fetch no less than 400,000 cowries, if not three times as much, which also happened, i.e., 1,200,000. The exchange rate in Gogo was mentioned by him with assurance. And Cà da Mosto, who had never seen cowrie in 1455 described *Cypraea moneta* correctly from hearsay and added specific information about their traject from the Persian Sea to Venice and from Venice by the desert route of the Western Sahara to the Niger.

The later date, when cowrie entered West Africa from the south, is almost as definite, though the medium of transportation by which this happened is much less certain. The Arab traders of the north represented the eleventh century world movement of Islam (its seventh century irruption had been quite brief and superficial). They were now keen to tap the sources of the gold that had been flowing since Roman times from the Upper Niger toward Carthage and Libya. Their cultural influence on the Upper and Middle Niger was paramount and cowrie, with which they were familiar from Arabia and India, was current in Mali, at least as far as Gogo in the east. The Arab trader was bred to the use of the mitkhal and its fractions, as well as gold and silver dinars and dirhems, and not limited like the 'unbelievers' to damba beans and takus for their gold weights. When in the fifteenth and sixteenth centuries he was faced with the Europeans on the coast, his mullahs felt their equals in trade, if not their superiors.

Fifteenth century Portuguese trade in Benin was a somewhat different proposition in the Arabs' eye, who deemed it an intrusion into their inland territory. The Portuguese established themselves on the Gold Coast where they traded in the African staple, gold, for a limited number of European goods: cloths, guns and powder, used sheets, hardware such as basins and knives, but mostly iron bars and rings of copper. Neither caravan slaves nor cowrie yet entered into the picture. And with the opening of the sea route to India in 1497, Portuguese commerce changed direction. Based on the islands of Fernando Po and St. Thome, the Portuguese turned the Bight of Benin into a Portuguese lake. Their purchases from the natives were now intended for use in their local island sugar plantations and for coastal trading. This brings us back to the two regions where the

Portuguese penetrated to some extent into cowrie-using areas: Benin and Ardra.

The insalubrious beaches from which Benin and Ardra themselves withdrew were not favoured for settlement by the Portuguese either. They preferred the islands off the coast or inland fairs that lay about sixty or seventy miles from the sea. They induced the inland natives to trade the goods they had to offer, including slaves. But the superior civilisation of Benin, heir to the religion, art, and statecraft of Ile-Ife, set narrow limits to Portuguese cultural expansion. Besides, the Arab traders from the far north would meet them there and bar further entry.

On Ardrasian matters, however, the Portuguese exerted a formative influence. The king himself had been brought up in a Christian monastery on St. Thome. A momentous feature of the cowrie currency resulted. The numerical denominations of that system, e.g., the designation of the smallest stringed unit of forty, the toque; the five toques of 200 shells, the galinha; the twenty galinhas of 4,000 shells, the cabess – all carry Portuguese designations. Important culture symbols such as the fetish have Portuguese names, as well as the administrative heads of any group or bearers of any port of importance, the *cabosseros*. It must be noted that the vernacular for the various cowrie units was also current in Dahomey. Yet the Portuguese terms were employed over the entire area of stringed cowrie money, including Dahomey itself.

Within a reasonably narrow span, sometime between the end of the thirteenth and the middle of the fourteenth centuries, cowrie then reached the Middle Niger; in the last quarter of the fifteenth century the Portuguese may also have found it in inland Benin. While on the Middle Niger it came undoubtedly from the Mediterranean by way of the northern desert route, its presence in Benin may have been due to seepage by Negro or Arab traders from the Niger in the north. In any case, this influx was later to be amply reinforced from overseas, rounding the Cape. The trickle of cowrie shells from the east coast by way of the valleys of the Congo may be ignored.

Our question regarding the origins of the cowrie currency in Africa, consisting of loose shells at first, probably mixed *moneta and annulus*, can now be partly answered. The when and where of its arrival renders it a certainty that Dahomey was *not* the originator of the cowrie currency system, although it soon incorporated it and became its protagonist. Of this crucial initial phase of a stringed cowrie currency in Dahomey we know, however, next to nothing, except for the fact that Whydah stringed its cowrie even before the Dahomean conquest. We have here in mind not the mere monetary use of loose cowrie shells, but that organised system of cowrie as a currency which, once it struck roots in Dahomey, became so notable an instrument of its national existence and of the regional economic organisation over a wide area of the Guinea Coast.

A recorded episode of economic history may be of relevance. The Portuguese square cloth money stamped in Lisbon with the royal arms of Portugal may have stimulated the monetary imagination of the new inland rulers of the Guinea Coast. Barbot's nephew, James Barbot, Jr., gave an intriguing on-the-spot report of Angola, printed as a supplement to his uncle's work about the Guinea Coast. Angola's secession from the empire of the Congo gave the Capuchin monks the chance of converting the natives and introducing an economic organisation with domicile in Lisbon. A comprehensive taxation system was based on the local administration which again was put in the care of a privileged native stratum, the Sonassen. The monetary systems of Angola were regionalised and were partly made into a royal monopoly. The shells current as money, the inferior simbos (*Olivetta nana*), were only partly of domestic origin; others were imported from Brazil. Of the domestic simbos, those of Loanda provenience were most valued for their beautiful colour. These favourite simbos were carried by native servants in straw sacks, which held a load of sixty-four pounds, to the Congo there to be exchanged for slaves and square cloths of different sizes made of the bark of a native tree. All things in Congo, James Barbot, Jr., wrote, are bought with these shells, even gold, silver, and provisions, adding that the use 'of coin either of gold or any other metal is suppressed and forbid in all Congo, as it is in some other parts of Africa'.[1] The Portuguese government in Lisbon, however, combined tax-farming with the monopoly of the issuance of fiat money stamped in Lisbon and thence introduced into Angola at an excessive profit to the tax-farmer and fiscal monopolist of this royal 'mint'.

The official value of the marked clouts (cloth money) was four times the value of the unmarked ones, the double-marked clouts being worth five to six times the unmarked clouts. Except for fourth century B.C. and ninth century A.D. Chinese experiments with paper money, no such ambitious schemes are anywhere on record on an empire scale. The intellectual influence of the Portuguese on Dahomean state finance should then not be underrated. The daring Guinean enterprise of regionally stable moneys may have originated from previous Angolan experiments. From the Niger empires of the north, greatly antedating Dahomey, no hint of such a sophisticated currency has reached us.

We must confess to ignorance of a more elementary kind, namely how in the first place these shells came to be moved physically in the mass from their homes along such vast trajects. Traditionally, the migration of the cowrie was confidently traced by ethnographers to the Indian merchants' interest in monetary gain. But trade is no explanation, since it needs itself an explanation in terms of demand. Admittedly, the profit, in Ibn Batuta's terms, was in the possible range of 100,000 per cent. This, however, leaves untouched, the main-spring of the transaction, namely why specifically for currency purposes cowrie was so much in demand in Africa. Nor does it answer the question of whence the purchasing power was forthcoming, capable and willing to be spent on a large scale in such a manner.

The economist is indeed at a loss to account for the emergence in an early society of an effective demand of first magnitude for a means of currency as such. The notion that economic developments are mainly referable to what we have become used to calling 'economic interests' is apt to be misleading. Rather, weighty events in the sphere of statebuilding and of economic organisation may have accounted for the introduction of currency systems in West Africa. This may have been the source of the demand for money objects to be used as currency and consequently of the finance capable of supplying the purchasing power for their acquisition. The economic historian may have to seek an explanation in the rise of new empires, or even in the need for a popular currency which would speed the functioning of local food markets.

NOTES

1.   James Barbot, Jr., *Churchill's Voyages*, London: 1732, p.518.

27

THE OUNCE IN EIGHTEENTH CENTURY WEST AFRICAN TRADE*

Marion Johnson

This paper is a by-product of a much larger study on the West African cowrie currency to be completed shortly. It has been necessary to try to understand the various other units of account which at one time or another were interchangeable for cowries. One such unit is the Trade Ounce, valued at 16,000 cowries in the late eighteenth century; the only account of the Trade Ounce available appears to be that by the late Karl Polanyi (1). Since some of Polanyi's conclusions appear to be untenable, this attempt has been made to reconstruct the history of this most important eighteenth century trade unit of account.

The eighteenth century Ounce represents an attempt to introduce a monetary system into what had hitherto been a barter trade on the Guinea Coast. One of the disadvantages of a barter system is that it is hard for either party to know if it has had the best of the bargain; and this is particularly serious where one or both parties is acquiring goods for further trade elsewhere. In the Guinea Coast trade, the African traders probably thought in terms of the local currency (gold dust or cowries or whatever it might be), while the European merchants thought, in part at least, in terms of the first or prime cost of their goods – the money which had been paid for them in Europe. Owners and shareholders in Europe were concerned primarily with the difference between the proceeds of the round voyage and the first cost of the trade goods with which a ship was loaded at the start of the voyage. They were not directly concerned with the details of the exchange rates between these trade goods and slaves on the west coast, nor in the details of the sale of slaves in the West Indies and the subsequent purchase of West Indian produce.

To some extent, the captains of trading ships used 'prime cost' as a basis for their own calculations. Throughout the eighteenth century,

*Reprinted by permission of Cambridge University Press from the *Journal of African History*, Vol. VII, No. 2, 1966.

especially when giving evidence in Europe, ships' captains refer to the cost of gold or slaves in terms of the prime cost of goods given in exchange.

It follows that the value of the gold or slaves had to be higher than the prime cost of the goods for which they were exchanged – otherwise trade could not have taken place. There seems to have grown up, as Polanyi has pointed out, a rough and ready reckoning that goods to the value of 40s. in England ought to buy gold to the (English) value of £4 on the West Coast of Africa. In fact, as we shall see, gold was frequently bought for less; the whole secret of the Guinea trade was to choose trade goods in such a way as to satisfy the African traders at the lowest possible prime cost.

Throughout the history of the Guinea trade, business was normally carried on, not in a single item of trade goods, but in an assortment. Even before the introduction of the Trade Ounce, it was understood, both on the Gold Coast[1] and at Whydah, that cheaper goods would only be accepted in transactions which also included more expensive goods. In both areas an elaborate system of equivalences grew up; on the Gold Coast these were tied to the amount of gold that could be purchased by a given quantity of a commodity; on the Slave Coast, where there was usually no gold trade, they were tied to the quantities which would purchase a slave.

An early stage in the development of the Ounce system can be seen in the accounts of the *Sarah Bonneaventure* in 1676 (2: 217 pf.) The Accounts include a ship's manifest giving the European prices of

Table I

Extract from the accounts of the 'Sarah Bonneaventure'

	Mark	Oz.	Ang.
45 musketts	1	1	7
20 iron bars, 16 per bendy[2]		2	8
10 firkins tallow		2	10
16 sheets		1	2
' barrels powder at 2 oz. 6a.[3] per barrel	1	1	8
12[4] sletias at 6a. per ps.		4	14
12 perpetuanso at 11a. per ps.	1	–	4
2 sayes at 22a. per ps.		2	12
½ one say			11
	5	1	12

goods; there follow accounts for the purchase of slaves, gold, and corn (for the use of the slaves). The purchases of slaves are recorded in terms of various trade goods given for small batches of slaves; in a few cases a small quantity of gold is also included in the purchase. No attempt has been made to reduce the figures to any common unit;

thus we read that, for example, three men and a boy were bought for two pieces of Says (an English woollen), two Perpetuanas (another English woollen) and four Paper Bralls (an Indian cotton); in this transaction, six ounces of gold were also received.

The purchase of gold in these accounts is covered by Table I. It is clear that by this date some of the goods already had customary gold values in round numbers of ounces and angels; others seem to have been subject to *ad hoc* bargaining, though the prices may include allowances for defective quality, etc.

From the information available, it is possible to calculate the cost per ounce in terms of the prime cost of each commodity (Table 2).

Table 2
Calculated prime cost of commodities

Commodity	Total cost	Cost of 1 oz. gold
Muskets	360s.	38s. 2d.
Iron bars	72s.	28s. 9½d.
Tallow	100s.	38s. 1d.
Sheets	37s. 4d.	33s. 2d.
Powder	220s.	23s. 2d.
Sletias[5]	143s.	29s. 4d.
Perpetuanos	288s.	34s. 11d.
Says	105s.	30s. 2d.
Total	1325s. 4d.	Average 31s. 9½d.

Evidently it was much more profitable to deal in gunpowder than in muskets – but the one would naturally not be in demand without the other.

The price of slaves at this date cannot usually be calculated, as most batches included women or children in addition to men. In two cases where four men were sold, the price works out at approximately 32s. and 33s. a head in prime cost of the goods. There is not enough information to calculate exactly the 'ounce value' of a slave by using the ounce and angel ratings used in the gold trade. By making reasonable assumptions as to the ounce rating for goods which were not exchanged for gold, based on their exchange rate for corn (which seems to have been close to Barbot's figure (3: p. 177) of one chest for one ackie or angel), it would seem that a rough equivalence of one ounce for an adult male slave underlies the figures; but there is no means of knowing whether any such calculation was made by the buyer. Some of the slaves were much cheaper than this – but these may have been in some way defective.

A unit-for-unit equivalence – one slave = one ounce of gold; one chest of corn = one angel or ackie – would have had obvious advantages for the African trader who had to keep his accounts in his head, or with the help of the simplest aids to memory. It is the African units of currency (benda, ounce, ackie) which came into use as the accounting system on the Coast. Phillips, in 1693-94 (4: p. 206), found that all accounts at Cape Coast were being kept in marks, ounces, ackies and takus.

By 1714, if not earlier, goods on the Gold Coast were being valued in ounces and ackies, even in transactions which involved no gold at all. A transaction at Commenda in 1714 (2: II, p. 187), will serve as an example:[6]

		Oz.	A.
Bartered for slaves:	14 gunns 7 per 2 oz.	4	—
Man at 4 oz.	60 lb. powder 20 per 5a.		15
Man at 3.4 oz.	40 lb. brass 2 per a.	1	4
	1 green p.p.t.a. 5a. each		5
	2 fir(kin) tallow 4a. each		12
		7	4

It will be seen that the ounce value of guns and tallow have not greatly changed since 1676; perpetuas have dropped from 11 ackies to five (a few years earlier there were many complaints (5) that English woollens had dropped to half their previous value on the Guinea Coast). At this period there were many complaints[7] that competitors were underselling the company (or vice versa) – offering goods for fewer ackies. There is also a corresponding complaint that they were raising the price of slaves – offering more ackies for them. Both complaints are couched in terms of ounces and ackies; the trade is no longer regarded as barter.

It is not possible to discover the prime cost of the goods involved in the Commenda transaction quoted above. Atkins, however, in 1721 (6: p.160) gives very full information. He quotes a transaction at Apollonia (Table 3), for which the prices can be calculated from his own figures. (Columns 3, 4, and 5 are so calculated to illustrate the transaction shown in columns 1 and 2.) Atkins himself speaks of buying slaves at Apollonia for four ounces, which he approximates to £8. The above is a model transaction, and is more profitable, even when paying 70 ackies. It all depends on the assortment. Atkins was paying more for slaves on the Gold Coast, but the exact prices cannot easily be calculated from his information.

Table 4 is an actual transation at Anomabu in 1728 (2: II, p. 121), the later columns being calculated from the invoice of the same voyage.

On another Anomabu transaction of the same voyage, the Ounce works out at about 38s., the total price in the latter case being 6½ oz. for a male slave. These figures are not far from the conventional 40s.

Table 3
Transactions from 'Voyage to Guinea'

	Ackies	Each	Prime cost	Value of 1 oz.
2 photees[8]	14	17s. 6d.	35s.	40s.
2 cotton ramals[8]	8	11s.	22s.	40s.
1 piece longee[9]	4	10s.	10s.	40s.
2 sletias	5	7s. 6d.	15s.	47s.
7 sheets[10]	7	1s.10½d.	13s. 1½d.	38s.
32 brass pans	32	1s.3d	40s.	20s.
A man slave	70		135s. 1½d.	31s.

Table 4
Transaction at Anomabu in 1728

		Oz.	Ac.	Total cost	Cost per oz.
1 large blue ell	@ 8 ackies		8	20s.	40s.
1 large green ell		8	8	20s.	40s.
1 large green purplet[11]		5	5	14s.	49s. 9½d.
2 large blue purplets		5	10	28s.	49s. 9½d.
2 buccaneer guns		5	10	30s.	48s.
12 brass pans		1	10	30s.	40s.
30 three-pound basins		2/3	1 4·	60s.	48s.
8 brass pans		1	8	20s.	40s.
3 kegs tallow		3	9	18s.	32s.
1 half-anchor spirits		5	5	12s.	38s. 5d.
5 sheets		1	5	9s. 2d.	29s. 4d.
		6	4	26s. 2d.	41s. 9d. (average)

value for the Ounce. It was always possible, by good fortune or by clever choice of goods, to have a lower value for the prime cost of an 'Ounce' of goods than the standard 40s.; but in times of heavy competition, the Ounce value of a cheap commodity would be brought down until it bore much the same relation to its prime cost as did the Ounce values of other commodities. Unfashionable commodities would also fall in Ounce value, as had occurred in the case of perpetuanas.

The 1740s, however, seem to have been a time when Ounce values were low. Two ships' captains, looking back in 1777 over their long experience in the Guinea Coast trade, told the Commissioners for Trade and Plantations (7: pp. 134, 145) that Ounces were running at about 30s. or thereabouts in 1744, and that an Ounce of gold could be purchased for 30-50s. worth of English goods in 1748. Their figures for the cost of slaves in the 1740s (6-8 oz., or £9-10) are in line with these figures, and are confirmed by contemporary evidence. In a note to an affidavit of 1753, the Ounce is defined as 'the nominal value set upon goods which cost about 40s. in Europe, but sold in trade upon the Coast of Africa at £4' (2: II, 362 ff). £4 was the value of an Ounce of gold.

The same figures –40s. for an Ounce of goods, £4 for an Ounce of gold – are still being quoted in 1777 (2: II, p. 502); but the figures conceal a complete change in the nature of the trade, and of the meaning of the Ounce. By this date, gold had become one of the items in the 'price list', expressed in terms of trade Ounces; it had become an imported trade good, not an item in the export trade. Mr. Chalmers, a ship's captain, stated: 'An ounce of gold is reckoned two ounces of trade, therefore if a slave cost twelve oz. of trade, in which an ounce of gold must be given, then ten ounces of trade are actually given, together with one ounce of gold equal to two ounces of trade' (7: p. 131). At first sight, it seems as if the trade Ounce has been devalued to about half the value of twenty years earlier.

Owing to the principle of Assortment, according to which the cheap goods were acceptable only if accompanied by more expensive goods, it is not possible to determine exactly the real value in terms of goods of the Ounce at any one time, or to compare quite exactly its value at one time with another, as the goods in an Assortment underwent some change from time to time. Quite a number of goods, however, continued to be included in Assortments right through the eighteenth century, and if there had been any large change in the real value of the Ounce, in terms of goods, this would certainly be reflected in the Ounce values of these goods. Some goods it is very difficult to compare, owing to standard practices of adulteration; as the King of Ashanti complained to Bowdich (8: p. 72), '. . . ten handkerchiefs are cut to eight, water is put to rum, and charcoal to powder. . .'.

It can be seen from Table 5 that for many of the goods, especially the cottons, there was a tendency for values to rise (in terms of ackies and ounces) between the 1720s and the end of the century – but by about one quarter or one fifth only. Other goods such as tallow and sletias (linen) went down in Ounce value in the same period. It is clearly not true that the Ounce was devalued to one half, in real terms, between the 1720s and the end of the century.

The alternative explanation is a very large increase in the price of gold on the Guinea Coast. There is a good deal of evidence for such a rise in the 1760s and 1770s. At this period the flow of gold was reversed; whereas previously gold had been exported from the Gold Coast, it was now being imported into West Africa. One Liverpool merchant, at least, in 1777 (7: p. 92) admitted to importing gold from Holland for the Guinea trade. Other merchants (7: pp. 129, 134 et. seq.) related that they had purchased gold at prices up to £5 10s. or £6 prime cost of goods per ounce of gold, on the coast to west of the Gold Coast proper.

Table 5
Value in ackies

Commodity	1676	1721	1728	End of 18th cent (9: p. 235).	1819 (10: p. 119)
Trading gun	3 +	4	4	6	–
Anchor spirits	–	–	10	12	16
Keg tallow	4 +	2½	3	2	–
Chintz	–	–	6 (15 yd.)	8 (12 yd.)	–
Old sheets	1	1	1	–	–
Brass pans	–	1	1	1	–
Cotton romal	–	4	6	6	6
Small Nicanee	–	–	5	8	–
Neganipaul	–	–	8	10	–
Bejutapaul	–	–	8	10	–
Chelloes	–	–	8	10	–
Photaes	–	7	6	8	–
Glasgow red Danes	–	–	–	8	6
Sletias	6	2½	–	2	–
Half Says	11	–	–	10	–
Perpetuas	11	–	5	–	–

Part of this rise in the value of gold was a direct result of the dispute between Fanti and Ashanti which closed the roads and cut off the Ashanti trade (11: 38 ff). There had, however, already been an increase in the buying of gold at Apollonia even before the dispute came to a head in 1765 (12: p. 40), and it was stated that this gold was bought for the purchase of slaves at Anomabu. In 1771, Brew at Anomabu (2: II, p. 541) was deploring the 'pernicious practice' which had 'of late crept into the trade of the Gold Coast, which is the giving of gold upon slaves'. 'Gold commands the trade', he wrote in August 1771 (2: II, p. 539). 'There is no buying a slave without one ounce of gold at least on it, and the windward coast has been so ransacked, that there is no such thing as getting gold, even though you sell your goods from 40 to 50% under prime cost. . . . The next year he was writing:

> There is no buying slaves now without you give 2 oz. of gold on each, to procure which, you must sell your goods 20% under prime cost and may think yourself happy to get it even at that rate. The black traders . . will not take the primest smoak taffty . . . but will oblige you to give seven ackies of gold in its stead, and they will have gold also for any article that is not in ready sale in the market; in short, the nature of the trade is so much altered that a man who was here but two years ago would be at his wits end to make a purchase (2: II, p. 547).

The trouble went back much more than two years, however; one of the ship's captains who gave evidence in 1777 remembered (7: p. 134) that it was in 1764, when he first sailed as captain, that the sellers began to demand gold for slaves.

This was not the first time that gold had flowed to the Gold Coast instead of the other way. Portuguese traders from Brazil, indeed, seem to have brought gold and tobacco throughout the century, but usually they traded at Whydah and not on the Gold Coast. In about 1710, however, for a short time, the Akwamu people began to demand gold for their slaves, instead of selling gold as they had done hitherto (13).

To understand the causes of this reversed gold trade, it would probably be necessary to know much more than is known at present about the flow of gold northwards across the Sahara. Although the immediate cause of the stoppage in gold exports in the 1760s and 1770s was undoubtedly the Ashanti-Fanti dispute, the fact that gold had begun to be demanded by the Fantis before their quarrel with Ashanti, and the fact that the gold trade never recovered to anything like its former volume on the Guinea coast, suggest that the flow of gold had been reversed. It was certainly reaching North Africa in some quantity at the end of the eighteenth century (14). Possibly the Ashanti policy of northward expansion was beginning to bear fruit. For whatever reason, Hippisley could write in 1764 (12: p. 40). 'Gold is no longer considered by the negroes in the careless light it was when the Europeans first traded with them. . .' Something had happened which brought the value of gold on the Guinea coast much more closely into relation with its value in Europe.

The value of the Trade Ounce at half a gold ounce, once established, remained at least as a formal value, so long as the Trade Ounce itself continued in use. Adams, who traded on the Coast in the years between 1786 and 1800, wrote in 1823 (9: p. 236): 'The value of goods in gold, on the Gold Coast, is estimated *pro forma* to be half the trade price, or half that price which they were valued when bartered for slaves. . .', but he goes on to say that it was often possible to obtain more than this for well-chosen goods. It seems likely that the price of gold had fallen again somewhat in the early nineteenth century; two separate estimates translate Trade Ounces, for the purpose of payment of 'stipends' to the King of Ashanti and others, as three-quarters of the gold value.

The decline of the Trade Ounce, in terms of gold, can throw light on the complaint, sympathetically reported by Dupuis (10: p. 123), of the King of Ashanti that he was being cheated in the prices of trade goods in which the Notes for the forts were paid. One payment on the Cape coast note, amounting to 24 oz. altogether, was made up as shown in

Table 6 (the Ounce value per unit is added for purposes of comparison).

Table 6
Payment on Cape Coast note

	Oz.	Ac.	Value per unit
66 lead bars	2	1	½ ackie
4 ankers rum	4	0	1 ounce
4 kegs powder	4	0	1 ounce
13 cottons	1	10	2 ackies
1 cotton bandanoe		8	8 ackies
2 taffeties	2	0	1 ounce
5 Glasgow Danes	1	14	6 ackies
1 Fathom scarlet		8	8 ackies
8½ pieces longcloth	4	4	8 ackies
3 Romals	1	2	6 ackies
5½ Manchester Toms	2	1	6 ackies
	24	0	

The Ounce values are reasonably in line with other Ounce values; but Dupuis, whose experience did not lie on the Guinea coast, listened with sympathy when the King of Ashanti told him: 'When I send gold to Cape Coast to buy goods, and the Governor does not know it, so I buy powder at two or three kegs to the ounce, and three ankers of rum to the ounce, and seven ackies for the best guns, and get 100 bars of lead for two ounces.' It is clear that the King of Ashanti is speaking of gold ounces. He also complained of the adulteration of his rum and gunpowder, which we know to have been normal trade practice, at least so far as spirits were concerned (9: p. 238). Dupuis, however, appears to have been completely ignorant both of the Trade Ounce and of the Trade conventions concerning adulteration.

By this time the Trade Ounce was reaching the end of its usefulness. Indeed, its survival in the payment of stipends may have been due to the fact that it was the subject of a written agreement in the Notes. After 1826 the Ounce seems to have gone out of general use, and values were usually quoted in dollars or in sterling.

NOTES

1.   In this paper, Gold Coast and Slave Coast are used in their eighteenth century sense to mean the coast west of Accra and east of the Volta respectively.
2.   *Benda*, a gold weight of two ounces.
3.   In this, and other tables printed in Donnan, some of the units have been given incorrectly. Donnan prints, for example, '4 Barrels powder at *2s. 6d.* per barrel', but totals this as 4 oz. 14 angels. The price of powder in the minifest is *55s.* a barrel. If *2s. 6d.* is amended to 2z6a (2 ounces, 6 angels) the correct total is

obtained. The table has been amended accordingly. There were 16 angels or angles to the ounce: this unit is later known as the ackie.
4.   Presumably a misprint for 13. Sleties. silesias. or platillas are folded pieces of Silesian linen.
5.   Calculated as 13 (see note 4).
6.   This table has also been amended. substituting oz. and a. for £ and s.. without which the addition is not possible. Donnan has also printed oz. for ackies in the prices of some items.
7.   For example. Benjamin Way's replies to Commissioners of Trade and Plantations. P.R.O. T.70 1 12 (Furley transcript).
8.   Indian cottons.
9.   Indian grass-cloth.
10. Second-hand.
11. Purplets (presumably perpetuanas) do not appear under that name in the invoice. The prices shown are given for large ranters. a woollen cloth.

REFERENCES

(1)   Polanyi. K.. 'Sortings and "ounce trade" in the West African Slave Trade'. *J. Afr. Hist.*. 3 (1964).
(2)   Donnan. E.. *Documents Illustrative of the History of the Slave Trade to America* (1930); reprinted Frank Cass. London (1966).
(3)   Barbot. J.. *Description of the Coasts of North and South Guinea* (1732).
(4)   Phillips. T.. 'Voyage of the *Hannibal*' in Churchill. *Collection of Voyages*. London (1732).
(5)   Royal African Company of England to Lords Commissioners of Trade and Plantations. letter dated 18 December 1707. P.R.O. T. 70 15 (transcript in Furley Collection. University of Ghana).
(6)   Atkins. J.. *Voyage to Guinea*. London (1735); reprinted Frank Cass. London (1970).
(7)   *Journal of Commissioners for Trade and Plantations* (1777).
(8)   Bowdich. T. E.. *Mission to Ashantee*. London (1819); 3rd. ed. with a new introduction by Ward. W. E. F.. Frank Cass. London (1966).
(9)   Adams. J.. *Cape Palmas to Rio Congo*. London 1823; reprinted Frank Cass. London (1966).
(10) Dupuis. J., *Journal of a Residence in Ashantee*. London. 1824; 2nd ed.. with a new introduction and notes. Frank Cass. London (1966).
(11) Priestley. M.. 'Richard Brew: an eighteenth century trader at Anomabu'. *Trans. Hist. Soc. Ghana*. IV. 1 (1959).
(12) Hippisley. J., *Essays on the African Trade*, London (1764).
(13) Letter from Director-General Haring to W.I.C.. Amsterdam. 15 August 1712. Furley transcript (I am indebted to Professor Ivor Wilks for this reference).
(14) Jackson. J. G.. *An Account of Timbuctoo and Hausa*. London. 1820; reprinted Frank Cass. London (1967).

28

SALT CURRENCY IN ETHIOPIA IN THE ZÄMÄNÄ MÄSAFENT*

M. Abir

'An unchanging feature of Ethiopian economy since the decline of the Aksumite Empire was the absence of coined money, and the use of gold, salt, and iron as the principal means of exchange' (1: p.260). In the Zämänä Mäsafent one hardly hears of iron as being a medium of exchange. Gold kept its importance. It was much in demand by merchants but was always scarce and the trade in this commodity was usually carried on in secret (2: p.426; 3: III, pp.30-31; 4: p.410; 5: II, p.559). The small quantities of gold produced in Ethiopia were exported either by way of Sennar or through the port of Massawa. Anyway, the overwhelming majority of the population of Ethiopia, throughout the period covered by this paper, was so poor that it could not afford to acquire gold. During the Zämänä Mäsafent, as in the past, trade in Ethiopia's markets was usually carried on by barter. However, in the more important trading centres the Maria Theresa Thaler was accepted by merchants. For smaller change people used pieces of cloth, black pepper, blue silk cord, beads and above all salt amolé.[1] Salt, having been essential for Ethiopia's economy (1: p.260; 6: p.214) since the Aksumite period and probably before it, retained its importance in the nineteenth century. The salt amolé might be considered to have been the official currency all over the Ethiopian highlands from Tegré to Kaffa and from Wällaga to Argoba (7: pp.260-1, par. 106; 8: II, p.414; 9: IV, p.125) and amolé merchants were to be found even in the remotest parts of Ethiopia (5: II, p.298; 7: pp.260-2). Taxation and tribute were in many cases paid in amolé. For certain articles only the amolé was accepted (10: p.261; 11: p.170; 12: II, pp.232, 233) and even when barter was practised the

*Abridged by the editors by permission of the author, and reprinted from 'Salt, Trade and Politics in Ethiopia in the "Zämänä Mäsafent" ' in the *Journal of Ethiopian Studies*, Vol. 1, No. 2, 1966. 'Zämänä Mäsafent' means 'the time of the judges (princes)', considered to be the period of the final decline of the Gondarine Empire in the latter part of the 18th century and the first part of the 19th century.

amolé served in many instances as the medium of exchange. It facilitated the inter-regional trade and was indispensable to the long-range caravan trade because the further the merchants penetrated into the interior the less were people ready to accept Maria Theresa Thalers, while the salt amolé was always welcomed.[2]

The amolé was, in the Zämänä Mäsafent, a block of salt similar in shape to a prism, about 20 cm. long and 2½ thick. In the centre it was about 5 cm. wide but only 2½ cm. at the ends. The 'legal' weight of an amolé was about half a kilo (14: I, p.302). Its colour was greyish and it was usually protected from damage by a strip of leather bound across it (7: p.118). During the rainy season the amolé became moist and tended to fall to pieces. Moreover, with continuous use, the amolé tended to depreciate in weight until finally it would not be accepted at its full value or not accepted at all and thus could only be used as raw salt. The difference in price between the amolé and raw salt was quite noticeable and people tried to preserve their amolé by burying them in ashes or by suspending them above a fire (11: II, p.170; 12: II, pp.232-3; 10: p.260).

The source of all the amolé in circulation in Ethiopia was the salt plains in the Taltal area nearly 100 miles south of Massawa and east of the Ethiopian plateau (14: pp.124-6; 13: I, p.302; 8: II, pp.58-9; 15: p.92). An ancient agreement existed between the Taltal and the people of Tegré by which the Tegreans were allowed to descend to the Taltal plains and extract as much salt as they could against a small payment. Thus each year great caravans left Agamé and Endärta under the protection of an important officer whose title was Balgada and who was entrusted with the protection of the amolé trade. (14; 2: p.325; 8: II, p.58). The Tegreans stayed for a few weeks in the Taltal area and then returned to the highlands with many thousands of amolé which they shaped into the accepted form. The Taltal themselves brought great quantities of rock salt to Agamé for sale to the local population who later formed them to the desired amolé (16: p.69; 8: II, p.59). The traveller d'Abbadie[4] estimated the quantity of amolé extracted each year (in the 1830s) from the Taltal salt plains to be the load of 3,000 mules and about 3,000 porters. A good mule could carry about 150-200 amolé while a porter usually carried about 40. Thus nearly three-quarter of a million amolé were added annually to the circulation in the Ethiopian highlands.[5] However, being very fragile and easily corroded, a great number of amolé went out of circulation each year and the number of available amolé probably did not increase very much from year to year. The danger of inflation was thus avoided especially in view of the expansion of trade in Ethiopia in the nineteenth century. In fact the value of amolé gradually increased throughout the century.

The most important centres for the amolé trade were the village of Fičo and the nearby town of Atsbi on the border between Agamé and Endärta overlooking the Taltal plains. Here amolé were exchanged mostly against cattle at a rate of 80 to 120 per thaler according to the season (8: II, pp.58-9; 7: p.385; 3: II, pp.25-6). From this area amolé were carried by donkeys, mules and porters to Antalo, Lasta, the Yeju and the Wällo areas. On the borders of Wällo the salt merchants from the north were met by caravans coming from Shoa. These caravans took the amolé into Shoa and beyond it to southern Ethiopia, the Sidama areas and even to Kaffa (17; 9: IV, p.125; 7: p.601, par. 106). Another route led from Atsbi to Ifag in Bägemdér and from there to Gondar. No less important was the route of distribution from Bägemdér to the market of Basso in Gojjam and thence to all the provinces of southwestern Ethiopia. The limit of amolé diffusion in southern and southwestern Ethiopia was probably the limits of the penetration of caravan merchants from the north, i.e. the Sidama lakes area on one hand[6] and Kaffa on the other. The population of Kullo (south of Kaffa), we are told, had no use for amolé, and there is no evidence to show any trade in amolé with the Negroid areas to the south and west of the Ethiopian plateau (7: pp.277, 537, pars. 118, 178).

The rate of exchange of amolé to Thaler differed according to the distance of any trading or administrative centre from Agamé and Endärta. Thus, whilst at Fičo up to 120 amolé were received for a Thaler, at Sokota or Adwa 50 to 70 were given per Thaler, in Bägemdér 30 to 40, in Gojjam and Shoa about 20 and at Saka (Enarea) 10 to 12 (8: I, p.453, II, p.59; 18; 11: I, pp.376-7, 379; 12: II, p.248; 3: II, Appendix p.32). However because of their increased value, the amolé reaching south-western Ethiopia were broken into four and sometimes even into six smaller units (7: pp.260-1).

The difference in the exchange rate was naturally the result of the cost of transportation and the damage caused to the fragile amolé on the road. Moreover, the amolé caravans were heavily taxed by governors and by customs authorities all along the caravan route.[7]

The income from the amolé trade was extremely important to the governors of Tegré and especially to the rulers of Agamé and Endärta. This income above all enabled them to defray part of the heavy costs of keeping a large army.[8] Moreover, with the growing importance of firearms in the nineteenth century, the rulers of Tegré, taking advantage of their position in the highlands and using the income from the salt trade, were able to acquire the largest stock of firearms which any one ruler in Ethiopia possessed. The bitter and continuous struggle for power in this area in the first half of the nineteenth century between the houses of Endärta and Agamé and between the descendants of Däjazmač Sabagadis, Ras Wäldä Sellasé and Däjazmač Wubé of Semén could be explained, to a certain extent, by this background as well as by the fact that the road from Edd and Amphila on the coast (around which European intrigues with Däjazmač Sabagadis, Däjazmač Wubé, Däjazmač Kasai and Balgada Araya Sellasé, centred) was connected to Agamé (19).

It is quite evident that the regular and continuous supply of amolé was vital to Ethiopia's economy and to the administration and government of the different provinces. The quantity of Thalers imported into Ethiopia was relatively small (20). Ethiopian exports hardly covered the imports and a certain quantity of Thalers was continuously taken out of circulation by the silversmiths of Ethiopia. Moreover, a number of rulers tended to hoard Thalers, while others used all the Thalers they could get to purchase firearms which were growing in importance in Ethiopia (20; 21: p.287; 16: XIII, p.286). The salt amolé, being produced in Ethiopia, did not present the same problems as the silver and thus they became almost indispensable for internal trade and for the needs of the government and administration of the country.

NOTES

1. Salt bar serving as currency, see below.
2. Of the salt currency used during the Portuguese period in Ethiopia see: (1: pp.261-262; 6: p.214-5).
3. The size, shape and protective cover of the amolé varied in different periods.
4. Travelled extensively in Ethiopia in the second quarter of the nineteenth century (7: p.385).
5. The quantity of amolé extracted each year from the Taltal plains has been intriguing a number of authors (6: pp.218-22). Munzinger, who was the governor of Massawa under the Egyptians reckoned that in the 1860s about 30 million amolé were added annually to the circulation. This estimate was taken up also by Arakel Bey, who inherited Munzinger's position at Massawa (G. Douin, *Historie du règne du Khédive Ismail*, tome 3, p.709). It is evident that Munzinger, as well as a number of Italian authors, mentioned by Pankhurst 'Primitive Money', greatly exaggerated the quantity of amolé sent to the highlands. They assumed that the salt mines were exploited throughout the year, forgetting that the salt plains were flooded during the rainy season and were unbearable even to the Danakils during the hot months of the year. In fact the mines were actually worked less than three months a year. Moreover, if one studies available figures regarding the income from the salt trade of some Ethiopian rulers in the nineteenth century (6: pp.210-20); and if one takes into account that the annual revenue of Däjazmač Kasai, ruler of Agamé in the late 1830s from all sources, was about 10,000 Thalers (7: p.28, para. 69), and that the market of Alio Amba, the most important in Shoa, which was the centre of amolé trade in that country, is said to have yielded to the government of Shoa 3,000 Thalers in cash and about 2,000 in kind annually (L.G. 185, No. 1440, Par. 18, Barker, 7.1.1842), one tends to think that the quantity of amolé extracted

each year from the Taltal area, according to Munzinger and some of the Italian sources, is nothing but the dream of imperialists who tried to convince themselves, as well as their governments that it would be profitable or economically feasible to conquer parts of Ethiopia. It is logical that the quantity of amolé introduced each year into Ethiopia depended upon the political, climatic and economic conditions in the highlands. Obviously, because of the instability of Ethiopia in the period covered by this paper, it is only to be expected that the supply of additional amolé greatly varied from year to year. But, in a country whose economy was dormant, having a population which numbered only a few millions, where the potential market for amolé was even much smaller, the variation could oscillate only within a limit, otherwise the market would be glutted with amolé and the value of amolé would have greatly fallen instead of gradually going up, as it did, throughout the nineteenth century. It seems therefore, that even if d'Abbadie minimises the production of amolé the average quantity extracted could not have been more than a few millions.

6.   According to D'Abbadie (7: p.421, para. 277), amolé were rare in Kambat.

7.   Because of the archaic system of customs which existed in northern Ethiopia the amount demanded at different custom barriers usually varied from place to place. However, Däjazmač Kasai in 1838 the ruler of a large part of Agamé used to take 20% of the salt amolé brought in by the caravans (7: p.28, para. 69).

8.   According to Nathaniel Pearce, *Life and Adventures* (London, 1831, II, 14), the customs on the amolé was not within the jurisdiction of the Negade Ras (farmer of the customs) but Ras Wäldä Sellassé of Tegré received it himself and used the amolé to pay his army and officials. The income in salt amolé received from taxation on market days was distributed by the Ras among his friends and his courtiers. According to Plowden (14: p.126), the Balgada had a custom house at the entrance to the Christian areas where he received the dues from the salt caravans coming from the Taltal areas. See also above for the income of Ras Kasai from the salt trade.

REFERENCES

(1)   Pankhurst, R., *An Introduction to the Economic History of Ethiopia,* London (1961).

(2)   Salt, H., *A Voyage to Abyssinia in the Years 1809, 1810,* London (1814); reprinted Frank Cass, London (1967).

(3)   Lefebvre, C. T., *Voyage en Abyssinie,* Paris 1845-51.

(4)   Parkyns, M., *Life in Abyssinia,* London (1853).

(5)   Cecchi, A., *Da Zeila alle frontiere del Caffa,* Rome (1886).

(6)   Pankhurst, R., 'Primitive Money in Ethiopia', *Bulletin de la Société des Africanistes,* (1964).

(7)   D'Abbadie, Antoine. Bibliothèque Nationale Paris, France Nouvelle Acquisition (F.N.A.), Vol. 21303.

(8)   Ferret et Galinier, *Voyage en Abyssinie,* Paris (1847).

(9)   Combes et Tarnisier, *Voyage en Abyssinie,* Paris (1838).

(10)   D.Héricourt, Rochet, *Second Voyage,* Paris (1846).

(11)   Harris, *The Highlands of Aethiopia,* II, p.170.

(12)   Johnston, C., *Travels in Southern Abyssinia,* London.

(13)   Rüppell, E., *Reise in Abissinien,* Frankfurt (1838-40).

(14)   P.R.O./F.O. Abyssinia 114, Plowden, 17th November 1947.

(15)   Isenberg and Krapf, *Journals,* London (1843).

(16)   Ministère des Affaires Etrangères. Memoires et Documents (AE.M & D), Vol. 61, Gilbert, 28th August (1861).

(17)   India Office, Bombay Secret Proceedings, Lantern Gallery (L.G.) 189, No. 2034, 12th December 1841.
(18)   L.G. 185, No. 1440, Barker, 7th January, 1842.
(19)   India Office, letters from Adin, Vol. 28, Christopher, 15th December 1843.
(20)   Pankhurst, R., 'The Maria Theresa Dollar in Pre-War Ethiopia', *Journal of Ethiopian Studies* (1965), I, No. 1.
(21)   D'Hericourt, *Voyage sur la Côte Orientale*, Paris (1841).

Index

Abyssinia, 81, 87
Accra, 137, 139
ackie, 291, 292, 294, 295, 297
Adan, kingdom of, 233
Adamawa, 149; exports of, 151; ivory, 162; trade, 158
Aden, 196; Gulf of, 84
Adulis, 85, 87
Agades, 129
Aksum, 83
Akwapim, 137
Al Dimaschki, 91
Al Fazari, 91
Al Husayn, 91
Al Masudi, 195, 196, 216
Al Zouhri, 97
ambergris, 196, 208
American War of Independence, 209
amolé, see salt amolé
Amratian, culture, 92; epoch 90
angel (or angle), see ackie
Anglo-Zanzibar, Treaty of 1873, 214
Angola, 109, 233, 236, 240, 243, 246, 247
Ankole, 28, 221
Arab slave-traders, 113
Arabia, 8, 9, 64
Arabs, 86, 89, 97, 195, 212
Ashanti, 66, 68n, 135, 136, 140, 145, 146n 167, 257
Asia, 5, 6, 10, 34, 64
Association for Promoting the Discovery of the Interior Parts of Africa, 42
Assyrians, 79, 80, 193
Atlantic slave trade, see slave trade
Azanian coast, 194

Badarian era, 92
Baganda, 16
Bambata, 9
Bamenda grassfields, 147-165
bananas, 5, 14, 17, 19, 31; beer (mbide), 15; cooking (matoke), 15; dessert (menvu), 15; roasting (gonja), 15; see also Musa acuminata and Musa balbisiana
banians, 87

Bantu, expansion, 27; speaking peoples, 22
Barbary coast, 63
Barbot, James, 275, 280, 287, 288n
Barbot, John, A., 43, 49n, 132, 140, 146n, 177n, 274, 282n
Bargash ibn Said, 214
bark-cloth, 267
barley, 5
barter, 253, 299
Barros, João de, 46
Basra, 196
Benin, 142; bronzes, 95
British South Africa Company, 59
Bronze age, 63, 90
beads, 150, 203, 238; aggry, 142; black and white slave, 160; chevron, 159; cylinder, 160; glass, 108, 185, 187; gold, 108
Bechuanaland, 56
beer bananas, see bananas
Benguela, 236
Benue, 155
Berbera, 227n
Berbers, 91, 96
Berlin Act of 1885, 220
Bornu, 43; empire, 42
Bosman, John, 276
Bosman, William, A., 132, 140, 146n
Bovill, E.W., 128
bracelets: brass and copper, 277
brass, 94, 150, 274; rods, 277
Brazil, 211, 219, 287
British East Africa Company, 220
Brussels Act of 1890, 167, 220
Buganda, 14, 19, 27, 66, 69n, 221, 267, 270
Bukedi, 28
Bunyoro, 28, 221, 267
Burton, R.F., 47, 157, 214, 218, 233, 282n
Bushman-Hottentot group, 22

Cairo, 198, 234-235
Calonne-Beaufaict, A.de, 45
Cambay (the region of Gujerat), 197, 198, 202
Cape Coast, 292, 296-297
caravans, long-distance, 255

carbon-14 dates, *see* radiocarbon dates
Carthage, 63, 285
Carthaginians, 89, 90, 96
cattle, 8; Sanga-type, 105
Chad, 63, 94, 130; lake, 81
channelled ware, 9; decorated pottery, 103, 105, 113n; population, 10
China, 64, 195, 196, 216, 225, 234
cire perdue, *see* lost wax technique
citrus fruits, 31
civet, 129
cloth industry in Ghana, 139
cloves, 213, 215, 224
coconut, 31; oil, 193; palms, 213
coffee, 267
Colocasia antiquorum, *see* coco-yams
Congo, 27-28, 226, 258; basin, 44-45; forest and savannah cultures, 7
cooking bananas, *see* bananas
copper, 92, 108, 150, 184-187, 189, 203, 236, 237, 239, 242, 275; age, 63, 90, 93; bangles, 108; croisettes, 185; ingots, 184; mines, 94; mining, 110; rings, 277, 285; rods, 277; trade, 109, 110, 247; wire, 285; working, 109
Copperbelt, 109-110
cotton cloth, 87, 152
Coupland, Sir Reginald, 206-207
cowrie, 129, 150, 156, 161, 187, 197, 203, 238, 276, 277, 281, 284, 288; currency 289
Cross River, 149, 154, 157, 274, 275, 276, 278
cultivation, 65
currency, metal, 278; native, 276; trade, 280-282
Curtin, Philip, D., 172, 173
Cushites, 79, 80

Dahomey, 66, 166, 262, 278, 284
Dapper, O., 50n, 241, 251n, 274, 276, 278, 280, 283n
Dar es Salaam, 218
debt collection, 154
dessert bananas, *see* bananas
dimple-based pottery, 9, 10, 12n, 103
Dioscorea alata, cayenensis, esculenta, rotundata, *see* yams
domestication, 4; centre of vegetative, 24
Dutch West India Company, 141, 143

ebony, 129

Egypt, 79, 92, 94, 95
El Bakouwi, 93
El Bekri, 89, 91, 93, 97, 98n
El Mansur, 129
Eleusine coracane, *see* millet
Elmina, 92, 135, 140, 141, 142
Emin Pasha, 273n
English African Company, 141, 143
ensete, 5, 8, 16, 26
Equatorial Africa, 3,
Ethiopia, 8, 9, 11, 48, 63, 65, 66, 69n, 197, 233, 299, 300, 301
exchange, local, *see* trade local

Fagan, B., 236
Fage, J.D., 131n, 166
fairs, 134
farsilah, 220, 221, 222, 226n
Fayum A culture, 4
Fernandes, Antonio, 107, 112
Fernando Po, 285
feudalism, 58, 62
feudal-type states, 58
Fezzan, 96
finger millet, *see* millet
fire-arms, 238
flintlocks, 150, 154, 155
Fort Jesus, 202
Freeman-Grenville, G.S.P., 199, 200, 233, 236
Fulani, 149; raids, 155

Galla, 201, 257
Gambia, river, 48
Gao, 129, 130
Ghana, 7, 35, 38, 64, 68n, 91, 130, 132, 134, 136, 137, 139, 140, 142, 143, 145; kingdom of, 127; markets in, 132; salt producing areas of, 137
gift-exchange, 153, 259
glass beads, *see* beads
Gluckman, M., 55, 66
gold, 86, 87, 90, 127, 129, 130, 136, 140, 141, 171, 189, 236, 290, 295, 299; bars, 285; mines, 91; trade, 110, 141; weights, 285
gold beads, *see* beads
Gold Coast, 92, 94, 281, 285, 290, 292, 295, 296
gonja, *see* bananas
Greeks, 86
groundnuts, 31
Guillain, M., 226n

Guinea, 127; coast, 24, 28, 256, 289, 292, 294, 296; Portuguese, 35
gum copal, 223, 246
gunpowder, 150, 154, 155, 238

Hanno's *Periplus*, 91
Herodotus, 90
Hittites, 95
Hutu, 72, 74

Ibn Batuta, 91, 199, 233, 284, 288
Ibn Khaldun, 91
Ibn Said, 91
Ibo, 257
Idrisi, 91
Ife heads, 95
Ile Ife, 286
India, 194, 195, 196, 208, 225, 285
Indians, 86
Ingombe Ilede, 107-109, 182, 184, 186, 189, 190, 236
iron, 88, 95-99, 115-123, 180-182, 189, 239, 267, 279, 299; age, 10, 79, 85, 105, 109, 179, 184, 187, 190; age cultures, 81, 107; bars, 277, 285; meteoric, 95; ore, 90; smelting, 63, 95, 111, 123; tools, 106; trade, 86, 116; working 63, 238
ironware, 164
Israelites, 193
ivory, 108, 111, 116, 140, 189, 193, 196, 241; discs, 268; royal monopoly in Ethiopia, 227n; trade, 159, 216-226
Ivory Coast, 92

Jeffreys, M.D.W., 46, 50n, 165n
Jenné, 130

Kabinda, 242
Kalomo culture, 105, 107; mounds, 180; sites, 109
Kamba, 203
Kangila, 106-107
Kano, 130
Kasai, 248
Katanga, 196, 236, 244, 245
Kazembe, 112-113
Kenya, 253
Khartoum, 5, 6, 224
Kikuyu, 220, 257
Kilwa, 107, 196, 198-200, 203, 210-211, 212, 214, 215, 217, 231, 233, 234, 236
Kintu, 15, 19-21, 27; myth, 25

Kismayu, 226
kola nuts, 140, 165-166
Kongo, kingdom of, 239-241; people, 258
Kumasi, 144, 145, 146n

labour, demand for, 172; division of, 156, 255
land distribution, 57; ownership, 70; tenure, 55-60, 62, 68n, 70
landlordism, 65
Leopard's Kopje, 106
Libya, 285
Lisbon yam, *see* yams
livestock, 72, 135, 136, 165
Livingstone, D., 45, 113, 116, 189, 191n, 218-219, 249n, 251n
lost wax technique, 95, 148
Lozi, 56
Loziland, 245
Luanda, 241, 242
Luba, 244
Lunda kingdom, 110

Madagascar, 21-22, 212
Mafia, 199, 235
Maghreb, 92, 93, 96
maize, 31, 41-51; milho grosso, 47; milho zaburro, 46
Makalian Wet phase, 5
malaguetta pepper, 129
Malawi, 103, 183
Maldive islands, 281
Mali, 130; kingdom of, 128, 285
Malindi, 199, 201, 202, 216, 226
manilas (also manillas), 276, 277, 278, 279, 282; brass, 161
Mansa Musa, 93, 128
Mapungubwe, 232
Maria Theresa Thaler, 299-302
mark, 292
markets: local, 143, 237, 253; periodic, 134; traditional, 255, 257, 261, 262, 263
Masailand, 216
Masai people, 220, 221, 258
Mashonaland gold mines, 112
matoke, *see* bananas
Mauny, R.A., 127, 128, 131n, 172, 177n, 236
Mauritania, 93
Mauritius, 209, 211
mbide, *see* bananas

means of exchange, *see* media of exchange
media of exchange, 161, 299, 300
menvu, *see* bananas
Meroe, 63, 80, 86
Mesolithic population, 4, 6; *see also* Stone age
metallurgy, 63
metalworking (in Ghana), 139
Middle East, 64
milho grosso, *see* maize
milho zaburro, *see* maize
millet, 5; finger (Eleusine coracane), 14
mitkhal (gold ducat), 285
Mogadishu, 196, 200, 202
Mohammad Askia of Songhai, 128
Mombasa, 196, 200, 202, 203, 204, 221, 226
monetary system of Angola, 287
money, 285; fiat, 287; Portuguese square cloth, 287
Monomotapa, 46, 107, 197; kingdom of, 112, 197, 201, 202
Moresby Treaty of 1822, 212
Mozambique, 47, 202, 208, 209, 210-211
Muhammad Ali, 217, 223
Murdock, G.P., 22, 24
Musa acuminata, *see* bananas
Musa balbisiana, *see* bananas
Muscat, 203, 213, 219
Mwami, 71, 72

Nakuru-Naivasha basin, 8
Napoleonic Wars, 210
Natal, 23
native currency, *see* currency
Naukratis, 80
Ndebele, 59
Negroids, 6
Neolithic age, 91; communities, 7; culture, 5, 7; farmers, 10; population, 6, 8; *see also* Stone age
New World crops, 28
New Kingdom (Egypt), 79
New Yam Festival, 36
Niger, 38, 66, 68n, 90, 127, 256
Nigeria, 7, 66, 68n, 90, 278
Nile valley, 79
Nilo-Hamitic tribes, 259
Nilotic languages, 87
Nok, 96; culture, 7
Northern Rhodesia, *see* Rhodesia
Nubia, 94, 95

Nubians, 87
Numidia, 96
Nyamwezi, 203, 246
Nyasa, lake, 110, 116; region, 204
Nyasaland, 46

oil palm, 147; plants, 3, 4
Oil Rivers, 157
Okanga, country, 240; market, 241
Old Calabar, 150
Oliver, Roland, 207
Oman, 195, 196, 202
Omani Arabs, 230
Oryza glaberima, *see* rice
ostrich feathers, 129
ounce, 289, 293, 298; gold, 294, 297; system 290; trade, 296, 297
Ovimbundu: people, 245; trade, 246, 261

Pacheco, Pereira, 35, 170, 177n, 274
palm oil, 152, 157, 165; trade, 150
Pangani, 220
Park, Mungo, 42
pastoralism, 6
Pate, 202, 235; Chronicle, 200
pax Britannica, 124
Pemba islands, 46, 212, 213, 215
Periplus of the Erythrean Sea, 21, 82n, 85, 87, 193-195
Persian Gulf, 214
Peters, Carl, 270, 271n
Petrie, W.M. Flinders, 79, 82n
Phoenicians, 93, 193
Pigafetta, Filipo, 44, 50n, 240, 251n
pineapples, 31
Pleistocene, 3
Polo, Marco, 216, 284, 285
Polynesian peoples, 37
pombeiros, 248n, 250n
Pondoland, 232
Portères, R., 42, 50n
Portugal, 201, 202, 247
Portuguese, the, 33, 41, 43, 45, 48, 64, 93, 113, 169, 170, 200, 203, 208, 239, 242, 278, 285
Portuguese East Africa, 235; India, 208
potatoes, 32; sweet, 147
price control, 154
prime cost, 289
Punt, 193

Quelimane, 209, 211, 212

radio-carbon dating, 5, 12n, 17, 97, 106, 236
Ramusio, Gian Battista, 41
raphia (also raffia), cloth, 242; palm, 147
Red Sea, 20, 81, 193, 197, 198, 234
redistributive system, 156
rent, 73
reversionary rights of the chief, 61; of the tribal community, 61
Réunion, 47, 209, 211
Rhapta, 193, 194, 226n
rhinoceros horns, 129, 193, 225
Rhodesia, 103, 106, 236; Northern, 246, 261
Rhodesian gold-fields, 195
rice, 31, 63, 135; Oryza glaberima, 63
Rio Real, 274, 276, 278
roasting bananas, see bananas
Rodney, W., 168-170, 177n
Roman, Empire, 207; law, 60, 70
Romans, 89
Rosebery, Fort, 115
Roseires, 81, 87
Rovuma River, 218
Royal Niger Company, 159, 164
rubber, 164, 215, 247
Rudolf, Lake, 19
Rwanda (also Ruanda), 9, 70, 73, 74, 248, 267
Ruwenzori: mountains, 25

Sahel, 92
salt, 86, 116, 137, 150, 151, 158-159, 171, 182-183, 247, 267, 268, 274, 299; amolé, 299, 302; mines, 130
Sanga-type cattle, see cattle
San Salvador, 233, 239, 240, 241
São Tomé (also St. Thome), 48, 285, 286
Sarah Bonneaventure, accounts of, 290
Sauer, C.O., 18, 23, 25, 26
Schweinfurth, George, 45, 50n
Senegal, 44, 127; river, 97
Sennar, 299
serfdom, 65
Seyyid Said, 204, 213; moves to Zanzibar, 217
Shebelle valley, 197
shilling, West African, 279
shifting cultivation, see cultivation
Shirazi colonisation, 196
Sidamo people, 25
Sierra Leone, 38
silk, 198

silver, 302
Slave Coast, 275, 276, 278, 281, 290
slave markets, 157; trade, 116, 138, 149, 156, 164, 166, 168, 169, 170, 172, 173, 206, 207, 214, 246
slavery, 65, 68n, 166
slaves, 43, 87, 108, 111, 129, 140, 152, 155, 196, 223, 239, 246, 290
smelting, 117; process, 123; techniques, 111
smithing techniques, 111
Sofala, 112, 196, 200, 232, 233, 235; trade, 199
Somali coast, 83
Somaliland, 84, 87, 257; British Protectorate of, 233
Songhai, 128; empire, 128, 129
sorghum, 5
Sotho people, 259
Speke, J.H., 218
stamped ware, 10
standards of value, 239
Stanley, H.M., 223, 242, 252n
Stanley Falls, 223; Pool, 240, 241, 242, 248
Stone age, 5, 10; see also Neolithic age and Mesolithic population
Suakin, 234
Sudan, 44, 63, 80, 86, 93, 134, 168, 221, 235, 278; zone, 27
sudd, 19, 81
Summers, R., 235
Swahili, 201, 212, 258; coast, 202, 203
sweet potatoes, see potatoes

Tabora, 217, 218, 222
Taghaza, 129, 130
taich, 19
Takoradi, 139
taku, 292
Taltal salt plains, 300
Tanzania (also Tanganyika), 14, 45, 103; coast of, 110, 113
Taodemi, salt mines of, 130
taros, see coco-yams
Taxation, 299
Tchad, see Chad
tenure: rights, 70, 72; system of, 71
Tete, 112-113, 236
Thebes, 79
Tegré (also Tigré), 5, 299, 300, 301
Timbuktu, 129, 130, 284
Tiv, 149, 279

tobacco, 147, 164, 267, 296
Togo, 38
tortoise-shell, 193, 196
trade, centres, 267; east-coast, 189, 190; local, 237; long-distance, 187, 237-248, 255, 257; regional, 134-135, 237, 255; routes 231-236; royal, 154
trade ounce, see ounce
Transkei coast, 232
Trans-Saharan trade, 95, 127-130, 168, 171, 260
Transvaal, 232
tribute, 299
Tripoli, 42
tsetse fly, 5
Tswana people, 259
Tutsi, 72, 73, 75, 76n

Ubangi river, 258
Uganda, 14, 16, 28, 231
Ujiji, 217, 218, 222
units of account, 268
Unyamwezi, 220
Unyanyembe, see Tabora
Upper Volta, 38, 93
Urundi, 9
Usambara mountains, 21
Ushi iron industry, 115-123

Vansina, J., 44, 50n, 179, 185, 191n
Vavilov, N.I., 25
vegeculture, 6
vegeculturalists, 4, 11
Venice, 129, 284, 285
Victoria, Lake, 270
Volta, region, 139, 149; river, 135

Wainwright, G.A., 19, 82n, 88n
Wällaga, 299
water yam, see yams
wax, 140, 208
wealth, accumulation and distribution of, 153
wheat, 5
Whydah, 290, 296

yams, 5, 31, 32-37, 147; cultivation of, 37; Dioscorea alata, 24; Dioscorea esculenta, 24; Dioscorea rotundata, 8, 25; Dioscorea Cayenensis, 8, 25; Guinea, 35; Lisbon, 34; water, 34
Yao, 203

Yoruba, 95, 174, 255, 278; culture, 284; kingdom, 262; markets, 256
Yorubaland, 255, 256-257

Zämänä Mäsafent, 299, 300
Zambezi, 23, 103, 107, 108, 109, 113, 188, 197, 201, 136; great lakes route, 28; region, 202; river, 56, 209; trade, 186; valley, 186
Zambia, 63, 103, 104, 107, 110, 111, 113, 181, 184, 187
Zanj, 195, 196; empire 199, 216
Zanzibar, 46, 196, 204, 215, 223, 225, 226; slave and ivory market, 204, 208, 210-214; traders, 219
Zeila, 234
Zimbabwe, 197, 208, 236; acropolis, 9, 105
Ziwa people, 235
Zulu empire, 69n